Tourism and Economic Development

Western European Experiences

Second Edition

Edited by Allan M. Williams and Gareth Shaw

JOHN WILEY & SONS

Chichester · New York · Brisbane · Toronto · Singapore

First published in Great Britain in 1988 by Belhaven Press
2nd edition 1991

Reprinted 1995 by John Wiley & Sons Ltd,
Baffins Lane, Chichester,
West Sussex PO19 1UD, England

National   01243 779777
International   (+44) 1243 779777

Other Wiley Editorial Offices

John Wiley & Sons, Inc., 605 Third Avenue,
New York, NY 10158–0012, USA

Jacaranda Wiley Ltd, 33 Park Road, Milton,
Queensland 4064, Australia

John Wiley & Sons (Canada) Ltd, 22 Worcester Road,
Rexdale, Ontario M9W 1L1, Canada

John Wiley & Sons (SEA) Pte Ltd, 37 Jalan Pemimpin #05-04,
Block B, Union Industrial Building, Singapore 2057

ISBN 0 471 94794 6

Typeset by Florencetype Ltd, Kewstoke, Avon
Printed and bound in Great Britain by
Biddles Ltd, Guildford and King's Lynn

Contents

List of Contributors

Knut S. Brinchmann	Nordland Research Institute, Bodø
Andrew W. Gilg	Department of Geography, University of Exeter
Justin Greenwood	Department of Administrative and Social Studies, Teesside Polytechnic
Morten Huse	Nordland Research Institute, Bodø
Russell King	Department of Geography, Trinity College, Dublin
Lila Leontidou	Department of Geography and Regional Planning, National Technical University, Athens
Jim Lewis	Department of Geography, University of Durham
David Pinder	Department of Geography, University of Southampton
Peter Schnell	Department of Geography, Westfälische Wilhelms-Universität Münster
Gareth Shaw	Department of Geography, University of Exeter
John Tuppen	Lyon Graduate School of Business
Manuel Valenzuela	Department of Geography, Universidad Autónoma de Madrid
Allan M. Williams	Department of Geography, University of Exeter
Friedrich Zimmermann	Department of Geography, University of Klagenfurt

List of Figures

List of Tables

Preface to the second edition

We were pleased to be invited to produce a second edition of this book less than eighteen months after it was first published. Hopefully, this reflects a growing awareness of the economic importance of tourism and of the need for comparative international research. Tourism is certainly one of the most dynamic industries in Europe, a continent which has witnessed revolutionary changes in recent months.

There has been neither the need nor the time to revise systematically the entire volume. However, individual authors have updated their particular contributions, and we have also been fortunate to find authors for a chapter on one of the Scandinavian countries. Their contribution on Norway represents an important extension to the geographical coverage of this volume.

Allan M. Williams
Gareth Shaw
June 1990

Preface to the first edition

This edited volume is the result of a joint venture by the Tourism Research Group and the Western European Studies Centre at the University of Exeter. It brought together the work of the Tourism Research Group on the role of tourism in economic development and the broader international interests of the Western European Studies Centre at a time of growing interest in tourism. Expansion of, and the creation of new forms of, tourism—even at a time of global economic recession—has led to considerable interest in the industry. Furthermore, in recent years, there has been a spate of tourism policy formulation at the local, regional, national and—somewhat hesitantly—the international level. It therefore seemed timely to undertake a broad review in order to identify the main outlines of the Western European experience of tourism.

This work has concentrated on the national and regional development of tourism and on the implications of tourism development for national and regional economies. The underlying aim was to identify those elements which were common to the experiences of all or most countries and those which were unique in some way. As such, the volume does not seek to provide a comprehensive view of all aspects of tourism and economic development. It also does not provide comprehensive coverage of all Western European states. Given the constraints of length, originally we had intended to cover most rather than all of Western Europe. The major omission—Scandinavia—was unintentional: we were let down by a contributor at the last moment. Nevertheless, we hope that this volume will contribute to the understanding of one of the most rapidly growing —and misleadingly stereotyped—sectors of the economy of Western Europe.

The writing and production of this volume has been assisted by several persons and institutions. We are grateful to the Western European Studies Centre and the University of Exeter Research Grants Committee which provided the resources for a conference in May 1987 that brought together many of the contributors to the volume. This presented a first opportunity to air and discuss particular and general themes which helped in no small measure to shape the contents of the final manuscript. In addition, Iain Stevenson and two anonymous referees provided useful initial advice on the outline of this book. Terry Bacon drew or redrew most of the maps with his usual skill and efficiency, while Tracey Reeves and Joan Fry took on the daunting task of typing and retyping the final manuscript. However, the usual disclaimer applies to this work in that all errors or misinterpretations in the final manuscript are solely the responsibility of the authors and the editors.

Allan M. Williams
Gareth Shaw
Exeter, December 1987

1 Tourism and development: introduction

Allan M. Williams and Gareth Shaw

1.1 The study of tourism and development

There has been increased awareness of the economic importance of tourism in the 1980s and this stems from a number of sources, including appreciation of how long-term structural changes in demand are leading to expansion of the service economy (Bell 1974). With increasing real incomes and leisure time there is growing demand for recreation and holidays, and this benefits tourism. Not surprisingly, therefore, tourism is often considered to be one of the economic sectors which has realistic potential for growth beyond the short term. The importance of this trend for employment is strengthened because of the relatively labour-intensive nature of tourism and the limited substitution — up to the present, at least — of capital in the production of tourism services (Gershuny and Miles 1983). Given the growth of large-scale and long-term unemployment throughout Western Europe in the 1980s, it is hardly surprising that policy-makers have seized upon tourism as a source of employment creation. At the same time, the increasing share of services in international trade has focused attention on tourism as a major contribution — either positively or negatively — to the balance of payments. In short, tourism — along with some other select activities such as financial services and telecommunications — has become a major component of economic strategies in many parts of Western Europe.

As tourism emerges from the shadows of economic policy to a centre-stage position, it has become imperative to evaluate its role in economic development. The industry is shrouded with myths and stereotypes, and there is a need to examine critically recent trends in tourism, its economic organisation and its contribution to economic development. There have been previous attempts to question whether tourism is 'a passport to development' (de Kadt 1979) or is 'a blessing or blight' (Young 1973) as well as more broadly based assessments of the economic, social and environmental impacts of tourism (Mathieson and Wall 1982; Pearce 1981; Murphy 1985). However, this volume seeks to make a distinctive contribution to the growing literature in this field by focusing in depth on recent trends in Western Europe.

Western Europe is a coherent unit for analysis for many reasons. Although, of course, there are international flows out of and into the region, Western Europe actually accounted for 64 per cent of all international tourists in 1988 (see Table 2.1 in Chapter 2). Compared with all other macro regions, there is a very intense level of international tourist flows within Western Europe, so that the fortunes of the tourist industry in particular countries are heavily dependent on movements from—and events in—other countries within the continent. The major exception to this is the quantitatively important (and economically even more significant) inflow of tourists from the United States. The events of 1986 testify to the importance of North American tourists because the sudden reduction in arrivals following the Chernobyl incident and the US bombing of Libya had a notable effect on the tourist economies of several European countries. To some extent, emphasis on international tourism tends to overstate the importance of Western Europe because the geographical scale of the United States and Canada means that, in comparison, similar-length tourist journeys are recorded as domestic tourist flows in these two countries. Nevertheless, it is also important to study Western Europe as a unit because there is a communality of policy interests. Most obviously, the European Community (EC) constitutes a single market for tourism and while EC policy initiatives in this field have been limited (see Chapter 13), the very existence of the Community affects the industry. At the level of demand, it facilitates international tourist movements while, at the level of industrial organisation, the free movement of international capital and labour is eased. There are also some instances of EC-wide policy measures for tourism, notably in Social Fund assistance for training and European Regional Development Fund (ERDF) grants for infrastructure (Pearce 1988). However, most tourism policy is formulated at the national rather than the EC level. Even so, the countries of Western Europe are interdependent in respect of state inter-ventionism. Policy measures in one country—whether to stimulate new forms of tourism, to influence the holiday destinations of nationals or to attract more foreigners—impinge upon competing tourist industries in other countries. This is underlined by the fact that while the income elasticity of demand for tourism may be strongly positive in the long term, in the short term total demand is (almost) fixed.

Having considered the geographical parameters of this volume, we now turn to a consideration of tourism itself. The definition of tourism is a particularly arid pursuit (but see Cohen 1974; Peters 1969). It is sufficient to note that in this volume tourism is understood to constitute travelling away from home for periods of more than 24 hours; the principal purposes are recreation or business activities, but may also include visiting family, educational motives or health reasons. Excursionism involves visits of less than 24 hours. Although the major focus of this volume is on tourism, its development and, indeed, its economic impact are linked with excursionism, and so the latter cannot entirely be excluded. While the definition of tourism may be an arid exercise, the definition of the tourist industry is crucially important. In most countries tourism is 'statistically invisible' and, usually, only the most obvious sectors or those exclusively devoted to tourists are enumerated in official tourism data. Inevitably, this tends to be the accom-modation sector and, perhaps, cafés and restaurants. Yet the tourist industry is far larger than this (see Murphy 1985, Chapter 1). Tourists also spend money directly on recreational facilities, tourist attractions, shops and local services. In turn, these have indirect effects on agriculture, wholesaling and manufacturing, while secondary rounds of spending of tourism income create induced linkages in the economy. This, indeed, is the basis for the research which has been undertaken on tourism multipliers (for example, Archer 1982). In this volume we have sought to encompass as broad a definition as possible of tourism but the constraints of space and of data inevitably mean that much of the discussion is centred on the accommodation sector.

This volume seeks to analyse the major changes which have occurred in Western European tourism in recent years. While Chapters 2 and 14 provide comparative overviews, the principal focus is provided by individual countries. This is justified by the emphasis we wish to place on domestic versus foreign tourism, and by the concentration of policy-making powers at this level. While space precluded the inclusion of chapters on all seventeen major Western European countries, the ten which have been selected represent the major types of tourism economies. While each chapter has been written so as to take into account the particular characteristics of tourism in each country, certain themes recur throughout. The most important of these are changes in the demand for tourism (international and domestic, by region, by season, etc.), the organisation of the tourist industry and its responses to demand changes, and the contribution of tourism to economic development.

The case studies concentrate on two levels of analysis—the national and the regional—and on the relationship between these. Any analysis which ignores either level is likely to be incomplete. National developments affect regional developments and vice versa. For example, the effectiveness of national marketing programmes, of national investment schemes and of international currency fluctuations influence the ability of regional tourist industries to attract tourists and to restructure in the face of changing market conditions. However, these interrelationships are not unidirectional for the attractiveness or effectiveness of the national tourist industry is in large part a sum of its regional components. Furthermore, the national and regional levels are also linked by capital and labour movements, both interregionally and internationally. This is illustrated in a case such as Austria (Chapter 8) for the national performance of the industry is usually an aggregate of decline in some regions and of rapid expansion in others. These and other relationships are addressed in the country studies which follow in Chapters 3–13. First, however, the remainder of this chapter outlines some of the essential elements in the relationship between tourism and development.

1.2 Tourism and development: national perspectives

The importance of tourism to national economic development can be measured in a number of ways, the most important of which are its contribution to the balance of payments, income/GDP, employment and other sectors of the economy (via indirect effects). The balance-of-payments contribution has received most attention. The importance of tourism in the 'invisibles' account in international trade has long been obvious in countries such as Spain (see Naylon 1967) where, indeed, it was promoted as part of a long-term economic strategy. It helps to pay for imports (whether of food, technology, capital or consumer goods) and this can be important both in economies in development (Greece, Spain, Portugal, etc.) and mature economies (such as the United Kingdom), which have a negative balance on merchandise trade. In this respect, the importance of tourism is usually greatest in small open economies, such as Cyprus or Malta, but it is also a source of vulnerability in such countries, especially when—as in the latter case—it is heavily dependent on a single foreign market (Oglethorpe 1985).

Estimates of the contribution of tourism to the balance of payments are usually based on direct tourist expenditure. However, this is a rather narrow (if relatively easily measured) indicator, for it excludes the indirect transactions which follow from tourism. Baretje (1982) therefore recommends the use of the broader concept of 'tourism's external account' (see Table 1.1), which includes a variety of economic linkages but, it must be emphasised, there are practical difficulties in seeking to operationalise this. The breadth of the definition makes it equally difficult to estimate the contribution of tourism to national income or GDP. In addition to the linkages suggested by Baretje, calculations of income or GDP also have to include the effects of domestic tourism which, in Northern Europe at least, sometimes exceed those of foreign tourism. There is also the even more intangible consideration of how tourism impinges on general lifestyles and expenditure patterns. International tourism can have a demonstration effect (see de Kadt 1979) leading to increased indigenous demand for new types of good or services, and these may be produced by domestic or by foreign companies.

While there has long been an interest in the contribution of tourism to the balance of payments, this has been surpassed in the 1980s by a concern for its potential employment creation. Again, there are practical difficulties involved in any evaluation of this role: some jobs in shops, recreation centres, etc., are only partly dependent on tourism, while there are considerable difficulties involved in tracing secondary linkages. Furthermore, jobs are not a homogeneous category to be measured in simple units—as with income or net foreign exchange earnings. Instead, there are a variety of job types and these can be classified as seasonal/all-year, part-time/full-time, family-labour/ waged-labour, voluntary/waged-labour, manual/non-manual, skilled/unskilled, etc. According to some stereotypes, tourism employment tends to be low-waged, seasonal, non-unionised, part-time and the preserve of family and/or female workers. This may hold true in some cases but, in most instances, it is at best a partial description (see Williams and Shaw 1988 on the United Kingdom). Jobs in tourism may be jobs in hotels, shops, government administration, air transport or factories, amongst others. The discussions on

Table 1.1 Components of tourism's external account

Expenditures	Receipts
Expenditures by tourists abroad	Expenditures 'at home' by foreign tourists
Transportation	Transportation
Investments (outward)	Investments (inward)
Dividends, interest and profits paid out	Dividends, interest and profits received
Commodity imports (tourism induced)	Commodity exports (tourism induced)
Capital goods	Capital goods
Consumption goods	Consumption goods
Salaries repatriated abroad	Salaries sent from abroad
Training	Training
Publicity and promotion	Publicity and promotion
Miscellaneous services	Miscellaneous services

Source: Baretje (1982, p. 62)

employment in Chapters 3–13 indicate the need to be critical of the quality of jobs generated by tourism, and to resist the political 'hype' surrounding its potential for job creation. The variety of experiences outlined in these chapters also emphasises the need to avoid stereotypes and excessive abstraction. Consideration of the tourism-related demand for manufactured goods underlines this point, for the impact depends on where the goods are produced, whether it is by craftsmen or factory workers, on the alternative work opportunities available locally, and on the evaluation of these jobs by the individuals and by the community.

While the previous discussion has stressed the need to examine individual cases in detail, it does not preclude identification of the key elements which condition the relationship between tourism and development. Amongst the most important of these are the type of tourism, the structure of the national economy, and relationships with capital and labour movements.

1.2.1   Types of tourism

There are many different types of tourists (see Krippendorf 1986) but, in terms of their contribution to economic development, the critical considerations are per-capita spending power and the forms of tourism in which they participate. The most important distinction is probably between domestic and foreign tourists, although there are also important differences within both categories. For instance, American tourists tend to have a high spending capacity so that, in most countries (see Chapter 6 for the example of Portugal), their economic contribution is far greater than their absolute numbers might suggest. In addition, there are also other differences between national groups and, indeed, amongst domestic tourists, depending on their incomes, duration of stay, mode of travel, range of activities and type of accommodation. Much of the debate on whether to pursue strategies of mass-tourism or quality tourism is based on these differences. This is a debate which is common in such diverse locations as Venice, the Algarve and South-West England. Any typology of tourism is subject to change and, for example, in the 1980s there has been the emergence of 'green' or environmentally-concerned tourists.

1.2.2   National economic context

It is also important to see tourism in context of the national economy for, as de Kadt (1979, p. 12) stresses, 'tourism is not a unique devil'. Instead, the ability of the national economy to benefit from tourism depends on the availability of investment to develop the necessary infrastructure (hotels, golf courses, etc.) and on its ability to supply the needs of tourists, whether for food, souvenirs or hotel beds. While the types of demand are conditioned by the types of tourism, there are also important differences in the capacity of particular economies to respond to these demands. In general, small economies are more likely to be dependent on imports, and the same is also true of economies where tourism is not very well developed and where, therefore, there are poor economies of scale for suppliers.

There is also an important relationship between development and tourism in that the former conditions the level of domestic demand. Increasing real

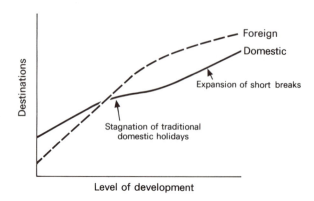

Figure 1.1   Hypothetical relationship between foreign and domestic
destinations corresponding to a changing relative balance ·
between short breaks and traditional holidays

incomes result in growing demand for tourism but this is distributed between
domestic and foreign destinations. Figure 1.1 suggests one hypothetical
scenario whereby domestic tourism is overtaken in relative importance by a
considerable expansion of foreign tourism. This shift can lead to a stagnation
in domestic tourism. However, with further increases in income and leisure
time, there may be a growth of second and third holidays—including short
breaks—and there may be sufficient demand for domestic resorts, to renew
growth in this sector. If, having reached saturation point, the growth of
foreign tourism also slows down, the gap between this and domestic tourism
may close. While the graph in Figure 1.1 is purely hypothetical, elements of
this relationship can be found in the experiences of several northern European
countries, including the United Kingdom.

1.2.3   *The organisation of capital: domestic versus foreign sources*

The role of tourism in national development also depends partly on the
organisation of capital and, in particular, on the penetration of international
capital. This assumed a number of forms and although foreign investment
initially may assist the development of tourism, it also leads to leakage of
income abroad through payment of royalties, profits and dividends. International capital can be involved in tourism development in a number of ways,
including direct ownership of facilities by large companies, individual ownership of second homes, and ownership of the means of transport (especially
airlines). In terms of the ownership of foreign facilities, hotels have been the
most obvious recipient of direct foreign investment. The largest hotel groups
are enormous and in 1986, for example, Holiday Inn owned 1,907 hotels
world-wide, followed by Quality Inns with 801 hotels. The largest European
groups were the United Kingdom's Trusthouse Forte (793) and France's Accor
(534) (*Financial Times*, 28 August 1987). Many of the major tour companies
also have interests in hotel chains. While direct ownership of hotels and of
other facilities is important, of even greater significance is the bargaining

power of large foreign tour companies such as Thomson, Tjaereborg or Schaernow-Reisen. For example, Thomson had 38 per cent of the UK package holiday market in 1989 and its sheer size allows it—and other major groups —to secure very low prices from subcontracting to nationally-owned hotel chains. Given the oligopolistic position of the tour companies in the delivery of tourists, especially when faced with large numbers of relatively undifferentiated hotels, their bargaining power is considerable (see also Chapter 3).

1.2.4   *International migration*

International migration also plays a role in the tourist industry and, in this, the experience of tourism is not dissimilar to that of other economic sectors, including manufacturing. The dominant international migration flows in Europe are from the South to the North (King 1984), and from less developed countries to Northern Europe (Castles *et al.* 1984). Countries such as the United Kingdom, France, Switzerland, the Federal Republic of Germany, the Netherlands and Sweden rely on the labour of an estimated 6 million immigrants. They occupy a variety of jobs including less well-paid posts in such services sectors as hotels and restaurants. Their role is twofold: the supply of a flexible labour force contributes to depressing wages in the tourist industry, while their remittances to their home countries contribute to the balance of payments and to the levels of consumption in those countries (King 1986). There is also an important link between tourism and the generation of emigration. Tourism contributes to familiarisation with foreign culture and life-styles (Lanfant 1980) and this may encourage emigration. There are some instances where tourists—or at least foreign settlers—have found jobs for locals abroad. Moore (1976) reports such a link in the Canaries where immigrant Swedes found jobs in Sweden for some of the local people.

1.3   Tourism and development: regional perspectives

The distribution of tourism is inherently uneven; not only is this polarised but, traditionally, it is concentrated in less urbanised areas. Therefore, as Peters (1969, p. 11) states, 'tourism, by its nature, tends to distribute development away from the industrial centres towards those regions in a country which have not been developed'. There are many studies which have illustrated the extent of such regional polarisation and the rapidity of the process. Quite apart from every single case study in this volume, previous studies of the United Kingdom (Duffield 1977), Greece (Buckley and Papadopoulos 1986) and Yugoslavia (Allcock 1983) reinforce this argument. What is surprising is not that tourism has featured in regional policy and regional development strategies (see Chapter 3), but that it has featured so little in these. Belatedly, however, local authorities are awakening to the possibilities of using tourism as a basis for regional development, as is evident, for example, in urban tourism projects in the United Kingdom and France.

The contribution of tourism to regional economies is measured in similar fashion to that for national economies. Its share of regional income or output can be estimated either in terms of direct effects or, via multiplier studies, of direct and indirect effects. The levels of interlinkages and dependency identified depend on the spatial scale of the analysis (Henderson 1976). Smaller tourist regions are more likely to be dependent on tourism than are larger regions, which are more likely to have more diversified economies. As tourism can be developed in a short time-span, and with only moderate levels of investment, its impact on a regional economy can be very rapid as, for example, Diem (1980) reports in the Val d'Anniviers in Switzerland. Here, a number of investments linked to a Club Méditerranée project resulted in a dramatic turn-around in the local economy in little more than a decade.

Tourism is also a major source of employment at the regional level. However, as Pearce and Grimmeau (1985) have shown for Spain, the numbers and types of jobs vary considerably between regions in relation to the structure of the tourist industry, especially its seasonality. The year-round tourism of the Costa del Sol provides more permanent jobs than does the summer tourism of the Costa Dorada. Seasonality is but one aspect of employment in tourism, and there is also a need—as at the national level—to consider whether jobs are full-time or part-time, and whether they provide professional or manual work. There is also a need to consider how jobs in tourism interact with other household employment: whether tourism wages are supplementary to or the principal source of income, and whether they are used to support another enterprise such as a farm or a small workshop. Alternatively the employment effects can be negative, and tourism may destroy the basis of other activities as, for example, Greenwood (1976) describes for an agricultural community in the Basque region. There is also the very real problem for many communities of the generational gap, so vividly described by Fraser (1974) in his study in southern Spain, but also evident in many Alpine communities (Kariel and Kariel 1982). Younger members of the family, lured by the easier wages and more glamorous lifestyles of tourist areas, may turn their backs on the traditional economy and, sometimes, society.

At the local level tourism can also have a very considerable impact on land markets. Tourism is highly polarised spatially, along the coastline, in a few cities or in some of the more picturesque inland areas. This is particularly evident along the Mediterranean coast where there is near-continuous urban sprawl, largely as a result of tourism (Gonen 1981). The demands of tourism may force up land prices, providing a windfall for local landowners and farmers, as, for example, in the Alps (Vincent 1980). However, rising land values can also cause difficulties for those locals who are not in the tourist industry but who need to build homes or establish businesses in these areas (see Andronicou 1979 on Cyprus, and Boissevain and Inglott 1979 on Malta). The highly polarised nature of development also generates intense environmental problems such as water and air pollution, water shortages, traffic congestion and destruction of traditional landscapes. This reduces the quality of life for locals as well as for tourists and, ultimately, may threaten the viability of the tourist industry intself. This is vividly illustrated in the Alps where the scars left by winter sports reduce the attraction of the landscape for summer visitors (see Chapters 7 and 8).

1.3.1   *Types of tourist*

As with national development, care must be taken not to overgeneralise about the role of tourism in regional development. This role is conditioned by a number of considerations. One important element is the number of tourists and whether they exceed the 'tourist carrying capacity' (de Kadt 1979) of a region. There are usually critical numbers of tourists which can be integrated into regional economic and social structures and, beyond this, any increase will result in a transformation of these structures. The regional economic effects are also dependent on the types of tourist attracted and, for example, Middleton (1977) shows the uneven regional distribution of (high-spending) foreign tourists compared to domestic tourists in the United Kingdom. Only a few cities and small regions benefit substantially from foreign visitors while other regions—such as the far South-West—suffer from their inability to attract foreign visitors. Similar trends can be observed in the Mediterranean countries where foreign tourists are usually much higher spenders, per capita, than are domestic tourists, although there may also be differences in consumption behaviour between groups of foreign nationals (see Chapter 6). For example, Weatherley (1982) has shown how the economic impact of domestic second home ownership—as opposed to foreign tourism—in the Sierra Morena, Spain, is weakened by a strong tendency for self-building and for buying food and other goods outside the region.

1.3.2   *Regional economic context*

The structure of the regional economy is also influential in conditioning the economic impact of tourism, and two elements are important in this. First, there is the question of whether the tourist development is integrated into an existing settlement or is on a greenfield site and, also, whether the scale of the development is such that it can be absorbed by or overwhelms the existing economy. In the Alps, for instance, there is a major difference between high-level ski villages, built beyond the traditional settlement line, and low-level centres where tourism is better integrated with existing villages (Barker 1982). Each of these types makes different forms of demands on local labour, capital and suppliers and, *in extremis*, a large specialist, high-level ski centre may be developed almost entirely by capital and labour from outside the local region.

This leads to the second question, which is whether the tourist industry is able to utilise local resources. For example, farm tourism—by its nature— mostly utilises local resources, in terms of capital, labour and food supplies (see Béteille 1976 on rural France). However, with the rapid expansion of farm tourism in Europe (Dernoi 1983), there is a tendency for the marketing and, therefore, some of the control of farm tourism to pass into the hands of tour companies. The critical importance of regional economic structures in the utilisation of local resources is highlighted by Loukissas's (1982) comparative study of Greek islands. The economic impact of tourism is most beneficial in the larger islands because these have more diversified economic structures, leakage effects are limited, and the pressures on the local population are reduced because tourism tends to be concentrated in specialised villages. In contrast, tourism tends to dominate the economies of the smaller islands, but may lead to unstable, short-term and dualistic development (see also Chapter 5).

1.3.3   Sources of capital

Capital in tourism development tends to be highly polarised between a few large groups and a mass of small, family-owned enterprises. The former will have access to the capital resources of large groups (for example, Thomas Cook to its parent, Midland Bank) or to banking or institutional capital (for example, Accor financed its 1987 expansion programme through a share issue to French banks). However, venture capital has been notoriously loath to invest in smaller tourist businesses which—sometimes wrongly—have been considered higher-risk activities than manufacturing firms. Instead, small tourist businesses may have to rely on public sector grants or loans (see Chapter 14) or, more commonly, on personal or family sources of capital (see Shaw, Williams and Greenwood 1987 on a Cornish case study); this can be a major constraint on business expansion. The polarisation of capital can also be a potential source of conflict between the different interests of small-scale and (often externally owned) large-scale segments of the industry and their labour forces, as Werff (1980) reports in the case of Pescara in Italy.

The sources of personal or family capital can be diverse but usually involve a transfer of resources from another economic activity, such as a small farm, fishing or transport business. One particularly important source of such capital—at least in southern Europe—has been the savings and remittances of emigrants and returned migrants, as King *et al.* (1984) and Mendonsa (1983a) report for southern Italy and central Portugal, respectively (see also Chapters 4 and 6). One final point to be emphasised with respect to capital is that most studies have concentrated on the accumulation of capital and new rounds of investment in tourism, while there has been little research on the restructuring of capital in existing tourist areas (with a few exceptions such as Weg 1982 on Scheveningen in the Netherlands).

1.3.4   Regional labour markets

The type of local economy and of tourist development also condition the impact of tourism on regional labour markets. It may be possible—if the development is small enough—to rely entirely on local labour but, failing this, a system of labour migration will develop. This can involve daily movements (from surrounding towns and villages), seasonal migration, or permanent in-migration. These have very different impacts on the local economy depending on whether extra housing and services are required, and also on how the migrant labour force distributes its expenditure between the locality and its home area (see Bernal *et al.* 1979 on the marked variations which exist between regional labour markets in Andalusia). Given that tourist regions often attract labour from less developed rural regions (see Cavaco 1980 on Portugal), the remittances they send back to these areas can ameliorate some of the features of uneven regional development.

This chapter has provided only a brief introduction to some of the relationships between tourism and economic development. Nevertheless, it has highlighted the complexity of the issues and relationships involved and the need to look in detail at particular cases, taking account of their regional structures and how these have evolved. In this respect, the case studies in this volume do indicate some of the major international and interregional differences which exist in the tourist industry of Western Europe. However, the way in which these and other relationships can be examined and compared depends on the availability of data, and this chapter concludes with a brief review of this topic.

1.4   Tourism data

The unreliability of tourism data is notorious and although there are usually quite good time series for individual countries or regions, international comparisons are fraught with difficulties (Chib 1977). Many commentators have argued for the need to develop reliable and internationally acceptable methods of data collection and presentation (for example, Baron 1983) and international organisations such as the OECD and the World Tourism Organisation have been active towards this end. However, there still remain considerable difficulties. Several of the authors in this volume provide commentaries on the statistical coverage for particular countries, while some general features are summarised below:

1. There are many sociological (for example, Cohen 1974) and economic considerations of what constitutes tourism (see Peters 1969). Tourism is usually considered to involve visits of more than 24 hours (but less than one year) for business or recreational purposes and has to be differentiated from shorter visits, known as *excursionism*, whether these involve national or international journeys.
2. In many countries, the data on international tourism may be more reliable than those on domestic tourism. The former may be enumerated at international frontiers and are probably more likely to be accommodated in officially registered premises.
3. Tourists may stay in any one of a number of forms of accommodation. Even discounting friends and relatives and the informal sector, this ranges from hotels, through boarding houses, holiday camps and camping sites, to rooms let in private dwellings. Data tend to be most reliable for hotels and large camping sites, and least reliable for the myriad of privately let rooms and small camping sites which are found in most countries.
4. Each national tourist organisation may record different types of information. For example, duration of stay, mode of travel, expenditure, age, socio-economic group and number of accompanying persons are all important aspects of tourism but these are not recorded in all tourist enumerations.
5. There are different ways of enumerating tourists: the census points can be international frontiers or the place of accommodation, while some countries also undertake special sample surveys. While international borders may seem the most reliable sources (for foreign tourists), relaxation of passport controls within Scandinavia and the EC have seriously undermined the value of these data.
6. Data on the economic aspects of tourism are even more problematic. Tourist expenditure can be estimated from social surveys or from bank returns, but both methods are incomplete and under-record prepaid transport, etc. (White and Walker 1982). There is also poor availability of

data on most tourism-related sectors other than accommodation and catering in most countries. Therefore, unless special firm-level surveys are undertaken (see Shaw, Williams and Greenwood 1987), estimates of the real importance of tourism to a national or regional economy can only be crude approximations. This applies equally well to expenditure as to employment data.

2 Western European tourism in perspective

Allan M. Williams and Gareth Shaw

2.1 Introduction: the emergence of mass tourism

The history of tourism can be traced via the spa towns of the eighteenth century and the railway-borne day-trippers of the late nineteenth century to the emergence of mass tourism in the twentieth century. As Krippendorf (1986, p. 131) writes:

Travel has become one of the most curious phenomena of our industrialized society. Travel occupies 40 per cent of our available free time, made up of 30 per cent for excursions and other short trips—note the week-end exodus from the cities—and 10 per cent for longer holidays. Human society, once so static, has gained true mobility.

This has partly been based on the requirements of business and, in a world of increased geographical mobility, the need to visit friends and relatives. However, holidays and leisure activities have been the primary motive and account for 70 per cent of international tourism (World Tourism Organization 1984, p. 44). Both domestic and international tourism have been based on rising standards of living (for most groups in many developed countries) and greater leisure time. There have been reductions in the working week, increased entitlement to paid leave, and increased numbers of retired or early-retired persons. For example, in the European Community (EC) there was a 10 per cent cut in working hours for manual workers in the 1970s, while annual paid holidays increased on average to about four weeks (Edwards 1981). At the global scale, it has been estimated that about 1,700 million people had the right to paid holidays in the mid-1980s (World Tourism Organization 1984, p. 45).

The combination of increases in real incomes and holiday leave need not automatically result in increased tourism. Instead, this is determined by the preferences of individuals. According to Murphy (1982), the goals of leisure time can be classified as physical (relaxation), cultural (learning), social (visiting friends and relatives) and fantasy. The last of these stems from the fact that, increasingly, people 'do not feel at ease where they are, where they work and where they live. They need to escape from the burdens of their normal life' (Krippendorf 1986, p. 131). Where people choose to go depends on their holiday preferences (sea or snow), their past experiences of tourism and, possibly, the desire to achieve social status through patronising the 'right' resorts. Whereas these used to be defined by the holiday activities of the royalty and the aristocracy, they are increasingly dependent on travel writers and on the advertising industry.

However, the growth of tourism depends on more than just the expansion of demand for it is partly supply-led. The costs of travel have declined especially because of the expansion of car-ownership and reductions in the real costs of air transport. For example, in 1949 it took 18 hours to fly from London to New York but, by 1979, this had been reduced to a minimum of 4 hours (Kahn 1979). Beyond this, the growth of demand enabled economies of scale to be realised in the costs of travel and accommodation. This has been reinforced by the emergence of package holidays, allowing tour companies to reduce their profit margins on particular elements of the holiday while maintaining acceptable levels of absolute profit. Increased competition between tour companies has also reinforced the downward pressures on costs, as has the shift from serviced accommodation to self-catering. There is, then, a strong positive demand for tourism and this is an especially 'deeply-rooted social custom in European countries, which have benefited from the good transport networks and from the variety of facilities, especially in the non-hotel category, which facilitate tourism for a broad range of social groups' (World Tourism Organization 1984, p. 32).

Tourism is characterised by a positive income elasticity of demand—demand rises proportionately greater than the increase in income levels. This is based on its status as a luxury good, compared to basic needs (such as food and clothing) on which the proportion of total expenditure tends to fall as incomes rise. Tourism figures prominently in the aspirations to and expectations of improvements in standards of living. This is aided by the nature of the product for there is a nearly infinite variety of places to visit, each of which is unique in some way. As Waters (1967, p. 59) states, 'the travel industry is not made up of people taking a once-in-a-lifetime trip. The average tourist is a collector of places, and his appetite increases as his collection grows'. Furthermore, the supply of tourism products is not fixed in any absolute sense for investment can create new tourist attractions, and these may be at an enormous scale; for example, Disneyland in the United States attracted some 11 million visitors a year in the late 1970s (Murphy 1985, p. 14).

There is little quantitative evidence on the elasticity of demand. In the mid-1960s Waters (1967) considered that in the United States $10,000 was a critical threshold in terms of household incomes and that, beyond this, there was a sharp rise in participation in tourism. More recently, it has been estimated that households in the EC spend about 7 per cent of their budgets on holidays (Commission of the European Communities 1985). This is a relatively high-income region and of course the proportion would be lower in less prosperous economies. Other than such fragmented statistical evidence, there is a dearth of reliable estimates of the precise nature and strength of the elasticity of demand for tourism.

An indication of demand, however, is provided by the numbers participating in tourism and, while deficient in some ways, these data do emphasise that strong growth has occurred. The most reliable statistics are those for inter-national tourists, which increased from 25 million in 1950, through 69 million in 1960 and 160 million in 1970, to 389 million in 1988. Comprehensive statistics are not available on domestic tourists but these are considered to account for 90 per cent of the total, which places the international numbers in perspective. Growth has not been constant throughout the post-war period

Table 2.1   International tourism: arrivals by region, 1950–88 (per cent)

Region	1950	1971	1975	1984	1988
Europe	66	75	71	67	64
North America, Latin America and the Caribbean	30	19	20	19	19
Africa	2	1	2	3	3
Asia/Pacific	1	3	5	9	11
Middle East	1	2	2	3	2
Total	100	100	100	100	100

Sources: Young (1973, p. 54); World Tourism Organization (1984, p. 36; 1986, p. 20; 1989, p. 273)

and can be disaggregated into three distinctive elements. There are long-term growth trends, cyclical movements and short-term erratics. The long-term growth trends show that a major expansion of international mass tourism occurred in the 1950s (increases of 10.6 per cent per annum) and 1960s but that there has subsequently been a slowdown. Growth in the period 1975–82 was only 3.8 per cent per annum but this recovered to 5–7 per cent a year 1984–8. Cyclical movements average about 6 or 7 years (World Tourism Organization 1984) while, as would be expected, erratic events such as oil price increases or bombings are largely unpredictable in their occurrence and in the duration of their impact. In the case of Greece, for example, the major erratics—all of which led to a downturn in foreign tourist arrivals—have been political instability in 1964, the *coup d'état* in 1967, the oil crisis and the invasion of Cyprus in 1974, oil price increases in 1980, and the sharp world recession in 1982–3 (Buckley and Papadopoulos 1986, p. 87).

Not all the world's major regions have shared equally in the expansion of tourism (see Table 2.1). The relative position of the Americas has slipped since 1950, although absolute numbers have risen, while the share of Australia and Asia has increased sharply. This partly reflects the emergence of the Japanese as an important group of tourists, but it also indicates the steady growth of countries such as Australia and India as tourist attractions. However, international movements are dominated by Europe, which is not surprising given the large numbers of relatively prosperous persons living in relatively close proximity to other countries. The share of Europe increased up to 1971, largely as a result of the growth of mass tourism in the Mediterranean region, but it has subsequently fallen, partly reflecting the lure of more 'exotic' destinations beyond the region. The next section considers some of the features of European tourism in greater detail.

2.2   Tourism in Western Europe

2.2.1   *Access to tourism*

The EC provides the most comprehensive set of comparative statistics on tourism in Western Europe, and although these data exclude some countries, they are used in this and the following sections. It has been estimated that 140 million persons in the EC took a holiday in 1985, some 56 per cent of the total population. Only 21 per cent habitually stay at home, while 23 per cent sometimes go away on holiday. Of those who went on holiday, 37 per cent went away once and 19 per cent took two holidays (Commission of the European Communities 1987, p. 16). Tourism is therefore a relatively widely shared experience within the EC, although one-fifth of the population—by choice or constraint—are not involved in this.

The ability to take holidays away from home is, of course, dependent on income. It is no surprise that while most of northern Europe recorded tourism participation rates in excess of 57 per cent, Ireland, Spain and Greece all had levels below 46 per cent, while in Portugal the rate was only 31 per cent (Commission of the European Communities 1987, p. 7). The reasons for not taking holidays away from home are mainly economic: only about one-fifth preferred to stay at home while almost half of those surveyed could not afford a holiday. As a result, there is a strong relationship between occupation and holiday-taking. According to the EC survey, while only 18 per cent of professionals stayed at home in 1985, 49 per cent of manual workers did so (Commission of the European Communities 1987, p. 19). Older persons, those with larger families and those living in rural areas are also less likely to take holidays away from home. The type of holiday taken is also influenced by occupation and income: for example, professionals are more likely than manual workers to take holidays abroad, to take longer holidays and to use air travel. Access to tourism is an important element in access to quality of life and/or to social well-being; as with access to housing or to services, it is fundamentally influenced by socio-economic structures. The differences between socio-economic groups appear to be greater in less developed economies—such as Italy or Spain—than in more developed ones such as Sweden (Travis 1982a). There are also other important differences amongst the Western European countries, as is shown in the following section.

2.2.2   Destinations and origins

There have been important shifts in the origins and destinations of tourist flows in the post-1945 period. Although these affect both domestic and international tourism, reliable comparative data are only available for the latter, which is unfortunate as over half of European tourism is domestic. This section, therefore, concentrates on foreign tourism, but domestic tourism is discussed in the individual case studies in Chapters 3–13.

Figure 2.1 summarises changes in the major destinations of tourist flows in the period 1960–80. Almost all the major countries of Europe experienced important increases in foreign tourist arrivals in this period. However, the greatest relative gains were in the Mediterranean states, with Italy, Spain and Greece experiencing large absolute and percentage increases. Portugal, however, had a mixed experience, with rapid growth in the 1960s being followed by stagnation in the 1970s as a result of recession and the political aftermath of the 1974 military coup. These Mediterranean countries benefited from the development of inclusive, low-cost package holidays. The growing importance of winter holidays in Switzerland and Austria is also evident, especially the rapid growth in the latter, based on successful marketing of lower-cost skiing holidays. Elsewhere, the United Kingdom and especially

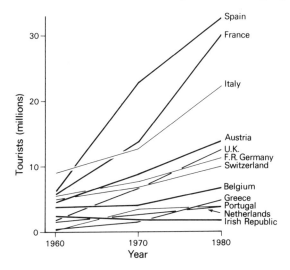

Fig. 2.1 Numbers of foreign tourists in Western Europe by country, 1960–80

Source: OECD reports

France experienced rapid increases in foreign tourist arrivals. While in France this can be explained by a variety of attractions (Paris, the Riviera, the Alps, touring and self-catering), in the United Kingdom London is still the dominant focus for foreign visitors (see Chapters 9 and 10).

Not all countries benefited equally from international tourist movements: for example, there was limited expansion in Belgium and the Netherlands (see Chapter 12) over the period as a whole; this is hardly surprising as they lack what were considered the main tourist attractions in this period—sea and sun, or skiing conditions. Even more remarkable is Ireland, which saw a decline in tourist arrivals. While partly accounted for by rising real costs, this was also probably the result of association with 'the troubles' in Northern Ireland. Another country which experienced difficulties is tiny Monaco, where 25 per cent of the Gross Domestic Product (GDP) is in tourism. Monaco had been a pre-war focus of élite tourism, but this specialised market segment was squeezed in the 1950s and 1960s by the growth of winter skiing holidays, while countries such as Spain and Greece provided fierce (and cheaper) competition in the market for Mediterranean tourism.

Some measure of the relative importance of foreign and domestic tourism is provided by Table 2.2. While not providing comprehensive coverage for Western Europe, it indicates major international differences. In particular, there is a group of countries where foreign tourists considerably outnumber domestic tourists, and this includes Portugal, Spain and Austria. The last named is especially dependent on foreign tourists, who outnumber domestic tourists by a ratio of three to one. The surprising ommission from this list is a Mediterranean country such as Italy (where domestic tourism is very strong). The special position of Austria (see also Chapter 8) is underlined by the very high ratio of foreign tourist overnight stays per head of population. At 11.6, this was considerably higher than the ratios for the next highest-ranked

Table 2.2   Nights spent by foreign and domestic tourists in all
accommodation in Western Europe in 1987 (in thousands)[1]

Country	Nights spent by foreign tourists	Nights spent by domestic tourists	Total nights
Austria	85,692	28,008	113,700
Belgium	10,064	20,719	30,783
Denmark	8,199	11,602	19,802
Finland	2,486	8,855	11,342
France[2]	36,144	82,073	118,217
FRG	32,862	207,599	240,461
Italy	106,491	243,083	349,574
Norway	5,456	11,361	16,818
Portugal	17,109	11,465	28,575
Spain[3]	92,444	46,276	138,721
Sweden	7,089	25,832	32,921
Switzerland	34,581	39,037	73,618

Source: OECD (1988, p. 164)

Notes: 1. There are variations in the sectors included.
          2. Excludes Pays de la Loîre, Champagne-Ardennes and Corsica.
          3. Hotels and camping only.

countries, Switzerland (5.6) and Spain (4.3) in the mid-1980s. Therefore, while
Spain has the largest absolute numbers of foreign visitors (grossly under-
enumerated in Table 2.2, see Note 3), their relative impact is potentially
greater in the Alpine region. The discussion here is limited to national data but
considerable regional differences exist within these countries. In Spain, for
example, more than half of the nation's total bed-space capacity is to be found
in just five provinces: the Balearics, Gerona, Barcelona, Málaga and Alicante
(Pearce and Grimmeau 1985). This and other aspects of regional differentiation
are discussed in the case studies which follow.

2.2.3   Types of tourist demand

The market for tourism is highly segmented and includes a number of
distinctive formations. In part, the relative success of particular countries in
attracting domestic and foreign tourists depends on their ability to 'deliver' the
type of tourism which is in demand. This, of course, is dependent on their
'resource' base so that it is not surprising that in 1977 Austria and Switzerland
had over 200 recognised winter sports resorts, while Portugal had only one
and Belgium had none (Winter 1979). Similarly, some countries have a
comparative advantage in terms of their climate or access to coastline. Beyond
this, cost structures, government policies and marketing strategies all
contribute to the ability of particular countries to capitalise on their tourism
resources. These tourism 'resources' are very heterogeneous and are not fixed,
with different types becoming popular over time. In the 1980s the major forms
include sunshine beach holidays, Alpine tourism, urban/cultural tourism,
business/conference tourism, and rural tourism.

The mainstay of twentieth-century holidays is still sea and sunshine beach-orientated tourism. While this dominates the domestic tourism industry in countries such as the United Kingdom, a major change has occurred with the expansion of international tourism along the coastline of southern Europe. Mediterranean holiday packages have become the model of mass tourism. These are based on low-cost charter air fares or (excluding Ireland, the United Kingdom and Scandinavia) self-drive to Mediterranean locations. The basic attractions are sun, sea, cheap wine and food, presented in a non-challenging, standardised international format. In recent years, additional recreational facilities such as golf courses and tennis courts have been added in the face of subtle changes in demand. Spain represents the most highly developed example of Mediterranean tourism, at least in terms of dependence on foreign visitors (see Chapter 3), but this model is also characteristic of substantial proportions of the foreign tourist market in Greece, Portugal, Italy and, to a lesser extent, France. The tourism resorts which are developed within this model tend to be little differentiated and Holloway (1983) terms them 'identikit destinations'.

Alpine holidays are the other main form of mass tourism. The roots of this lie in the nineteenth century when the Alps were visited for summer relaxation by the wealthy élites of Europe (Barker 1982). By the mid-nineteenth century, development of the international railway network and the emergence of the first modern tour company, Thomas Cook, was leading to increased tourism although this was still restricted to the middle classes and to exclusive resorts such as Montreux and Merano. Early in the twentieth century, winter tourism increased in importance, boosted by the first Winter Olympics which were held at Chamonix in 1924; by 1933, winter visits accounted for 44 per cent of the Alpine total. Finally, since the late 1950s there has been growth of mass tourism based on inclusive package holidays (see also Chapters 7 and 8). This has been stimulated by rising standards of living which have allowed more families to enjoy second holidays, which is often the priority allocated to skiing as opposed to sunshine holidays. There are many different forms of resort and, for example, Préau (1970) differentiates between resorts based on existing settlements, such as Chamonix, and greenfield development of resorts such as Les Bellevilles. The latter are often situated at very high altitudes, as at La Plagne in France, so as to secure more reliable snow conditions. Of course, not all tourism in either the Alps or the Mediterranean is mass package tourism. Large numbers of visitors make their own travel and accommodation arrangements in both cases.

Urban tourism contains two distinctive strands: cultural tourism and business/conference tourism. Every major European city benefits in some way from one or both of these, with London (59.5 million overnight stays in 1985) and Paris (15.8 million overnight stays) being the principal beneficiaries (*Financial Times*, 8 June 1987). Cultural tourism is based on diverse features ranging from archaeological remains, through outstanding architecture, to museums, art galleries and other attractions. The scale of such attractions can be enormous: for example, the European Disneyland in construction near Paris is projected to attract 10 million visitors a year, leading to the construction of 5,000 hotel rooms. This type of tourism usually plays a secondary role to other forms of tourism with, for example, cities being visited from nearby beaches. It has also benefited from the boom in short-break second and third holidays which, in turn, are generated by increased real incomes. However, it should be emphasised that some cities—notably London and Paris—are the focus of primary holiday activities, being especially attractive to non-European tourists, particularly from North America and Japan. The growing importance of this market segment is illustrated by the case of France where an estimated 17 per cent of visitor nights in 1978 were accounted for by short leisure stays, which were often in cities (Tuppen 1985; see also Chapter 10).

Urban tourism is also supported by business and conference travel; this accounts for almost as large a proportion of overnight stays in France (15 per cent) as do short leisure breaks (Tuppen 1985). Business and conference travel are of growing global importance both because of the need for increasing international contacts in an internationalised economy and society (Lawson 1982), and because business and conference travel are used as an employee perk. For example, it has been estimated that about one-third of the United Kingdom's top 1,000 companies use some form of travel perk to reward their staff. The *Financial Times* (2 September 1986) summarised the advantages of this:

Whatever the reason for the corporate travel trip—be it purely as a sales conference or as a reward for good work—the lure of a cruise in the Caribbean or a weekend in Paris has an attraction that other forms of incentives find hard to beat. . . . What an incentive trip delivers is an individually tailored fantasy which cannot be bought in an ordinary package. . . . Conference and incentive travel also offers a more prosaic reason for popularity in that it often includes spouses and sometimes children. An overseas travel trip with spouse is an added bonus that can sometimes help justify the long hours put in on the company's behalf.

In the United Kingdom alone, companies spent an estimated £145–200 million on incentive travel in 1985. Seventeen companies each spent in excess of £500,000. Short trips in Europe were common, accounting for 80 per cent of the total, with Paris being the most popular destination. On a global scale—including North American and Japanese companies—London is the top-ranked city.

Conference travel has become big business, although estimates of this are notoriously unreliable. Law (1985b) has estimated that in 1984 there were some 14,000 international conferences and that the United Kingdom attracted a major share of these (see also Chapter 9). However, according to a *Financial Times* estimate for 1985, Paris was the leading venue for international meetings, followed by London, Brussels and Geneva (see Figure 2.2). Some of these conferences are organised on a massive scale and, to date, the largest meeting held in the United Kingdom—the International Rotary gathering at the National Exhibition Centre, Birmingham—attracted 23,000 delegates (Law 1985b). Given that this meeting alone generated over £6 million of revenue and that business tourists spend about three times as much per day as do holiday tourists (Lawson 1982), it is not surprising that there has been a rush to develop conference centres. The Vienna Centre, for example, combines conference and exhibition facilities, and has fourteen halls catering for meetings with between 50 and 4,200 delegates. It cost £165 million to build and is not expected to make a real profit. Yet it provides 120 full-time jobs directly and large numbers of indirect jobs in the city's hotels, restaurants, shops and places of entertainment. A much smaller conference centre in Brighton is estimated to generate £30 million in revenue, to provide 43 per cent of hotel bookings, and to sustain 2,650 full and part-time jobs in the town (Law 1985b).

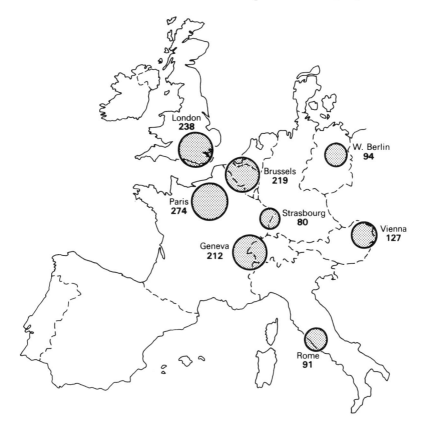

Fig. 2.2 International conferences in major European cities, 1985
Source: Financial Times, 2 September 1986

2.2.4 Seasonality

Seasonality is not exclusive to tourism—for example, it also occurs in fishing or in food processing—and it is also not typical of all branches of tourism. However, it is often a feature associated with the tourist industry. Seasonality arises both from the timing of holidays (traditionally in the summer, at Christmas, or perhaps at Easter) and from the seasonal nature of some forms of tourist attraction, especially summer sun and winter snow. According to the World Tourism Organization (1984,p. 43):

The most specialized destinations (some beach, mountain, hunting or fishing destinations at certain times of the year, etc.) are usually the most seasonal because of the seasonal factor associated with tourist utilization of their basic resources. Tourist destinations supported by large urban centres, while having high points of activity, have more continuous operation throughout the year because they depend upon a more diversified demand.

The pattern of seasonality in the Western European tourist industry is shown in Figure 2.3. Although important regional differences are averaged out

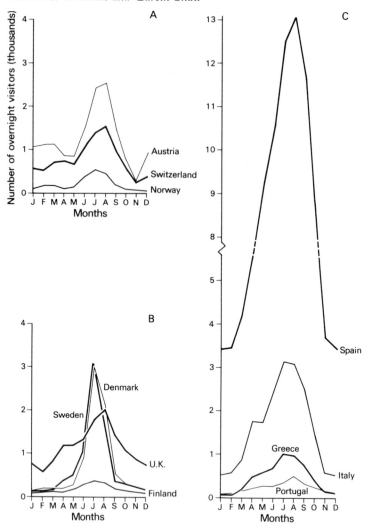

Fig. 2.3   Seasonality in the Western European tourist industry, 1983
Source: OECD (1985)

in national data, these indicate the significance of seasonality in almost every country. The figures only cover foreign tourism but domestic tourism usually has a similar, if less sharply peaked, pattern. There is a small group of countries which have double peaks in tourism; these are Austria, Switzerland and (to a lesser extent) Norway, countries with ski seasons and summer walking/touring seasons. A second group of countries, the Mediterranean destinations, displays the classic pattern of peak summer tourism. A third group, consisting of most of the northern European countries, also has single seasonal tourism peaks.

As the graphs in Figure 2.3 are drawn on absolute scales, it is difficult to assess the degree of seasonality. However, the proportion of tourist arrivals which occurs in the two peak months of the year gives a relative index of seasonality. In Sweden, Denmark, Italy and Greece, over 35 per cent of tourists arrive in two months. This is climatically determined, in part, either in a negative sense because of the harshness of the winter (as in Scandinavia) or in a positive sense because of the attractions of the summer (as in the Mediterranean). Given their double peaks, Switzerland and Austria occupy intermediate positions on this index. The countries with the lowest degree of seasonal peaking—between 24 and 27 per cent—are the Netherlands, the Federal Republic of Germany and the United Kingdom. In all three cases, cultural and business tourism are relatively important and these are less affected by climatic conditions. This pattern is borne out by the results of the EC tourism survey. Whereas 62 per cent of main holidays were begun in July or August, this only applied to 20 per cent of other holidays; the latter are more likely to involve urban tourism and less likely to involve beach tourism (Commission of the European Communities 1987, p. 31). Finally, it is interesting to note that Spain has a relatively low index (29 per cent), indicating a measure of success in attracting tourists out of season to enjoy the relatively mild winters in the far South, especially in Andalusia (see Chapter 3).

The impact of seasonality on the accommodation sector is made clear in Skojoldelev's (1984) study of the Scandinavian countries where, in 1981, room occupancy rates varied between 48 per cent (Denmark) and 61 per cent (Finland). The economic implications of this and of other features of tourism are considered in the following section.

2.3   Tourism: economic structures

The tourist industry is exceptionally heterogeneous and combines large numbers of small businesses or self-employed persons (partly dependent on tourism) with large-scale companies. Over time the industry has been subject to two major tendencies: internationalisation and concentration. There are several reasons for this, including the possibilities of selling a package of services rather than an individual product, economies of scale in purchasing and advertising, the internationalisation of travel, and the need to reduce costs in the face of intense competition. In this section, three interrelated features of the economic structure of tourism are considered: the international environment of the trading of tourism services; ownership patterns; and the structure of the accommodation sector.

2.3.1   *The internationalisation of tourism*

With the increase in international tourism, it was perhaps inevitable that internationalisation of the provision of tourism services would also occur. This can take many forms, including direct ownership, long-term subcontracting, or short-term agreements for the provision of transport, accommodation, tourism attractions and supporting services such as car rental. The importance of such international groups as Holiday Inns, Avis car rental, the Centre Parc holiday centres, and tour companies such as Thomson and Tjaereborg, bear testimony to the importance of internationalisation. Although little researched as yet, these companies influence the international distribution of jobs, international profit remittances, and local versus international expenditure on inputs of goods and services.

There has undoubtedly been an internationalisation of tourism but this has not occurred in an environment of unfettered competition. The service industries have tended to be excluded from most international trade agreements. For example, both the EC and the GATT negotiations have largely concentrated on trade in manufactured goods and only in the late 1980s have the service industries secured a prominent place on the agenda for trade liberalisation. Most of the barriers to trade in tourism services have been of the non-tariff type, and there have been a number of these (World Tourism Organization 1984, pp. 10–11):

1. Specific quantitative or qualitative restrictions: a 'quota' on tourism trade.
2. Non-tariff import charges: charges over and above normal customs charges.
3. Participation in trade by the administration: subsidies to discourage travel abroad.
4. Administrative and customs procedures and specific administrative prices: specific procedures which by their length, complexity and cost discourage international tourism.
5. Concessionary transport costs for tourists.
6. Prevention of the establishment of foreign-owned service industries.
7. Discriminatory practices against foreign airlines.

Taken together, these practices suggest that tourism services operate in a relatively restricted international market. This is in the face of increased concentration of ownership in the industry and the internationalisation of activities.

2.3.2   Ownership patterns

While this section mainly focuses on the concentration of ownership, it is important to stress that most tourist enterprises are small scale. In France, for example, 80 per cent of tourist firms employ fewer than ten people (Tuppen 1985). This form of ownership depends on the type of tourism involved, the speed at which the industry developed and the availability of local, as opposed to external, capital sources. Despite this, the most impressive feature of ownership patterns since 1945 has been increased concentration of ownership. This has involved both horizontal (the takeover of similar businesses) and vertical (the takeover of linked businesses) expansion. Examples of the latter include airlines buying hotels, hotels buying car-rental companies, and tour companies buying travel agencies. Linkages between these elements of the industry already exist, and vertical expansion is a logical extension of ownership and control. As has already been discussed, this offers cost advantages and guaranteed market shares or supplies in the face of intense competition in a multi-product, multinational industry.

One of the most impressive features of the industry has been the growth of major tour companies. These and other companies are widely used and, in the EC as a whole, it is estimated that 13 per cent of all holidays involved tour-company packages; most of these involved travel by plane to a foreign seaside destination, that is, the classic Mediterranean holiday package (Commission of the European Communities 1987, p. 47). Although these companies have international activities, their markets are virtually completely segmented by the nationality of the tourist: for example, German tour operators cater essentially for German tourists. There are, however, differences in the organisation of the sector even within the countries where tour companies are most important, that is, the United Kingdom, Scandinavia and the Federal Republic of Germany. The major companies are Neckermann Versand of the Federal Republic of Germany (which has its own travel-agency subsidiary), Tjaereborg of Denmark (which has its own airline and hotels), and Thomson of the United Kingdom (which has its own travel-agency chain and transport subsidiaries). In some cases the tour companies are in foreign ownership: for example, Caravela of the United Kingdom is owned by the Portuguese airline, TAP.

There is intense competition in this market segment and large companies have considerable cost advantages. First, because they sell 'bundles' of services—flights, accommodation, insurance, car hire, supplementary tours and activities—they can reduce margins on single items while maintaining overall profits. Second, because of the size of their operations—Thomson, for example, sold over 3 million holidays in 1986—they are able to sign large-scale, low-cost airline and hotel contracts, or even purchase their own accommodation and means of transport. For example, in the early 1970s, large tour companies were reputed to be paying Spanish hoteliers no more than £0.40 per capita per day for full board.

The keen competition amongst tour companies was particularly evident in the United Kingdom in 1985 when, following a sharp downturn in the holiday business (by some 6 per cent), the market leaders, Thomson, reacted with price cuts of up to 20 per cent. In the opinion of the *Financial Times* (4 November 1986), 'Thomson was able to take this step because a massive investment in new technology had enabled it to cut operating margins and cope with a large increase in volume of business.' As a result, Thomson increased its market share from about 20 per cent to 30 per cent, and other tour operators had to cut their prices and profit margins in the ensuing price war. However, a combination of low prices and sharply reduced growth led to a major crisis in the UK package-holiday industry during 1989.

Internationalisation and concentration of ownership can also be seen in the hotel sector. A league table of the largest international hotel groups shows that these have been dominated by American companies (Table 2.3). Only Club Méditerranée and Novotel of France, along with Trusthouse Forte and (its subsidiary) Travelodge of the United Kingdom, maintained a European presence amongst the American giants until recently. Some of the groups are very large scale: Holiday Inn, for example, owns far more hotels within the United States than abroad. Indeed, a 1986 league table of *all* hotels would show Holiday Inn (1,907) well in the lead, followed by Quality Inns (801) and Trusthouse Forte (793) (*Financial Times*, 28 August 1987). However, US dominance has been weakened by the (UK) Bass Group's acquisition of Holiday Inns during 1989. Some of the chains also belong to larger groups, notably Sheraton Hotels which is owned by ITT. Indeed, one of the most potent indicators of global shift in recent years has been the decision by ITT to disinvest partly from its traditional telecommunications interests in order to concentrate on more lucrative investments in financial and other services, including tourism.

Table 2.3   Transnational corporations and tourism, 1978

(a) Leading multinational hotel chains

Company	Nationality	Number of hotels abroad
Holiday Inn	USA	114
Inter–Continental	USA	74
Hilton International	USA	72
Sheraton Hotels	USA	64
Club Méditerranée	France	56
Trusthouse Forte	UK	53
Novotel	France	45
Travelodge	UK	34
Ramada Inns	USA	33
Hyatt International	USA	20

(b) Transnational hotels abroad by country/region of origin

Country	No. of parent groups	Transnational-associated hotels abroad	Percentage of total
USA	22	508	49.6
France	8	156	15.2
UK	13	147	14.5
Other European countries	14	87	8.5
Japan	7	23	2.2
Other developed market economies	8	65	3.9
Developing countries	9	37	3.6

(c) Transnational-associated hotels abroad, by main activity of parent group

Parent group	No. of transnational corporations	Transnational-associated hotels abroad Number	Transnational-associated hotels abroad Percentage
Hotel chains associated with airlines	16	277	27.1
Hotel chains independent of airlines	56	687	67.0
Hotel development and management consultants	3	15	1.5
Tour operators and travel agents	6	46	4.5
Total	81	1,025	100.0

(d) Number of transnational-associated hotels and rooms in selected host countries

Country	Hotels	Hotel bedrooms
Canada	99	23,318
Spain	58	14,883
FRG	51	13,691
USA	38	11,777
France	30	8,978
UK	28	8,631
Italy	29	8,439
Japan	9	5,835
Switzerland	24	5,314
Netherlands	27	5,271
Greece	15	4,630
Belgium	25	4,592

Source: UNCTC (1982)

These large, international hotels sell more than just a single product (accommodation), a brand image and invariable standards. Most large, modern hotels sell a package of on-site and off-site services (Dicken 1986). On-site services include conference facilities, leisure facilities, restaurants and bars, while off-site services include transport to and from airports, sales of theatre and sports tickets, car hire and organised tours. According to one estimate, hotels obtain only 51 per cent of their income from providing accommodation, while 40 per cent comes from meals and bars, and the remainder from other services (World Tourism Organization 1984, p. 58). Over time there has been a coalescence of the ownership of such services. This is prevalent at the level of the transnational hotels, for many of the large hotel chains are linked with airlines, tour operators, or management consultancies (see Table 2.3).

There are several different types of transnational hotel groups according to the United Nations Centre on Transnational Corporations (UNCTC 1982). One group—already mentioned—involves ownership by airline companies. Examples (in 1978) are TWA which owned Hilton International, Pan American which owned Inter-Continental, and Iberia which owned Hotels Husa and Entursa. A second group consists of large transnational groups which are not directly associated with airlines, and examples are Club Méditerranée and Trusthouse Forte. A third group are the specialist hotel development and management companies, such as Hotel Management International of the United Kingdom, but these are not of major significance. A fourth group is made up of hotel chains which are part of a larger enterprise; an example is Rank Hotels of the United Kingdom which belongs to a larger leisure group (see also Table 9.3). Hotels owned by tour operators and travel agents are the fifth type of group. These are particularly important in Western Europe and examples include Thomsons of the United Kingdom, Vingresor of Sweden and Hotelplan of Switzerland (the last, in turn, is owned by the Swiss retailing group, Migros). Each of these different types of hotel group has different long-term interests and strategies but, together, they increasingly dominate hotel provision.

Travel agencies are also subject to concentration and internationalisation although, again, particular companies almost exclusively serve national market segments. The UK market is dominated by a few large companies such as Thomas Cook and Lunn Poly, which, in turn, belong to larger groups such as Midland Bank and International Thomson. A similar pattern exists in other Western European countries, and in the Federal Republic of Germany, for example, Touristik Union International is the leading travel-agency company. There is also evidence of growing internationalisation of ownership. One example is the 1986 takeover of Melia, the Spanish travel agency (with 197 branches) and hotel group, by SASEA, the Swiss holiday company, and Interpart Holding of Luxembourg. This is a sector where there is growing competition from two sources. First, there is a move by airlines and other companies to bypass the travel agencies through such measures as walk-on flights and direct ticket sales. Second, there is competition from other high street retailers diversifying into travel-agency business; the Gelmoli department store group in Switzerland was an early leader in this field (Young 1973), while W.H. Smith is a United Kingdom example.

2.3.3   *The accommodation sector: polarisation tendencies*

It is important to consider this sector separately because it is 'accommodation, more than any other component, which dictates the sort of tourism industry a country can expect' (Young 1973, p. 98). The supply of accommodation is, of course, both determined by and helps to determine demand. Whether accommodation is in second homes, rented villas, private homes, camping or large hotels has a major influence on the types of tourist attracted, the duration of their visits, and the types and quantities of job created and income generated. These differences are underlined by considering for example, the differences between tourism in much of the Costa del Sol (based on large hotels) and in Denmark, where second homes are relatively important. Europe dominates the world hotel industry, having some 9.5 million bed-places in 1983 which accounted for 50 per cent of global capacity (World Tourism Organization 1986, p. 40). In addition, there are an estimated 16 million bed-places in supplementary accommodation, but this figure must be viewed cautiously given the paucity of the statistics. Non-hotel accommodation is particularly important in the Mediterranean and Alpine regions because, according to the World Tourism Organization (1984, p. 64):

In these countries the quantitatively high demand, also very diversified with regard to socio-economic origin, available income, motivation, etc., has made it necessary to diversify the supply, which has exceeded the possibilities of the hotel business in this regard. This has given rise to inns, company sites, apartments, holiday towns, houses, spas, etc., which have basically met the desires and economic possibilities of each segment of demand.

The emphasis on hotels versus supplementary accommodation is somewhat misleading, for there are strong polarisation tendencies within both of these. In terms of hotels, there seems to be a general expansion of large hotels and hotel chains. Some of these may be parts of international chains (see the previous section) but the transnationals only account for 2.2 per cent of all hotel capacity in Western Europe. Nevertheless, large hotel chains are increasing in importance because they possess a number of advantages, including projection of a brand image, access to large advertising budgets, economies of scale in purchasing, and—increasingly—computer reservation systems. In Europe only a quarter of the trade of international hotels is based on holiday-makers, while half are business travellers and 15 per cent are conference participants (World Tourism Organization 1986, p. 51). Smaller hotels are finding it increasingly difficult to compete, especially if they lack facilities such as private bathrooms, bars and swimming pools which are becoming a part of standard expectations. The smaller establishments have to compete, instead, in terms of price (cutting their margins to the minimum, often through relying on unpaid family labour) or offering a distinctive product: this may be highly personalised service, exceptional cooking or, as in farm holidays, participating in household activities.

Self-catering holidays have experienced similar polarisation tendencies. Until recently, rented houses and apartments were dominated by small-scale businesses, characteristically by entrepreneurs owning one or two properties. While this is still dominant in some areas, there has been increased profession-alisation and commercialisation of the sector. This may involve either greater reliance on large commercial booking agencies (which have access to computerised systems) or the emergence of large-scale ownership. Lower-quality and individually owned self-catering accommodation is likely to find it increasingly difficult to compete in this market. An important part of the self-catering market is accounted for by second homes. In 1985 these accounted for approximately 7 per cent of all principal holidays in the EC, and the figure for all holidays is likely to be even greater. Second homes are even more important in particular countries, accounting for over 10 per cent of all holidays taken in the Netherlands, Denmark, Spain, Italy and Greece (Commission of the European Communities 1987, p. 38). This is largely divided into discrete national markets but there are signs of internationalisation. This is probably most strongly developed in Spain, where there has been a major influx of property investment from northern Europe, especially from the United Kingdom and Federal Republic of Germany. This has even generated international development and sales agencies. For example, several large British construction companies build and sell houses in Spain, while Fincasol (a British-owned agency in Málaga) sells new and renovated dwellings, mainly to British clients. The Elliot Property and Leisure Group plays a similar role in Portugal (see Chapters 3 and 6).

A new dimension has been added to self-catering by the growth of timeshare. By the end of 1989 there were already an estimated 150,000 timeshare owners in the United Kingdom, and Spain was their favoured foreign destination (*Financial Times*, 5 January 1990).

2.4   The economic role of tourism

The structure of tourism and the role it plays in economic development have fascinated analysts for some time. Indeed, the challenge is summarised most succinctly in the titles of two books on the subject: *Tourism: passport to development?* (de Kadt 1979) and *Tourism: blessing or blight?* (Young 1973). The answer obviously has to be conditional. It can be positive or negative,

Table 2.4 International tourism and the national economy in Western Europe, 1986

Country		Tourism receipts as a % of	Tourism expenditure as a % of
	GDP	Exports of goods and services	Imports of goods and services
Austria	7.4	18.1	10.5
Belgium and Luxembourg	2.0	2.2	3.0
Denmark	2.1	5.9	6.3
Finland	0.9	3.0	5.2
France	1.3	5.2	3.6
FRG	0.7	2.1	7.4
Greece	4.6	23.2	4.1
Ireland	2.7	4.5	4.1
Italy	1.6	7.7	2.3
Netherlands	1.3	2.2	5.1
Norway	1.5	3.7	8.1
Portugal	5.4	15.6	2.9
Spain	5.2	25.9	3.5
Sweden	1.2	3.3	6.2
Switzerland	4.0	8.3	7.3
UK	1.5	3.8	4.2

Source: OECD (1988, p. 84)

depending on the criteria used for evaluation (for example, growth versus equity), on the nature of the industry and on the nature of the local economy. In this broad review, therefore, it is only possible to outline some of the salient features of international comparisons of the economic impact of tourism in terms of income, balance of payments, employment and some broader economic relationships. More detailed evaluations have to wait until the following chapters. As with other aspects of international comparisons, it is easier to comment on international than on domestic tourism.

2.4.1   Gross domestic product and national income

Measuring the contribution to GDP of tourism receipts is difficult because the major component of the latter—domestic tourism receipts—is not known for most countries. However, it has been estimated that domestic tourism expenditure is five to ten times greater than international tourism expenditure (World Tourism Organization 1984, p. 2). In addition, the difficulties are aggravated because there is a lack of a common international methodology for data collection (see Chapter 1, Section 1.4). These reservations should be borne in mind in the ensuing discussion. It has been estimated that tourism directly accounted for 4 per cent of GDP in the nine countries of the EC in 1979 and, taking into account multiplier effects, this figure rises to 10 per cent (Commission of the European Communities 1985). In individual countries, tourism can account for a significant share of income generation. For example, the English Tourist Board has estimated that in 1985 tourists in England spent about £10 billion and that about half of this came from overseas visitors. Given the levels of expenditure involved, it is not surprising that governments have been keen to attract overseas visitors, while trying to retain the tourist expenditure of their nationals. France has been particularly successful in this for, in 1983, French tourists only spent 38 billion francs abroad compared with 260 billion francs at home (Tuppen 1985).

The OECD (1986) provides a useful summary of the importance of international tourist receipts in Western Europe, based on estimates provided by national governments (Table 2.4). As would be expected, tourism makes its greatest contribution to GDP in the countries of mass tourism, that is, in the Alps and the Mediterranean. Austria is most heavily dependent on tourism, 7.4 per cent of GDP being attributed to this source. In Switzerland tourism is of lesser relative importance because of the smaller number of tourists and the role of multinational manufacturing and financial activities in the national economy. Amongst the Mediterranean destinations, international tourism is most important in Spain and Portugal, and least important in Italy, again reflecting the relative importance of the manufacturing sector in the latter. In contrast, international tourism receipts are of relatively minor importance in the Federal Republic of Germany and most of Scandinavia—but this is partly compensated for by the strength of their domestic tourism.

Other than employment, income is the major benefit of tourism to local communities. Hence, Clement (1967, p. 79) wrote that:

the rapidity with which tourists spend money over a given span of time is an important factor. It tends to reflect not only net income from tourism but also the efficiency of the travel plant—that is, the success of a country in getting tourists to spend a fair amount of money in relation to their length of stay.

This expenditure provides direct income which, via the multiplier effect, is amplified by indirect income. The total income generated can be considerable. For example, Law (1985a) reports that annual tourist expenditure in the early 1980s amounted to £16 million in Nottingham, £58 million in Merseyside and £56.6 million in Glasgow. The multiplier effects in these cases are unquantified. Some of the more reliable estimates of multipliers are provided by Archer (1977) who has calculated that the tourism income multiplier is about 1.68–1.78 in the United Kingdom. As with employment, the precise effects depend on the structure of the local economy and the tourist industry. Arguably, the local multiplier effects are greatest in larger and/or specialised tourist economies, because these are more able to support linked specialist services and manufacturing. In contrast, a tourist economy dominated by 'branch plants' is more likely than one dominated by small indigenous firms to be dependent on external services or products purchased by company head-quarters. In many cases the extent of income leakage can be considerable, especially if the tourist projects are large scale and exceed the capacity of the local economy. For example, very little of the capital invested in developing resorts such as Playa de los Americanos (Tenerife) originated locally.

Finally, with regard to income, it can be noted that the effects of tourism can be considerable in cases of farmhouse tourism. In regions of small–scale farming, money from tourism may be critical in helping maintain a family on the land in the face of limited returns from agriculture. This varies in importance within Europe, and the largest proportions of farms offering tourist accommodation tend to be in Scandinavia (for example, Sweden, with 20 per cent) and the Alps (for example, Austria, 10 per cent). In contrast, the role of farm tourism is usually limited in the Mediterranean countries of mass tourism: for example, only 0.4 per cent of Spanish farms participated in this (Murphy 1985).

2.4.2   *International tourism and the balance of payments*

Tourism is a major source of income for many countries and in 1980 accounted for roughly a quarter of total trade in services. Moreover, in the 1970s international tourism income grew considerably faster than international merchandise trade (Ascher 1983). Not surprisingly, tourism has been actively promoted in a number of countries specifically so as to increase foreign exchange earnings and improve the 'invisibles' component of the balance of payments. The negative side of this is spectacularly illustrated by the Federal Republic of Germany, where in 1985 the tourism invisibles account amounted to a deficit of DM 24.5 billion, equivalent to about one-third of the visible trade surplus. The overall position in Western Europe is summarised in Table 2.4. There is a clear North-South pattern: tourism expenditure by nationals accounted for between 3 and 10 per cent of all imports of goods and services in most northern European states compared with 4.1 per cent or less in the Mediterranean countries. In contrast, the pattern is almost perfectly reversed when considering tourist receipts relative to exports and services. Over 15 per cent of all exports derive from tourism in the Mediterranean countries (except Italy, which has important manufacturing exports), compared with less than 6 per cent in most northern European countries. Foreign exchange earnings from tourism have been significant in the industrialisation of southern Europe since 1960, effectively financing the imports of raw materials and technology for the manufacturing sector. They were particularly important in Spain in the 1960s when they accounted for almost half of export earnings (UNCTC 1982). Finally, note that the Alpine states occupy a special role in these international flows, being significant sources and recipients of foreign tourists expenditure. In general, while the growth of tourism receipts in Europe has been considerable (about 8 per cent per annum) this has been less than in the world tourist economy as a whole (World Tourism Organization 1984, p. 13).

A measure of the magnitude of the receipts and expenditure involved in international tourism is given in Table 2.5. In absolute terms, the largest net earners are Italy and Spain, while the Federal Republic of Germany and the Netherlands have the largest net deficits. Countries such as the United Kingdom and Switzerland have relatively small net balances which conceal very large flows of receipts and expenditures. These data confirm the argument of the Commission of the European Communities (1985) that tourism generates a net distribution of wealth from the North to the South of Europe, and from the richer to the poorer states. The obvious exceptions to this tendency are the Alpine states, which are geographically and economically in the centre of these financial exchanges. With the expansion of mass tourism, there is considerable evidence that the relative and absolute magnitude of the gap between the net financial revenues of the recipient and donor countries has increased over time. While most of the financial flows occur within Europe, an estimated \$8.5 billion of receipts (exclusive of air fares) originated outside the

Table 2.5 Receipts from and expenditures on international tourism in Western Europe, 1987 ($ millions)

	Receipts	Expenditure	Balance
Austria	8,703	5,501	3,202
Belgium	3,002	3,947	−945
Denmark	2,219	2,849	−630
Finland	821	1,509	−688
France	12,000	8,611	3,389
FRG	7,801	23,567	−15,766
Greece	2,290	510	1,780
Ireland	844	807	37
Italy	12,160	4,530	7,630
Netherlands	2,705	6,422	−3,717
Norway	1,244	3,056	−1,812
Portugal	2,147	423	1,724
Spain	14,780	1,952	12,828
Sweden	2,030	3,772	−1,742
Switzerland	5,382	4,363	1,019
UK	10,196	11,869	−1,673

Source: OECD (1988, p. 82)

continent in 1985, notably in the United States (European Travel Commission 1986).

Finally, a note of caution is required in interpreting these estimates, for the balance-of-payments surplus can be reduced by foreign 'leakage' effects. These are particularly significant for those economies which have weakly developed service and manufacturing activities that are required to supply the needs of foreign tourists. Amongst the most important leakage effects are:

1. Imported goods, particularly food and drink.
2. The foreign exchange costs of foreign imports for the development of tourist facilities.
3. Remittances of profits abroad by foreign companies which own hotels and other tourist facilities.
4. Remittances of wages by expatriate workers.
5. Management fees and royalties for franchised businesses.
6. Payments to overseas airlines, tour companies and travel agents.
7. Overseas promotion costs.
8. Extra expenditures on imports by nationals resulting from earnings from and the demonstration effect of tourism.

It is difficult to obtain precise estimates of these income leakages, especially of extra expenditures on imports by nationals. One such estimate for Italy in 1975 is reported by Mathieson and Wall (1982): whereas receipts were $2,578 million, leakages reduced net earnings to $1,528 million.

Table 2.6   Direct and indirect employment in tourism in France and the
United Kingdom, 1984/5

	France (1984)[1]	UK (1985)
Hotels	127,722	287,500
Restaurants	157,242	188,600
Travel agencies	19,250	NK
National tourism administration	400	NK
Other sectors of the tourist industry	127,900	736,900

Source: OECD (1986, p. 182)

Note: 1. Employees only

2.4.3   *International tourism and employment creation*

Estimating the employment provided by tourism is a difficult task, made more
complex by varying national data–collection practices. Nevertheless, there is
no doubting the importance of tourism as a source of jobs. The Commission
of the European Communities (1985) estimated that tourism provides 5
million direct jobs in the then ten member states of the EC, and between 10
and 15 million direct and indirect jobs. World Tourism Organization (1984, p.
81) estimates for Europe as a whole suggest that tourism and tourism-related
jobs account for 15.5 per cent of total employment. This proportion remained
fairly constant during most of the 1970s, reflecting a shift to self-catering
accommodation and attempts by employers to shed labour in order to reduce
production costs in a highly competitive industry. For individual countries,
consistent comparative data are only available on hotels and restaurants and the
latter, of course, do not exclusively serve tourism. Indeed, data on France and
the United Kingdom (Table 2.6) show that employment in travel agencies,
administration and 'other sectors' of the tourist industry may equal or exceed
that in hotels and restaurants.

Table 2.7 provides a summary of the available data on employment in hotels
and restaurants, but these must be treated cautiously, given differences in
coverage. Not least, the official data fail to record the large numbers of casual
workers in the industry and its links with the informal economy. Nevertheless,
they give some measure of the importance of employment in tourism and also
underline the dominance of female workers in most countries (the exceptions
being France, the Netherlands and Portugal).

Employment in tourism is also important because, in the face of recession in
the European economy, it has been one of the four most consistent sources of
job growth in recent years. For example, in France there was a 4 per cent per
annum growth rate in tourism employment between 1975 and 1982. Whether
or not employment in tourism will continue to expand in the same way in
future is debatable. While demand for tourist services is likely to increase,
productivity changes are likely to reduce the growth in jobs. Amongst the
more important changes are shifts from serviced to self-catering accommodation and the automation of kitchens. There is also the question of whether the
jobs are filled by nationals or by immigrants, and this largely depends on the
scale of tourism, the types of job available, and the labour-market alternatives.
Few countries keep accurate records on this aspect but the proportion of

Table 2.7 Employment in tourism in selected Western European countries, 1987

	% male	Total
Austria	37.4	116,695
Belgium[1,2]	NK	175,734
Finland[2]	20.6	63,000
France[1,3]	54.2	752,209
FR Germany[1,2]	37.2	992,000
Greece[1,2,4]	NK	42,028
Norway[1,2]	26.0	50,000
Netherlands[1]	54.8	120,700
Portugal[5]	52.7	32,899
Sweden[2]	36.0	86,100
Switzerland[1,2]	NK	181,100
UK	38.9	803,100

Source: OECD (1988, p. 173)

Notes: 1. 1986
    2. Hotels and restaurants only
    3. Considerable underestimate which does not include self-employed
    4. Employees covered by the Hotel Employment Insurance Fund
    5. 1984

immigrant labour employed in hotels and restaurants can be considerable: for example, 18.3 per cent in Sweden, 23.6 per cent in the Federal Republic of Germany and 37.8 per cent in Switzerland in 1982–3.

Turning to local economies, different methodologies make it very difficult to evaluate the employment created by the industry on this scale. Therefore, at best there is only fragmented evidence available: for example, Law's (1985a) review of selected local areas in the United Kingdom found estimates that the National Exhibition Centre in Birmingham provided, directly and indirectly, 3,922 jobs, while visitor expenditure in Glasgow supported 3,610 direct jobs and about 5,000 jobs in total. Even in these large cities, tourism makes an important contribution to employment, while it is totally dominant in many small, specialised tourist areas. Few detailed studies have been undertaken of tourism employment in the United Kingdom (see Williams and Shaw 1988). In one of the most detailed, Archer (1977) has shown that, in North Wales, an indirect job is created for every nine new direct jobs in tourism. At 1970 prices, expenditure of £20,900 was necessary to generate nine jobs.

The actual quality of jobs in the tourist industry is a matter of debate. Most jobs are semi- or unskilled, and in Spain, for example, it has been suggested that this accounts for about 98 per cent of all employment. This has generated considerable criticism of the quality of jobs in tourism. Recently, this led the Chairman of the English Tourist Board to retort that there are still many 'who believe that a job in the tourism industry is in some way less of a job than one in manufacturing industry' (quoted in *Financial Times*, 15 July 1986). The debate is a difficult one, especially at a time of high unemployment with limited job alternatives available. Furthermore, while direct employment in tourism (in bars, hotels, restaurants, etc.) may be mostly unskilled, indirect employment (in supply industries, producer services, etc.) may be highly skilled and well rewarded).

The same distinction between direct and indirect employment is necessary in considering the distribution of jobs between males and females. Some sectors of tourism are clearly dominated by women, especially in serviced accommodation. Bed-makers and cleaners in small and large hotels invariably seem to be women. The same tendency is even more marked in small-scale, rooms-to-let accommodation. For example, Hadjimichalis and Vaiou (1986, p. 17) writing about tourism on the Greek island of Naxos, state that

rooms-to-let is a household operation run almost entirely by women. They are rooms within or near the family house which are rented during the summer. Cleaning rooms and serving guests is regarded as an extension of daily housework, 'naturally' women's work. Negotiating prices and making contracts with the authorities is usually left to men.

Bouquet (1982) reports similar male–female divisions of labour in the farmhouse bed and breakfast trade in the South-West of England.

Skill-levels and male/female ratios are only two of the characteristics of the labour force. Other important features include full-time/part-time ratios, seasonality, wages, and the geographical origins of the work-force. All of these clearly depend on the nature of the local economy and the scale and ownership of tourist enterprises. For example, Barker (1982, p. 407) writing about high-level, specialised ski resorts in Alpine France states that the 'combination of corporate capital, distant investors and a state-planning mechanism has limited the participation of the valley populations chiefly to un-skilled, seasonal occupations'. There is some evidence available on these matters. For example, Cavaco (1980) reports that only 58 per cent of the labour force in the town of Faro (Algarve) has been drawn from the surrounding districts; this is a reflection of specialisation in tourism and the large scale of tourism developments relative to the size of local labour markets (see also Chapter 6). Nevertheless, such data as are available are fragmented and often unsuitable for comparative purposes.

2.5   Tourism: some broader economic considerations

The review of the economic role of tourism presented in this section is limited to brief comparisons of simple economic indicators. These are sufficient to indicate important differences in terms of the absolute and relative economic importance of tourism in various European countries. However, the relationship between development and tourism is more complex than this, as we suggested in the methodological review in Chapter 1. The complexities of the relationships are such that they are best investigated in the context of particular case studies. This is the focus of the following chapters, and here it is only possible to indicate some major themes.

2.5.1   *International tourism and dependency*

Tourism has been criticised as a strategy for economic development because it is associated with dependency upon external—and often fickle—sources of growth (de Kadt 1979). The choice of tourist destination is susceptible to large fluctuations from year to year, either because of recession in northern Europe reducing overall demand (as happened in the mid-1970s), or because of changes in the competitiveness of individual countries. This may arise from political uncertainty as, for example, in Portugal, where the number of foreign tourists was halved between 1974 and 1976, following the coup of 1974.

Considerable fluctuations in demand are also likely to result even from small price changes in tourism in particular countries. This is because the products of the mass tourist industry—whether Alpine skiing or Mediterranean sea and sun—are little differentiated. Instead competition is centred on prices so that even small price changes, following, say, a currency devaluation or revaluation, can have a considerable impact on tourist numbers. Spain provides an example of the positive and negative aspects of this process. While devaluation of the peseta in 1959 was a key in the development of Spanish mass tourism, occasional price 'leaps', such as that in hotel prices in 1984–5, have had a detrimental effect on competitiveness.

2.5.2   Tourism and polarisation

The development of tourist facilities tends to be spatially polarised. Given the nature of mass tourism—whether beach or ski activities—this leads to even greater concentration, as can be illustrated by the case of Yugoslavia. Whereas in 1953 only 29 per cent of overnight stays were in seaside centres, by 1980 (when Yugoslavia could be considered a major focus of Mediterranean mass tourism) 68 per cent of overnight stays and 86 per cent of foreign tourists were in seaside resorts (Allcock 1983). Nowhere is tourism more spatially concentrated than in Spain; in the Balearics, one-fifth of all jobs are in hotels and restaurants and, allowing for a multiplier of about 1.5, this takes the proportion nearer to one-third.

Mass tourism brings about intense local pressures in terms of congestion, the need for new infrastructure and pollution. The congestion involves overcrowded roads in the tourist season and over-use of tourist facilities to the point that their attractive power is threatened (see, for example, Marinos 1983 on the Greek island of Zakynthos). Rapid tourist development also requires substantial investment in roads, airports, water and sewerage plants in order to move tourists in and out of the resorts and to keep them adequately serviced. Where the latter fails, pollution of the air, of water supplies or of the seas may follow, again threatening the viability of the tourist resort. The extent of the pollution threat should not be underestimated; for example, the 4.5 million visitors to the Austrian Alps each year leave behind them an estimated 4,500 tonnes of rubbish. Given that mass tourist resorts are little differentiated in terms of their facilities, bad publicity for a health risk or an outbreak of food poisoning in a particular area can lead to a disastrous switch of tourists to other resorts in the following season.

Tourist developments can also conflict with industrial or agricultural developments competing for the same 'optimum' sites (on the coast, for example), limited water supplies and, possibly, limited labour reserves. Tourism may provide jobs but it can attract labour away from agriculture, leading to abandonment of some marginal farming areas. In Portugal's Algarve, for example, the growth of hotels on the coastline in the 1960s and 1970s was matched by population losses of about 30 per cent or more in municipalities located only 50–65 km inland (Cavaco 1980). At the same time, good agricultural land, near tourist resorts, may be left uncultivated, being held speculatively in expectation of future development gains. In addition, tourism may bring rapid cultural change as commercial values and products replace traditional values and locally crafted goods. Usually the speed of the change—and the scale of mass tourism—allow little time for adjustment by the local populace.

There is not a simple linear relationship between the growth of tourism and of the economic benefits for the local community. In the initial stages tourism may create more jobs for locals while increased demand for food leads to intensification of agriculture. Later, with further development, negative consequences may become more apparent. These include overcommitment of resources to tourism diverting investment from other sectors, congestion, pollution, in-migration of labour, and conflicts with other land uses.

2.5.3   *The linkages of the tourist industry*

Few industries have such widespread linkages as does tourism. There have been a number of attempts to measure these links in terms of the indirect employment, output sales or income generated by tourists. Most of these studies are based on the income multiplier, 'a coefficient which expresses the amount of income generated in an area by an additional unit of tourist spending' (Archer 1982, p. 236). While the usefulness and the reliability of multipliers have been severely criticised (see Archer 1977; Bryden 1973; O'Hagan and Mooney 1983), they emphasise the importance of the industry's linkages. The results obtained are obviously dependent on the nature of the local economy and the scale of analysis, but the tourism income multipliers for a number of towns, counties and regions in the United Kingdom are mostly of the order of 1.24–1.47 (Archer 1982, p. 241). Multiplier estimates can also suggest the differential economic impact of different types of tourist staying in different types of accommodation. However, they are aggregate estimates which fail to take into account such considerations as non-local versus foreign ownership of capital, the employment of migrant or immigrant labour, and diseconomies related to polarisation. Not only do these influences vary among countries but they also do so between adjacent resorts. For example, Barker (1982) has shown differences in the extent of local business involvement in high-altitude and low-altitude skiing centres in the Alps.

Looking beyond these aggregate figures, it is clear that tourism has a significant influence on a number of economic sectors, including transport, retailing, wholesaling, manufacturing, agriculture and producer services. A particularly important issue is the influence of tourism on arts and crafts; views are strongly divided between those who see tourism as a force for conservation and those who see it as destructive. A balanced summary is provided by de Kadt (1979, pp. 14–15):

Even though curio production, 'airport art', and performances of fake folklore are of course stimulated by tourist demand . . . frequently arts, crafts, and local culture have been revitalized as a direct result of tourism. A transformation of traditional forms often accompanies this development but does not necessarily lead to degeneration. To be authentic, arts and crafts must be rooted both in historical tradition and in present-day life; true authenticity cannot be achieved by conservation alone, since that leads to stultification.

Another important area for discussion is the relationship between agriculture and tourism. Tourism obviously provides a market for agricultural products but there are other links, as is epitomised by farm tourism. Farmers can provide accommodation—either serviced or self-catering—as well as tourist attractions such as involvement in farm activities or horse-riding. These can be important sources of farm income, sometimes matching or surpassing the returns from agricultural activities. Such a diversification of farm activities may require a new division of labour within the family. Access to such additional income may enable a family to maintain an otherwise unprofitable farm. The tourism income may be invested in farm modernisation or simply to subsidise the farming activities. Access to supplementary income need not involve farm tourism for members of the family may take up jobs in tourism outside the farm. The overall balance between benefits and disadvantages is far more complex than this, however; it also depends on whether the seasonality of tourist and family work is complementary and on whether tourism forces up the price of farm land and labour.

In summary, the relationship between tourism and development—whether in rural or urban areas—depends on many conditional factors. Above all, it depends on the nature of the tourist industry itself and the nature of the local, regional or national economy. There is, therefore, great diversity, as the following case studies of particular countries illustrate.

3 Spain: the phenomenon of mass tourism

Manuel Valenzuela

3.1 The effects of mass tourism on the Spanish economy: a positive balance

The most outstanding features of Spanish tourism after the Second World War have been a rapid growth in the number of visitors and the incorporation of domestic and foreign middle and lower-class social groups. This expansion is based on external factors such as generalisation of paid holidays, rising living standards and a rapid increase in air travel; but social and economic conditions in Spain (cheaper prices, absence of labour conflicts, etc.), as well as the official policy of promoting tourism through financial credit and publicity campaigns abroad, have also contributed. The regime of General Franco set considerable store by tourism, regarding it not only as a valuable economic resource but also as a means of securing tacit acceptance of his dictatorial rule by European countries (Cals 1983, p. 15).

On the eve of the Civil War of 1936–9 foreign tourism to Spain was still relatively small scale, involving little more than 200,000 tourists. The major expansion in volume came after the 1950s, with an increase from 2.5 million visitors in 1955 to 43.2 million in 1985, and to 47.4 million in 1986. Of the last, only around 30 million are tourists as opposed to excursionists or travellers in transit (especially Portuguese and North Africans).

As can be seen from Table 3.1, the increase in the number of tourists continued until 1973, with a reduction between 1973 and 1976, reflecting the economic crisis in a sector which was particularly affected by rising oil prices. After 1983 there was a further increase in tourism which has made Spain the second most important country in world tourism (with 8.8 per cent of all tourists and 10.5 per cent of all foreign exchange earnings); in 1986 it was surpassed in terms of the volume of tourists only by France. Another significant indicator of the position occupied by Spain in world tourist flows is the fact that approximately 50 per cent of foreign tour operators sell holidays to this country.

Domestic Spanish tourism, expanding as a result of higher standards of living and increased car-ownership after the mid-1970s, has also contributed in no small part to the growth of mass tourism. Indeed, in the 1980s 40 per cent of Spaniards already participated in tourism; of this number, 90 per cent took their holidays in Spain in 1985.

The fact that Spanish tourism has experienced largely uninterrupted growth, reflects its intrinsic strength as much as that of the economy as a whole. Hence,

Table 3.1 Foreign visitors to Spain, 1955–86

	Number of visitors	Index
1955	2,522,402	100
1960	6,113,255	242
1965	14,251,428	565
1970	24,105,312	956
1975	30,122,478	1,194
1980	38,022,816	1,507
1984	42,931,658	1,702
1985	43,235,362	1,714
1986	47,388,793	1,879

Source: Anuario de Estadísticas de Turismo

it is not surprising that tourism has been favoured by successive policy-makers. The role that tourism played in balancing some of the structural deficiencies of the Spanish economy in the 1960s (lack of industrial investment, a commercial deficit, low consumption capacity, etc.) is well known. Even the advent of democracy in the mid-1970s, at the height of a global economic crisis, has not substantially changed the attitude of Spanish governments. Ideology seems to have little influence on the importance attached to tourism and the policies developed for the industry.

In the last three decades tourism has made a substantial contribution to the Spanish economy and its share of GDP—around 10 per cent—underlines this. Equally important is its contribution to the accumulation of foreign exchange reserves, without which Spanish development in the 1960s would have been much more problematic. In this way, tourism has stimulated several sectors of production, but especially accommodation (hotels and restaurants have secured about half of the economic growth generated by tourism), followed by transport, travel agencies, recreation and commerce (Alcaide 1984, p. 34). Since 1970, official input–output tables for tourism (produced every four years) have made it possible to trace the impact of tourism on the national economic system as well as providing estimates of the multiplier effect of tourist spending; the latter has been calculated at around 2.5 (Instituto Español de Turismo 1978). Tourism provides a stimulus to virtually the whole of the economy through the process of secondary expenditure effects. It has also contributed to capital development, derived from the savings of residents as much as from foreign investment; this has mostly been channelled into real estate. In some periods, tourist investments have accounted for approximately 10 per cent of the gross formation of fixed capital (Figuerola 1983, p. 24).

The most important economic effect of tourism at present is its contribution to employment creation, whether directly or indirectly. Partly due to tourism, the 1960s flow of emigrants to Europe has been stemmed. However, poor working conditions, seasonality and a low level of skill content are widespread in most tourist jobs (Cals 1974, p. 121). Tourist activities directly employed 500,000 persons in the mid-1960s; this increased to 1 million in 1975, and it is usually accepted that tourism accounts for 11 per cent of the economically active. In absolute terms, tourism in 1986 was responsible for 1,234,000 jobs (740,000 direct and 494,000 indirect). Nevertheless, of all the economic changes

Table 3.2   Foreign exchange earnings of tourism in Spain, 1975–86

	Earnings ($ millions)	Index (1970 = 100)	% of value of exports
1975	3,404.2	165	25.1
1980	6,967.7	339	20.5
1985	8,150.8	397	35.8
1986	12,058.0	587	44.6

Sources: Secretaría General de Turismo y Contabilidad Nacional de España

brought about by tourism, the most spectacular is the generation of foreign exchange earnings; these have been a critical element in the balance of payments (Table 3.2).

Following the stagnation of growth in the mid-1970s, the position of tourism in the Spanish economy strengthened after 1983, and it had become the principal economic sector by 1986. A number of economic indicators corroborate this; it is a prolific source of foreign currency (1.67 trillion pesetas, equivalent to $12.058 billion, in 1986), surpassing Italy and France in this respect, and contributes 11 per cent of GDP. The beneficial effects on the commercial balance have increased further, with tourism earnings providing 44.6 per cent of all exports, and being more than double the commercial deficit.

3.2   Intense geographical concentration: a major feature of Spanish tourism

Three countries have together contributed more than 50 per cent of Spain's foreign tourists in most years: France, the United Kingdom and the Federal Republic of Germany (Table 3.3). Despite their minor importance at present, non–European tourists (mostly North American or Japanese) are being encouraged because their spending capacity is far superior to that of the Europeans; they are also more likely to participate in inland and quality tours (cultural tourism, hunting, golf, etc.). In contrast, the 'average' profile of European tourists is more modest. They visit Spain in the peak holiday period and generate relatively low income, compared with the world average. This is largely due to the manner in which tour operators control tourist demand and contribute to strong geographical concentration of both demand and supply. In fact, the coastal regions and the Spanish archipelagos (Balearic and Canary Islands) offer a very attractive environment to northern European tourists: a dry and sunny climate, picturesque landscapes and inexpensive meals. Promotional campaigns, emphasising the bright and pleasant climatic conditions, contribute to this image. This is stressed in the current official slogan of Spanish tourism ('Everything under the sun'), while commercial names with climatic connotations (for example, Costa del Sol) are given to many seaside resorts (Figure 3.1).

Efforts to break the dominance of the regions with the most sunshine have not been very successful, as is evident in surveys of the motivations of foreign tourists in Spain. In 1985, 82.1 per cent of tourists still confessed that their

Table 3.3   Arrivals of visitors in Spain by country or region of origin, 1955–86

| | Percentage of all visitors | | | | | | | |
	1955	1960	1965	1970	1975	1980	1985	1986
Benelux	2.8	2.9	4.0	6.2	7.9	6.3	5.9	5.8
France	36.8	41.8	45.2	36.6	31.1	26.5	25.4	23.8
FRG	4.6	5.4	7.3	8.6	14.1	12.3	13.1	12.6
Portugal	6.9	5.7	7.0	10.9	11.8	24.0	17.9	20.1
Scandinavian countries	1.0	1.6	2.0	3.6	4.0	2.6	3.7	3.9
UK	13.2	10.2	9.5	11.3	11.3	9.5	11.6	13.6
USA and Canada	8.8	8.5	5.1	4.8	3.7	2.5	2.7	2.0
Other countries	25.9	23.9	19.9	18.0	16.1	16.3	19.7	18.3

Source: Anuario de Estadísticas de Turismo

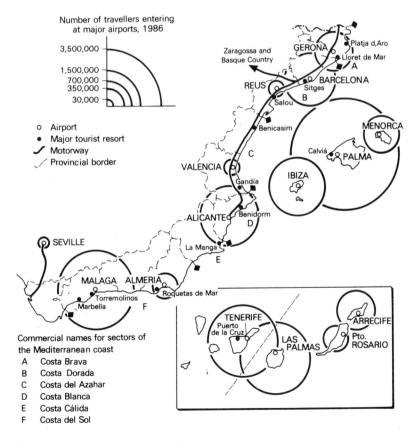

Fig. 3.1   Major features of Spain's leading tourism regions

Table 3.4   Regional distribution of travellers using hotels in Spain, 1985

	Total	Foreign tourists Total	(%)	Domestic tourists Total	(%)
Andalusia	5,214,418	2,814,565	15.5	2,399,853	15.2
Aragón	903,191	779,899	0.8	123,292	4.2
Asturias	368,143	342,302	0.2	25,841	1.8
Balearics	3,342,989	509,293	18.3	2,833,696	2.7
Canaries	2,066,225	601,473	9.4	1,464,752	3.2
Cantabria	344,523	306,939	0.3	37,584	1.6
Castille-La Mancha	1,018,267	763,859	1.6	254,408	4.1
Castille-León	1,956,610	1,612,510	2.2	344,100	8.7
Catalonia	4,695,398	2,134,797	16.5	2,560,601	11.5
Extremadura	540,071	472,688	0.4	67,383	2.5
Galicia	1,251,722	1,093,590	1.0	158,132	5.9
Madrid	3,331,148	1,970,338	8.8	1,360,810	10.6
Murcia	450,982	366,489	0.5	84,493	2.0
Navarra	275,880	241,752	0.2	34,128	1.3
Basque country	795,155	599,921	1.3	195,234	3.2
La Rioja	158,945	145,229	0.1	13,716	0.8
C. Valenciana	2,476,709	1,463,663	6.5	1,013,045	7.9
Total	34,051,006	18,543,710	100.0	15,507,296	100.0

Source: INE, *Movimiento de viajeros en establecimientos turísticos*, 1985

chief reason for coming to Spain on holiday was to enjoy the climate, even though there are variances according to the tourists' countries of origin; this reason is most important for the British and Germans and least important for the Italians. Apart from the seaside resorts, the foremost attraction is Madrid, which combines the attractions of a big city (museums, palaces, first-class hotels, luxury shopping, etc.) with good air links with the rest of Europe. It is also the 'door to Europe' for most North and South American tourists. The historic cities of the interior are also widely visited by excursionists either from the nearby coasts or from Madrid.

The regional distribution of tourists—whether foreigners or Spanish nationals—is far from homogeneous, as is evident for hotels at the level of the autonomous regions in 1985 (Table 3.4 and Figure 3.2). Andalusia, with more than 5 million visitors, is the leader, followed by Catalonia (4.6 million), Madrid (3.3 million), the Balearics (3.3 million), Valencia (2.5 million), and the Canary Islands (2 million). There is a rough balance between Spanish and foreign travellers in all the regions, except the Balearics and the Canary Islands where foreign tourism dominates.

Data on overnight stays provide another measure of geographical concentration (Table 3.5). The importance of the Balearic Islands for foreigners is evident, accounting for up to 40.7 per cent of overnights. However, for hotel overnights there is a more stable relationship as shown in Catalonia and Valencia, while significant fluctuations between 1985 and 1986 highlight the instability of tourist flows. The regional distribution of domestic tourists— 56.8 per cent of whom preferred seaside holidays in 1985—is more evenly distributed amongst the tourist regions, except the archipelagos. However, there is some domestic preference for the region of Valencia (23.3 per cent of

a) Number of visitors in hotels, 1985

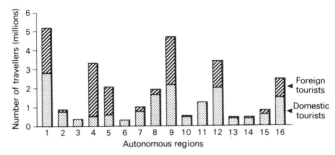

b) The provinces of Spain

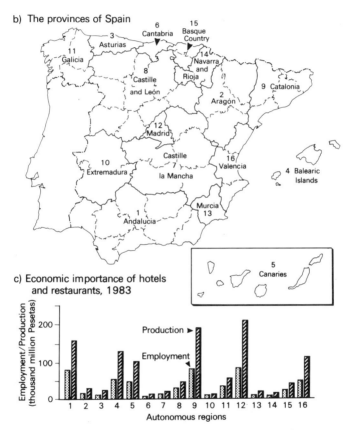

c) Economic importance of hotels and restaurants, 1983

Fig. 3.2 Hotel visitors and the economic role of hotels and restaurants in Spain: regional features

Source: INE, *Movimiento de viajeros en establecimientos turísticos*, (1985); Banco de Bilbao, Renta Nacional de España

Table 3.5   Foreign and domestic overnights by tourist area in Spain, 1985–6

| | Foreign tourist overnights | | | | Domestic tourist overnights | | | |
| | In hotels | | Other | | In hotels | | Other | |
	1985	1986	1985	1986	1985	1986	1985	1986
Andalusia	13.5	13.2	11.6	11.7	15.6	15.3	17.8	18.3
Balearics	18.3	22.6	39.7	40.7	6.9	7.3	1.5	2.7
Canaries	12.4	18.4	18.9	17.7	6.0	6.3	1.1	3.7
Catalonia	23.0	20.6	14.8	15.2	14.7	14.1	17.9	16.8
C. Valenciana	24.4	16.2	7.9	8.3	16.5	13.5	23.3	18.4
Other areas	8.4	9.0	6.1	6.4	40.3	43.5	38.4	40.1
Total (%)	71.9	72.4	28.1	27.6	8.3	6.2	91.7	93.8
(millions)	280.5		78.9		42.1	41.8	464.2	630.0

Source: Instituto Español de Turismo

Table 3.6   Foreign hotel visitors in the main tourist provinces in Spain, 1986

| Province (region) | % of all visitors | Country/region of origin (%) | | | | |
		FRG	UK	France	North America	Other
Alicante (C. Valenciana)	40.3	2.7	20.7	3.5	11.0	62.1
Balearics (Balearic Islands)	84.8	26.7	31.7	7.4	0.9	33.3
Barcelona (Catalonia)	51.1	13.3	10.8	11.2	10.3	54.4
Gerona (Catalonia)	69.0	35.3	12.1	17.6	2.5	32.5
Granada (Andalusia)	47.3	12.5	8.7	13.1	24.7	41.0
Málaga (Andalusia)	82.8	5.7	17.5	6.8	10.8	59.2
Madrid (C. de Madrid)	40.8	4.4	5.0	5.5	24.6	60.5
Las Palmas (Canaries)	66.7	44.5	16.0	3.2	1.5	34.8
Santa Cruz de Tenerife (Canaries)	76.0	21.6	40.7	6.9	1.3	29.5
Seville (Andalusia)	41.6	11.6	5.6	12.0	30.3	40.5
Tarragona (Catalonia)	48.8	26.6	31.3	14.0	1.9	26.2
Valencia (C. Valenciana)	25.7	10.5	10.3	17.1	14.4	47.7
Zaragoza (Aragón)	15.4	10.3	0.1	1.2	0.7	87.7

Source: Instituto Nacional de Estadística

other overnights in 1985), followed by Andalusia and Catalonia. Domestic tourists also have a stronger preference than foreign tourists for other destinations, including the mountains of the interior.

There are important variations in the geographical preferences of tourists, according to their country of origin (Table 3.6). West German and British tourists are the major foreign sources of tourists; the British are in a majority on the Costa Blanca (Alicante), the Balearics and the Costa del Sol, while West Germans predominate on the Costa Brava and the Canary Islands. The French continue to be important on the Costa Brava and the Costa Blanca. North American tourism is increasing in volume and is already significant in inland areas (Madrid, Seville and Granada), but is also important in Alicante and Málaga, seaside resorts which attract the elderly.

3.3 Tourism and a new territorial model of development

The Spanish regime in the 1960s realised that the development of coastal tourism offered considerable economic advantages, and for this reason a number of measures were introduced to promote tourism. There was even a special law to facilitate the creation of new tourist settlements in the zones most favoured by spontaneous tourism, the so-called *Centros y Zonas de Interés Turístico Nacional* Act of 1963 (Valenzuela 1985). Nevertheless, the administration limited itself to sectoral intervention (coasts, marinas, natural spaces, etc.). Furthermore, no regional planning mechanisms existed even in those areas where the risks of congestion were considerable (for example, the Balearic Islands). A high price has been paid for this lack of foresight because valuable spaces have been lost, such as forests and rich agricultural land. For the same reason, the development of tourism has been accompanied by a number of negative environmental impacts and a serious deficiency in collective infrastructure.

The state paid more attention to communications so as to ensure there was sufficient accessibility to the tourist zones. This was one of the objectives of the Development Plans (1960s and mid-1970s). Although only two-thirds of the planned coastal motorway axis has been completed (see Figure 3.1) this has linked the Mediterranean coast, as far as Alicante, with the European motorway network. A lack of motorways in other regions is an obstacle to further expansion, given the importance of road traffic in Spain. Airports have also been improved and expanded in response to the requirements of charter tourism which, by 1986, accounted for 29.8 per cent of the total, although the regional distribution is uneven with the Costa del Sol and the archipelagos being most important. However, the supply of other basic infrastructure (water supply and sewers, for instance) has in many cases fallen behind demand. An inadequate supply of water is a particular problem in the Canary Islands, and it has been necessary to rely upon sea–water desalination.

The supply of accommodation is the critical element in the organisation of tourism and the chief component of the built environment of tourist settlements. Accommodation tends to be varied, and different types of villa, bungalow, apartment and hotel exist in the same zones (Morales Folguera 1982) (Table 3.7). In Spain, as a whole, the official supply of tourist beds had increased to 1,697,408 by 1985; there were 1,014,022 in hotels and similar establishments (59.7 per cent), 385,378 on camping sites (22.7 per cent) and 298,008 in declared apartments (17.6 per cent). Besides these, there are substantial numbers of undeclared beds; although difficult to quantify, according to some estimates there could be as many as 9.3 million lodgings, consisting of apartments and villas to let, including second homes.

In the undeclared sector it is difficult to distinguish between tourist lodgings which are rented out seasonally and homes used by the owner and his family throughout the year. Owning a house or an apartment in a coastal resort is a widely held aspiration in all social classes. It can even be argued that the 'weekend home' is part of the mythology of what constitutes general progress and this helps explain the expansion of second homes in recent decades, especially in the areas near the larger cities (Valenzuela 1976; Canto 1983) and in the tourist regions (Miranda 1985). However, renting of second homes to tourists also constitutes a degree of 'unfair' competition with declared premises.

Table 3.7   Regional distribution of tourist lodgings (registered beds) in Spain, 1986

	Hotels	Percentage of the total Apartments	Camping	Touristic rate[1]
Andalusia	12.44	12.07	11.80	14,797,00
Aragón	2.45	0.22	3.11	2,162.10
Asturias	0.96	0.01	4.30	1,005.20
Balearics	26.40	22.60	0.40	21,006.50
Canaries	8.98	37.36	0.38	13,312.00
Cantabria	1.24	0.34	5.34	983.20
Castille-La Mancha	1.55	0.05	0.95	1,150.30
Castille-León	3.57	0.10	4.39	3,130,00
Catalonia	20.20	17.10	43.68	16,696.70
Extremadura	0.86	–	0.62	660.50
Galicia	3.31	0.29	4.36	2,940.10
Madrid	5.60	1.71	3.50	9,652.30
Murcia	1.16	2.18	2.08	1,187.30
Navarra	0.64	0.03	0.46	798.10
Basque country	1.34	0.07	2.27	1,857.30
La Rioja	0.34	0.01	0.77	323.30
C. Valenciana	8.67	5.77	12.28	8,130.40

Sources: Secretaría General de Turismo; Banco Español de Crédito, *Anuario del Mercado Español,* 1986

Note: 1. This is obtained by calculating the number of places in hotels and camping × prices × days opened during the year (Spain = 100.000)

There has been considerable growth of foreign investment in the second-home market, and there are already more than 1 million foreign–owned dwellings on the Spanish coast. In 1986 alone foreign investments in real estate and housing totalled 195 billion pesetas, 80 per cent of which belonged to tourists. It is estimated that foreigners buy approximately 50,000 dwellings a year in Spain. Investment in the larger cities is speculative and comes from international firms, but in the tourist zones it involves individuals investing their savings in a dwelling, initially for seasonal use but ultimately as a place for retirement.

The large-scale settlment of retired foreigners on the Mediterranean coast and in the Canary Islands started in the 1970s, especially in the Costa Blanca (Gaviria 1977b) and in parts of the Costa del Sol, such as Marbella and Mijas (Jurdao 1979); it has spread subsequently as the ageing of the European population feeds demand. In places, permanent foreign residents threaten to overrun the capacity of municipal services which were designed for smaller local populations. In the last four years, Marbella alone has received 55 billion pesetas in real estate investment, mainly from the United Kingdom and France. Altogether, there are moe than 500,000 foreign–owned second homes on the Costa del Sol and the Costa Blanca. The remainder are divided amongst the Costa Brava, the Balearic and the Canary Islands. The majority of the owners are British (30 per cent), or German (25 per cent). One indicator of the recent hectic round of foreign purchasing is the emergence of new types of property acquisition such as 'lease-back' and 'time-sharing'. Both of these are mostly controlled and organised from abroad and they lack a clear regulatory framework in Spain. Time-sharing is of particular concern to the hotels as it competes head-on for short visits. Nevertheless, the growth of second homes can help reduce the acute seasonality experienced in tourist areas as it is the main factor in determining whether tourists become permanent settlers (Bosch 1987, pp. 133–6).

Tourism has contributed to urbanisation ever since the middle of the nineteenth century when, among the middle and upper classes, summer holidays became fashionable. The first tourist towns—such as San Sebastián and Santander on the north coast, and Málaga, Alicante and Palma de Mallorca on the Mediterranean—developed on the basis of their climatic conditions, their surroundings and astute promotion. Alicante, for example, became known as the 'Playa de Madrid' when, after the inauguration of a direct railway link in 1858, it became fashionable with the middle classes of Madrid, not least because seabathing supposedly had healing properties (Vera Rebollo 1985). There were similar reasons for the take-off of tourism in Málaga, whose fame as a 'winter resort' spread throughout Europe at the turn of the nineteenth century, at about the same time as Palma de Mallorca.

In contrast to these older resorts, the specialised 'leisure towns' of the 1960s' tourism boom are very different, for their spatial organisation and economies are subordinate to tourism. Many are based on small, existing farming or fishing settlements, as in the case of Torremolinos, Benidorm or Lloret de Mar. However, some developed at a distance from existing municipal centres, and can be regarded as newly created settlements: examples include Platja d'Aro (Costa Brava) and Playa de San Juan (Alicante). Benidorm is the archtypical 'leisure town', its tourist development having been planned from the 1960s (Gaviria 1977a, pp. 1, 24–31), while its thousands of enterprises in the hotel sector, transport, retailing and other services are totally dedicated, directly or indirectly, to tourism. Benidorm, with 125,000 registered bed-spaces (33,000 in hotels), receives 3 million tourists annually while its permanent population is only about 33,700. In the peak season it can accommodate 300,000 tourists but, on the other hand, it is one of the 'leisure towns' which least suffers from seasonality because of its effectiveness in attracting elderly tourists (an estimated 700,000 in 1986).

Other types of tourist settlement also line the coast, ranging from 'marinas', linked to new sports harbours, to exclusively residential urbanisations. There are vast urban areas covering hundreds of hectares and many involve high-quality urban projects, with some even having been declared *Centros de Interés Turístico Nacional* (for example, La Manga, Sotogrande or Dehesa de Campoamor). They boast good-quality residential accommodation and a variety of select sporting opportunities (golf, riding, sailing, etc.). In contrast, some urbanisations involve illegal plots of land in non-zoned areas and possess hardly any infrastructure (Diputación Provincial de Valencia 1983).

In some municipalities the new tourist settlements already occupy a major part of the space available for development, as in Calviá (Balearics), Calpe (Alicante) or Mijas (Málaga). Not surprisingly, these are widespread along the coastal fringes. Foreign capital has a strong preference for such developments which consequently have been labelled 'neo-colonialist'. Frequently, they have poorly-defined residential landscapes and this constitutes one of the major challenges to town and country planning in these regions. Studies exist of tourist settlements on the Mediterranean coast as a whole (Zahn 1973) and of particular regions such as the Costa Brava (Barbaza 1966, pp. 618–24), and Valencia (Miranda 1985), as well as of the Canary Islands (Gaviria 1974, pp. 275–383) and of the Costa de la Luz (Fourneau 1979, pp. 145–61).

3.4   The economic effects of specialisation in tourism on regional development

Tourism has traditionally been considered to be a means of reducing regional economic disparities, even though it exhibits extreme coastal concentration (Pearce 1981, pp. 59–60). In Spain, the economic effects of tourism have mostly been evaluated on a national scale, and there has been comparative neglect of regional perspectives.

3.4.1   *Tourism as an instrument of change in regional economic structures*

Tourism may benefit production and employment creation in a region by means of three effects—direct, indirect and induced (Lecordier 1979). However, econometric techniques have not yet captured the full extent of the structural change which occurs in the productive structures of tourist regions. Input–output tables for tourist regions, such as Andalusia or the Canary Islands, do underline the importance of tourism. Nevertheless, it has not been possible to assess fully the impact of the activities such as air transport, which are closely connected with mass tourism. Similarly, the full impact of tourist expenditures is not known except for the contracts between tour operators and hoteliers. Furthermore, it is difficult to estimate the multiplier effect of tourist expenditure because a large proportion of the goods consumed is imported from other regions or countries (Rodríguez Marín 1985, pp. 253–61). However, it can be stated that the regional economic effects of tourism broadly reflect the contrasts in tourism supply and demand, and this is confirmed by the weight of tourism in regional GDP and by the contribution of the regions to Spain's total Gross Value Added (GVA) from tourism (Table 3.8)

The sector of tourism which has been most thoroughly researched is hotels and restaurants, not least because of data availability. The Balearics (24 per cent) and the Canary Islands (13.8 per cent) stand out for their contribution to regional production, measured in terms of GVA. The impact of tourism is less clear in larger regions such as Andalusia or in diversified economies, such as Catalonia or Valencia, where the weight of the hotels and restaurant sector in the regional economy hardly differs from the national average. Yet, at the provincial level, tourism contributes 9 per cent in Gerona (Costa Brava) and 10.5 per cent in Málaga (Costa del Sol).

Hotels and restaurants have considerable intersectoral links. In Andalusia, for example, input–output analysis has shown that hotels and restaurants provide a strong impulse to the regional economy, not only in terms of GVA (61.2 per cent of production) but also because there is a low level of imports from outside the region (Cuadrado and Aurioles 1986, pp. 57–8). In Valencia, input–output analysis has shown that hotels and restaurants are the branch of the service sector which possesses the greatest propulsive power for the regional economy (Denia and Pedreño 1986, pp. 394–5).

Table 3.8   Tourism and regional economic structures in Spain, 1985

	Economic impact of hotels and restaurants				Regional weight of tourism	
	Production (GVA)[1]		Employment		in regional	in the national
	Millions	(%)	Number	(%)	GDP	tourist GVA[1]
Andalusia	160,658	5.9	84,715	5.2	15.1	18.6
Aragón	26,219	3.4	15,285	3.9	4.7	1.6
Asturias	21,780	3.3	12,296	3.3	3.5	1.1
Balearics	131,149	24.0	58,052	21.7	51.3	11.3
Canaries	10,690	13.8	47,325	11.0	19.4	6.5
Cantabria	12,646	4.1	6,869	4.0	–	–
Castille-La Mancha	200,232	2.8	14,673	3.2	4.1	1.4
Castille-León	43,678	3.2	30,294	3.7	5.1	3.1
Catalonia	192,859	4.4	86,914	4.3	10.7	21.2
Extremadura	11,593	3.2	9,211	3.3	4.7	0.8
Galicia	58.783	4.4	33,060	3.3	6.3	3.7
Madrid	211,478	5.8	88,668	5.6	3.8	2.4
Murcia	18,267	3.9	10,066	3.7	5.5	1.2
Navarra	9,016	2.7	5,369	3.2	3.5	0.5
Basque country	39,930	2.7	22,143	3.3	3.8	2.4
Rioja	4,216	2.4	2,875	3.2	2.7	0.2
Valencia	117,208	5.2	53,017	4.4	8.8	8.8
Total	1,188,403	5.3	584,291	4.9	100.0	100.0

Source: Banco de Bilbao. *Renta Nacional de España*, 1985; Instituto Español de Turismo

Note: 1. Gross Value Added

The effects of tourism on real-estate activity are of particular geographical interest, even if the economic benefits are more questionable (owing to the leakage of some of the income from the sale of land and property). Among 'local' agents, large landowners have derived most gross benefits, either from the sale of the agricultural land to developers or by becoming promoters themselves. However, the resulting value added hardly benefits the economy of the tourist region for the landowners are mostly absentees (Mignon 1979, pp. 69–72). There have been even greater benefits for the developers who have commercialised either rural land in the expectation of development or land already subdivided into plots for development, or who have converted existing buildings to tourism-related businesses. All of these types of real-estate business have attracted investment from the wealthiest regions (Madrid, Catalonia and the Basque country) and from abroad.

In the Canary Islands West German investment has been responsible for the development of one of the most distinctive leisure towns in Spain (Maspalomas-Playa del Inglés in Gran Canaria). The initial stimulus for this was the fiscal advantages provided for West German investment in 'under-developed countries' by the Strauss Act (1968). More recently, West German capital has spread throughout the archipelago, although it is currently most active on Lanzarote, developing leisure towns such as Costa Teguise and Puerto del Carman (Rodríguez Marín 1985, p. 265). Prospective profits from tourism-related real-estate business have provided a strong stimulus for the building trade, especially on Tenerife, where it was responsible for 72 per cent of construction in 1979–80 (Cabildo Insular de Tenerife 1983, p. 73).

The origin of investment in real estate on the Costa del Sol is more diversified but West German, Belgian, British and French capital have secured greater economic benefits from these than has Spanish capital. Not least, this is because Spanish legislation places few restrictions on foreigners' acquiring real estate because of the priority accorded to obtaining foreign exchange in the face of an endemic balance-of-trade deficit (de Kadt 1979, p. 19).

Tourism does not always have positive economic effects. There is intense conflict along the Mediterranean coast between tourism and traditional economic activities, many of which are centuries old, such as fishery, salt mines and, above all, agriculture. Tourism competes for land, water and labour, usually to the detriment of these other activities. One consequence has been the difficulty experienced in recruiting farm workers in the hinterlands of the tourist zones and this has hindered agricultural commercialisation (Mignon 1979, pp. 127–9). The implications are even graver if account is taken of the way that these other activities have, over the centuries, shaped a cultural space which is valued, fragile and of great scenic importance. Furthermore, the imprudent exploitation of water resources threatens the survival of intensive agriculture (fruit trees, early vegetables, sub-tropical products, etc.) on the Costa del Sol, in Almeria and on the Canary Islands. Agrarian structures have literally been torn apart as residential settlements have invaded vineyards, as has occurred, for example, at Marina Alta in Alicante.

Until the present none of the regional plans has been guided by the principles of preserving the environment and of complementing traditional activities with tourism. There are economic reasons why such plans are necessary, for many complementary activities are profit-yielding and are competitive in EC markets. Agricultural activities should also be viewed positively from a tourist perspective, for they create an attractive landscape and supply fresh consumer products which help reduce dependence on imports; this problem is especially grave in the archipelagos (Salvá 1984, p. 227). All of this highlights the urgent need for the regional authorities (responsible, at present, for regional planning) to establish clear criteria for the spatial zoning of tourism and other activities in the coastal areas, following the principle of complementarity. The recent production of White Papers on tourism in some regions (Catalonia, the Balearics and Andalusia) point in this direction, although they have not yet been effective. There are fears that stricter territorial controls might deter investors in tourism. On the other hand, many coastal municipalities have introduced changes in their city planning in order to avoid the loss of their most fertile agricultural land, as has happened on many previous occasions (Valenzuela 1986a).

3.4.2   *The contribution of tourism to regional labour markets*

There have been considerable demographic changes in the provinces of mass tourism, with their populations growing at above average rates between 1960 and 1985 (Table 3.9). Gerona is an exceptional case, with the population multiplying almost threefold in this period. The demographic growth is mainly a consequence of in-migration. The number of in-migrants among the resident population of the single-province tourist areas (Costa Brava, Costa Blanca and the Balearics) had already reached 25–30 per cent, according to the

Table 3.9 Demographic evolution in the main tourist provinces of Spain, 1960–85

| | Number of inhabitants | | Increase | |
	1960	1985	Absolute	1960 = 100
Alicante	711,942	1,216,413	504,471	171
Balearics	443,327	680,955	237,628	154
Gerona	177,539	465,888	288,349	262
Málaga	775,167	1,137,782	362,615	147
Santa Cruz de Tenerife	490,655	700,884	210,229	143
Spain	30,430,698	38,398,246	7,967,548	126

Source: INE population censuses

1981 census. Emigrants from Murcia have a preference for neighbouring Alicante, which has also attracted in-migrants from the eastern provinces of Andalusia (Granada and Jaen) and from Castille-La Mancha (Albacete, Ciudad Real, etc.). Andalusia and Murcia also dominate emigration to the Balearics, while the most underdeveloped provinces of Andalusia (Granada and Jaen) provide the least-qualified labour working in hotels and catering on the Costa Brava. The three provinces mentioned above are among the first ten with respect to the volume of in-migration in 1961–82, although the biggest contingent arrived between 1962 and 1973 (Santillana 1984, p. 29).

Migration to the tourist zones in the less developed regions (Andalusia and the Canary Islands) has a different pattern. The coastal regions of the province of Málaga (Costa del Sol) have received a major part (40 per cent) of their in-migrants from the province itself, with most (33 per cent) of the remainder from the rest of Andalusia. Marbella and Fuengirola have probably derived the greatest demographic increases from this process (López Cano 1984, p. 74).

To some extent the effects of tourism on regional labour markets can be deduced from the increasing weight of the tertiary sector in the economies of the tourist provinces. Hotels are the best-known example of directly created tourism employment, although this type of accommodation is now in decline. Table 3.10 shows the distribution of hotel jobs by region, differentiating maximum (50 per cent of which is seasonal) from permanent employment. These figures highlight the extent of seasonality in hotel employment which, in the low season, can fall to as little as one-fifth of that in the peak season in the Costa del Sol and the Balearics, and to 30 per cent in Alicante. Only the Canary Islands have no pronounced seasonality in tourism.

The regional distribution of employment in hotels and restaurants is indicated in Table 3.8 (see also Figure 3.3). This type of employment is dominant only in the smaller regions and in specialised tourist areas, reaching 21.7 per cent in the Balearics. In Alicante, hotel and restaurant jobs represent only 6.2 per cent of the total, in Málaga 10.5 per cent and in the Canary Islands 11 per cent. However, these relatively modest figures do not reflect the real extent of the dependence of labour, for tourism affects many sectors of the economy. Building activity provides an example; in the most touristic provinces (indicated in Table 3.11) its share of employment is over 1.5 times that of the national average, reaching a maximum in Málaga (11.6 per cent).

Table 3.10   Regional distribution of hotel employment in Spain, 1985

	Permanent employment	High season employment	(%)
Andalusia	8,965	16,004	12.3
Aragón	1,846	3,296	2.5
Asturias	637	1,137	0.9
Balearics	19,059	34,021	26.2
Canaries	5,812	10,373	8.0
Cantabria	890	1,589	1.2
Castille-La Mancha	1,157	2,064	1.6
Castille-León	2,705	4,829	3.7
Catalonia	15,018	26,808	20.7
Extremadura	634	1,132	0.9
Galicia	2,458	4,389	3.4
Madrid	4,288	7,653	5.9
Murcia	850	1,517	1.2
Navarra	458	818	0.6
Basque country	1,382	2,467	1.9
Rioja	220	393	0.3
Valencia	6,340	11,319	8.7
Total	72,719	129,809	100.0

Source: Secretaría General de Turismo, *El empleo en el sector hotelero*, 1985

The overall contribution of tourism to improving standards of living and to family income can be assessed. Tourism is directly responsible for the Balearics and Gerona occupying, respectively, first and second place amongst the fifty Spanish provinces in the league table of per-capita income. The situation in Alicante is less clear but family income is still 6 per cent higher than the national average. Traditionally Málaga and Tenerife were backward regions, but tourism has contributed to an improvement in their positions to 28th and 30th place, respectively. The effects of tourism on standards of living in particular communities is more difficult to assess; however, in Valencia

Table 3.11   Employment linkages of tourism in specialised tourist areas in Spain, 1985

	Tertiary sector Employment	(%)	Building industry Employment	(%)	Hotels and restaurants Employment	(%)
Alicante	173,697	44.6	36,667	9.4	24,217	6.2
Balearics	175,039	65.3	25,830	9.6	58,052	21.7
Gerona	92,089	48.9	18,521	9.8	16,916	9.0
Málaga	159,166	60.4	30,583	11.6	27,754	10.5
Santa Cruz de Tenerife	130,241	61.8	20,226	9.6	22,713	10.8
Spain	6,015,396	50.6	958,430	8.1	584,291	4.9

Source: Banco de Bilbao, *Renta Nacional de España*, 1985

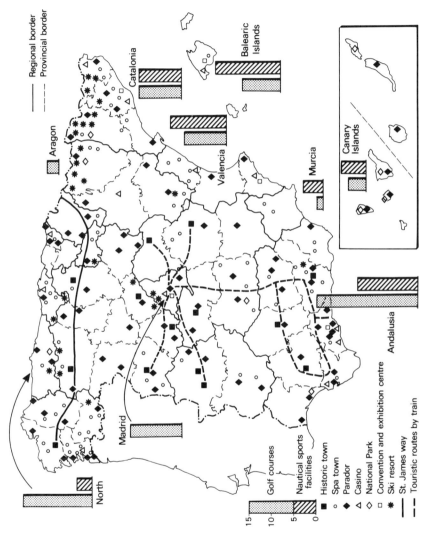

Fig. 3.3 Major tourism resources in Spain

most touristic municipalities do occupy leading positions in listings of per-capita income (Esteban and Pedreño 1985).

3.5   Policies to combat seasonality and regional concentration

The seasonality of demand and regional concentration constitute the two major problems of Spanish mass tourism. Measures have been adopted to ameliorate both, but with uneven results.

3.5.1   *Quality improvement and diversification in response to seasonal demand*

Expert opinions agree that the priorities for policies should be measures to broaden out seasonal demand and to secure higher-spending customers through improving the quality of supply (Figuerola 1986). In practice, except for the retirement boom in Alicante and the Costa del Sol, achievements have been modest. More has been achieved in terms of improving the availability of those complementary recreational activities which are essential for attracting higher-income and more active tourism. In the hotel business itself, there have been programmes to develop integrated services. Moreover, specialised tourism is being increased through the promotion of particular interests (for example, painting and computing); Club Méditerranée has been a pioneer in this, and the approach has been imitated elsewhere, with the mushrooming of club resorts (Gutiérrez 1985, pp. 157–67).

Provision of select sports facilities is important in attracting middle and high-income tourism. There is a move to link golf courses to luxury hotels (Parador del Golf) or to large residential–tourism developments such as Nueva Andalucía (Málaga) and Almerimar (Ortega Martínez 1986, pp. 44–5). In the same way, marinas have been a decisive promotional attraction in many residential complexes, sometimes incorporating traditional Mediterranean architecture. The supply of diversified and select sporting opportunities (submarine fishing, regattas, polo, etc.) has a key role in shaping tourist flows and in improving quality (Esteve 1986, pp. 237–66). Without doubt, the Costa del Sol has the finest and largest number of sports facilities linked with the development of residential areas and high-level tourism (Valenzuela 1982).

Another element in the expansion of quality tourism is 'talasotherapy', which has a long tradition in a number of internationally famous tourist centres (Estoril, Knokke, etc.). In Spain 'talasotherapy' has been practised since the late nineteenth century at a number of coastal resorts (Cadiz, Mar Menor, Alicante, etc.). At present, only the wealthiest tourists have access to such specialised luxury facilities, such as those at the Biblos Hotel (Mijas). There will probably be greater demand for cure-bathing in the future as the European population ages and third-age tourism continues to increase.

Spain's administration has also undertaken the construction of exhibition and conference halls in order to diversify the industry (Figure 3.3). This has been favoured by many hotel-owners who offer well-conditioned installations for conferences and conventions. Besides the high-spending propensity of conference attenders, this type of tourism also meets the double challenge of improving quality and reducing seasonality.

3.5.2   Developments in the interior and the spatial extension of tourism

The interior of Spain relies on high-quality tourism and a variety of attractions, and this could provide a solid base for developing alternative activities and generating new tourist flows. Unfortunately, no detailed inventory of inland touristic resources exists for Spain as a whole, only for some regions (Marchena 1986). At present, the promotion of inland tourism is a preoccupation of all levels of public administration (local, regional and state) but, thus far, the results have been modest in the face of powerful competition from seaside resorts.

Historically, the first measure to encourage inland travel was the construction of *paradores* (state-owned hotels): this policy dates from the 1920s but was intensified in the 1960s, marking an outstanding chapter in the work of the Ministerio de Información y Turismo. Its contribution, although worthwhile, lacked clear aims and criteria, and it was mainly a prestige operation. The central government was even more active in the promotion of winter tourism through the *Planes de Desarrollo* (Presidencia del Gobierno 1976, pp. 75–8). This provided subsidies for tourist enterprises and for infrastructural improvements in those skiing resorts which had the greatest potential for attracting foreigners (the Pyrenees and the Sierra Nevada) or those most frequented by visitors from the largest cities (Ariza and Villegas 1984; Valenzuela 1986b). A number of ski resorts did spring up in the 1960s as a result of official aid but priority was given to rapid growth while ecological criteria and a concern for territorial equilibrium were lacking. This resulted in a number of problems in mountainous regions such as Alto Aragón and Valle de Aran (López Palomeque 1982). Nevertheless, the ski resorts do provide facilities which are complementary to coastal tourism. At the regional level, skiing is particularly important in Andalusia — which boasts the southernmost ski resort in Europe, the Sierra Nevada (Solynieve) — and Catalonia, where some of the Pyrenean resorts (for example, Baqueira Beret) have a cosmopolitan clientele. The *Generalitat de Cataluña* (Government of Catalonia) has channelled financial assistance to the ski resorts — 1.075 billion pesetas in 1985 alone — for artificial snow facilities and promotion abroad.

The autonomous regions have emphasised the promotion of 'green' and 'nature' tourism, through creating and widening their networks of parks and natural reserves, while marketing new tourist products (excursions on foot, on horseback, boating, etc.). The northern regions have been pioneers in this and thus have the most attractive and well-preserved rural resorts (in Asturias and Cantabria). Meanwhile, Andalusia has undertaken a pilot study of the recreational potential of the Sierra de Cazorla natural park.

There are even greater possibilities for promoting tourism related to game-hunting for which excellent conditions exist in the South and central Spain (López Ontiveros 1981). Hunting could become a useful tool for economic regeneration in many depressed and virtually unpopulated areas in the interior. The autonomous government of Castille-La Mancha, the region that contains one of the best-endowed hunting-grounds in Europe (Montes de Toledo), has already realised this.

Rural tourism is currently a line of action being pursued by some autonomous governments; this could lead to either the rehabilitation of country houses and hamlets or to the building of new residential facilities. This second option has been chosen by the *Junta de Andalucía* in the promoting of *villas turísticas*, the first of which is already functioning in the picturesque region of the Alpujarras, in the heart of Sierra Nevada. This boasts many natural and cultural conditions for the development of a stable tourism, little more than 100 km from the Costa del Sol (Calatrava 1984, pp. 310–12). The rehabilitation of old buildings is also being considered in the cases of Extremadura and Asturias (Bote 1985).

Cultural and historic-artistic attractions have drawn excursionists to the historic cities in the interior of the country which are within easy reach of the coastal tourist centres (Granada, Cordoba), or of Madrid (Toledo, Segovia) or areas situated along the main routes (Burgos, Trujillo). Historic and almost forgotten routes are being opened up, such as the Camino de Santiago (Figure 3.3), with the aim of generating tourist itineraries—by car or on foot—and this may represent a new model of cultural tourism (Herrera 1984). All in all, the interior offers many rich and stimulating attractions, but it remains to be seen whether they can compete with the powerful attractions of the coastal areas.

3.6   A Conclusion for the 1990s: The Challenge of Quality

After years of continuous growth in the indicators measuring the economic effects of tourism on the Spanish economy (such as foreign currency earnings and GDP), the sector has again plunged into crisis during the 1989 season. In 1988 the number of foreign tourists had grown by 7.2 per cent over 1987 levels (54,178,150 visitors). By then earnings had reached $16,686 million (2,000 billion pesetas), being equivalent to 9.5 per cent of GDP. In contrast, a reduction of 5–6 per cent in the number of tourists was likely for 1989, and this has mostly resulted from the tour-operator controlled segment of the market.

Hotel enterprises and chains have been strongly affected by this tendency, as the market climate has changed from one of overbooking to serious under-occupation. In those specialised tourist regions, such as the Balearic and the Canary Islands, which are most heavily dependent on tour-operators, a 10 per cent market decline was likely during 1989. The magnitude of the crisis is evident if July occupancy levels are compared for 1988 and 1989 for selected resorts (Table 3.12). Given that the weather has been very variable and exceptionally rainy in all the Mediterranean coast during the autumn, the mean occupancy rate for the whole year is expected to be even lower.

The reasons for these changes are many and complex, and can only be summarised briefly here. Beside some probably temporary causes such as a stronger peseta or the threat of terrorism at some resorts, there are some structural faults in the Spanish tourist industry, which neither the private sector nor the public sector tourism administrations (national, regional and local) have succeeded in eradicating. The most important of these has been the loss of competitivity of Spanish tourist 'packages', by some 1.5 percentage points during the last two years, in relation to direct competitors such as Tunisia, Yugoslavia and Turkey, and the surplus supply of bed-spaces, some of which constitute illegal provision. At this point, reference must also be made to the phenomenon of time-share which has become enormously popular amongst British and Scandinavian tourists, even though this form of ownership lacks proper legal regulation in Spain. From the point of view of the hotel organisations (ZONTUR and *Federación de Empresarios de Hotelería*),

Table 3.12   Hotel occupancy levels in July 1988 and 1989

Tourist Resort	Level of occupancy July 1989 (%)	Percentage change in occupancy level, July 1988–9
Benidorm	80	−15
Gerona	60	−30
Costa del Sol	78	−12
Mallorca	60	−15
Menorca	70	−17
Ibiza-Formentera	70	−15
Gran Canaria	60	−20
Lanzarote	55	−21
Tenerife	75	−10

Source: ZONTUR

the time–share system is competing with and causing serious damage to the hotel sector.

In addition to these reasons for the decline of tourism, the current crisis in the industry also has much deeper roots. In particular, the loss of quality has been emphasised by both professional and academic critics. Strong concentration of tourists in some resorts has had serious adverse effects on the environment and the landscape, as well as on the quality of life in these areas (on transport, personal services, etc.). The excessively low prices of holiday packages also contributed to the pressure on the natural and the built environment.

The key to resolving this crisis lies in improving Spain's tourism image. The central administration, via the *Instituto de Promoción del Turismo* (TURESPAMA), spent over 13,000 million pesetas in 1988 on promoting Spain as a tourist destination, and this was in addition to the 8,000 million pesetas spent by the autonomous governments. However, as already indicated, the upgrading of the industry requires more far-reaching developments both in and outside the hotel and apartment sectors. Many voices can now be heard demanding such changes. Rediscovery of the traditional quality of service is one example of such changes, and it has to be linked to improved professional training. It is also important not to neglect the quality of the complementary supply, in such aspects as infrastructure (roads, telephones, sewage, etc.) and services, as well as the environment and landscape of the tourist resort. Improvement of the supply side also requires diversification, with the development of sport and leisure facilities in and around the tourist resort, so as to make golf, riding or sailing widely accessible and not just to a small élite of wealthy customers. In the same way it has been proposed that traditional seaside tourism should be linked with inland tourism, based on the rich cultural and natural landscape of the latter.

Some progress has been made in the upgrading of coastal tourism in Spain. Preservation of unspoilt coastal landscapes and restoration of less seriously damaged ones are the major aims of the recently approved *Ley de Costas* (1988). This established free public access to all the beaches, dunes, cliffs and marshes adjacent to the sea and prohibited any new construction within 100 metres of the shore. Important progress has also been made by the *Ministerio de Obras Públicas y Urbanismo* (MOPU) in the restoration of beaches on some coasts where the sand had almost disappeared (e.g., Maresme coast in Catalonia). In this region the sea-front of Barcelona has been newly designated for tourism and leisure uses, as a part of an urban restructuring plan with a view to improving urban tourism facilities for the 1992 Olympic Games. Similarly, in Andalusia, the decision to hold a World Exhibition at Seville in 1992 has been the catalyst for improvement of the whole Huelva Coast (*Costa de la Luz*), situated an hour from Seville. Here, new tourist resorts are being promoted (e.g., *Costa Doñana*) and old ones are being refurbished (e.g., *Isla Canela*).

In order to counterbalance the crisis in foreign tourism, domestic tourism has been encouraged by the institutions which provide social tourism opportunities to those on low incomes. After 1985 the new *Ministerio de Asuntos Sociales*, through the *Instituto de Servicios Sociales* (INSERSO), has promoted tourism programmes for at least half a million pensioners. Between October and April, those aged over 65 can travel to and stay for fourteen days in any one of a selected number of seaside resorts at very low prices. During the 1989–90 season the same Institute has also launched a programme of spa tourism, whereby approximately 13,000 pensioners will have the possibility of access to two-week holidays at about thirty spas located throughout Spain.

Finally, it is worth mentioning a recent study of the *UNO Economic Commission for Europe* (CEPE), which has emphasised that by the year 2000, tourism will be *the* major sector of the service industries. It is highly desirable that by that date mass tourism in Spain should have attained its ideal structure, both from the point of view of its economic weight and its environmental and social integration.

4 Italy: multi-faceted tourism

Russell King

4.1 Introduction

Italy is one of the oldest, most established and most diversified tourist countries in the world. As White (1987) points out, the country has strong claims to be the first home of tourism, for it was the patrician families of Ancient Rome who built the first second homes, inventing the idea of the holiday at their coastal and country resorts. Later, Italy's widely recognised cultural and historical attractions brought the first impetus to European leisure travel as élite visitors started to stream in during the eighteenth and nineteenth centuries; no young English or German gentleman could be considered fully educated until he had visited Italy on the 'Grand Tour'. During the present century, and especially since the Second World War, Italy has seen dramatic expansion away from the aristocratic and cultural bases of tourism to embrace the mass markets of beach and ski tourism. Nevertheless, the artistic and architectural heritage of many cities remains as an important feature on the itineraries of many tourists and visitors. Overall, Italy today not only has the largest number of foreign visitors (including day excursionists) of any country in the world and the second largest number of foreign tourists in Europe, but it also possesses a tourist industry that is more diversified than that of any other country.

Italy counts on two major resources to attract the bulk of its tourists. These are its climate and its cultural heritage. Other attractions include its beaches, its many thermal resorts, its centres of religious pilgrimage such as Assisi and Loreto, its beautiful mountain and hill scenery, and, more nebulously, the Italian 'way of life' (Cole 1968; Perez 1986).

The climatic attraction is essentially twofold: the mountain areas are frequented for their snow in winter and for their fresh climate in summer; the coastal areas are tourist magnets because of their heat and reliable sun in summer. The most popular coasts are the Ligurian Riviera and the Adriatic Riviera around Rimini. Also quite important are the Neapolitan and Amalfitan coasts of Campania; the north-east corner of Sicily, especially Taormina; and the Sardinian Costa Smeralda.

With regard to historic sites, Italy is undoubtedly one of the richest, if not *the* richest, in the world. Tuscany alone has more classified ancient monuments and artistic treasures than any other European country (Quilici 1984). The peninsula and the islands of Sicily and Sardinia are rich in ruins whereas most of the finest medieval towns are in the North, either in the Po Plain or in the

Fig. 4.1 Tourist resources and activities in Italy.
Sources: Cole (1968, p. 159); White (1987, p. 556)

northern third of the peninsula. In the latter two regions there are not less than thirty cities which in any other country would be classed as outstanding. Pride of place naturally goes to Venice and Florence, and further south of course to Rome, but there are also Turin, Mantua, Pavia, Parma, Verona, Bologna, Padua, Pisa, Siena and many more.

Figure 4.1 shows some of the main places and areas of touristic importance in Italy. The major feature of the map is the concentration of tourist attractions and facilities in the northern half of the country. In the South the incidence of tourism is much more scattered. Thus, tourism reinforces the spatial dualism in the economic geography of Italy, adding to the economic domination by the

Table 4.1   The supply of tourist accommodation in Italy, 1970–80

	1970			1980		
	Enterprises	Bed-spaces	(%)	Enterprises	Bed-spaces	(%)
Hotel sector: total	41,290	1,332,530	41.6	41,697	1,569,733	33.9
Hotels: de luxe	64	15,822	0.5	53	13,111	0.3
1st class	582	81,380	2.5	715	110,670	2.4
2nd class	3,184	271,363	8.5	4,409	408,489	8.8
3rd class	6,543	334,757	10.4	8,162	409,289	8.8
4th class	8,037	218,090	6.8	8,608	227,559	4.9
Pensioni: 1st class	113	4,895	0.2	119	5,045	0.1
2nd class	1,277	47,250	1.5	1,452	54,906	1.2
3rd class	7,299	195,335	6.1	7,440	197,177	4.3
Locande	14,191	163,638	5.1	10,739	143,487	3.1
Non-hotel sector: total	1,204	1,871,421	58.4	2,009	3,061,157	66.1
Private rented accommodation	–	989,852	30.9	–	1,944,905	42.0
Youth hostels	66	6,657	0.2	108	8,958	0.2
Campsites	1,138	476,922	14.9	1,901	853,002	18.4
Other	–	397,990	12.4	–	254,292	5.5
All accommodation types	42,494	3,203,951	100.0	43,706	4,630,890	100.0

Source: ISTAT, *Annuario Statistico Italiano*, Rome, 1971, pp. 261–3; 1981, p. 217

Note: For private rented accommodation and 'other' categories, numbers of enterprises are not
published

North which already exists, and has existed for some time, in the fields of
agriculture and industry.

4.2   Sources of data

In its *Annuario Statistico* the Italian Central Statistics Agency ISTAT publishes
every year quite detailed statistics on the tourist industry. These data are
continuous since 1949 and cover two broad areas: the supply of hotel and other
accommodation; and the influx and movement of the tourists themselves. The
figures are published at national level and for each of Italy's twenty regions.

Italy's supply of tourist accommodation—the most extensive of any
European country—is classified into two broad sectors: hotel-type enterprises
(*esercizi alberghieri*) and non-hotel enterprises (*esercizi extralberghieri*). Each of
these is further subdivided: see Table 4.1. For each of these detailed accommodation types columns of data are presented on the number of enterprises
and of rooms, beds and bathrooms. In 1984 a new system of star classification
both for hotels and other forms of tourist accommodation was introduced,
including new minimum standards and size criteria for hotels (for details, see
Perez 1986); however, this has yet to find its way into the official statistics.

The movement of tourists and visitors in the above types of accommodation,
for each region, is recorded according to the following parameters: number of
arrivals, number of overnights spent, average length of stay, month of arrival
and departure, and nationality (including Italians). Data specifically on Italian

domestic tourism are more restricted to numbers of people taking a holiday by socio-economic group and by regions of origin and destination. Moreover, these data on internal tourism tend to be the product of specific surveys carried out by ISTAT and other bodies and are not monitored on an annual basis. Data on the movement of Italian tourists abroad are exiguous.

4.3   Supply of accommodation

Italy offers nearly 5 million bed-spaces for tourists and visitors in the various kinds of accommodation listed in Table 4.1. Of these, 1.6 million, roughly one-third, are in the hotel sector (which also includes *pensioni* and *locande*), two-fifths are in rented accommodation, and one-fifth are in the campsite sector. Table 4.1 sets out this supply in more detail and notes trends for the period 1970–80 (changes in data availability prevent a more up-to-date comparison), while Figure 4.2 portrays the regional distribution of the three major types of tourist accommodation for 1984.

The regional map shows that the total stock of bed-spaces is highest in a group of regions—Trentino-Alto Adige, Veneto, Emilia-Romagna, Tuscany —which lie adjacent to the main centres of population in the industrial North-West. The north-western regions of Lombardy and Liguria are themselves important, the former because of its mountain, lake and ski attractions, the latter because of its coast. In central Italy Latium and Abruzzi are also quite important. Latium is the region in which Rome is situated, whilst Abruzzi has the dramatic scenery of the Apennines, including a national park and several ski resorts, and a string of beach resorts popular with Roman holiday-makers. South of these two regions the quantities of tourist accommodation are much lower. Figure 4.2 also shows the differential regional importance of accommodation types. Hotels are relatively more important in Trentino, Emilia-Romagna, Campania and Sicily; rented accommodation dominates in all northern and central regions except Piedmont and Umbria; campsite bed-spaces are relatively more prominent in Apulia, Calabria and Sardinia.

Returning to Table 4.1, it can be seen that the total increase in bed-spaces of 1.43 million between 1970 and 1980 was mainly accounted for by the 1.19 million increase in the non-hotel sector. In fact the hotel sector saw its share of total bed-spaces decrease from 41.6 per cent to 33.9 per cent over the decade. The decreases in the importance of hotel-type accommodation were most marked at the polar ends of the quality spectrum, with absolute numbers of both enterprises and bed-spaces falling for de luxe hotels and *locande*. These trends have continued into the 1980s; by 1984 there were, for instance, only 6,255 *locande* with 30,760 bed-spaces. Legislation in force since 1984 provides for the eventual elimination of the *locanda* and *pensione* categories: the enterprises will either close down or be upgraded to lower-class hotels. De luxe and first-class hotels have become less important as tourism in Italy makes the transition to a mass phenomenon; the decline of quality hotels has been well documented on both the Ligurian and Adriatic coasts by Titi (1980). The accommodation types which have shown most consistent increases have been rented accommodation and campsites; in both cases available bed-spaces approximately doubled between 1970 and 1980.

The pattern of expansion and contraction of accommodation types also varies regionally. The growth of tourist accommodation since 1970 has been

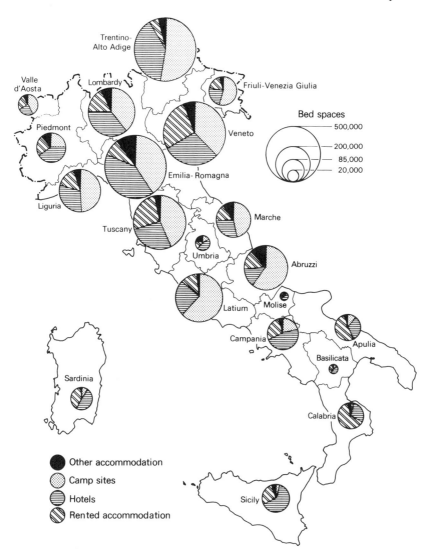

Fig. 4.2 Regional provision of tourist accommodation in Italy, 1984

Source: ISTAT, *Annuario Statistico Italiano*, 1986

strongest in Trentino-Alto Adige and the South, and weakest in the North-West and central Italy, whose relative shares of national totals have declined for all three major accommodation types. Particularly dramatic has been the growth of campsite accommodation on the southern mainland. Nevertheless these figures should not be allowed to obscure the fact that compared with the rest of the country, the South remains profoundly underprovided with tourist accommodation. Even though the region contains two-fifths of Italy's surface area, three-quarters of its coastline and 36 per 'cent of its population, it accounted in 1984 for less than 19 per cent of the national total of tourist bed-spaces and only 11 per cent of tourist arrivals.

The single biggest problem of the Italian hotel industry is its generally low utilisation index, below that for most other European countries. Such a lack of balance between the production and consumption of tourist facilities is largely, but not entirely, a reflection of the seasonality of demand for tourist accommodation. This is in turn related to two broad controlling factors: seasonal variations in climate, summer having obviously the most favourable holiday weather (except for winter sports); and the availability of free time linked to holiday leave, school holidays, and so on.

At the national level the crude utilisation index, obtained by dividing the total potential overnights (number of bed-spaces × 365) available in hotel-type accommodation by the number of nights the beds were actually occupied, was 28.8 per cent in 1984. The *net* utilisation index, taking into account the seasonal closures of some establishments, was naturally higher—38.5 per cent. These figures have generally been improving over the last fifteen years (in 1970 they were 26.3 and 34.9 per cent respectively), although they have been falling during the last couple of years (in 1982 they were 30.0 and 40.6 per cent respectively). Moreover, the indices vary by hotel category, by region and, of course, by month. Table 4.2 spells out some of these variations in more detail, averaging the figures for the four most recent years for which data are available in order to iron out year-to-year fluctuations.

Crude occupancy rates are 5.5 times as high in August (67.9 per cent) as in November (12.3 per cent); for ten months of the year both crude and net rates

Table 4.2   Italian hotel sector: utilisation indices by class of establishment, month and region, 1981–4 (annual averages)

Hotel types	Crude[1]	Net[1]	Month	Crude[1]	Net[1]	Regions	Crude[1]	Net[1]
Hotels	29.9	39.5	January	15.5	26.1	Piedmont	27.1	32.6
De luxe	43.1	50.4	February	18.4	30.2	Valle d'Aosta	26.2	33.3
1st class	39.4	48.4	March	18.7	29.2	Lombardy	27.5	32.4
2nd class	31.5	41.9	April	23.7	33.5	Trentino	25.8	28.6
3rd class	28.7	39.8	May	24.4	31.3	Veneto	31.2	49.9
4th class	23.7	29.8	June	37.8	41.0	Friuli	24.5	34.3
			July	54.8	56.6	Liguria	30.9	40.5
Pensioni	27.5	45.6	August	67.9	70.5	Emilia	28.4	55.2
1st class	36.3	48.5	September	39.5	45.7	Tuscany	35.5	48.2
2nd class	30.0	43.8	October	21.1	31.7	Umbria	32.0	33.2
3rd class	26.5	46.1	November	12.3	21.7	Marche	20.6	33.5
			December	13.1	22.6	Latium	40.5	45.5
Locande	23.9	28.8				Abruzzi	19.0	24.6
			Year	29.2	39.3	Molise	26.8	28.9
Total	29.2	39.3				Campania	32.2	46.7
						Apulia	26.0	29.6
						Basilicata	17.1	24.8
						Calabria	21.2	27.2
						Sicily	32.2	27.2
						Sardinia	32.4	38.1
						Italy	29.2	39.3

Source: after Vaccaro and Perez (1986, pp. 156–9)

Note: 1. For explanation of 'crude' and 'net' utilisation indices see text

remain below 50 per cent; only in July and August are they higher. Regarding hotel type, luxury and first-class hotels have relatively high rates of usage; the lowest indices are recorded by fourth-class hotels and *locande*. In between, the middle-ranking hotels and *pensioni* have average values, but with greater differentials between crude and net rates, probably reflecting the way in which *pensioni* react to the seasonality of demand by closing down for dead-season periods (Vaccaro and Perez 1986). Regionally, too, there are wide variations. Occupancy rates are generally highest in the major tourist regions (see Figure 4.2) of Veneto, Emilia-Romagna, Tuscany and Latium; they are particularly low in southern mainland regions like Abruzzi, Basilicata and Calabria. Calabria's occupancy rates, for instance, are half those of Tuscany. The low southern rates are partly a reflection of the lower efficiency of the tourist industry in this part of Italy, and the fact that hotel-owners are more willing to survive on lower incomes (given the lack of alternative entrepreneurial outlets), and partly due to the South's greater reliance on summer beach tourism. By contrast, regions like Latium, Emilia-Romagna, Veneto and Tuscany not only have a more efficiently managed beach holiday industry, but also include a large number of cities (Rome, Florence, Pisa, Siena, Bologna, Venice, Verona etc.) which attract year-round cultural visitors.

In addition to the fundamental problem of seasonality, there are also other reasons why Italy's supply of hotel accommodation remains relatively under-used. More and more people, especially Italians themselves, are holidaying outside the traditional hotel networks in private boarding-houses, rented accommodation, holiday villages and campsites. This has put particular pressure on regions like the Ligurian Riviera where the hotels are old and often in need of substantial repair and modernisation—an upgrading which is difficult to achieve with declining clienteles. Italy as a whole remains a country of medium-sized and small family-run hotels. National hotel chains such as Jolly Hotels or the state-owned Agip Motels have emerged only recently. The only real infrastructure for mass tourism is on the Adriatic coast and, to a lesser and more fragmented extent, on the Ligurian Riviera. The type of tourism with heavy foreign investment in big hotels, bringing in tourists by cheap charter flights, has never been so important in Italy as it has in Spain. Although it is true that the standard of accommodation has steadily improved, Italy is still left with a legacy of mostly old-fashioned hotels with low occupancy rates.

4.4 Tourist flows

Figure 4.3 graphs the growth of tourist flows to the hotel and non-hotel sectors for the period 1958–84. The effects of the two major oil-induced recessions appear as relatively minor interruptions in the overall upward trends of the curves, although the stagnation of the 1980s may prove to be more enduring.

Again, however, there are marked spatial variations in this pattern of growth. Figure 4.4a shows that the strongest growth has occurred in a scatter of regions, indicating once more the diverse nature of Italian tourism. Latium contains the ever-popular tourist magnet of Rome which is not only Italy's single most important tourist locality but also acts as a gateway and stopover point for tourists and travellers aiming at other destinations. Valle d'Aosta and

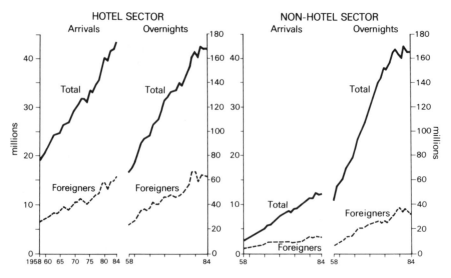

Fig. 4.3   Tourist arrivals and overnights in Italy, 1958–84

Source: ISTAT, *Sommario di Statistiche Storiche 1926–1986*, Rome, pp. 252, 255

Trentino-Alto Adige are the only two Italian regions which lie entirely in the mountains and whose tourist strength relies on mountain activities such as skiing and 'scenic tourism'; these two regions also enjoy good connections with adjacent countries so that French, Swiss, German and Austrian tourists find it convenient to holiday there—a convenience which is further enhanced by the fact that Valle d'Aosta is mainly Francophone and the northern part of Trentino-Alto Adige is German-speaking. Sicily and Sardinia are Italy's two island regions whose unique insular character offers the discerning tourist something rather different. Interestingly, the four peripheral regions with high tourist growth patterns are the four 'special statute' regions created as regionally autonomous units by the 1948 constitution: as self-governing units for forty years, they have long experience of promoting themselves— apparently effectively—on the national and international tourist markets.

Regions where the absolute number of tourist overnights declined during 1974–84 embrace three northern and three southern regions (Figure 4.4a). Again, these are polar types: industrial regions containing big cities (Turin, Milan, Trieste, etc.) which have lost popularity as Italian holiday-makers have ventured farther afield; and remote rural southern regions whose appeal has never been very strong, especially to foreign tourists.

The seasonal pattern of overnights reveals a marked concentration in the summer months and is, of course, responsible for the uneven occupation of hotel beds and other facilities noted earlier. More than 50 per cent of total tourist overnights are recorded in July and August, more than 70 per cent in the four months between June and September. Domestic tourists are more seasonally concentrated than foreign tourists, especially in the month of August. Seasonality is more marked in the non-hotel sector which, for Italians, sees 70 per cent of overnights registered in July and August alone, reflecting the tradition, also widespread in other countries such as France and

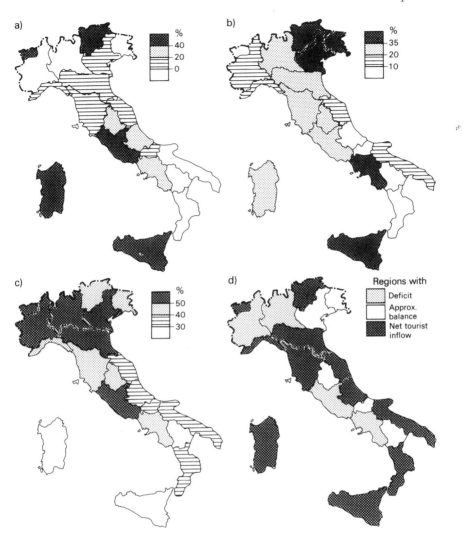

Fig. 4.4 Regional aspects of Italy's foreign and domestic tourism: (a) change in total tourist overnights (all types of accommodation), 1974–84; (b) foreigners' share of tourist overnights, 1984; (c) proportion of the population taking holidays; and (d) regional balance of domestic tourism, 1985

Source: ISTAT, *Annuario Statistico Italiano*, 1975, pp. 338–9; 1986, pp. 44, 459

Spain, of taking a month by the sea. Overall, the number of overnight stays (in all types of accommodation) in August, the peak month, is thirteen times that in the trough month of November.

4.4.1   Foreign tourists

The number of tourist arrivals from abroad recorded via the official accommodation network grew steadily until 1980, since when it has increased more unevenly. There were 8.5 million foreign tourist arrivals in 1960, 12.7 million in 1970, 17.9 million in 1980 and 19.9 million in 1985. The total number of foreigner overnights also reached a maximum (103.3 million) in 1980, since when it has fallen back and fluctuated; it was 97.6 million in 1985. The foreign proportions of total tourist arrivals and total overnights have remained fairly constant in recent years at around 35 per cent and 30 per cent respectively. As far as types of accommodation are concerned, foreign tourists (except the Dutch) opt more for hotels than do the Italians who have a preference for rented accommodation and campsites. Foreigners are overrepresented in de luxe and first-class hotels and, at the other end of the price and quality spectrum, youth hostels.

The nationalities of foreign tourists recorded in Italian accommodation (and therefore excluding foreign day excursionists and visitors who stay outside the official accommodation network) are given in Table 4.3. Included in this table are all countries supplying at least 100,000 tourists. The list of tourist nationalities is long, reflecting Italy's status as a 'mature' tourist country, able to attract tourists from all Western European countries as well as from North America, Australia, Japan and elsewhere. However, one supplier dominates

Table 4.3   Foreign tourists in Italy, by major nationality

| | Annual average for 1980–4 | | | Growth in |
	Arrivals	Overnights	Average length of stay (nights)	overnights 1970–84 (%)
France	1,961,397	7,536,298	3.8	+25.6
FRG	5,588,650	42,596,537	7.6	+59.3
Netherlands	527,346	4,130,299	7.8	+33.5
Belgium	474,384	3,176,045	6.7	+52.4
UK	1,298,496	6,953,688	5.4	+30.2
Denmark	168,481	996,786	5.9	−23.0
Sweden	226,047	1,308,383	5.8	−7.2
Switzerland	1,020,841	5,940,622	5.8	+43.9
Austria	1,083,934	7,320,014	6.8	+55.9
Yugoslavia	139,838	609,822	4.4	−26.5
Greece	161,503	629,938	3.9	+46.1
Spain	501,381	1,089,095	2.2	+103.0
USA	1,952,600	5,302,320	2.7	−18.0
Canada	202,993	626,360	3.1	+9.2
Brazil	126,889	357,768	2.8	+22.1
Argentina	174,243	498,570	2.9	+13.4
Israel	157,741	366,123	2.3	+101.6
Japan	253,258	570,988	2.3	+53.4
Australia	232,881	636,464	2.7	−62.1
All countries	18,180,966	97,738,583	5.4	+41.1

Sources: ISTAT, *Annuario Statistico Italiano*, 1971, p. 271; ENIT, *Turismo Internazionale nelle Regioni Italiane*, Rome, ENIT Rapporto 5/1986, p. 10

the picture, West Germany being responsible for 31 per cent of foreign arrivals and 44 per cent of foreign overnights recorded in the 1980s.

Whilst there has been a 41 per cent increase in foreign overnights during the fifteen years 1970–84, this rate has varied greatly from country to country, and in some countries (Denmark, Sweden, Yugoslavia, the United States) tourism to Italy has actually fallen off. For statistical reasons the biggest increases recorded in Table 4.3 are for countries starting from low base levels (Spain, Israel); more quantitatively important have been the strong increases in major sending countries like the Federal Republic of Germany, Austria and Belgium, all with at least a 50 per cent growth in tourist overnights.

Length of stay varies remarkably from one country to another. Generally northern European tourists have the longest stays, reflecting their participation in week-long (or longer) sun-seeking package holidays, whereas southern European and overseas visitors have much shorter stays (2–4 days on average), reflecting their tendency either to come on weekend visits (Greece, Yugoslavia) or to spend a short time in Italy as part of a European tour (Japanese, Americans, Australians).

The proportion of foreign to Italian tourists varies greatly from region to region in Italy, with a general tendency to diminish from north to south, as would be expected given increasing distance from Italy's continental neighbours and near-neighbours (the main source areas for Italy's foreign tourists) and the generally less publicised nature of the South as an international tourist destination. Figure 4.4b shows this general pattern. In the three north-eastern regions, 40–44 per cent of overnights are accounted for by foreigners, and the proportion steadily declines southwards to Calabria. Two southern regions which interrupt the pattern are Campania (39 per cent) and Sicily (37 per cent): these are the southern regions with well-established international tourist resorts (Amalfi, Positano, Sorrento, Capri, Taormina, Cefalù) and world-famous archaeological treasures (Paestum, Pompeii, Herculaneum, Agrigento, Syracuse, etc.). The other notable exception to the north-south trend is Valle d'Aosta. In this tiny frontier region less than one-tenth of overnights are accounted for by foreigners. Most of its tourism is made up of Italians' ski holidays; most foreign visitors merely pass through the region en route to the Mediterranean via the Mont Blanc tunnel and the St Bernard passes (Janin 1982).

The monitoring of foreign tourists through statistics supplied by overnights recorded in officially recognised tourist accommodation has certain short-comings: it misses out day excursionists who flock over Italy's northern frontier for picnics, hiking, shopping, sightseeing and skiing; and it fails to record foreigners who stay in private houses or in other kinds of clandestine accommodation. Also relevant here are the large numbers of Italian emigrants, some of whom have taken foreign nationality, who return to their native land for holidays but who do not normally use tourist-type accommodation, staying instead with their relatives. An alternative method of recording foreign visitors and tourists is through the statistics collected at entry points—frontier stations (road and rail), ports and airports. In 1985 the number of foreigners who crossed Italy's frontiers in this way reached a record figure of 53.6 million, a considerable increase over recent years (cf. 33 million in 1970, 36 million in 1975, 47.8 million in 1980). These figures are substantially higher than the numbers of foreign visitors recorded through the hotel and tourist accommodation networks (just under 20 million foreign arrivals in 1985), mainly because of the extraordinarily high number of excursionists. In 1985, for instance, day excursionists numbered 28.6 million, or 53 per cent of non-Italians crossing the frontier. This leaves a residue of 25 million entrants defined as tourists—visitors who stay more than 24 hours. However, the fact that this number still exceeds by 5 million the number of tourists recorded in officially registered accommodation implies that many foreign visitors, perhaps one-fifth, stay outside the official accommodation network in unregistered accommodation or with friends and relatives.

4.4.2   Domestic tourists

Internal tourism accounts for 71 per cent of overnights recorded in officially registered accommodation. Domestic tourism has been sustained by rapidly increasing prosperity since the 1950s. In 1959 only 13 per cent of Italians took a holiday of at least four days' duration; by 1985 this proportion had risen to 46 per cent. Clearly, there remains considerable potential for further growth in the domestic holiday market.

ISTAT's survey data on Italians' holidays in 1985, the most recent available, show that those with the greatest propensity (and financial ability) to take holidays are professionals, managers and clerical workers (70 per cent of whom do so). Much lower proportions were evident for farmers (15 per cent), pensioners (30 per cent) and manual workers (41 per cent). Regionally, there was a broad difference between the inhabitants of northern Italy, 54 per cent of whom took holidays in 1985, and southerners, for whom the figure was only 32 per cent; Figure 4.4c gives the full regional pattern. These regional differences are not purely a function of spatial variations of disposable income, for they are also related to customs: taking a holiday is less a part of the southern Italian way of life than it is in the more 'European' North of Italy.

Nearly all Italians holidaying in their own country arranged their holidays themselves, eschewing package arrangements or the services of travel agents, while well over two-thirds of holiday trips were in the family's own car. This predominantly informal, non-institutionalised approach to domestic tourism is also reflected in the kinds of accommodation used. Still considering domestic holiday trips of at least four days' duration, 25.5 per cent of overnights were spent in the houses or flats of friends or relatives, 22.2 per cent in hotels, *pensioni* and *locande*, 21.6 per cent in privately rented accommodation, 17.7 per cent in 'second homes' and 9.2 per cent in campsites. The second-home phenomenon is becoming increasingly widespread in Italy as more and more city and town-dwellers invest in second (and even third) homes by the sea, in the countryside or in the mountains. Statistically, the high proportion of Italian dwellings vacant and therefore potentially identifiable as second homes (19.9 per cent in the 1981 population census) is exaggerated by large numbers of rural dwellings abandoned by rural–urban migrants and by emigrants living abroad.

Most Italian domestic tourism is intraregional and thus fairly local. There are relatively few long hauls and little to match the French 'rush to the Mediterranean', partly of course because northern Italy, unlike northern France, enjoys a good summer climate. The main patterns of tourist movement are diverse but well established: residents of inland districts travelling to take their holidays by the sea; residents of the coast and of lowland districts travelling to the fresher air of the mountains for *villeggiatura* holidays in farmhouses, second homes or holiday villages; residents of the northern industrial belt travelling to the Alps for short-stay winter skiing holidays. Few Italians are 'culture-lust' tourists, unlike foreign visitors, especially the Americans and Japanese. Intraregional tourism is particularly dominant in Sardinia, Sicily, Calabria and Apulia, four large, isolated southern regions with a sufficient range of holiday attractions to keep most of their holiday-makers relatively near to home.

Figure 4.4d divides the twenty Italian regions into three categories in terms of their balance of domestic tourist movements: deficit regions, inflow regions and regions in balance. 'Deficit regions' are those whose outflow of tourists exceeds to a significant extent the inflow of tourists from other regions; they are Piedmont, Lombardy, Latium and Campania. All of these are regions of important tourist attraction, but their most significant feature is that each contains one of Italy's four cities of more than 1 million inhabitants — Turin, Milan, Rome and Naples. Furthermore, Lombardy in particular has several other large industrial cities, as well as Milan, which act as reservoirs of population from which people need to escape for their holidays. Net tourist inflow regions are those which attract more visitors than they export. These are regions with a good range of tourist facilities — beach resorts, cultural centres, mountain scenery — and which lack large industrial agglomerations or big cities. In the southern regions in this category the net inflow is basically a product of the low propensity of residents of those regions to holiday outside the region, combined with the attraction of visitors from other regions. In the case of northern and central regions like Tuscany, Emilia-Romagna and Trentino-Alto Adige, the net inflow reflects the product of significant outflows being outweighed by more massive inflows. Finally, there are five regions in approximate equilibrium. These regions are a mixed bunch. For example, Basilicata and Molise are small, mainly rural regions whose inhabitants have a low propensity to take holidays anyway and an even lower tendency to venture beyond the regional borders; this is balanced by weak powers of attraction for holiday-makers originating from other regions. Umbria, a land-locked region, loses many of its holiday-makers to coastal resorts; but this is balanced by visitors who appreciate the region's fine hill scenery and cultural and pilgrimage centres.

4.5 The economic importance of tourism

Tourism has always been a major income earner for Italy. In the post-war period, however, its importance has grown considerably. This growth has been more or less continuous, although its rhythm has been interrupted by various factors, both internal and external. Thus the rapid growth of tourism receipts in the 1950s and early 1960s was curbed by domestic inflationary problems during 1963 and then by the West German recession of 1967. The impacts of the two oil-price recessions have already been mentioned: the effect on tourist receipts was broadly in line with the impact on numbers of tourists arriving.

As Manente (1986) has pointed out, the competitiveness of Italian tourism in the international market rests essentially on two variables: the disposable income available to potential visitors to Italy in the major sending countries (a positive elasticity of 1.44); and the price of the Italian 'tourist product' measured against those of its main competitor countries (negative elasticity of 1.28). The interaction of these two variables shows that Italy was generally attractive as a tourist destination until the late 1970s, but that after 1980 the rising value of the Italian lira (now linked to the European Monetary System), the increasing cost of living in Italy, as well as a range of other events (strikes, urban terrorism, the 1980 earthquake), caused Italy to lose its competitive edge rather badly.

4.5.1   Macro-economic impact of tourism

Table 4.4 shows Italy's foreign exchange earnings and losses from tourism over the past fifteen years. Earnings broadly represent the expenditures of foreign tourists in Italy, losses what Italians spend abroad. The figures quoted are at current prices and the real increases, for all three columns, will have been considerably less; indeed in some years (for example, 1974 and 1981) the real gross earnings from foreign tourists actually fell compared with the previous year. Nevertheless the overall importance of tourism to the Italian economy remains critical. In recent years the net receipts from foreign tourism have covered between half and two-thirds of Italy's deficit on visible trade (emigrant remittances being the other major invisible item). Table 4.4 also sets out the foreign exchange gains and losses recorded by the Banca d'Italia and the Ufficio Cambi for the major tourist currencies, averaging the annual figures for 1980–5. Interestingly, the United States contributes slightly more than the Federal Republic of Germany, in spite of the considerable numerical dominance of tourists from the latter country (Table 4.3). The conclusion must be that American tourists are much more lavish in their spending habits when on holiday.

A mounting threat to Italy's net tourist position is the growing tendency for Italians to take their holidays abroad. Unfortunately information on Italians holidaying abroad is still scarce. Data for 1982 show that 6.8 per cent of the Italians who took holidays went abroad; a quarter of these holidayed both abroad and at home (Barucci 1984). The most popular foreign country for Italian tourists was France (17.7 per cent of Italian overnights spent abroad), followed by Yugoslavia (10.8 per cent), Spain (9.6 per cent) and the United Kingdom (8.6 per cent). Most of Italy's foreign holiday-makers come from the North; northerners tend to be more travel-oriented (apart, of course, from the southern emigrants who travel out of necessity rather than pleasure), and are richer and closer to adjacent popular countries than the southerners. Table 4.4 shows that negative financial balances are recorded from Spain and Portugal; the same picture would hold for Yugoslavia, Greece and Turkey were data available. Although it is difficult to imagine tourism as a deficit item in the Italian balance of payments in the foreseeable future, it seems likely that the real value of the surplus will be consistently whittled down.

Calculations by Manente (1986) show the very considerable impact of tourism on the Italian economy in terms of expenditures by tourists, value added and employment. In 1984 tourist expenditures on hotel and other accommodation (331.4 million overnights) and on other consumables amounted to Lit. 43,138 billion. This comprises expenditure both by foreign and Italian tourists in Italy, the former having a higher mean daily expenditure

Table 4.4   Italy's foreign exchange earnings from tourism, 1972–85
(Lit. billions)

Year	Earnings	Losses	Balance	Selected countries (annual averages, 1980–5)	Earnings	Losses	Balance
1972	1,466	520	946	France	770	497	273
1973	1,628	667	961	FRG	2,343	280	2,063
1974	1,815	626	1,189	Netherlands	101	23	78
1975	2,216	676	1,540	Belgium	30	14	16
1976	2,728	735	1,993	UK	434	215	219
1977	4,310	986	3,324	Ireland	8	3	5
1978	5,440	1,229	4,211	Denmark	15	6	9
1979	6,961	1,446	5,515	Sweden	36	8	28
1980	7,828	1,501	6,327	Norway	17	4	13
1981	8,773	2,336	6,437	Switzerland	611	141	470
1982	11,343	2,857	8,486	Austria	278	101	177
1983	13,784	3,202	10,582	Spain	48	154	−106
1984	15,099	3,686	11,413	Portugal	1	1	(−)0
1985	16,722	4,360	12,362	USA	3,443	1,100	2,343
				Canada	105	8	97
				All countries	12,258	2,990	9,268

Sources: Barucci (1984, p. 233); ISTAT, *Annuario Statistico Italiano*, 1985, p. 446; 1986, p. 457

per head (Lit. 87,640) than the latter (Lit. 66,400). However, domestic tourists' expenditure has to be modified downwards by the amount they would have spent (on food, etc.) had they stayed at home; when this is done the net daily expenditure of Italian tourists falls to Lit. 57,000 per head.

Tourist expenditures, whether by foreign or national visitors, can be analysed in the Italian official statistics by category of consumption, and by the sector of origin of the goods consumed (Table 4.5). The importance of 'transport and communications' and of 'other goods and services' (which includes hotels and other tourist accommodation) is highlighted for category of spending, while 'commerce, hotels, etc'. dominates in the sectoral column. Some differences between foreigners' and Italians' patterns of spending may also be pointed out—for instance, foreigners spend more on clothing when on holiday in Italy, whilst Italians tend to be more mobile within Italy, thereby consuming more energy products. In terms of total spending, foreigners spent Lit. 15,122 billion, whilst Italians spent Lit. 28,016 billion (which falls to Lit. 24,044 billion if the quota which would have been spent if Italians had stayed at home is deducted). Domestic tourist expenditure represents 6 or 7 per cent (depending on whether the net or gross figure is taken) of total household expenditure per year.

Moving on to value added: in 1984 tourism contributed Lit. 17,786 billion in terms of its direct effects, and Lit. 28,072 billion if the indirect effects are also taken into account. This latter figure represents 4.8 per cent of total national value added, and 40 per cent of it is made up of foreign tourists' contributions. More than half the value added contributed directly by tourism is to be found in the 'commerce, hotels, etc.' sector of the economy, with another 17 per cent in 'transport and communications' and 13.5 per cent under the heading

Table 4.5 Economic impact of tourism in Italy by category of consumption and sector of origin, 1984 (percentage)

Category of consumption	Distribution of tourist expenditure		Sector of origin	Distribution of tourist expenditure		Value added		Employment	
	Foreign	Italian		Foreign	Italian	Direct	Direct and indirect	Employees	Self-employed
Food and drink	3.2	8.2	Agriculture	0.8	2.4	1.1	8.3	9.9	20.9
Tobacco	1.3	1.6	Energy products	8.2	13.6	2.6	2.8	1.1	0.0
Clothing and shoes	10.2	1.1	Manufactures	21.6	14.1	6.5	12.8	17.2	4.8
Housing, energy	0.6	2.2	Construction	0.0	0.0	0.0	0.6	1.1	0.3
Furniture, linen, etc	2.4	0.4	Commerce, hotels etc.	50.9	49.6	58.1	42.2	45.5	57.6
Health services	0.7	0.8	Transport communications	10.2	10.3	17.2	15.2	14.3	7.5
Transport, communications	19.5	26.5	Credit, insurance	1.1	0.2	1.0	6.3	1.8	0.0
Recreation, entertainment	7.5	9.5	Renting of accommodation and other services	7.2	9.8	13.5	11.8	9.1	8.9
Other goods and services	54.6	49.7							
	100.0	100.0		100.0	100.0	100.0	100.0	100.0	100.0

Source: Manente (1986, pp. 329, 332, 337, 341–2)

'renting of accommodation and other services'. The biggest indirect effects are on agricultural and manufactured produce. The importance of tourism for certain categories of manufactured goods can hardly be overstressed. Italy would not lead the world in the manufacture of products like power boats, beach apparatus and ski equipment if these tourist and recreational activities were not firmly entrenched in the leisure lives of many Italians and foreign tourists to Italy.

Tourism accounts for the direct employment of 790,000 individuals (1984), a high proportion of whom—44 per cent—are categorised as independent workers, i.e. employers or self-employed. Two-thirds of those directly employed in tourism work in the 'commerce, hotels, etc.' sector, 12 per cent in 'transport and communications', 11 per cent in 'renting of accommodation and other services', and 7 per cent in the manufacture of specifically tourist products such as souvenirs, pleasure-boats, and so on. When individuals indirectly employed by tourism are included, the total tourist employment figure rises to 1,216,000, or 5.8 per cent of the total national labour force. The predilection for self-employment in the tourist sector is revealed by the fact that 8.7 per cent of the national total of such jobs are accounted for by tourism. The main indirect employment links are to be found in farming (a notional 163,000 individuals) and manufacturing industry (90,000). Table 4.5 gives the percentage sectoral distribution of employees and self-employed workers in tourism, showing that the independent workers predominate more in manufacturing, transport and communications.

It should be stressed, however, that these are official figures and take no account of unregistered and clandestine employment. The tourist industry, with its fragmented structure and seasonal and part-time nature, has many opportunities for such 'unregistered' employment. Therefore the real employment impact of tourism probably exceeds 1.5 million and could be as high as 2 million. The extra employment would include illegally hired hotel and restaurant workers, many from Third World countries such as Ethiopia and the Philippines (these clandestine immigrants are particularly important in Rome and other big cities), unregistered family helpers in family-run businesses, domestic and predominantly female producers of souvenirs and other goods sold in tourist shops, and the thousands of street-hawkers (many of them from African countries) who ply their precarious trade to tourists in big cities, cultural centres and beach resorts the length and breadth of the country.

The analysis of tourism's contribution to the Italian economy through value added and net foreign exchange earnings must be modified slightly by taking into account imports brought in to satisfy foreign tourists' spending in Italy, imports to satisfy domestic tourists' demands (net of what those demands would have been had they stayed at home), and also exports to satisfy the demands of Italian tourists abroad (but this last item is very small). Imports thus defined amounted to Lit. 4,704 billion in 1984 (10.9 per cent of total tourist expenditure), of which 55 per cent was due to energy products (petrol, heating oil, etc.), 33 per cent to industrial products and 10 per cent to agricultural imports (Manente 1986).

4.5.2   *Tourism and regional and local economic development*

The contribution of tourism and recreational activities to regional development in Italy has rarely been rigorously analysed, probably because of the surviving orthodoxy that industrialisation should be the motor of regional economic growth. The emergence in recent years of remarkable economic prosperity and dynamism down the eastern coast or 'Adriatic strip' owes a great deal to the growth of an almost continuous ribbon of tourist resorts from the Po Valley to Molise. Yet the recent abundant literature on the remarkable economic growth of the 'Third Italy'—that region interposed between the now deindustrialising north-western industrial triangle of Turin–Milan–Genoa and the economically backward South—pays scant attention to the role of tourism, preferring instead discussions of 'diffuse industrialisation' and economic decentralisation (Arcangeli, Borzaga and Goglio 1980; Brusco 1982; Fuà 1983; Secchi 1977).

In the course of development, Italy's coastal areas have attracted migrants from other parts of the country, mainly from the hilly interior of the peninsula and the South. The map of population change since the 1950s shows the coastal strip to be an unbroken ribbon of continuous growth (Dematteis 1979). However, given the diverse nature of Italian tourism, its economic and demographic impact is not restricted to coastal areas. Towns and cities famous for their cultural attractions, such as Florence and Rome, tend to be demographically more dynamic than similar-sized industrial cities like Turin or Milan, whose populations are now declining. Even within the coastal setting, the subdivision of the tourist market by price and locality enables obvious contrasts to be drawn between, for instance, the higher-class resorts of the Ligurian Riviera and the mass appeal of the Adriatic coasts (Tinacci 1969).

Tourism's impact on rural Italy, at least in terms of direct effects, is most marked in upland areas. Since the 1960s the ski boom has transformed dozens of small mountain villages in the Alps into winter sports centres, joining the older-established élite resorts of Cortina d'Ampezzo, Sestriere and Courmayeur. Not only has skiing transformed the landscapes of many mountain districts, it has also altered the seasonal regimes and lifestyles of both local inhabitants and the holiday-makers—winter and early spring being the periods of peak activity (Bonapace 1968). Outside the Alps, the possibilities for skiing development are much more limited. Nevertheless, Landini (1973) has pointed to the emergence of a 'skiing conurbation' in the high Abruzzian Apennines east of Rome. Aside from skiing, rural tourism has made most impact in the Sylvan landscapes of Tuscany and Umbria, where there are well-established if scattered colonies of British and German residents and second-home owners. Here, too, Italian second-home ownership has burgeoned, to the obvious disadvantage of locals wishing to buy property. The phenomenon has involved both the renovation of old, abandoned houses, either in villages or in the open countryside, and the construction of new dwellings and holiday complexes, not always, it must be said, in a carefully planned way. Some rural districts, especially those near to the coast or in high-altitude, attractive mountain country—areas where the pressures for weekend and holiday homes are greatest—have been scandalously developed (Pedrini 1984).

The fragmented structure of the Italian tourist industry, with 250,000 different companies and enterprises (hotel-owners, car-hire concerns, travel agents, etc.) and the relative lack of multinational and foreign capital involvement (unlike in Spain, for instance), means that tourism is often quite well integrated with local and regional economies—although there are some exceptions to this generalisation. Family effort has often been the organising principle behind many tourist enterprises, such as a beachside bar, pizzeria or small hotel. In other cases the solidarity of the family as both a social and an economic unit enables the dovetailing of two or more activities, different members working on a full or part-time basis in different sectors, perhaps from a residential base on a farm in the agricultural hinterland. Especially in the South, injections of remittances or migrant savings accrued from a period of foreign work by one or more members of the family enable the establishment of a tourist enterprise on the coast. King, Mortimer and Strachan (1984) have studied the case of the Calabrian resort of Amantea where returned migrants, mainly from Venezuela, have played a leading role in investing in small hotels, apartment blocks, restaurants, and the like, in the evolving local tourist economy.

4.5.3   Tourism and the development of the Mezzogiorno

Over the period since the 1960s, tourism has become increasingly discussed as an economic policy to develop the South. Many economic planners have argued that the labour-intensive tourist industry, with its spinoffs into private accommodation, small restaurants, crafts, shops, local transport, and so on, is better suited to the needs of the underdeveloped and labour-rich South than the heavy capital-intensive industrial policy pursued in the region in the 1960s and 1970s (King 1981).

Unfortunately, hopes that tourism might function as a 'leading sector' in the South's development have largely been misplaced. Results have been modest despite some financial and planning support from the Cassa per il Mezzogiorno, the government's southern development agency, which operated between 1950 and 1984. As early as 1957 the Cassa had recognised the potential for tourism and loan funds were offered for building, enlarging and modernising hotels and holiday villages, most effort being concentrated into selected areas of tourist development (Gambino 1978). Loans of up to 70 per cent of admissible costs were available, to be repaid at 3 per cent interest over 20 years. By the early 1980s, Cassa finance had contributed to the construction and modernisation of 14,000 hotels, resulting in a net addition of 65,000 rooms. Such improvements have undoubtedly had an impact, but the fact is that tourism in southern Italy has yet to 'take off'. In spite of fast, and mostly free, motorways, the Mezzogiorno is still considered too far for car-bound tourists from central and northern Europe, especially when regions like the Italian lakes, Venice and Tuscany offer such attractive 'intervening opportunities'. Spain, Greece, Yugoslavia and Turkey, all cheaper and in some cases more exotic, have taken much of whatever tourist flow might have been channelled to the Mezzogiorno. Only in Campania is the 'tourist index' (number of tourist beds per thousand local population) above the national average.

Several authors have provided diagnoses of why the hoped-for tourist bonanza in the South has not so far happened (Alhaique 1975; Campagnoli-Ciaccio 1979; Di Majo 1982; Monti and Vinci 1984). First and foremost is the lack of a coherent national tourist policy within which tourist planning for the Mezzogiorno might be set. Second, and following on from this, tourist loans have been distributed not according to rational criteria of carefully considered spatial planning but according to criteria of political favouritism and clientelism — following, in other words, the well-established patterns of agricultural and industrial loan and grant allocation of earlier phases of southern development policy. A reflection of the minimal attention paid to proper planning controls is the untidiness of much of the South's coastal landscape and the failure to provide good, clean tourist environments for visitors. Another aspect of the generally poor quality of the planning environment has been the lack of attention paid to effective publicity and to the proper training of local personnel in tourist service activities. Generally the character of southern tourism has become polarised between, on the one hand, big hotels built for an élite clientele and, on the other, the burgeoning of second homes around the coast, many stretches of which have been ruined. Locally run hotels, often poor in quality and inefficient, have been squeezed out; yet this is the sector which needs assistance and improvement if the long-term benefit of tourism to the region is to be maximised.

In some respects, part of the touristic development of the South has replicated the earlier experience of the industrial policy: the creation of so-called 'cathedrals in the desert', or large capital-intensive enterprises unrelated to the context of their locational setting, with low involvement of local capital and an even lower integration with the local economy. In Sicily the general lack of services has paradoxically led to a juxtaposition of new tourist areas with industrial zones, so that infrastructures for one can also serve the other (for example, water, power, motorways); this has happened in spite of obvious problems of visual, atmospheric and possible marine pollution (Campagnoli-Ciaccio 1979).

Nearly a third of tourist revenue from the South returns to the owners of capital in the North, mainly in Rome and Milan, but also abroad. Instead of improving living standards by reviving agriculture and other local activities, the big hotels, many of them built with public money, tend to become self-contained complexes: seasonal ghettos for rich northerners into which the local population rarely enter except as servile workers. Unlike the situation in northern and central regions like Emilia and Marche, traditional economic activities like agriculture, fishing, artisan crafts and commerce have drawn almost no benefit from tourism in the South. Only construction labour, plus the usual low-grade service jobs like cleaners and waiters, have impinged on the local labour market. Ironically, many southerners still migrate north to work in the tourist industry there.

4.6 Tourism, planning and the future

In spite of 'tourist saturation' in Venice and Florence and in spite of 'wall-to-wall people' shoehorned into segmented beaches in the summer in places like Rimini and the Lido di Roma, the future of Italian tourism is likely to be a scenario of stability rather than one of dramatic growth or decline. The main period of rapid tourist growth is probably over: this was the era of the 1960s and, to a somewhat lesser extent, the 1970s. During the decade 1966–75 the number of tourist overnights spent in Italy increased by 47 per cent; during 1976–85 it grew by only 17 per cent. As White (1987) says, there will be no newly created Riminis or Viareggios, although the established reputation of such existing resorts should ensure their healthy survival. Growth in home tourism is now sluggish as more and more Italians holiday abroad; prospects for a boom in foreign tourism remain poor because of strong competition from other Mediterranean countries which can often offer a similar package of tourist attractions at a lower price than Italy. Where some expansion seems possible is in the newer forms of tourism: camping, agritourism and conferences. The average attendant at a conference in Italy stays five days and spends 50 per cent more than other holiday-makers. Moreover congress-goers are often accompanied by spouses, families and secretaries. However, conferences are demanding to organise and it seems that only the big cities, the major cultural centres and resorts, and a very few specialised locations such as Bellagio on Lake Como which houses the Rockefeller International Conference Center, have the capacity and appeal to organise them. Agritourism has been much discussed (see, for example, Castagnari 1975; Desplanques 1973; Parente 1980) but it has yet to make much of an impact outside the Dolomites, Tuscany and Umbria and certainly has yet to achieve as widespread and entrenched an importance in Italian rural life as it has in France.

The major changes in the future of Italian tourism are likely to be organisational. During the 1970s powers in the fields of tourism planning and administration of the local industry passed to the newly-formed regional governments. A *legge quadro* or 'framework law' for tourism was finally passed in 1983 and, at least theoretically, regional administrations will have the flexibility to introduce innovations such as attractive off-season packages and holiday arrangements for special categories such as pensioners. Regions also have the responsibility for identifying areas to be developed for, or protected from, tourism; for the preservation and rehabilitation of historic town centres and specific monuments and artistic treasures; for the classification of hotels (within the national framework described earlier); and for the co-ordination of the activities of their various provincial tourist boards (Enti Provinciali di Turismo) and local tourist boards (the so-called 'Pro-Loco' agencies).

All the signs are that most regional authorities are working hard to promote tourism, with the northern regions being the most effective (Lazzeretti 1986). Some useful initiatives are beginning to surface. For instance, the Veneto region is successfully promoting off-season tourism in Venice, and putting together week-long itineraries within the region. Particularly at the regional level, tourist planners and administrators are increasingly conscious of the 'social function' of tourism (see, for example, Brunetta 1976). This involves both viewing the industry in a much wider framework, as an integral and vital component of an overall regional economic strategy, and also targeting some of the benefits of tourism at particular groups such as the unemployed, old people, part-time farmers, etc. (Becheri 1986). At a national level the two critical structural tasks to confront are the 'deseasonalisation' of Italian tourism, and the diversion of many more tourists to the South (Demarinis 1979). These are only slowly being achieved. Over recent years there has been a very slight tendency to spread the seasonal distribution away from the peak months with, for instance, a growing number of Italians favouring March and April breaks, and an increasing proportion of foreign visitors preferring the 'shoulder' months of March, May, September and October. Whilst the South has significantly increased its share of tourist accommodation, this has not been reflected in an equivalent increase in overnights, with the result that much new capacity remains underutilised. The ironic situation thus persists that hotel occupancy rates remain lowest, due to the high seasonality factor, in the region which climatically has most to offer in terms of winter, spring and autumn holidays.

Much will also hinge on whether the existing central agencies for tourism can be made to function better. A Ministry of Tourism exists but it is understaffed, underfunded and carries little power within government. Moreover, the *legge quadro* has not clearly defined all the relative responsibilities of the Ministry and the regional governments (Fuscà 1983). Two other central tourist organisations, ENIT (the national tourist organisation) and CIT (the government-run travel agency) are also in less than satisfactory positions. ENIT is ripe for reform, given the way that tourism has changed since its foundation in 1919. It, too, remains chronically underfunded when compared to its sister organisations in other European countries (Demarinis 1972). Since regional devolution some of its functions have been taken over by the regional tourist offices, but it still has a co-ordinating role and maintains its national offices abroad and at frontier stations. CIT was nearly closed down when it made heavy losses as an out-of-date agency in the 1970s; now, with ninety offices in Italy and abroad, it has a more progressive attitude to selling holidays in Italy.

However, reforms in Italy have a habit of being endlessly discussed but not often put into practice. For the foreseeable future tourism is likely to have to rely, as does the rest of the country, largely on individual effort and talent. This formula may not enable the country to extract the maximum economic return from its touristic resources in the short term, but perhaps in this lies part of the endless appeal of Italy for tourists: that the country has not ruthlessly exploited tourism to the point where it becomes counter-productive.

4.7 Conclusion

The time-lag in the formal publication of Italian tourism statistics means that complete survey data are not available for the period since 1985. However, preliminary indications are that after a period of stasis lasting up to 1986, the last couple of years have witnessed an increase in touristic activity, with American tourists leading the recovery. Hotels in Rome and in Venice reported an 80–90 per cent rise in visitors from the United States over the period 1986–8.

The perspective on tourism in Italy in the late 1980s is that the country's bucolic image is beginning to become a little tarnished. Environmental abuse has dulled the attractiveness of the Italian landscape, especially in coastal regions, whilst the emergence, in the summer of 1989, of a 10-metre thick layer of slimy algae in the Adriatic Sea kept many visitors away from popular east coast resorts between Trieste and Ancona (Scobie 1989). The spectacular rise in the Italian 'green vote', in a country where the balance between political forces is usually delicately set, will almost certainly focus more attention on these environmental problems in the future.

The tourists themselves must take a share of the blame for Italian environmental deterioration. The sheer weight of numbers that mass tourism brings upsets the fragile equilibrium which allows a priceless artistic heritage to survive in the modern world. Florence receives, but no longer successfully absorbs, 7 million tourists per year, more than 20 times the city's population, whilst in Rome over 18,000 visitors stream through the Sistine Chapel in a single day. Dubbed the 'new barbarians', tourists in Italy are accused of damaging artistic treasures and introducing indecorous standards of dress and behaviour. High heels gouge out the tesserae of Roman pavements, frescoes deteriorate under the assault of the humid breath of a multitude of admirers, and fast-food restaurants proliferate in historic town centres to cater for the appetites of the tourist hordes. In the summer of 1987 in Florence alone the following instances of desecration occurred: Giambologna's statue of the Rape of the Sabines was badly damaged, a hoof was broken off a marble horse in Ammannati's Fountain of Neptune, and the toenails of Michaelangelo's David in front of the Palazzo Vecchio were painted red (Walsh 1987). Tourism is generally thought to represent progress, but tourists picnicking all over St Mark's Square in Venice or walking around the streets and churches of Rome in bathing costumes cause offence—and are now fined. Italy naturally wishes to keep the tourists—and the foreign exchange—coming, but there is also a need to respect and to safeguard the landscape and the artistic heritage of one of Europe's most diverse and rich tourist environments.

5 Greece: prospects and contradictions of tourism in the 1980s

Lila Leontidou

If Greece is one of the cradles of Western civilisation and the gateway to both Europe and the Middle East, this is hardly evident in the nature, destination and seasonality of tourist flows. Instead, the country's mild climate (ranging from continental in the North to Mediterranean in the South), its natural beauty and especially the clear sea are preferred to its culture, heritage, myths and historic monuments. Tourist flows increased in the 1950s after the Second World War and the Civil War had ended and the country's infrastructure was partially restored. Then tourism expanded rapidly, especially in the 1970s, after a phase of concentrated state policy and given changing economic circumstances. Its nature, rhythm, regional polarisation and informalisation trends, however, were transformed only very slowly.

If tourism is a 'statistically invisible' industry, this is especially so in the case of Greece. Documentation of its nature, rhythm and impact is incomplete, due to the 'hidden' aspects of many activities and transactions. The state of research also makes the following summary presentation somewhat selective and fragmented. However, the identification of important regional and local economic features of tourism in Greece is possible on the basis of primary material and existing research.

5.1 Greece in international tourism

5.1.1 Types of tourism and travelling

As the Italian and Iberian peninsulas tend to become congested during the summer months, the Balkan coast, and especially Greece, presents a claim to a major role in the future of European tourism — at least according to the Greek Five-Year Plans (see, for example, Doxiadis Assoc. 1974; CPER 1976, pp. 54–62).[1] Its 15,000 km coastline, of which 3,000 km of sandy beaches and attractive bays are suitable for swimming, has an estimated capacity of 6–9 million swimmers a day during the peak season, while it accommodated only about 1.5 million in the 1970s (CPER 1976, pp. 47–8, 136). Major attractions include the 337 inhabited Greek islands scattered in the Aegean and Ionian seas of the Mediterranean (with 1.4 million of the 9.8 million Greek population in 1981); many traditional villages; areas of physical beauty and ecological importance; and, of course, a wealth of ancient and Byzantine monuments. Some developed areas already present signs of congestion and environmental

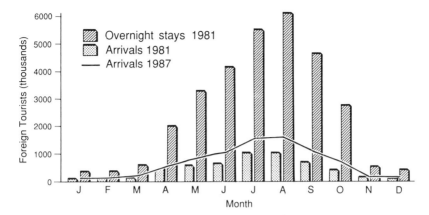

Fig. 5.1 Arrivals and overnight stays of foreign tourists in Greece, 1981 and 1987

Sources: Adapted from *Statistical Yearbook of Greece*, 1985, 1987 (arrivals); NSSG (1985) (overnights)

deterioration, particularly due to a lack of planning control, which has been systematic in Greek history (Leontidou 1977). Greater Athens, in particular, is rapidly losing its popularity among tourists.

Visitors to Greece usually combine sightseeing with relaxation, but rest and recreation rather than exploration and cultural tourism seem to be their priorities. The nature of Greek tourism is thus rather specialised; its seasonality is among the most extreme in Europe and, moreover, is increasing with time. Extreme peaks occur during the summer months for both the arrivals and overnight stays of foreign tourists (Figure 5.1). In 1981, 61.6 per cent of arrivals and 66.7 per cent of overnight stays were concentrated between June and September, and the rate of arrivals had increased by 1987 to 65 per cent.

The small number of Greeks travelling abroad makes Greece a country of tourist destination rather than of origin. The population is actually discouraged from travelling abroad by the imposition of strict foreign exchange controls. For many years, the annual foreign exchange allowance was only \$250; in the 1980s, this rose gradually, especially for travel within the EC. Emigration and repatriation complicate the study of actual vacation or short-term travelling, especially after 1977, when emigration statistics were no longer collected by customs authorities. However, it seems that the number of Greek travellers is rising and was 1.54 million in 1985 (Figure 5.2). Their proportion in the total population increased sharply during the years of economic development, the early 1960s (from 1.7 per cent to 5.6 per cent). In the 1980s the proportion of travellers stabilised at about 14.5 per cent of the total population (adapted from EOT and NSSG data).

5.1.2 Foreign visitors

International tourist flows, as evidenced in arrivals and receipts, expanded consistently until the late 1970s. Two major exceptions were during the world recession in 1974 and in 1967–8, the first years of dictatorial rule. After every

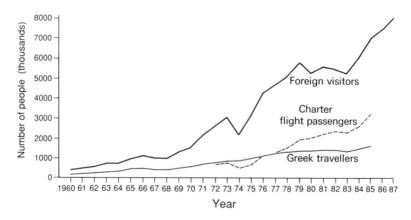

Fig. 5.2   Foreign visitors, domestic travellers and charter-flight passengers in
Greece, 1960–87

Source: Adapted from *Statistical Yearbooks of Greece, 1960–87*

decline, however, the country has recovered remarkably (Figure 5.2). The
number of foreign tourists almost doubled every five years, and rose from
58,238 in 1951 through 471,983 in 1961 and 2,103,281 in 1971, to 5,577,109 in
1981. There is a certain difference if cruise passengers and Greeks residing
abroad are excluded from the definition of 'foreign tourist'. By 1987 arrivals
had risen to 8,053,052 or 81 per cent of the Greek population, among whom
465,435 were cruise passengers visiting the islands (NSSG). The growth of
package-holiday mass tourism is indirectly indicated by the increase of charter
passengers from 16 per cent of the total in 1970 to 31 per cent in 1977 and 46
per cent in 1985 (Figure 5.2).

These numbers are still low in comparison with other European countries,
and the share of Greece in total arrivals in all Mediterranean countries was until
recently only 3 per cent. However, whereas in the latter group arrivals grew
by 8.4 per cent annually, the rate for Greece was almost double this (16.4 per
cent in 1960–75 and 8.3 per cent in 1975–87). Consequently, the country
increased its share of total arrivals in the OECD European countries from 2.2
per cent in 1970 to 3.5 per cent in 1982 (CPER 1987, p. 83).

Foreign and domestic tourist nights spent in all types of registered accommodation (including camping) grew by 19.8 per cent per annum in 1970–8,
and by 2.3 per cent in 1981–6; they were estimated at 45,968,811 in 1986
(provisional EOT data). Nights spent by foreigners also increased as a
proportion of total nights from 44 per cent in 1970 to 70 per cent in 1978
(Singh 1984, pp. 64–6), and 77 per cent in 1986 (Table 5.4). Furthermore, a
series of surveys by EOT, covering the 1966–85 period, found that the
average length of stay varied by nationality, but had grown from 11.4 days in
1967 to 12.6 in 1977–8 and 14 in 1984–5 (Fragakis 1987).

The national origins of foreign tourists are shown in Table 5.1. The largest
numbers originate in Europe, which increased its share from 63.4 per cent in
1971, through 74.5 per cent in 1978, to 89.9 per cent in 1987, of which 77 per
cent were from the EC. In the 1970s this was especially due to tourists from
Scandinavia and Yugoslavia and, in the 1980s, to visitors from the United

Table 5.1 The origin of foreign tourists to Greece, 1971–87

	Arrivals (%):						Nights spent (%):[1]	
	1971	1975	1978	1981	1984	1987	1981	1985
UK	13.85	12.10	11.51	19.12	18.90		23.10	21.42
FR Germany	11.52	15.05	11.65	12.39	15.65		19.44	20.66
France	7.88	8.47	7.78	5.88	7.35		7.47	7.85
Italy	6.19	5.22	4.80	4.47	5.95		3.50	4.42
Denmark	2.07	1.90	2.87	2.62	2.25		2.66	3.05
Netherlands	2.64	2.25	2.73	3.37	3.49		4.01	5.63
Spain, Portugal	.57	.76	.66	.74	.78		.65	.70
Rest of EC	1.98	1.71	2.19	2.03	1.94		2.36	2.30
EC COUNTRIES	46.69	47.47	44.20	50.62	56.32	69.50	63.18	66.02
Yugoslavia	5.36	9.84	11.52	12.47	4.77	5.06	1.81	.97
Austria	2.20	3.11	3.37	2.91	4.31	3.30	3.88	4.37
Sweden	2.62	4.15	5.70	5.00	3.52	3.21	6.95	4.77
Switzerland	2.50	2.53	2.84	2.85	2.84	1.55	3.43	3.74
Norway	.27	.74	1.25	1.90	1.93	1.66	2.97	3.02
Finland	1.14	1.70	1.82	1.92	2.43	2.36	1.68	3.12
Rest of Europe	2.60	2.48	3.44	3.46	3.63	3.30	4.41	2.51
NON-EC EUROPE	16.71	24.55	29.94	30.51	23.43	20.43	25.12	22.49
USA	24.66	17.37	11.49	6.37	8.60	2.84	4.24	4.73
Canada, Lat.Am.	3.64	2.42	2.71	2.30	2.27	1.32	1.49	1.62
Asia	3.90	4.16	6.31	6.06	5.41	3.38	3.49	2.72
Africa	2.15	1.88	2.83	1.82	1.83	1.06	1.51	1.40
Oceania	2.21	2.07	2.41	2.22	2.00	1.38	.96	1.02
USSR	.04	.07	.11	.10	.13	.10		
REST OF WORLD	36.60	27.98	25.86	18.87	20.25	10.07	11.70	11.48
Total	100.00	100.00	100.00	100.00	100.00	100.00	100.00	100.00
Total number[2]	1,780,415	2,640,282	4,468,269	5,044,392	5,521,032	7,644,868	31,495,674	35,617,451

Source: Adapted from *Statistical Yearbooks of Greece* 1976, 1987; NSSG (1986, 1987); and EOT unpublished data.

Note: 1. In all types of accommodation, including camping.
2. Excluding cruise passengers.

Kingdom, the Federal Republic of Germany, France and Austria. Whereas in 1963–73 Greece was 'dependent' on the United States for the inflow of tourists and on Italy for their outflow (Komilis 1986, pp. 52–4), this is no longer so. The flow from the United States in 1970 was 13 times higher than in 1953 (Alexandrakis 1973, p. 154) but, thereafter, its share in arrivals dropped from 27 per cent in 1970, through 11 per cent in 1978, to 7 per cent in 1985. The share of US citizens in nights spent was considerably lower–8 per cent in 1978 and 4.7 per cent in 1985 (Table 5.1).

5.2   Political change and tourist policy

5.2.1   *The emergence of tourism as a public policy concern, 1950–67*

Infrastructure has been actively developed by the Greek government since the late 1950s, but tourism began to feature in policies and programmes in the early 1960s, when its potential for economic development was realised. Legislation permitting incentives for tourist developments began with LDs 3213/1953, 3430/1955, 4171/1961 and 276/1969 (TCG 1981, pp. 74–5; Singh 1984, p. 131). During the 1960s state assistance to tourist enterprises involved, in particular, loans for building accommodation units. Direct investment in infrastructure to facilitate communications and create opportunities for the private sector also helped tourist development.

The main executive public organisation for the development and promotion of tourism and for the formulation and implementation of policy has been EOT, the National Tourist Organisation of Greece. It became an autonomous agency in 1950, but its origins can be traced back to 1929. Its role was both supervisory and developmental, involving planning, promotion, education (for example, the School of Tourist Professions), construction and management of accommodation and infrastructure, and financial assistance for private tourist businesses. Promotion was undertaken by a network of offices in Greece and abroad, as well as through the organisation of summer festivals.

The policies of EOT were only marginally influenced by other bodies until 1983, when EOT came under the direct surveillance of the Ministry of National Economy and Planning. The Ministry of the Environment influenced tourism through land policy and building controls. The Ministry of the Interior controlled the tourist police, collected data, and co-ordinated local services. The Ministry of Culture is responsible for the maintenance of museums and monuments. Finally, the School of Tourist Professions is supervised by the Prime Minister's Office. Consequently there has been a highly varied administration for tourism, and policy has tended to lack co-ordination until recently.

5.2.2   *Policy during the dictatorship, 1967–74*

Tourism played only a minor role as Greece was emerging from under-development in the mid-1960s. Regional policy was not promoted at the time. Indeed, for a long period, developed and even congested areas received incentives for tourist development. In 1951–64 the largest share of public investment in tourism (56 per cent) was allocated to construction of accommodation and its management. By contrast, infrastructural work predominated in 1965–74 (Komilis 1986, p. 165), reflecting a major change of policy during the late 1960s.

Greater emphasis on tourist development followed the imposition of dictatorial rule in Greece in 1967, involving construction, financing and promotion. A simultaneous emphasis on the construction sector was not incidental: house-building, as well as tourism, was used as a means of 'heating up' the economy. Such goals were incorporated into the 1968–72 Five-Year Plan more explicitly than in its predecessor. All former legislation on tourism was consolidated into a single LD, 1738/1973, providing special concessions for hotels in the form of tax and depreciation allowances (Singh 1984, p. 131).

The initiative for tourist development shifted to private enterprises, and state activity was limited to the provision of infrastructure to facilitate their operation (Alexandrakis 1973, p. 180). Meanwhile, the banking system and government incentives were mobilised to boost the private sector. The average annual rate of growth of tourist loans rose from 11.3 per cent in 1960–6 to 26.7 per cent in 1967–73 (Komilis 1986, p. 166). Private investment in tourism rose sharply during the dictatorship, while public investment declined during the first years, as is indicated in Table 5.2. Foreign investment hit a peak in 1968, when it rose to 66.1 per cent of all investment in tourism (from 4 per cent during 1962–7) and 37 per cent of total foreign capital investment in all sectors of the Greek economy. This was mostly US capital (51.8 per cent of the total in 1968–70), although West German, Swiss, and French sources were also important (Alexandrakis 1973, p. 181). Foreign investment was mostly concentrated in hotel businesses, especially in coastal locations. Consequently, it is possible to talk of a speculative upsurge and the 'sellout' of several Greek coastal areas to foreigners during the dictatorship.

Regional imbalance was blatantly reinforced by government policy at this time. Public investment in tourism tripled during the early 1970s, in relation to the previous period, but the share of Greater Athens increased from 49 per cent to 52 per cent. Investment was also directed to other cities and to already

Table 5.2 Public and private investment in tourism in Greece, 1957–70 ($ thousands)

	Public[1]	Private[2] domestic	Private, foreign[3]	(%)	Total
1957	1,100	300	134	8.74	1,534
1958	6,600	5,100	889	7.06	12,589
1959	8,500	8,400	635	13.62	17,535
1960	8,500	8,400	47	0.28	16,947
1961	10,400	7,900	407	2.18	18,707
1962	6,900	15,100	1,208	5.21	23,208
1963	7,300	10,300	229	1.28	17,829
1964	4,000	8,100	1,391	10.31	13,491
1965	7,800	9,100	844	4.76	17,744
1966	9,700	10,700	1,151	5.34	21,551
1967	6,800	17,600	0	0.00	24,400
1968	8,100	35,100	84,430	66.15	127,630
1969	13,100	57,400	13,468	16.04	83,968
1970	14,100	65,900	6,100	7.08	86,100
1957–61	35,100	30,100	2,112	3.14	67,312
1962–67	42,500	70,900	4,823	4.08	118,223
1968–70	35,300	158,400	103,998	34.93	297,698

Source: Alexandrakis (1973, p. 179)

Note: 1. Financed by government budget and EOT, incl. infrastructure
      2. Financed by banks only
      3. Foreign: projects approved by Ministry of Co-ordination

developed tourist areas such as Salonica, Crete and Khalkidiki (Komilis 1986, p. 166). Mass, large-scale tourism was promoted, and a goal of 13 million foreign tourists was set for 1982 (CPER 1972).

A peculiar type of domestic tourism also appeared during the dictatorship: summer vacations in 'mobile homes'. This came about following legislation allowing for prefabricated construction on plots smaller than those specified in existing by-laws. It has been estimated that by 1973 about 100,000 such houses had been erected, especially by low-income groups in areas around Greater Athens, notably in Salamina (Polychroniadis and Hadjimichalis 1974).

5.2.3   Recent policy trends, 1974–89

After the fall of the dictatorship (1974), tourism increasingly featured in the successive Five-Year Plans as a means of dealing with foreign exchange problems and the chronic trade deficit, and as an appropriate strategy for economic development. Public sector participation in investment increased especially after the effective nationalisation of Olympic Airways on 1 January 1975. Domestic interests were also given greater priority at this time. The 1976–80 Plan emphasised the role of local capital and of small non-hotel tourism as a means to local development. Subsequently, the 1983–7 Plan carried through the same policy of discouraging large units and foreign capital. It also set goals for public involvement where 56 per cent of investment would be public and 44 per cent would be private (Greek Parliament 1984, p. 62). Legislation also emphasised the development of small lodgings with less than 80 beds (TCG 1981, p. 78). This policy was reversed recently, as outlined below.

Some concern with regional policy has begun to emerge. Already by the 1980s further development in Greater Athens was to be discouraged (Leontidou 1981, p. 66). In addition, the gradual decentralisation of EOT and management of its property by local authorities and mixed 'popular base' companies was considered. At the same time, new legislation, especially LDs 1116/1981 and 1262/1982, treated tourist investments along with industrial ones. The former law introduced grants in place of tax exemptions, as well as regional criteria, subdividing the country into four areas (TCG 1981, pp. 75–6). Both laws, however, continued to stress as criteria the viability of investment rather than the reduction of congestion, and often encouraged financing of traditional buildings in all areas. Though congested areas were delimited by ministerial decision in 1983, the 1983–7 Five-Year Plan for Economic Development and investment realised under LD1262/1982 (Table 5.8 and analysis below) did not promote regional development. Locality considerations were also not mentioned in 'social tourism' programmes, which annually has helped about 100,000 less affluent citizens to take low-cost vacations since 1983 (TCG 1981, p. 60; CPER 1987, pp. 95–100).

In 1987, finally, a Ministry of Tourism was established.[2] EC policy also started to have some impact alongside national policy. The Integrated Mediterranean Programmes, as well as the new Five-Year Plan for Economic Development 1988–92, tend to promote 'selective' tourism (MNE 1988) in large hotels with additional services.[3] This policy to attract higher-income tourism is combined with a reorientation toward decentralisation and a creeping 'privatisation' of the tourist sector.[4] Areas for tourist development are

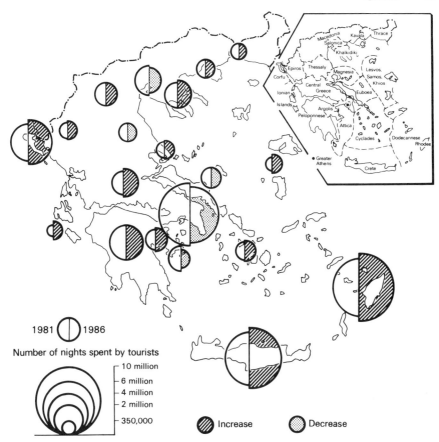

Fig. 5.3 The regional distribution of demand (overnight stays) in Greece, 1981–6

Source: Adapted from NSSG (1985, pp. 44–9) and unpublished EOT data for 1986

also delimited by LD 1650/1986 on the environment. Overseas promotion (advertising campaigns, pamphlets and posters) is being intensified with the aim of attracting off-season and higher-income tourists. However, only 18 per cent of tourists surveyed in 1986 claimed to have been influenced by advertising campaigns, while 34 per cent had been influenced by friends and relatives (EOT, cited in Papachristou 1987). This stresses the importance of return visits and the need to improve the quality of tourist services in Greece. Tourist agents and tour operators influenced 24 per cent of choices, and their impact will be evident in the following analysis of the concentration of various national groups of visitors in particular localities.

5.3 Regions and localities

5.3.1 *The regional distribution of demand*

Existing information on regional structures will be updated in this section, on the basis of primary material analysed within standard administrative

Table 5.3 The distribution of tourists, by nationality, in selected areas in Greece, 1984 (per cent)

Nationality of origin	Greece	UK	Austria	Belgium	France	FRG	Yugoslavia	Denmark
Total nights spent	11,017,091	6,803,916	1,474,401	665,877	2,778,399	6,232,307	347,697	887,983
Athens centre, suburbs	13.70	4.00	5.40	11.30	18.40	5.50	12.40	8.50
Attica coasts	2.20	5.40	1.70	9.00	12.10	1.80	3.90	1.30
Pieria: Makrygialos-Platamon	1.70	0.00	2.20	0.20	0.20	1.90	27.90	0.10
Salonica-Agia Trias	8.20	0.50	1.20	1.10	1.00	1.30	26.70	0.50
Corfu	3.00	28.70	8.70	5.40	4.70	6.40	1.60	3.90
Northern Crete	5.00	17.20	17.80	19.70	10.80	7.80	1.40	4.20
Rhodes	4.10	17.90	18.00	17.90	2.40	20.30	3.30	27.30
Kos	0.70	3.90	2.10	1.90	0.40	4.20	0.40	11.30
Rest of Aegean islands (Cyclades etc.)	3.70	2.30	4.90	3.10	2.30	3.20	0.90	4.90
Rest of Greece	64.84	19.96	36.07	31.89	48.85	32.05	22.08	17.69
TOTAL CONCENTRATED TOURISTS*	13.70	63.80	35.80	48.90	41.30	20.30	67.00	38.60

Source: Adapted from NSSG (1987, pp. 96–126).

* Concentration of each nationality of over 10 per cent in a certain locality.

Table 5.3 The distribution of tourists, by nationality, in selected areas in Greece, 1984 (per cent)

Nationality of origin	Switzerland	Italy	Spain	Norway	Netherlands	Sweden	Finland	USA
Total nights spent	1,317,458	1,470,827	214,118	943,627	1,544,269	1,568,760	1,074,707	2,078,846
Athens centre, suburbs	6.00	24.80	63.10	2.90	7.30	3.90	4.50	49.70
Attica coasts	1.20	6.30	1.70	2.10	2.80	2.40	2.00	8.50
Pieria: Makrygialos–Platamon	0.70	0.40	0.10	0.00	0.50	0.00	0.10	0.10
Salonica–Agia Trias	0.50	2.20	3.10	0.20	0.90	0.50	0.30	2.60
Corfu	3.60	9.80	2.70	0.40	7.30	2.40	1.90	4.30
Northern Crete	27.30	7.50	4.40	13.10	33.60	20.90	21.20	6.30
Rhodes	18.30	8.30	3.60	53.00	20.00	39.90	46.10	4.20
Kos	9.20	0.90	0.10	15.50	8.90	19.20	14.00	0.40
Rest of Aegean islands (Cyclades etc.)	10.10	4.30	3.60	3.80	2.30	1.70	4.80	4.50
Rest of Greece	28.35	40.82	17.53	14.12	21.80	9.99	10.50	27.58
TOTAL CONCENTRATED TOURISTS*	55.70	24.80	63.10	81.60	53.60	80.00	81.30	49.70

boundaries. Sub-regions are delimited in relation to tourist attractions (Figure 5.3). Mainland Greece is treated separately from the islands, and from the two largest cities — Greater Athens and Salonica. A qualitative stepwise investigation has been adopted, so as to avoid the traps of data and information 'intransparencies', especially with respect to unrecorded accommodation. In any case, it should be emphasised that domestic tourist demand is not adequately reflected in overnight stays — the main unit of the following analysis — as Greeks have access to additional accommodation outlets. Relative preferences rather than absolute numbers of domestic tourists can be concluded from such spatial analysis.

A first approach to the regional concentration of demand (overnight stays) by nationality shows that in 1984 visitors from northern Europe flocked to certain localities, while Mediterranean nationalities had a more dispersed pattern of preferences, or opted for cultural tourism (Table 5.3). The most dispersed pattern of preferences was evidenced by Germans and Italians. Italian and French citizens seemed to opt for exploration as much as for vacation tourism: they mostly used non-organised forms of travel, and moved between two and four times during their visit (EOT 1979). The Spanish tended to prefer cultural tourism, concentrating in Greater Athens (Table 5.3). By contrast, northerners, such as Finnish and Swedish tourists, tended to congregate in few areas, especially on the island of Rhodes, which was actually developed as an area for mass tourism by Swedish tour operators (TCG 1981, p. 106). Mediterranean and US visitors displayed a preference for Greater Athens.

During the 1970s there was remarkable stability in the regional pattern of tourist demand, which poses questions about the control exercised by tourist agents, charter flights and package holidays. Certain flows were entrenched, and their direction was not easily modified for long periods, either at the regional or the international level (Komilis 1986, pp. 51, 104–6). Demand was concentrated in Greater Athens and three tourist islands: Rhodes, Crete (northern coast), and Corfu (Table 5.4 and Figure 5.3). Domestic tourism did not compete with foreign tourism either in regional terms or by type of accommodation. By 1986 foreigners were overrepresented in the Dodecanese (Rhodes), Crete, Corfu, Attica and Khalkidiki, while Greeks were more represented in the largest cities, the mainland, and islands near the coast such as Sporades and Euboea (Table 5.4).

Changes since the 1970s involved a fall in the popularity of Attica and a shift of foreign tourists' preferences from the larger towns towards Corfu, northern Crete and Khalkidiki (Komilis 1986, pp. 136–7). Nights spent in Greater Athens declined dramatically by 2 million in 1981–6, and the popularity of Attica has continued to fall: 40 per cent of tourists preferred it in 1983, 33 per cent in 1984, 30 per cent in 1985 and only 25 per cent in 1986 (unofficial estimate, Papachristou 1987). Islands near Athens (in Attica, Euboea) and the city of Salonica also lost popularity. Capacity in Attica declined proportionally in the late 1970s (Leontidou 1981, pp. 67–8) and, in the 1980s, three luxury hotels closed down and a central historical hotel began to rent out rooms to Greeks as residences. It is peculiar, in view of these trends, that a huge Sheraton hotel complex is scheduled to open in Phaleron. Tourist flows are now directed to islands, especially to the Dodecanese, which gained nearly 3 million overnight stays in 1981–6, and Crete, which gained 2 million (Table 5.4). Corfu, by contrast, gradually lost its attraction after 1987.

Table 5.4 Regional distribution of demand (overnight stays) in Greece, 1981–6[1]

	1981 (%)	1981 Foreigners as % of total	1986 (%)	1986 Foreigners as % of total	1981–6 difference
Greater Athens	20.67	74.45	14.34	69.83	−1,896,480
Salonica (Nomos)	4.62	44.54	3.86	48.82	−124,214
Rest of mainland Greece					
Central Greece[2]	3.05	41.16	3.77	51.34	480,243
Argolis	2.68	80.12	2.59	77.31	89,503
Rest of Peloponnese	5.73	54.63	5.38	53.15	118,643
Epiros	1.61	33.09	1.73	35.89	134,061
Thessaly[3]	1.40	26.38	1.22	26.79	−17,509
Khalkidiki	3.04	80.13	3.56	85.17	386,029
Rest of Macedonia[4]	2.74	36.31	2.57	39.93	58,276
Thrace	1.14	17.22	1.16	20.44	65,962
Aegean islands					
Dodecanese	17.37	95.97	22.00	95.36	2,972,898
Cyclades	1.82	73.32	1.98	70.93	161,383
Lesvos, Samos, Chios	1.41	66.23	1.59	74.51	153,892
Rest of eastern islands					
Attica (Hydra, Kythira, etc.)	3.06	80.12	1.60	87.49	−523,130
Euboea	2.16	44.99	1.84	50.76	−40,879
Magnesia (Sporades)	1.46	42.25	1.58	46.96	125,104
Kavala (Thasos)	1.45	50.19	1.25	55.63	−21,699
Crete	14.73	91.90	17.53	93.13	2,007,925
Ionian islands					
Corfu	8.94	93.59	8.78	92.72	362,713
Zante, Kephalonia, Lefkada	0.91	55.23	1.66	72.95	390,833
Total	100.00	74.63	100.00	76.94	4,883,554

Sources: Adapted from NSSG (1985, pp. 44–5, 48–9); and unpublished provisional EOT data for 1986.

Notes: 1. Includes camping.
2. Excluding Attica and Euboea.
3. Excluding Magnesia.
4. Excluding Salonica, Kavala and Khalkidiki.

5.3.2 *Capacity and types of accommodation*

Infrastructure and accommodation facilities improved rapidly in the post-war period throughout Greece, but especially in the largest cities and in the islands. The composition of tourist accommodation changed as follows: using the mid-1960s, standard types of lodgings predominated; yachting appeared from the late 1960s; bungalows and apartment hotels emerged in the early 1970s, and from the mid-1970s, organised cruises and summer villas appeared, along with a strong tendency for foreigners to purchase private homes (Zacharatos

1986, p. 84). Capacity in 1986 included 5,488 hotel units with 359,377 beds, 46,251 rented rooms with 97,795 beds, and a large number of unauthorised rooms (cf. below; Papachristou 1987). The number of small cruise ships hired by better-off tourists grew slowly, from 1,200 in 1975 to 1,700 in 1987. About 600 cruise ships changed to the Turkish flag recently, due to the more favourable conditions offered for tourist development (Papachristou 1987). The number of yachts which called at Greek ports increased from 1,737 in 1960 (38 per cent under the Greek flag), through 16,249 in 1970 (only 9 per cent Greek), to 29,098 in 1977 (30 per cent Greek).

As with demand, hotel capacity was sharply concentrated in Greater Athens (17.2 per cent of beds in 1985), Rhodes (14.8 per cent) and Crete (13.9 per cent) and, to a lesser extent, Corfu (6.7 per cent; Table 5.5). This concentration has changed little since 1963 (Komilis 1986, pp. 102–3). Auxiliary accommodation facilities, such as camping and rented rooms (officially registered), also

Table 5.5   The structure of tourist capacity in Greece by region, 1985

Hotel[1] Beds (HB), Camping (C), Rented Rooms (RR, beds)	Total capacity		Regional distribution (%)	
	Beds	%	HB only	C + RR (% of total)
Greater Athens	62,129	12.10	17.17	3.77
Salonica (Nomos)	13,826	2.69	2.22	44.07
Rest of Mainland Greece:				
Central Greece[2]	24,153	4.70	4.59	33.86
Peloponnese	59,201	11.53	10.72	36.95
Epiros	11,744	2.29	1.67	50.60
Thessaly[3]	8,088	1.57	1.37	41.15
Macedonia[4]	39,146	7.62	5.92	47.33
Thrace	5,746	1.12	0.95	42.26
Aegean islands:				
Dodecanese	57,578	11.21	14.79	10.58
Cyclades	34,106	6.64	4.47	54.40
Lesvos, Samos, Chios	15,750	3.07	2.42	46.60
Rest of eastern islands				
Attica (Hydra, Kythira, etc.)	20,962	4.08	3.38	43.78
Euboea	20,389	3.97	3.46	40.91
Magnisia (Sporades)	18,111	3.53	2.72	47.79
Kavala (Thasos)	13,276	2.58	1.56	59.08
Crete	62,071	12.09	13.91	22.00
Ionian islands:				
Corfu	30,267	5.89	6.67	23.26
Zante, Cephalonia, Lefkada	17,066	3.32	2.02	58.76
TOTAL %		100.00	100.00	33.33
Absolute number	513,609		348,171	

Source: Adapted from NSSG (1987, p. 35–9).

Notes: 1. Includes hotels, bungalows, motels, furnished suites, guest rooms, boarding-houses, inns.
       Excludes: 2. Attica, Euboea;   3. Magnisia;   4. Salonica, Kavala.

increased rapidly, especially in certain areas: in 1985 they provided 59 per cent of total beds in the Kavala-Thasos area, 59 per cent in the Ionian Islands excluding Corfu, 54 per cent in the Cyclades, and 48 per cent in the Magnesia-Sporades area. By contrast, they were less important in the main tourist areas: Greater Athens (4 per cent), the Dodecannese (11 per cent), Crete (22 per cent), and Corfu (23 per cent); see Table 5.5. This correlates with the regional preferences of native and foreign tourists. The latter tended to prefer hotel accommodation, especially luxury and Class A hotels (Singh 1984, pp. 76–7).

A large concentration of auxiliary accommodation in some regions, by contrast, is indicative of the predominance of domestic tourism. Approximately 90 per cent of the clients of rented rooms are Greek. Domestic tourism is difficult to measure, because it is far less dependent on overnight stays in hotels and related accommodation. Greeks usually prefer rooms to let, the houses of relatives and, of course, second homes. The regional distribution of second homes can be deduced indirectly from the distribution of houses found empty during the population censuses. Their spectacular increase everywhere, in both absolute and relative terms, is shown in Table 5.6.[5] As domestic tourism originates mainly in Greater Athens and Salonica, second homes predominate on the fringes of the metropolitan areas (especially Attica, 54 per cent), and in the nearby eastern islands (Cyclades 50 per cent).

5.3.3 *Regional polarisation, seasonality and informalisation*

The spatial polarisation and concentration of different nationalities and types of accommodation in specific localities is a feature of mass tourism. In fact Greeks are excluded from certain well-known regions by inaccessible hotel prices; these cater for organised tourism and are far more expensive for individual (domestic) visitors. Concentration of mass tourism in seaside centres and underutilisation of the mainland is evident in both capacity and demand. Beaches and recreation spots rather than ancient and historical sites are preferred. In the mid-1970s, 50–60 per cent of foreigners' hotel nights were spent in coastal summer resorts and only 6–7 per cent near archaeological sites, while another 25–30 per cent were spent in Greater Athens (CPER 1976, p. 184).

This type of demand intensifies seasonality. Auxiliary accommodation in standard lodgings is withdrawn from the market during the winter, while hotels are utilised to capacity during the summer and remain underutilised or unutilised for the rest of the year. Many islands are deserted for long periods during the winter. Of 82,346 hotel beds in 1970, 34.4 per cent operated on a seasonal basis (for 3–9 months). Of these, about two-thirds were located on the islands and one-third in the rest of Greece, except Athens, Piraeus and Salonica, where hotels operate all year round (Alexandrakis 1973, p. 174). National estimates in 1984[6] indicated that hotel occupancy rates were unsatisfactory, even during the peak period, reaching 82.1 per cent in July and 91.4 per cent in August. The highest average annual rates were in Crete (79–81 per cent) and eastern Rhodes (79 per cent), and the lowest in Athens (26 per cent).

Occupancy rates of hotel units appear low, especially in those regions where cheaper beds are offered in the market. The relationship between hotel and auxiliary lodging facilities in Greece is 1:0.76 compared to 1:2–1:3 in other

Table 5.6   Empty residences in Greece by region, 1961–81

	Empty houses as % of total:			1981 Absolute no.	% of all empty houses
	1961	1971	1981		
Greater Athens	0.00	7.50	17.65	213,397	20.82
Salonica (Nomos)	0.00	12.31	21.33	75,164	7.33
Rest of mainland Greece					
Central Greece[1]	10.64	16.32	24.94	51,832	5.06
Peloponnese	13.03	24.72	32.52	139,750	13.64
Epiros	10.12	19.36	25.73	32,455	3.17
Thessaly[2]	5.25	13.37	21.55	39,246	3.83
Macedonia[3]	2.70	15.54	24.83	104,398	10.19
Thrace	0.00	9.98	15.41	18,130	1.77
Aegean islands					
Dodecanese	25.52	29.12	32.09	19,157	1.87
Cyclades	33.22	40.85	50.36	30,004	2.93
Lesvos, Samos, Chios	25.94	33.37	40.56	47,337	4.62
Rest of eastern islands					
Attica (Hydra, Kythira, etc.)	21.77	39.61	53.54	110,858	10.82
Euboea	11.68	17.68	28.20	22,003	2.15
Magnesia (Sporades)	14.38	20.81	29.02	23,010	2.25
Kavala (Thasos)	4.89	17.11	24.84	13,744	1.34
Crete	13.21	20.01	26.31	55,801	5.44
Ionian islands					
Corfu	14.52	23.97	29.60	13,264	1.29
Zante, Kephalonia, Lefkada	26.18	27.36	37.23	15,332	1.50
Total	7.52	16.88	25.63	1,024,882	100.00

Sources: Adapted from the NSSG population censuses 1961, 1971, 1981 and the building censuses (vols of censuses and *Statistical Yearbook*, 1985, pp. 34, 279)

Notes: 1. Excludes Attica and Euboea
2. Excludes Magnesia
3. Excludes Salonica and Kavala

European tourist countries (CPER 1976, pp. 30–2; 1989). This is deceptive, however, since it ignores the large sector of unrecorded rooms for rent. The registration of rented rooms forming part of private houses started in 1972, but only a small percentage of owners have complied thus far. Undeclared rooms in private homes—whether empty or inhabited in the winter—exist in all tourist regions. There are also larger undeclared units of 80–100 beds, known as 'para-hotel' businesses (*paraxenodokhia*). According to various estimates, the ratio of official to unofficial beds ranges from 1:3 to 1:1.[7] In 1975 it was officially admitted that, due to undeclared rooms, overnight stays were underestimated by at least a quarter (CPER 1976, p. 28). In the mid 1980s, in addition to the 406,000 beds in hotels and officially declared rooms, there were at least 450,000 beds in 230,000 undeclared rooms, with a further 200,000 added during the last two years.

Such inconsistencies between official data and actual capacity abound in areas where illegal building occurs. Real estate accumulation and building without a permit outside authorised settlement plans have been widespread processes in Greek cities and villages, involving a variety of social classes (Leontidou 1990). In tourist localities, as opposed to metropolitan areas, property accumulation and illegal building are petty speculative rather than popular activities. After the mid-1970s, property accumulation underwent a form of decentralisation, as real estate investment was diverted from Greater Athens, the rest of Attica, and Salonica to peripheral regions. As it became profitable to be a seasonal landlord in the islands and other tourist resorts, investors turned from urban apartments to small furnished houses in provincial Greece, which were often unauthorised. These forces were triggered off during the period of dictatorial rule, but the practice continued in the following decade. Residents built in unauthorised areas, and pressurised the authorities for 'post-legislation'. The Land Laws, especially LD 1337/1983, which taxed land according to the size of properties, became a counter-incentive for large organised development, and led to an increase of small units. 'Auxiliary' but sub-standard rooms were built illegally and later 'legalised', although some remained undeclared and uncontrolled.

The main tangible negative environmental effect of informalisation is unplanned development and overburdening of infrastructure and the environment, since small as well as large units require a share of the coastline, parking and facilities. Therefore, although small inns and houses are not necessarily sub-standard, they can lead to sub-standard tourism. Competition between land uses is usually resolved to the detriment of agricultural activities, with the abandonment of land and the fragmentation of farming in tourist areas. In most cases the agricultural sector has declined where tourism has developed, and the case of Rhodes is typical in this respect (TCG 1981, p. 67; see also Komilis 1986, p. 38). In a few localities, however, the tourist diet and demand did lead to the intensification of agriculture. But even where the produce is summer fruit and vegetables, as in Crete, imported foodstuffs are the norm.

The conflict between tourist and industrial sites, on the other hand, usually sparks off political debate and local social movements. It is interesting that both in Pylos in 1975 (Vaiou-Hadjimichalis and Hadjimichalis 1979, pp. 181–96) and in the debate in Delphi in June 1987 on the location of an aluminium factory, part of the local population mobilised against the Ministry of Culture. They opted for industrial development rather than protection of the archaeological and cultural heritage and the environment, implying an indifference to tourism. Such an attitude was especially surprising in Mykonos, the island which has three-quarters of the total nights spent in the Cyclades. In 1975 the local population mobilised against a proposed regional plan (Kalligas *et al.* 1972), protesting that protection of traditional housing was an obstacle to 'economic development', and demanding greater permissiveness in building permits (Romanos 1975, p. 201). The alternative posed to protection was not industrialisation, but speculative building.

5.4   A note on income and employment

5.4.1   *Research difficulties and 'intransparencies'*

Given intense segmentation and illegality, tourism has been underestimated in Greek economic and geographical research. Undeclared activities confuse data matrices, and there is a hidden economy in tourism, which is much more pronounced than in other consumption or production sectors. The recent Five-Year Plan, 1983–7, recognises the need to obstruct the action of intermediaries and the tourist 'black economy' (Greek Parliament 1984, p. 59), but this is a formidable task. Besides evading taxation and controls, non-registrations in tourism also have an impact on research and policy formulation. Additional difficulties in assessing the economic impact of tourism stem from the complicated nature of the industry. It has been conceptualised as an export industry where the purchaser consumes the product on the spot (Singh 1984, p. 26). Elsewhere it has been argued effectively that it should be treated as a specific form of private consumption or final demand rather than as an industry or sector of the economy (Zacharatos 1986).[8]

If tourism is generally criticised as an uncertain developmental strategy (de Kadt 1979), in Greece it is particularly associated with dependence on external political and economic fluctuations, and is highly specialised and seasonal. Its fragility and dependence on socio-political conjunctures has recently been evident in President Reagan's 'travel proclamation' issued in June 1985; after a TWA highjacking, this curbed US tourism in Greece. The Chernobyl accident in early 1986 has also had adverse effects throughout Europe. In addition, the negative impact of tourism on localities is especially evident where seasonality is acute. Even the positive impacts—economic revitalisation and the development of cultural contacts—can have negative aspects: increased communication between previously isolated areas and the outside world is torn by the contradictions of the demonstration effect, which increases the propensity of Greeks to consume non-essential, luxury goods, and their desire to travel. In general, however, the external effects of tourism have been considered positive in Greece (Alexandrakis 1973, pp. 183–97; Singh 1984).

5.4.2   On the economic impact of tourism at the national level

The lack of any specific study of patterns of tourist expenditure complicates evaluation of economic impact. Available figures underestimate foreign exchange receipts, as they only refer to foreign exchange transactions recorded by the Bank of Greece. These are much lower than actual tourist consumption, which includes unofficial transactions (Zacharatos 1986, pp. 65–6, 89; Singh 1984, p. 85). Even so, the available information shows that tourist receipts maintained a high rate of growth in 1960–78—21.4 per cent per annum—while exports, invisible receipts and current account receipts grew by only 16 per cent (Singh 1984, pp. 86–9). Tourist receipts grew from \$49.3 to \$1,326.3 million between 1960 and 1978, while receipts per arrival doubled in the same period from \$140 to \$282 (Singh 1984, pp. 92–3).

Average tourist expenditures have always been low in Greece by international standards. In 1970 they were \$13 daily (compared with \$16.80 in Portugal, \$15.70 in Spain, and \$13.70 in Turkey; Alexandrakis 1973, p. 156). Expenditures per visit were \$120 in 1968 (compared with \$130 in Italy and \$170 in Spain; Alexandrakis 1973, p. 157). This can be attributed to cheap services, especially in the informal sector, as well as to the type of tourism. It seems that medium or even low-income tourists keep visiting Greece. In recent years per-capita expenditure has fallen consistently, and the number of nights spent in hotels has remained stable (Table 5.7). In the mid-1980s foreign

Table 5.7 Foreign tourists' expenditures in Greece, 1983–6

	1983	1984	1985	1986
Arrivals	4,778,477	5,523,192	6,573,993	7,024,779
Expenditures, total ($ million)	1,175	1,312	1,428	1,833
Average per-capita expenditure ($)	246	238	217	261
Nights spent in hotels	32,429,206	32,705,115	33,919,174	33,740,110

Sources: Adapted from NSSG (1985) and Parachristou (1987)

tourists tend to prefer auxiliary accommodation and consider Greece a place for cheap vacations: in a 1985 survey (EOT 1985) 66 per cent of respondents found the cost accessible, 29 per cent low, and only 5 per cent high. Tourism expenditure abroad by Greek nationals was also low, and only constituted 3.4 per cent of all imports of goods and services (OECD 1985).

Special studies of the economic effects of tourism in Greece raise reservations with their image of tourism as a 'passport to development' (de Kadt 1979). The net impact of tourism was calculated recently by subtracting the negative impact (foreign exchange expenditure) from the positive one (total receipts from foreign tourism); the balance was positive and had grown from $170 million in 1970 to $1,186 million in 1978 (Singh 1984, pp. 177–8). Other analyses have shown that the share of tourist receipts in GDP increased from 1.6 per cent in 1960 to 2.4 per cent in 1970, and 4.9 per cent in 1978 (Singh 1984, p. 98). Later estimates indicate that tourist receipts have decreased to 3.4 per cent of GDP (OECD 1985). By contrast, as much as 16.4 per cent of all exports came from tourism. According to the same source, international tourist financial flows (receipts minus expenditures) gave a positive balance of $1,006 million in 1984. The positive impact of tourism on the balance of payments is manifested in its contribution to total invisible receipts, which increased from 18 per cent to 32 per cent in 1960–78 (OECD 1985, pp. 95–6). Tourist earnings have covered about one-fifth of the balance of current transactions in many years, and this rose to 24 per cent ($492 million) in 1986 (Papachristou 1987).

5.4.3 Employment and family work strategies

It is relatively easy to identify employment in hotels, restaurants, transport (including travel agencies), recreational and cultural services in the Greek censuses, but much more difficult to analyse other sectors of the tourist industry, such as national tourism administration which in some countries exceeds employment in the former sectors (Williams *et al.* 1986, 16–17). Greek tourist enterprises are small scale. Between 1969 and 1978 the average size grew from 2.2 to only 2.5 employees per hotel and restaurant establishment, and decreased from 3.4 to 3.3 employees per recreational and cultural service establishment. Only the size of transport establishments expanded, growing from 14.7 to 16.6 employees per establishment (adapted from NSSG censuses).

It is difficult to construct an accurate indicator of direct employment in tourism, as all sectors, except hotels, serve local residents as well as visitors. The labour force recorded in hotels and restaurants, recreational and cultural services and transport increased by 59,679 persons over the period 1961–71, and by 88,460 over the period 1971–81, and grew from 6.1 per cent to 10.5 per cent of total employment in Greece. Two more detailed studies during the late 1960s, though difficult to compare because of their different methods, give compatible estimates. Direct employment in tourism was estimated at 23,500 in 1966 (Spartidis 1969) and this was corroborated by a 1970 study by the Ministry of Co-ordination (1971), which found 26,100 working in the sector. Thereafter, employment grew considerably and, by 1984, employment in hotels alone had risen to 50,000 (OECD 1985). The Five-Year Development Plan 1988–92 estimated employment in all types of accommodation in 1987 to be 118,000 at peak period, rising to 180,000 if indirect employment is added (CPER 1987, pp. 135–6). Amongst these, about 25,000 qualified and 50,000 less skilled labourers were employed in hotel businesses (Greek Parliament 1984, p. 61).

Official employment censuses do not show a particularly marked seasonality. Monthly fluctuations in 1978 showed 12 per cent of the labour force to be temporary in restaurants and 54 per cent in hotels. According to the Hotel Employees' Insurance Fund, seasonality was higher during the 1970s and has not improved over time (Komilis 1986, pp. 127–35). In the larger cities (Athens, Salonica, Patras, Volos, Larisa) monthly fluctuations were almost negligible, as these centres cater for domestic and commercial movements as well as tourism. By contrast, some tourist towns (Heraklion, Rhodes, Ayios Nicolaos, Corfu) have experienced considerable peaks in employment from May to November, especially in July and August. Even more acute peaks occurred in small seaside settlements.

High seasonality in hotels and restaurants particularly affects the female labour force. While female participation in the labour force decreased in the country as a whole over the period 1961–81, it doubled in sectors associated with tourism but is very low in transport. The increase would be even greater if unrecorded employment were included. Jobs in accommodation are dominated by women (bed-makers, cleaners, servants, etc.) especially in unrecorded rooms and the informal sector, where such jobs come 'naturally' as an extension of housework. Indeed, the attraction of 'housewives' into tourist employment has been a government proposal since the mid-1970s (CPER 1976, pp. 51–2). In the Greek islands the division of labour according to gender involves women taking care of the guests and rooms (usually parts of family houses), and men collecting the clients at the port (usually accompanied by their sons), negotiating prices and, where the rooms are declared, contacting the authorities.

Seasonality is both an economic and a socio-cultural problem. In fact, the cultural impact of tourism should be discussed in this context, but only a brief reference can be made for what seems to be one of the most crucial issues for a country such as Greece. Tourism breaks up certain long-entrenched traditions and introduces cultural continua, having both negative and positive impacts on localities. The changing role of women in areas incorporated into the tourist market, influences family strategies and creates new classes on the societal and cultural level.

Table 5.8 Hotel capacity, 1983, and new investment by region, 1983–8

	Hotel[1] beds 1983		New beds 1983–8		New investment 1983–8	
	Abs. no	%	Abs. no	%	Abs. no	%
Attica and Piraeus	71,125	22.33	162	1.15	94998890	0.76
Salonica (Nomos)	8,903	2.80	0	.00	0	0.00
Rest of Mainland Greece:						
Central Greece[2]	16,169	5.08	194	1.37	141524263	1.13
Peloponnese	36,037	11.31	967	6.85	590303389	4.70
Epiros	5,614	1.76	405	2.87	356699718	2.84
Thessaly[3]	4,977	1.56	585	4.14	68043621	0.54
Macedonia[4]	19,108	6.00	1290	9.14	1352310780	10.78
Thrace	2,915	0.92	299	2.12	406357344	3.24
Aegean islands:						
Dodecanese	43,896	13.78	2438	17.27	2372449007	18.91
Cyclades	12,550	3.94	733	5.19	634293635	5.05
Lesvos, Samos, Chios	6,754	2.12	1272	9.01	1182152190	9.42
Rest of eastern islands						
Euboea	10,810	3.39	450	3.19	294571021	2.35
Magnisia (Sporades)	7,668	2.41	440	3.12	675096342	5.38
Kavala (Thasos)	5,301	1.66	299	2.12	173932977	1.39
Crete	39,760	12.48	2771	19.62	2675012604	21.32
Ionian islands:						
Corfu	20,713	6.50	1459	10.33	1264162164	10.07
Zante, Cephalonia, Lef	6,215	1.95	357	2.53	266646844	2.12
TOTAL	318,515	100.00	14,121	100.00	12548554789	100.00

Source: Adapted from NSSG (1985) and MNE (unpublished series of investment realized on the basis of LD 1262/1982 until April 1988).

Notes: 1. Includes hotels, bungalows, motels, furnished suites, guest rooms, boarding-houses, inns.
Excludes: 2. Attica, Euboea; 3. Magnisia; 4. Salonica, Kavala.

5.5 Economic aspects of regional polarisation

The importance of tourism in Greek economic development has been considerable. This was less evident until the mid-1960s, as Greece rose to semi-peripheral status in the world economy, but later emphasis on tourism added a certain dynamism in the 1980s. As the bulk of expenditure occurred in the countryside and the islands, moreover, tourism affected previously isolated areas more than developed urban centres. Most of the Greek islands were inaccessible in the 1950s, and their economies were characterised as a mixed monetary and bartering system (Alexandrakis 1973, pp. 196–7). They were then connected with Piraeus and Athens by sea and air transport, and later were interconnected (though the communication systems still remain radial and centralised on Athens). Finally, several islands have been directly connected with European cities by charter flights. By the late 1970s, more than 50 per cent of charter arrivals already occurred at island airports such as Rhodes, Kos, Corfu, and Heraklion (Singh 1981; NSSG).

Unequal development is pronounced in tourism, as has already been shown. At a deeper level of analysis, the apparent decentralisation of activity is highly polarised spatially, being concentrated in a few localities (with resulting congestion) and absent in other areas with remarkable natural and cultural resources. In the former type of localities tourism can be advantageous from the residents' viewpoint, or it can disrupt labour markets, and overload social infrastructure and the environment as, for example, has occurred in Rhodes (TCG 1981, pp. 67–72). The impact of spatial polarisation on regional development and new trends of diffuse urbanisation in the 1980s (Leontidou 1990) have yet to be investigated. Mass tourism, if highly seasonal, can create an inverse type of polarisation, as it disrupts local communities and labour markets, and undermines population growth. However, there are several possible outcomes depending on the locality and the type of tourism. Polarisation at the intraregional level is also possible, as in the case of Rhodes where social segregation between tourists and inhabitants has been observed (Loukissas 1977).

Polarisation is apparently intensifying through investment in already congested areas which, ironically, is still going on during a period when decentralisation goals have been explicitly set. Table 5.8 underlines the impact of LD 1262/1982 on tourist development by region. The law specifies non-assisted areas according to certain criteria, and excludes large cities from incentives policy. With the exception of Attica and Salonica, however, new investment in 1982–8 was directed towards areas which already had considerable tourist capacity: the Dodecanese (especially Rhodes, 19 per cent of investment), Crete (21 per cent), Macedonia (especially Khalkidiki, 11 per cent of investment) and Corfu (10 per cent). The correlation coefficient between existing (1983) and new (1983–8) hotel beds by region (including cities) in Greece is as high as 0.90, and even if total existing capacity (including campings, rented rooms etc.) is compared with new beds, the coefficient remains at 0.85. This analysis indicates that new investment is attracted to already developed areas. The question of whether it creates any growth poles, should be addressed separately for different types of accommodation and tourist development.

Greek Five-Year Plans from the mid-1970s have considered small-scale tourist development to be advantageous from the viewpoint of the local population, while large-scale developments were found to drain local income. According to the Khalkidiki Regional Plan, only 19 million out of 126 million drachmas (15 per cent of the total) gained in hotel tourism remained in the locality, and only 27.5 per cent of employees were recruited from the local population (OAOM and Assoc. 1976, vol. 1, pp. 335–48). The operation of small-scale local tourist developments and inns was generally promoted by the government after the mid-1970s in order to assist regional development by channelling additional income to the local population, family units and small businesses. In retrospect, the economic impact of the growth of small-scale tourism was positive, as the amount of income remaining within localities increased. However, the environmental impact was rather negative, as the quality of services and of the environment deteriorated, segmentation intensified, and illegal building and unrecorded activities mushroomed.

The regional developmental effect of tourism, however, is complex and contradictory and has yet to be adequately studied. Congestion and environmental deterioration have diverted tourists from Athens, 'the City of the Gods', but has not dispersed them: they still flock to Rhodes, Crete, and other centres. In these, as well as other peripheral localities, contradictions emerge from seasonality, regional polarisation and segmentation on several levels: most importantly, domestic versus foreign tourist resorts (approximately the mainland versus the islands), and formal versus informal activities in tourism. This creates a virtual impasse in both analysis and policy.

Notes

1. Main abbreviations used in the paper: CPER—Center of Planning and Economic Research; EOT—National Tourist Organisation of Greece; LD—Legislative Decree; NSSG—National Statistical Service of Greece; RD—Royal Decree; TCG—Technical Chamber of Greece; YPEHODE—Ministry of the Environment, Regional Planning and Public Works.
2. The Ministry of Tourism supervises EOT, the Xenia Hotels, the Summer Festivals, the casinos, but not Olympic Airways. The role of EOT was reviewed recently, and its modernisation is being sought, with the introduction of tourism higher education courses and the review of its entrepreneurial role with the creation of *Sociétés Anonymes* in certain areas, and the combination of central with local intervention in tourist development (MNE 1988, p. 33).
3. Additional services include conference rooms, recreation and sporting grounds, etc. Information about the provisions of the 1988–92 Development Plan, which has not been published except for a brief document (MNE 1988), was kindly provided by Panagiotis Komilis (CPER). Information about the Ministry of Tourism and its policy, especially the Integrated Mediterranean Programmes, was kindly provided by Dimitris Kavadias (EOT).
4. The Integrated Mediterranean Programmes encourage large investments (over 300 million dr.) in hotels of rank 'A' or above, with additional services, in under-developed areas (earmarked as 'D' areas). About 29 per cent of the expenditures of the Programmes approved by EOT will be directed towards infrastructure, especially for marine tourism and sailing. As for the 1988–92 Development Plan, it explicitly refers to the attraction of higher-income tourism and to the dominant role of private investment in the creation of large tourist complexes, including those with recreation and sports facilities (MNE 1988, p. 33). To this effect, some of the limits set by LD 1262/1982 were relaxed. Its impact on regional structure is studied in the final part of this chapter (Table 5.8).
5. A word of caution is required here. The large numbers of empty residences on the islands also reflect the existence of abandoned dwellings, and the building boom in 1976–9 created excess empty houses all over Greece, especially in the cities.
6. The NSSG and EOT calculate the ratio of bed-nights occupied to bed-nights available on the basis of the number of beds actually available each month.
7. The 1:3 estimate by the Greek Chamber of Hotels is calculated on the basis of hotel beds (excluding auxiliary accommodation). It may be an exaggeration, given their vested interest in the control of this flourishing para-hotel business. In Corfu 20,000 hotel beds are thought to correspond to 60,000 additional undeclared beds. This is an average which rises in undeveloped areas: for example, Casiopi in Corfu is believed to have 60 official and 4,000 unofficial beds. They are not only offered on the spot. Undeclared rooms have appeared in British brochures advertising summer vacations in Greece! The cost is considerably lower, being no more than one-third that of hotels at the most, especially after the latter suddenly increased their prices by 32 per cent in the summer of 1987.

8. This suggests a new way of treatment in place of earlier approaches to tourism as an industry with intersectoral linkages in the Greek economy: tourism should be treated as a separate column of final demand in input–output tables (Zacharatos 1986, pp. 47–55). Earlier approaches, using 1960 data (Alexandrakis 1973, pp. 183–8) showed that backward linkages were weaker in tourism than in manufacturing. However, tourism created stronger linkages than had been suggested, including, for example, dynamic effects such as the appearance of industries producing basic metal products for hotel construction, leading to a decrease of such imports. Tourism was also considered significant because linkages were created by exogenous money brought into the economy with a relatively small promotion cost. It was calculated through regression equations that each $1 of promotion would foster approximately $16 of tourist receipts. In 1975 the percentage of intermediate inputs created by tourism was calculated at 20 per cent compared to 13 per cent in services, 40 per cent in transport, and over 68 per cent in manufacturing (CPER 1976, p. 34).

6 Portugal: market segmentation and regional specialisation

Jim Lewis and Allan M. Williams

6.1 Introduction

Portugal is particularly poorly represented in the English language research literature on tourism because, as in so many matters, it lies in the shadow of its much larger neighbour, Spain. Except for some case studies of rural change in the Algarve—such as Bennett (1986) or Jenkins (1979)—which touch upon tourism, the industry has been virtually ignored by researchers outside Portugal. Even within the country, there are few substantive published studies except for Cavaco's (1979; 1980; 1981) pioneering work. Yet there are many features of Portuguese tourism which merit further investigation. First, there is the economic importance of the industry; by 1987 international visitors generated a net inward balance of $1,727 million for the economy, receipts were equivalent to some 4.1 per cent of GDP and 13.3 per cent of exports of all goods and services. Second, the industry exhibits a high degree of regional polarisation in terms of capacity and types of employment which reflects market segmentation. Third, since the initial formation of official Portuguese tourist policy, the government has consistently favoured the development of luxury tourism (see Cavaco 1979). Consequently, tourism in Portugal has developed in a different manner from that in neighbouring Spain. This is highlighted by the simple fact that there are more hotel beds in Spain's Costa del Sol than there are in the whole of Portugal. Finally, the development of tourism in Portugal has been marked by a very uneven course, with a disastrous decline in the mid-1970s being followed by slow recovery and then, in the mid-1980s, rapid expansion.

This chapter aims to provide a broad introduction to the Portuguese tourist industry and is divided into five main parts. First, there is a review of its national-level evolution, followed by an analysis of the changing regional pattern of tourist arrivals and provision. This leads to an analysis of the national and regional economic features of tourism. Particular attention is paid to the relationship between market segmentation and the character of employment provided by tourism. Finally, current developments in policy are reviewed in relation to the future of tourism in Portugal.

6.2 The development of tourism

The first significant development of tourism in Portugal was based around the thermal spas of the interior, such as Vizela, Vidago, Curia and Luso. These became popular with both foreign visitors and the emerging indigenous Portuguese middle class after the mid-nineteenth century. Even by the early twentieth century beach tourism was little developed, and was mostly limited to daily visits from large urban centres, such as Oporto, Coimbra and Lisbon, to nearby beaches at Foz do Douro, Figueira de Foz and Belém, respectively (Cavaco 1979). The Algarve was little developed; even the best-known resort at that time, Praia da Rocha, had only one inn and a few *pensões* (boarding houses) in 1933, and these were frequented exclusively by wealthy families from Lisbon and the Alentejo. Portuguese tourism remained mainly based on domestic markets into the 1930s, and there were only about 36,000 foreign visitors each year.

During the 1950s the number of foreign tourists increased from 70,700 in 1950 to 353,000 by 1960, and between 1955 and 1963 alone foreign exchange receipts quadrupled. This was actively encouraged by state aid after 1952 to promote foreign tourism (Cunha 1986). Despite the difficulties caused by the major devaluation of the Spanish peseta in 1958—a move designed to promote Spanish tourism but which also inhibited the movement of Spanish tourists abroad—the policy seems to have been moderately successful.

The most significant phase in the expansion of Portugal's international tourist trade was the period 1963–74, when its growth comfortably exceeded the average for the OECD countries. Portugal benefited from the general expansion of demand for tourism in Western Europe, combined with falling costs—especially as a result of the expansion of package holidays. Expansion was brought to a halt by the 1973 devaluation of the dollar, a rise in transport costs and the recession which followed the 1973–4 oil crisis. While all European tourist destinations suffered from these events, Portugal also had the much publicised political uncertainty which followed the 1974 military coup. In 1973 there had been over 4 million foreign visitors, and this number was not exceeded until 1977. The 41 per cent fall in tourist bed-nights in hotels and guest houses (see Figure 6.1) which occurred in 1975 constituted a major setback for the economy as a whole. This was only partly compensated for in economic terms, by a sharp rise in domestic tourist bed-nights in 1974–6, generated by a temporary increase in real purchasing power and the use of vacant hotel rooms to house some of the thousands of *retornados*—refugees from Angola and Mozambique (Lewis and Williams, 1984). Since the late 1970s international tourism has revived and has steadily expanded to account for 15 million bed-nights by 1988—four times the number of 1970.[1]

The nature of the tourist industry also changed during these years, with a shift to more luxurious hotels and away from *pensões*, whose numbers are actually falling (Table 6.1a). By 1988 over 47 per cent of foreign tourists stayed in three-star (or superior) hotels, compared to only 33 per cent of domestic tourists (Table 6.1b). Together with the expansion of second homes, apartments, motels, tourist villages and camping, this led to considerable change in the types of accommodation being provided in response to growing market segmentation. There was a 35 per cent expansion in the number of hotels in the period 1965–84, most of which occurred in higher-quality hotels (that is in three, four or five-star units), so that 78 per cent of hotel bedrooms had their own bathrooms by the mid-1980s. This has also been supplemented by marked increases in other forms of up-market accommodation, including tourist apartments, motels and *pousadas* (state-owned inns). These developments are firmly associated with the shift to beach tourism and to rapid

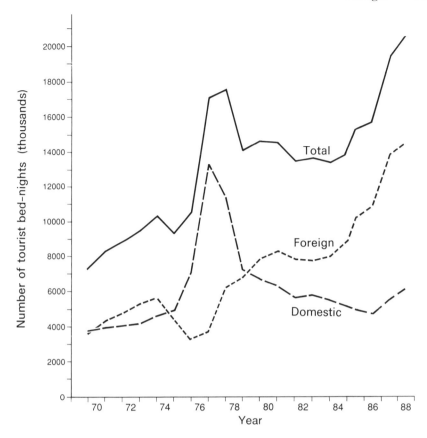

Fig. 6.1   The number of foreign and domestic bed-nights in hotels in
                Portugal, 1970–88

Source: Direcção Geral do Turismo (1986; unpublished statistics for 1987, 88)

expansion of the Algarve: only 13 per cent of *pensões* are in coastal regions,
compared with 44 per cent and 57 per cent of five-star and four-star hotels and
57 per cent of hotel apartments. In addition there have also been developments
of other forms of tourism, including an expansion of camping (the number of
official campsites increased from 61 in 1973 to 87 in 1982) and of second
homes. Time-sharing or co-ownership schemes have also become important
recently, especially in the Algarve, fostered by companies such as Elliot
Property and Leisure Group. More recently, further diversification has been
secured by the development of *turismo de habitação*, based on short stays in
historic houses in northern and central Portugal.

    Despite the changing nature of the Portuguese tourist industry it has
remained highly seasonal. In 1972, 44 per cent of all tourists arrived in the
three peak months of July, August and September, and this had risen to 47 per
cent by 1980, and to 48 per cent by 1984 (see Figure 6.2a). This increased
seasonal peaking has occurred despite strong growth in the winter sunshine
tourist market with the Algarve and Madeira, in particular, proving attractive

Table 6.1   Development and domestic/foreign utilisation of tourist
accommodation in Portugal
(a) Development of hotels and other forms of tourist accommodation 1965–87

	1965	1970	1975	1980	1987	% change 1965–87
Hotels	212	263	258	266	320	+50.9
Hotel apartments	–	–	24	33	47	
Tourist apartments	–	–	–	62	–	
Tourist villages						
Motels	–	–	17	13	15	
Pousadas	–	17	22	26	32	
Inns	–	76	75	68	62	
Pensões	1,029	1,019	1,003	988	988	– 4.0
Total	(1,320)	1,375	1,429	1,456	1,464	10.9

(b) Portuguese and foreign visitors' use of hotels and other forms of
accommodation, 1988

Type of accommodation	Foreign		Domestic	
	thousands	(%)	thousands	(%)
Hotels (total)	7,391	50.9	2,439	40.6
Five-star	2,123	14.7	321	5.4
Four-star	2,878	19.4	692	11.5
Three-star	1,919	13.2	945	15.7
One and two-star	459	3.5	480	7.9
Hotel apartments	2,001	13.8	387	6.4
Motels	61	0.4	71	1.2
Pousadas	198	1.4	57	0.8
Inns	199	1.4	105	1.7
Pensões	1,168	8.0	2,250	37.4
Tourist Villages	1,611	11.1	279	4.6
Apartments	1,897	13.1	433	7.2
Total	14,527	100.0	6,015	100.0

Source: (a) Instituto Nacional de Estatística (1985a; 1985b); (b) Direcção Geral do Turismo
(Unpublished Statistics)

to British and Scandinavian tourists. However, this has been counterbalanced
by the increasing importance of Portugal, especially the Algarve (Lewis and
Williams 1988), as a mass tourist summer destination. The lower per-capita
expenditure and environmental pollution problems associated with this have
become a matter of serious concern in the mid-1980s.

6.2.1   *Market segmentation: domestic and international sources*

While foreign tourists are pre-eminent in terms of both visitor numbers and
income generation in Portugal, domestic tourism represents a significant
market segment. Simply in terms of bed-nights (in hotels etc.), there have
been periods in the 1970s when domestic visitors (including rehoused *retornados*)

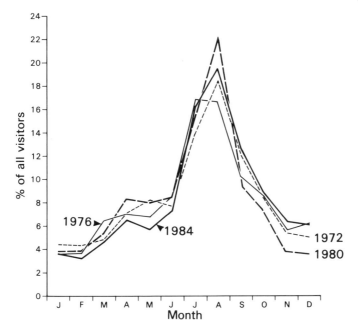

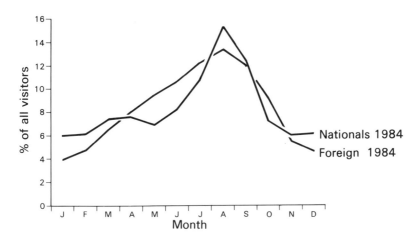

Fig. 6.2 Seasonality trends in Portuguese tourism: (a) changing patterns of seasonality, 1972–84; (b) seasonality patterns for national and foreign tourists, 1984

Source: Direcção Geral do Turismo (1986)

have outnumbered foreigners (see Figure 6.1). Even after the boom in foreign tourism in the 1980s, domestic tourists still accounted for 29 per cent of all recorded hotel nights in 1988, and there are some types of holiday in which they were dominant; for example, the Portuguese accounted for 90 per cent of guests in holiday villages (camps) and 55 per cent of campers (Direcção Geral do Turismo 1988). However, there is very low participation in tourism within Portugal in general. In 1978 only 19 per cent of the Portuguese took holidays away from home; by 1986 this had risen to 28 per cent, which represents a major increase, but the level is still substantially below northern European averages. The low participation is a consequence not only of low per-capita incomes but also of highly polarised incomes and access to leisure. Thus while only 34 per cent of the population had any paid holidays at all, over half of these had 23 days or more! The relatively low level of development of Portuguese domestic tourism is also confirmed by the lack of professionalism and institutionalism in the organisation of the industry. Most Portuguese families arrange their own holidays, with only 4 per cent relying on travel agencies (Direcção-Geral do Turismo 1988), and there were only 539 such agencies in the whole of the country in 1984.

The most reliable evidence on where the Portuguese take holidays comes from a household survey undertaken in 1987. This suggested that only 7 per cent went abroad for holidays, comprising 2 per cent who went to neighbouring Spain, a further 2 per cent to France and 2 per cent to the rest of Europe. Given the weakness of the escudo on international exchange markets, the preference for adjacent countries is hardly surprising. Within Portugal, the major change in domestic tourism, in line with foreign tourism, has been the shift from thermal resorts since the Second World War. Aged hotels, a lack of modern sporting facilities, the isolation of many spas and a growing preference for beach holidays have all led to a shift to coastal resorts. Although thermal spas are now dependent on Portuguese nationals for over 90 per cent of their trade, few visitors stay for more than a few nights, so the spas have continued to decline in importance (Cunha 1986). In coastal resorts the Portuguese tend to rely more on either camping or lower-quality hotel and boarding-house accommodation than foreign visitors do: 37 per cent of domestic tourists, compared to only 8 per cent of foreign tourists, stay in *pensões* (Table 6.1b). There is also considerable reliance on second homes, especially in the Algarve and the Costa do Sol, east of Lisbon (see Cavaco 1981; Williams 1981) and on renting rooms in houses not registered with the tourist authorities.

A further important feature of domestic tourism is that seasonality is much less marked. Accurate data are only available for this in terms of bed-nights spent in hotels, apartments and *pensões* (see Figure 6.2b). Yet it is clear that in 1984 domestic tourism was spread much more evenly throughout the year. Generally, there are relatively more domestic tourists in winter and more foreign tourists in summer. The exception to this pattern is August which has 15.4 per cent of all domestic tourists, reflecting the tradition of taking holidays in that month.

The international tourist market is highly segmented. In the first instance there is a fundamental division between excursionists and tourists (as defined in Chapter 1). In 1987 excursionists outnumbered tourists by 10,072,000 to 6,101,700. The bulk of excursionists (approximately three-quarters) are from Spain. Historically, this balance has been variable and in 1973, for example, tourists outnumbered excursionists by one-and-a-half times. Much of the recent growth of excursionism can be accounted for by rising real incomes in Spain, a more relaxed political relationship between the Iberian neighbours, and price differentials for some commodities leading to considerable cross-border movements for shopping purposes. Indeed, some Portuguese border towns, such as Miranda do Douro and Vilar Formoso, have prospered as a result of this trade.

Table 6.2   Tourist bed-nights spent by selected foreign nationals in hotels, apartments and tourist villages in Portugal, 1960–88

	1960		1980		1988	
	Thousands	(%)	Thousands	(%)	Thousands	(%)
FRG	86	6.9	1,557	16.2	2,006	13.8
Spain	110	8.8	964	10.1	1,233	8.4
UK	278	22.3	2,681	28.0	5,073	34.9
Netherlands	39	3.1	985	10.3	1,162	8.0
USA	150	12.0	458	4.8	630	4.3
France	220	17.6	521	5.4	725	5.0
Sweden	29	2.3	455	4.7	549	3.8
Total	1,246	100.0	9,580	100.0	14,527	100.0

Sources: Direcção Geral do Turismo (1986); and unpublished data for 1988

While excursionists usually outnumber tourists, the latter are clearly more important in economic terms. Between 1940 and 1984, the total number of nights spent by foreign tourists in Portugal increased from 500,000 to 36 million. The total number of tourists is also increasing strongly and since 1978 had more than doubled to reach 6,101,700 by 1987. Over time, the composition of the international tourist trade has changed significantly (see Table 6.2). The dominant feature is the expanding share of the United Kingdom in the Portuguese market which, between 1960 and 1988, increased from 22 per cent to 35 per cent. This is matched by a decline in the relative importance of US tourists (as in many other European countries) and French tourists. Spanish tourist numbers have fluctuated in relative importance over time, West German and Dutch tourists increased considerably in number in the 1960s and 1970s before levelling off in the 1980s, while the Scandinavian countries have become more important as sources of tourists. These changes are important because they affect the overall pattern of market segmentation.

Different groups of foreign tourists have very distinctive holiday patterns in terms of length of stay, type of accommodation, reliance on commercial travel agencies, and seasonality (see Table 6.3). The Spanish and the Italians have relatively short stays, a highly peaked seasonality and are inclined to organise their holidays independently (many drive to Portugal and arrange their own accommodation on arrival). For the Italians, this is likely to be in hotels or *pensões*, but the Spanish are likely to rely on camping or a number of 'unspecified' alternatives (presumably in the informal sector). Another group is made up of tourists from countries such as Belgium, the Netherlands, France and the Federal Republic of Germany. For these the average stay is 10–14 days, their visits are highly peaked in the summer and they show a relatively high propensity for camping holidays and, to a lesser extent, hotels, while about half to three-quarters use travel agencies to arrange their visits. The Brazilians are superficially similar to this group but, given their ties through emigration, they are much more heavily reliant on friends and family for accommodation. The Swedes (and other Scandinavians) and the British form another distinctive group. They also have relatively long stays, but because of their severe domestic winters, visits between October and April are relatively common, so that their seasonality is less peaked. They rely mainly

Table 6.3 Market segmentation: major features of the holidays of selected groups of international tourists in Portugal, 1984/7

Country of origin	1987 Average length of stay (no. of days)	Percentage of holidays taken in three peak months	1984 Percentage staying in Hotels, etc.	Camping	Apartments	Other	Percentage using travel agencies to organise their holiday
Spain	4.3	41	13	21	5	61	39
Italy	6.1	59	53	26	4	17	53
Brazil	7.1	37	32	1	1	66	71
Belgium	9.8	57	42	28	11	19	70
Netherlands	14.2	50	29	39	17	15	79
France	9.6	55	43	17	17	23	71
FRG	12.2	49	37	34	12	17	56
USA	9.7	37	67	0	5	28	75
UK	11.6	39	45	4	34	17	92
Sweden	12.1	33	70	3	24	3	93

Source: Direcção Geral do Turismo (1984) (1988)

on hotels or apartments for accommodation and frequently come on package holidays, leading to a heavy dependence on travel agencies. Finally, American tourists have low seasonal peaking, and a heavy reliance on hotel or other accommodation (being the friends or family of many returned emigrants). Such segmentation is of fundamental importance for each group makes a different contribution to economic development.

6.3   Regional segmentation of the Portuguese tourist market

This section of the chapter outlines the regional shifts in the Portuguese tourist market and some of the ways in which regional sub-markets are differentiated. Between 1974 and 1988 the main feature of the regional growth of tourism has been an impressive increase in numbers going to the main centres: that is the Algarve (Faro *distrito*), Lisbon and Madeira. The number of foreign visitor bed-nights spent in Faro quadrupled to 7,035,016 while the numbers in Lisbon and Funchal both increased by almost 1 million to 3,137,816 and 2,517,810 respectively. Most of this expansion occurred in the 1970s and visitor numbers were relatively static in the early 1980s, but then increased. Absolute increases in the other regions have been much smaller, although in percentage terms they have been broadly similar. Consequently, the overall share of the foreign tourist market held by the three main centres has remained static at a level of 86 per cent. The next ranked *distrito*, Oporto, had only 14 per cent of foreign bed-nights in 1987.

The regional distribution of domestic tourists is quite different from that of foreigners; there is a greater geographical spread and the Algarve is far less prominent. Absolute numbers of visitors to most *distritos* have remained static or actually decreased between 1974 and 1988. The one region which has avoided this fate is Madeira, which shared in a general expansion in the mid-1970s but where the number of domestic tourists has since remained stable. The influence of falling living standards in Portugal in the 1980s can be seen in the substitution of types of holiday. While the number of hotel and *pensão* holidays taken by nationals has fallen, there have been considerable increases in the numbers of bed-nights spent on campsites. The global total for the domestic market has increased from 1,421,000 in 1974, through 2,984,000 in 1977, to 4,924,458 in 1987. These increases have been spread fairly evenly between *distritos*, except that Leiria (which has resorts such as Nazaré) has seen a tenfold gain. However, in absolute terms, Setúbal (1,340,077) and Faro (870,053) are the main centres for camping.

Distinctive regional markets have developed and their major characteristics, as of 1984, are shown in Table 6.4. Lisbon has the largest stock of accommodation (approximately a quarter of the total), but it is distinctly up-market, with, for example, 43 per cent of all five-star hotel accommodation. Given its role as the administrative and economic capital of Portugal, it attracts large shares of both domestic and foreign tourists. However, their stays are relatively short; domestic 'tourists' are often on business trips, while foreign visitors make short cultural tours of the city. Nevertheless, these attractions remain strong all year round so that there are relatively high bed-occupancy rates.

The Algarve is the second largest tourist region in Portugal with about one-fifth of bed-spaces. It has a relatively broad spread of accommodation types,

Table 6.4 Regional features of Portuguese tourism, 1987

District/region	% of all hotel and *pensão* beds	% of all hotel beds	% of all five-star hotel beds	% of all *pensão* beds	% of all bed-nights at camping sites	% of all foreign hotel bed-nights
Aveiro	4.3	3.4	0.8	5.1	7.0	1.2
Beja	0.6	0.1	–	1.2	0.6	0.1
Braga	3.9	4.3	–	4.0	1.1	1.3
Bragança	1.1	0.3	–	2.7	0.3	0.1
Castelo Branco	1.2	0.6	–	2.2	0.2	0.1
Coimbra	3.3	2.7	–	4.2	6.5	1.6
Evora	0.9	0.4	–	1.5	0.5	0.6
Faro	21.2	21.7	20.6	11.2	25.0	35.2
Guarda	1.3	0.7	–	2.6	0.9	0.3
Leiria	4.0	3.2	–	6.4	10.6	1.4
Lisbon	24.2	29.7	42.5	22.5	12.0	26.6
Pontalegre	0.8	0.6	–	1.2	0.1	0.3
Porto	7.9	9.0	10.1	9.0	7.8	4.0
Santarém	3.7	3.3	–	5.5	1.0	1.3
Setúbal	2.9	1.1	–	3.4	19.8	1.6
Viana do Castelo	2.2	1.9	–	3.2	5.8	1.0
Vila Real	1.9	1.8	–	2.6	0.5	0.2
Viseu	2.8	1.9	–	5.2	0.4	0.3
Azores	2.0	1.5	–	2.8	NA	0.9
Madeira	9.8	11.8	26.0	3.5	NA	21.9
Total	100.0	100.0	100.0	100.0	100.0	100.0

District/region	% of all domestic hotel bed-nights	Average stay by domestic tourists (no. of days)	Average stay by foreign tourists (no. of days)	Hotel occupancy rates	% of total *distrito* employment in hotels and *pensões* (1984)
Aveiro	4.0	2.3	2.4	18.2	0.4
Beja	0.9	1.6	1.2	24.8	0.1
Braga	4.4	2.2	2.7	22.1	0.3
Bragança	1.4	1.4	1.1	17.6	0.4
Castelo Branco	2.0	2.1	1.7	20.3	0.4
Coimbra	4.9	2.0	1.9	29.9	0.3
Evora	1.2	1.3	1.1	35.5	0.3
Faro	9.4	2.7	7.1	47.7	8.4
Guarda	1.7	1.3	1.1	21.0	0.4
Leiria	4.3	2.0	1.6	21.4	0.5
Lisbon	28.0	2.1	2.8	41.8	1.0
Pontalegre	1.4	1.6	1.2	30.8	0.6
Porto	12.0	2.0	2.1	30.9	0.3
Santarém	2.6	1.5	1.8	17.1	0.4
Setúbal	3.2	2.3	3.1	27.3	0.3
Viana do Castelo	2.2	1.7	2.5	22.8	0.4
Vila Real	2.4	2.1	1.3	17.9	0.4
Viseu	3.0	1.9	1.2	15.3	0.3
Azores	3.9	3.1	3.5	35.4	0.8
Madeira	7.1	5.1	9.2	65.2	4.8
Total	100.0	2.1	4.0	37.4	0.9

Source: Instituto Nacional de Estatísticas (1985a); DGT 1988

including both camping sites and luxury hotels, hence it has a broad market. While it does attract domestic tourists, its primary appeal is to foreign tourists and it accounts for one-third of those visiting Portugal. Domestic tourists stay for relatively short periods—perhaps reflecting the importance of weekend breaks in second homes (Williams 1981)—but foreign tourists, many of whom have come on package holidays, stay an average of seven days. Given its relatively mild winter climate, Faro attracts visitors throughout the year and, hence, has relatively high occupancy rates. The Algarve has attracted a more up-market segment of tourism than most Mediterranean countries. From the very beginning there was considerable emphasis on the development of such facilities as golf courses, tennis centres and riding stables. Vale do Lobo typifies such developments, and it has a championship golf course, the Roger Taylor tennis centre, a selection of swimming pools and 700 villas.

The island of Madeira represents the élite end of the Portuguese tourist market. While it has about one-tenth of all bed-spaces, these are concentrated in the upper brackets so that it has about one-quarter of five-star hotels but very few *pensões*. Its major market is foreign visitors and, given the high cost of flying to the island, average stays are relatively long—9.2 days for foreigners. Given the equable year-round climate it attracts large numbers of tourists throughout the year and numbers deviate little from about 20,000 per month. The industry has been relatively static in the late 1970s and the 1980s with little new investment until the decision by North American interest to build the $35-million Meridian-Madeira hotel, with over 200 bedrooms (*Tempo Econômico*, 23 July 1987).

The rest of Portugal has only a small-scale tourist industry. Domestic visitors outnumber foreign ones, average stays are short, and occupancy rates are extremely low, being around one-fifth of capacity. Within this group the coastal *distritos* of central and northern Portugal, such as Aveiro, Coimbra, Leiria, Setúbal and Viana do Castelo, stand out as popular summer resorts for the Portuguese, and this is reflected in their relatively large share of camping places. These resorts mainly serve their immediate hinterland, and over one-half of Portuguese tourists take their holidays in either their *distrito* of residence or in an adjacent *distrito* (Direcção Geral do Turismo 1986). Other important centres of tourism in the interior are spa towns such as Luso and Geres, which have been faced with a vicious downward cycle of lack of investment and falling demand.

6.4   Tourism and the national economy

It is notoriously difficult to estimate the importance of tourism in the national economy. However, Cunha's (1986) estimate that tourism accounts for some 5–7 per cent of GDP does not seem unreasonable, and is comparable to the Secretaria de Estado do Turismo's (1986) estimate of 5.9 per cent of GDP in 1982 and to da Silva's (1986) estimate of 7 per cent of value added. This share exceeds that of the electricity, gas and water companies, and approaches the share accredited to agriculture. The importance of tourism to the Portuguese economy is further emphasised by considering its role in the balance of payments, investment and employment.

6.4.1   The balance of payments

Receipts from international tourist expenditure have grown steadily (in terms of current prices) throughout the 1970s and 1980s (except for 1975–6). International tourist expenditures have grown more slowly, being depressed by the weakness of the escudo; consequently, the gap between receipts and expenditure has widened (Figure 6.3). By 1987, receipts were 302,550 million escudos and expenditure was 59,590 million escudos yielding a balance of 242,960 million escudos. If the receipts are calculated in terms of constant 1970 prices, then they show a much smaller gain from 6,368 million escudos to 16,617 million escudos, while expenditures in real terms have been largely static since 1979. There are also a number of 'leakage' effects which serve to reduce the net contribution of tourism to the economy. While no accurate data are available on these, they are likely to include expenditure on imported consumer and capital goods, profit remittances from foreign-owned hotels and other tourist businesses, payments to foreign tour companies and promotion costs abroad. According to da Silva's (1986) estimate, imports account for approximately a quarter of all expenditure by national and foreign tourists — a not inconsiderable leakage.

Nevertheless, the positive balance on international tourism has played a vital role in helping to cover at least a part of Portugal's enormous visible trade gap. This coverage has varied over time but has generally tended to increase since 1975, being equal to 20.6 per cent in 1983 and 51.1 per cent in 1987. The importance of tourism is also underlined by the fact that, in most years, it contributes more to the balance of payments than does the leading industrial sector, textiles. Indeed, it is usually only surpassed in importance as a source of foreign exchange earnings by emigrant remittances. Within this total, different segments of the international market have varying importance. In 1984, UK visitors accounted for 35 per cent of bed-nights but their spending power is relatively low and they contributed only 20 per cent of receipts. In contrast, French and West German visitors spend relatively large amounts per capita, while the Spanish contribute only 3 per cent of receipts (this may be a considerable underestimate because of unregistered currency exchanges). The largest contributors, however, are US visitors, providing a staggering 33 per cent of receipts although only accounting for 6.4 per cent of bed-nights (Instituto Nacional de Estatística 1985a).

6.4.2.   Investment

While the Portuguese tourist industry is now firmly based on foreign tourists, direct foreign investment has played a relatively minor role in developing tourist facilities. Over time this role has diminished and there was a particularly sharp reduction in foreign investment in 1975, following the 1974 coup (Table 6.5). Indeed, pre-coup levels of foreign investment were only surpassed in current price terms as late as 1984. This pattern has changed in the mid-1980s with a flood of foreign investment being attracted into new forms of facilities, especially in the Algarve. While statistical data for this period are not yet available, a number of examples serve to illustrate the size and nature of some of these recent investments. Shell Oil has spent £6.6 million on building a 700-bed holiday village as an extension to the Vilar do Golf complex at Quinta do

Table 6.5　Sources of investment in tourism in Portugal, 1973–86

	1973	1977	1981	1986
		(millions escudos)		
1. National capital	2,440	844	4,910	23,553
(a) Personal	1,357	358	2,077	13,330
(b) Credit	1,061	474	2,631	10,205
(i) Fundo do Turismo	158	26	260	756
(ii) Caixa N. Crédito	70	12	1	–
(iii) Caixa G. Depositos	183	168	747	3,021
(iv) Banks	459	189	1,355	4,534
(v) Particular sources	192	79	269	1,894
(c) General state budget	23	12	202	18
2. Foreign capital	507	152	244	3,392
(a) Personal	112	152	244	3,076
(b) Credit	395	–	–	316
Total	2,947	997	5,154	26,945

Source: Direcção Geral do Turismo (1986, 1988)

Lago. Meanwhile, indicative of a general increase of interest in leisure and recreational investments, the Elliot Property and Leisure Group of the United Kingdom has opened a new water park at Porches, west of Faro. Probably the largest undertaking is Vilamoura near Faro; the 1,600-hectare site will eventually include four golf courses and a 1,000 berth marina. However, hotels (and similar accommodation) have not been particularly attractive to foreign investors who, even in 1987, only accounted for 13 per cent of total investment in this sector. Instead, the vast majority of hotels are in Portuguese ownership and large hotel groups such as D. Pedro and Torralta subcontract to international tour companies.

While foreign investment was static in the late 1970s, domestic investment recovered rapidly from a low point in 1977, increasing by some 300 per cent per annum. This has involved both personal capital and credit from the banks or other financial institutions in broadly similar amounts. In some cases the investors are industrial companies seeking to diversify their activities—such as the investment by the Petrogal oil group in the Meriden Hotel in Lisbon. Banks remain the leading source of credit but the roles of the Caixa Geral do Depositos and the Fundo do Turismo have also expanded. As much of the tourist industry is small scale, it offers considerable opportunities for small-business formation relying on personal or family savings. This may sometimes include emigrants' use of their remittances, as King *et al.* (1984) noted in Italy. For example, Mendonsa (1983a; 1983b) shows that returnees in Nazaré are more likely than non-migrants to rent rooms to tourists. Although less important than investments in fishing-equipment or transport, almost a quarter of his sample of returned migrants had invested in commercial establishments oriented to tourism. By doing so they have added to the range of 'coping strategies' traditionally adopted in this small fishing-town and have contributed to the general trend towards increasing economic and social polarisation.

6.4.3   Employment

Perhaps the greatest contribution of tourism to the Portuguese economy is in terms of employment. According to the Plano Nacional de Turismo 1986–9, there were some 145,000 jobs in tourism in 1985. Of these 26 per cent were in hotels, *pensões* and camping sites, 70 per cent were in restaurants, 2.5 per cent were in travel agencies and 1.2 per cent were in public sector administration. These data are not entirely reliable for they underestimate employment in car-hire firms, sporting and other tourist attractions, while the figure for restaurants is, at best, a crude approximation. Only the data for accommodation can be considered with any confidence. These show that in 1984, 67 per cent of accommodation-related jobs were in hotels, 19 per cent in *pensões*, and 8 per cent in hotel-apartments. Clearly, hotels are the most important source of jobs in this subsector of the tourist industry.

With the expansion of the industry, employment numbers in the accommodation sector expanded by almost half in the period 1969–86. There has also been a small shift from male to female employment, which were almost in balance by 1984. At the same time—and a clear indicator of the changing structure of the industry—the proportion of non-paid labour diminished from 13 per cent to only 5 per cent by 1984. However, formalisation does not necessarily mean increased professionalisation. While no accurate data are available on this, Cavaco's (1981) study of the hotels in the Costa do Estoril showed that only 16.5 per cent of male and 8.2 per cent of women employees had more than a basic primary school education. Only the larger hotels recruit from the hotel schools.

While employment has increased over time, it has fallen relative to the number of guests. For example, in the 1970s employment per bed in better-quality hotels fell by some 20 per cent (Cavaco 1981). This reflects a shift to self-catering holidays, self-service facilities in hotels and a general substitution of capital for labour in such diverse activities as catering and cleaning. To some extent, the up-market shift in accommodation has contributed to employment expansion, for employment 'densities' (that is, relative to the number of beds) vary by subsector (Table 6.6). The employment ratio for hotels is more than double that for *pensões* with, not surprisingly, the largely self-serviced motels and hotel-apartments providing the fewest jobs. However, there are also considerable variations within each of these types, especially in that five-star hotels provide four times as many jobs as one-star hotels and almost twice as many as four-star hotels. Portugal's strategy of favouring up-market tourism may, therefore, have some beneficial employment effects, although a strategy of mass tourism may have produced a larger global employment figure.

Employment in tourism represents different degrees of formalisation, ranging from full-time work for professionally trained personnel to the single family combining running a small guest house with a number of other activities. Such pluriactivity is relatively common in Portugal (see Lewis and Williams 1986b, for the example of industrial employees). The transfer of savings from waged employment into other activities is quite common, especially in the case of investment in land and agriculture, and Bennett (1986) indicates that some such transfers occur from tourism employment to farming in the Algarve. Furthermore, Lewis and Williams (1986a) have shown that returned migrants in central Portugal also tend to favour investments in cafés, bars and *pensões* as one productive use of their savings. However, according to

Table 6.6   Employment ratios and tourism as a secondary economic activity by accommodation type in Portugal, 1984

	number of jobs per bed	% of those employed in tourism for whom this is a secondary economic activity
Hotels	0.38	0.30
Five-star	0.64	–
Four-star	0.39	–
Three-star	0.30	–
Two-star	0.21	–
One-star	0.15	–
Hotel apartments	0.23	0.24
Tourist apartments		3.88
Motels	0.23	5.96
Holiday villages		0.88
Pousadas	0.76	2.96
Inns	0.35	–
Pensões	0.15	17.77
Four-star	0.20	–
Three-star	0.14	–
Two-star	0.14	–
One-star	0.13	–
Total	0.28	3.80

Sources: Direcção Geral do Turismo (1986); Instituto Nacional de Estatísticas (1985a)

official statistical returns, only some 3.8 per cent of those employed in tourism regard this as their secondary activity. Given the tendency to underestimate double job-holding in official statistics, and given that many may regard their tourism job as a primary activity, the true extent of pluriactivity is probably far greater. Nevertheless, even these limited data indicate the importance of pluriactivity (17.7 per cent) for those engaged in running *pensões*. In these cases tourism-related work is but one element in the overall household strategy.

6.5   Tourism and regional development

Portugal has a highly polarised regional economic strcuture (Lewis and Williams 1981; Ferrão 1985). The two main nodes of industrial development are the Lisbon and Oporto metropolitan regions, although there is also a substantial spread of small and medium-sized firms throughout the coastal region, between Braga and Setúbal. Agriculture is poorly developed, especially in the interior, and only now is there any significant shift to more intensified and commercialised farming geared to exports. Tertiary activities are probably the most polarised economic sector, and both private and public services are highly centralised in Lisbon and, to a lesser extent, Oporto.

Tourism development partly reinforces this broad pattern of uneven regional development, in that it is heavily concentrated in the littoral region, where the Costa do Estoril is effectively part of the larger Lisbon metropolitan region.

However, tourism also serves to modify the nature of the general regional pattern, especially in the case of Madeira and the Algarve which have not shared in the recent industrialisation of the country. These two districts obtained 6.5 per cent and 32.7 per cent respectively of all investment in hotels in 1981, considerably greater than their share of all investment (Secretaria de Estado do Turismo 1986). While precise data are not available on the contribution of tourism to these regional economies, there is some fragmented information on the regional features of the industry.

6.5.1   *Tourism and regional income*

Estimates of the income generated by tourism are not available at *distrito* level. However, the regional government in semi-autonomous Madeira does provide estimates of the receipts earned by tourism from both national and foreign visitors (*Madeira* 1982). These show that receipts increased from 288 million escudos in 1967 to 898 million in 1974 and 4,140 million in 1982 (de Freitas 1984). In the 1970s and 1980s tourism earnings almost equalled Madeira's visible trade gap and exceeded emigrant remittances.

Tourism is of exceptional importance to the Madeiran economy, but is also highly significant in some parts of mainland Portugal. The distribution of visitors (especially of foreigners) and of up-market tourist facilities suggests that tourism is of greatest absolute economic importance in Lisbon and Faro *distritos*. While the relative importance of tourism in Lisbon *distrito* is likely to be limited, it is of considerable importance in the Costa do Estoril sub-region. However, it is undoubtedly of enormous relative importance in the Algarve where manufacturing industry is little developed (only 28 per cent of total employment in 1981, compared to 47 per cent employed in the tertiary sector). Tourism can be of considerable importance in particular communities. For example, in Nazaré, other than formal tourist businesses, about half of all households had rooms to let. These provided, on average, an extra $500 in income at a time when mean annual household income was only $3,160 (Mendonsa 1983b, p. 228). The ownership of housing is therefore crucial in the ability to share in the benefits of tourism, and serves to exclude many lower income households from these.

6.5.2   *Regional employment in tourism*

The employment data for hotels, *pensões* etc., confirm that the economic benefits of tourism are highly concentrated. Of a total employment of 32,899 in this sector, only four *distritos* have more than 1,000 and together they account for three-quarters of all the jobs: the Algarve has 30.8 per cent, Lisbon 25.9 per cent, Madeira 12.9 per cent and Oporto 5.5 per cent. In contrast, several interior *distritos* have less than 400 persons employed, with Beja having the exceptionally small number of 89 (Figure 6.4a). The importance of tourism employment in some regions is underlined by the percentage of all jobs which are in the accommodation subsector. In Madeira and the Algarve, 5 per cent and 8 per cent, respectively, of all employment is in hotels or *pensões*, while in no other *distrito* does the proportion exceed 1 per cent.

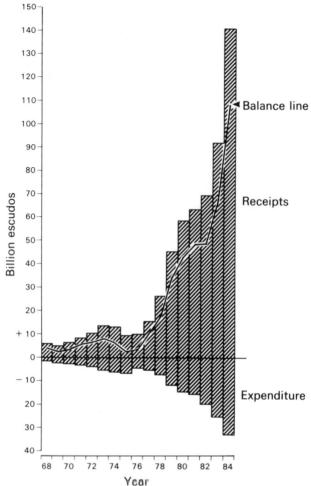

Fig. 6.3 International receipts from and expenditure on foreign tourism in Portugal, 1968–84

Source: Direcção Geral do Turismo (1986)

This broad pattern of regional employment can be further disaggregated to take into account employment densities and seasonality. These are effectively conditioned by the types of tourist attracted and the types of accommodation available. Employment densities are considerably higher in Madeira, Faro and Lisbon than in the rest of Portugal, with ratios of 0.32–0.37 being recorded in these areas. This reflects the less pronounced seasonality in these areas, generally higher bed-occupancy rates, and the relative importance of higher-quality accommodation. The data on seasonality show a very complex pattern (Figure 6.4b). However, Madeira has a notable lack of seasonality, with only a 1.9 per cent difference in employment levels between January and July. Lisbon also has a year-round tourist industry and only has a seasonal employment shift of 7 per cent. In contrast, Faro has rather more peaked seasonality in the tourist industry and has an employment gain of 29.9 per cent in the summer.

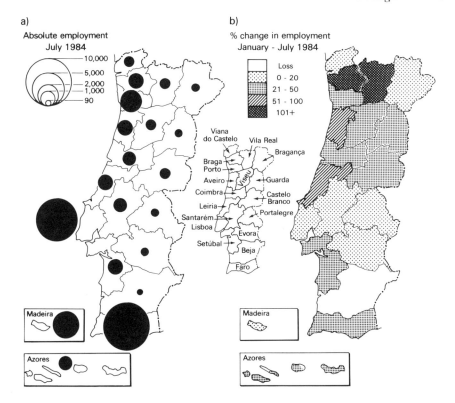

Fig. 6.4   Employment in Portuguese hotels, *pensões*, etc.: (a) absolute
employment, July 1984; (b) percentage employment change,
January–July 1984

Source: Instituto Nacional de Estatístícas (1985a)

The remaining *distritos* have highly variable employment shifts ranging from
−4.3 per cent in Beja to 123.1 per cent in Vila Real. While there is no obvious
explanation for these variations, they do tend to be greater for the central and
northern coastal *distritos* which would be expected to have increased tourist
activity in the summer. Other aspects of the regional distribution of employment are discussed in Lewis and Williams (1988).

6.6   Tourism policies in Portugal

The transformation of the Portuguese tourist industry has been accompanied
by major shifts in the priority attached to it in government policy. Thus in
1952, one traveller commented that

the Portuguese government has little time to spare for encouraging tourists. I say this
because their official Tourist Office, under the control of the Secretary of Information,
is a distinct contrast with the offices of most other Western European countries.

Outside of Lisbon, in fact, with the exception of Tomar and Estoril, the visitor would, I suggest, do better to seek independently for advice rather than at the local information office (Cooper 1952, pp. 193–4).

Within a decade this had changed markedly, as was evident in the emphasis given to tourism development in the Intermediate Development Plan and the Fourth Development Plan in the late 1960s and early 1970s. The greatest priority was given to attracting foreign tourists and to developing up-market tourism, and credit was made available to build the hotels which could facilitate this.

Over time, a comprehensive organisation has been created within the Secretaria de Estado do Turismo to develop Portugal's tourist industry. As of 1987 this had five divisions: the Direcçao Geral do Turismo, responsible for international relations, for tourist information and with administering (licensing, etc.) the supply side of the industry; ENATUR, a public enterprise responsible, amongst other things, for managing the *pousadas*; the Fundo do Turismo, responsible for financial assistance; the Instituto Nacional de Formaçao Profissional, responsible for professional training, including the tourism schools at Lisbon, Faro, Oporto and Funchal; and the Instituto de Promoçao Turística, established in 1987 to be responsible for promotion abroad. It has eight foreign offices as well as a number of other representatives. Other than promotion and co-ordination, the most important role of the Secretaria is that of financial assistance. The Fundo do Turismo has both financial and fiscal measures at its disposal. There are four main financial aids: direct loans at low rates of interest (these vary regionally, favouring less-developed areas such as the Douro Valley); subsidisation of bank loans, which may be for up to a value equivalent to two-thirds of the fixed assets of a project; outright grants (not used in practice); and, since 1987, they act as a channel for European Regional Development Fund (ERDF) grants for up to 50 per cent of the costs of a project. The main fiscal measures are designed to give tax relief on investment. When first introduced in 1957, the relief could extend over 25 years, but since 1983 it has been limited to total tax exemption for 7 years, followed by 50 per cent exemption over a further 7 years. This was particularly important in the development of new hotels during the 1960s boom. Together, these measures constitute a considerable degree of financial aid. In contrast, government investment in essential infrastructure—such as water, waste treatment and roads—has tended to lag behind demand, especially in the Algarve. This has been somewhat ameliorated recently, especially with the availability of European Investment Bank and ERDF assistance to build new roads, extend airports and provide improved water treatment plants in Madeira and the Algarve.

In recent years there has been a reassessment of policy and the rush to attract foreign tourists has been somewhat modified. The *Plano Nacional de Turismo* 1986–9 set out four major objectives for the industry:

1. To increase tourism so as to contribute to the balance of payments by
    (a) increasing external receipts;
    (b) increasing earnings, and
    (c) increasing foreign investment.
2. To contribute to regional development by
    (a) creating priority zones for tourist development;

(b)developing spa towns; and

(c)implementing measures which favour regional development.

3. To contribute to the quality of life in Portugal by

(a)increasing domestic tourism;

(b)increasing agritourism;

(c)increasing *turismo de habitação*; and

(d)supporting social tourism.

4. To contribute to conservation of the national and cultural heritage by

(a)organising a more balanced use of space between tourism and other needs;

(b)protecting the natural environment, especially flora, in the littoral;

(c)defining the optimum numbers of tourists in particular areas;

(d)protecting regional and urban traditional architecture;

(e)preserving monuments; and

(f) developing artisanal crafts and supporting folklore.

This is a wide-ranging set of objectives but, despite the apparent conflicts between some of the aims, the government has decided not to prioritise them. As such, it is difficult not to believe that the greatest weight will tend to be given to the first objective—if only because of national economic necessity. However, other developments can also be expected, especially in terms of tourism in rural areas. The *turismo de habitação* programme (involving rural houses of great character) already has 1,500 bed-spaces available and in 1987 there were an estimated 84,000 overnights in these. Elsewhere, there are specific projects to develop rural tourism, as in the north-east Algarve, a zone which lost approximately 50 per cent of its population between 1950 and 1981 (Faisca 1985). Rural tourism is now being promoted in this isolated area as a means to encourage artisanal crafts, and upgrade social and physical infrastructure, as much for the benefit of the local inhabitants as for the potential tourists (Pinto 1984).

6.7 Conclusions

The rapid development of Portuguese tourism in the 1960s and early 1970s also saw a transformation in the nature of the industry. Domestic tourism and spa tourism gave way to foreign tourism and beach tourism, attracting a higher-income segment of the market than neighbouring Spain. Demand slumped badly in the mid-1970s and recovery thereafter was hampered by economic conditions in the major markets. Nevertheless, by the mid-1980s there was evidence of very rapid expansion at rates unrivalled elsewhere in Western Europe, apart from in Greece. Tourism currently accounts for about 6 per cent of GDP, employs well over 200,000 persons and is a vital element in international trade.

The industry has developed very unevenly between regions and there are distinct regional specialisations. In absolute terms, tourism is most important in Lisbon and this reinforces existing structures of regional inequality in Portugal. In contrast, the considerable absolute and relative importance of tourism in Madeira and the Algarve partly modifies the low level of overall development in these regions. However, even in these cases, the tourist industry adds on new layers of inter- and intraregional polarisation rather than contributing to a generally more spatially equitable distribution of growth.

Not surprisingly, the current major policy concerns are to secure a more even 'spread' of the industry, in terms of market segmentation, seasonality and geographical space. Increased reliance on the UK market is a concern because of the problems of overdependency on a volatile market (highlighted by the bankruptcy in 1987 of two companies—Biggles Travel and Jetwing—which sent tourists to Portugal) and because of the low-spending propensity of British visitors. Moutinho (1982) is amongst those who urge more selective promotion to diversify the market and to attract more high-spenders from countries such as the United States. Greater temporal spread is also being sought, especially for the Algarve, particularly in the 'shoulder' months. In this respect, UK visitors—with a distinct preference for winter holidays— make a welcome contribution to a more even distribution of visitors between seasons. Finally, an attempt is being made to attract foreign visitors to lesser-known regions, such as the Costa Verde of the North. Rural tourism, *turismo de habitação* and agritourism are also being promoted so as to encourage the spread of tourism to the interior.

Of the three major regions, Madeira currently faces the greatest problems. Climatic and topographical conditions make it difficult to expand the tourist industry either *in situ* or intraregionally. In contrast, the Algarve still offers considerable scope for further development. Although there is mounting concern about the environmental problems associated with the industry, further rapid growth is likely. This will probably involve more investments in water-based and other recreational facilities and intraregional shifts from the centre to the less-developed western and eastern zones. The latter will be encouraged by the opening of a bridge at Castro Marim, providing much easier access from Spain. Finally, Lisbon offers opportunities for further development of cultural and urban tourism. There may also be some scope for expansion of business and conference tourism, and the acute lack of specialised conference facilities is being partly remedied by the construction of two new conference centres in the city and at Estoril. Tourism seems likely to continue to increase in importance in Portugal, but further expansion will also renew the pressures on regional economic imbalance and on the environment.

Note

1.   The primary sources of data on tourism in Portugal are the *Estatísticas do Turismo* published annually by the Instituto Nacional de Estatísticas (INE). There is usually a one to two-year delay in the publication of these data. The *Estatísticas do Turismo* volumes report both the results of special annual censuses of hotels, camping sites and other forms of accommodation, and data collected by other bodies on the entry of foreigners at frontier crossings and the receipts and expenditures recorded by the banks. Normally the reports cover the number of border crossings, the average length of stay, the origins of the tourists, the total number of bed-nights by accommodation type, and the number of employees on 31 January and 31 July. The precise level of detail available varies by sector but is greatest for hotels and boarding-houses. These are categorised according to their official classifications and information is presented on the numbers of rooms/beds available, employment, receipts and expenditure, investment, overnights, length of stay and rates of occupation. In most cases the data are disaggregated to the level of the eighteen mainland *distritos* (districts) and the Azores and Madeira, but in a few instances the

finer spatial disaggregation of the *concelho* (municipality) is used.

In addition, the Direcção Geral do Turismo publishes an annual report, *O turismo em 19 . . .* While mainly based on the data collected by INE, this sometimes presents the information in a different format, including some previously unpublished materials from INE. It also draws on specially-commissioned sample surveys such as those on the holidays of the Portuguese and the nature of foreign tourism, presents information on holiday tours, travel agents and *turismo de habitação*, and reviews recent legislation.

7 Switzerland: structural change within stability

Andrew W. Gilg

7.1 Brief history of tourism in Switzerland

Even though Hannibal dented the myth of the Alps as an inhospitable barrier full of trolls and fearsome weather, it was not until the days of the 'Grand Tour' that Switzerland began to be seen as a desirable place to visit in its own right. Even then the Alps were but a scenic backdrop on the journey between the great cities of Europe. Gradually, however, more and more travellers and, more importantly, writers, poets and artists began to appreciate the scenic beauty of the Alps and the pre-Alpine lakes, and visits specifically to Switzerland began to be popular from around 1850 onwards, with Thomas Cook leading the first package tour in 1863 (Gilg 1983). At the same time, climbers began to extol the Victorian virtues of climbing the hitherto unscaleable peaks of the Alps. By the end of the nineteenth century, another dimension to Swiss tourism was added with the growth of specific resorts devoted to health cures, notably tuberculosis. By the early twentieth century, therefore, the Swiss tourist industry had been created, based on three types of tourism: first, genteel tourism in the grand hotels to be found along the shores of lakes like Geneva and Thun, for example the resorts of Montreux and Interlaken; second, mountaineering centred in Alpine valley resorts like Grindelwald and Zermatt at the foot of the picturesque peaks of the Eiger and Matterhorn, respectively; and third, health-based tourism centred in resorts like Leysin and Davos which were normally placed on sunny Alpine terraces above the foggy lowlands.

Until this time tourism, apart from mountaineering, had been mainly passive, but gradually the delights of winter sports became apparent, often to the younger, healthier members of families taking health cures. To fill the empty hours, they invented skiing and ice-skating as new types of recreation. However, in spite of the development of new ways of scaling the mountains in the inter-war years, for example *téléphériques*, winter sports remained the preserve of the wealthy. In the post-war years however, as Table 7.1 shows, increasing affluence and mobility allowed millions rather than thousands of people to participate in winter sports, and it was this development above all that was to change the nature of Swiss tourism (Schilling *et al.* 1974).

The first twenty-five post-war years set the scene for modern Swiss tourism, for since 1970 the overall number of nights spent in Switzerland has remained fairly static (Table 7.1). However, within the overall pattern of static demand, a number of changes have occurred which have concerned the Swiss,

Table 7.1   Some changing aspects of Swiss tourism, 1935–85

	Beds (thousands)	Bed-nights (millions)	Occupancy rate (%)	Percentage of bed-nights accounted for by Swiss		
				All year	Summer	Winter
1935	137	12	24	56	51	58
1945	108	14	36	84	57	86
1955	116	20	44	47	54	44
1965	178	29	45	39	43	37
1975	223	31	39	40	42	40
1985	225	34	42	41	43	40

Source: Office Fédéral de la Statistique Suisse (1986a, pp. 92–3, 111 and 113)

namely an increasing emphasis on the winter season, thus causing new problems of seasonality; more visits to the Alps rather than the lowlands, thus creating regional imbalances; more self-catering and thus a lower economic multiplier; more emphasis on foreign capital and foreign ownership of second homes, leading to inflation of land values; and finally, an increasing reliance on foreign workers, with a subsequent leakage of the economic benefits of tourism. These changes and the problems they have created are now considered in more detail.

7.2   National trends in Swiss tourism since the 1970s

The gradually changing nature of Swiss tourism is shown in Figure 7.1a, which demonstrates a slow but steady rise in the supply of beds since 1977, but only in the self-catering sector, which includes second homes, camping and caravanning and youth hostels. The demand for these beds has, however, changed erratically, with a rapid increase in the early 1980s being followed by a fall in the mid-1980s (Figure 7.1b). Much of the change can be accounted for by a rise in the number of foreigners in the early 1980s (Figure 7.1d), although they still account for fewer nights than the Swiss, and to a lesser extent by a greater increase in self-catering in the early 1980s (Figure 7.1c). In the late 1980s there has been a general levelling off, both of supply and demand.

In general, the major problem of the last 10 years has been an expansion of supply in excess of demand (see Table 7.2), since the overall supply of beds has risen by nearly 25 per cent but the overall level of demand has only risen by 9.5 per cent. These overall figures, however, conceal major structural changes. First, in the hotel sector, demand has continued to grow both internally and externally, while the supply has been slightly reduced; none the less, significant spare capacity exists. Within the hotel sector, the health cure trade has declined in both supply and demand. Second, in the self-catering sector a major increase in supply has not been matched by a similar increase in demand, with the shortfall in camping and caravanning being particularly severe. Third, the demand for self-catering has increased at almost twice the rate as the demand for hotels. Fourth, and finally, a significant difference emerges between Swiss and foreigners in the type of demand for self-catering, with the Swiss favouring camping and caravanning, while the foreigners have deserted this sector.

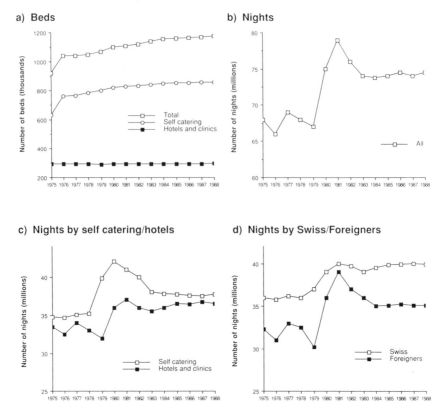

Fig. 7.1   Changes in the structure of tourist accommodation in Switzerland, 1975–88

Source: Office Fédéral de la Statisique Suisse (1986c, p. 4) and Swiss Tourism in figures 1989 (Swiss Tourism Federation)

If the picture in 1985 alone is examined, some further structural features of the Swiss tourist industry emerge. First, hotels only account for 24 per cent of beds but for 46 per cent of bed–nights, and a still larger proportion (57 per cent) of all foreign bed–nights. Second, camping and caravanning account for 23 per cent of beds but only for 9 per cent of bed–nights. Third, self-catering apartments and second homes are more popular with Swiss than with foreigners.

In economic terms, the most significant feature is that the largest single number of bed–nights is accounted for by the 20.3 million bed–nights (out of a total of 75 million) spent by foreign tourists in hotels in 1985, since this is the sector with the largest multiplier and the highest potential for foreign currency earnings. However, there are significant expenditure differences between national groups of foreign tourists (Table 7.3). For example, the West Germans account for nearly half of all bed–nights but less than a third of hotel nights, and only spend 66 francs per night. The countries whose tourists spend proportionately more nights and money than their share of visitors would suggest are the United States and Japan and, to a lesser extent, the United

Table 7.2 Capacity and demand in Swiss tourism, 1975–85

Type of Accommodation	Capacity (beds)			Swiss demand (thousands of nights)			Foreign demand (thousands of nights)			Total demand (thousands of nights)		
	1975	1985	Change (%)	1975	1985	Change (%)	1975	1985	Change (%)	1975	1985	Change (%)
Hotels	277,366	275,365	– 0.7	12,915	14,013	+ 8.5	18,987	20,320	+ 7.0	31,902	34,333	+ 7.6
Clinics	6,797	6,785	– 0.2	1,306	1,295	– 0.8	370	366	– 1.1	1,676	1,661	– 0.9
Sub-total	284,133	282,150	– 0.7	14,221	15,308	+ 7.6	19,357	20,686	+ 6.9	33,578	35,994	+ 7.2
Self-catering apartments and second homes	320,000	375,000	+17.2	13,500	13,935	+ 3.2	8,000	10,065	+25.8	21,500	24,000	+11.6
Camping and caravanning	185,000	270,000	+45.9	3,550	4,913	+38.4	2,650	2,044	–22.9	6,200	6,957	+12.2
Group lodgings	122	214	+75.4	4,400	5,051	+14.8	1,800	1,912	+ 6.2	6,200	6,963	+12.3
Youth Hostels	9,308	7,925	–14.9	301	334	+11.0	451	475	+ 5.3	752	809	+ 7.6
Sub-total	636,308	866,925	+36.2	21,751	24,233	+11.4	12,901	14,496	+12.4	34,652	38,729	+11.8
Total	920,441	1,149,075	+24.8	35,972	39,451	+ 9.9	32,258	35,182	+ 9.1	68,230	74,723	+ 9.5

Source: Schweizerischer Fremdenverkehrsverband, *Fremdenverkehr in der Schweiz*, Berne, 1986, p. 16.

Table 7.3   Pattern of tourism by foreign visitors to Switzerland, 1985 and 1988

Country of origin	Number of bed–nights (millions)	(1988)	(%) of total	% of bed-nights in hotels spent by foreigners	Expenditure per head per night (francs)	Mean length of stay all accommodation (days)
FRG	14.4	(14.8)	41.0	29.5	66	5.0
USA	3.6	(2.3)	10.0	16.1	98	2.2
Netherlands	2.8	(3.0)	8.0	3.9	68	5.8
UK	2.7	(2.6)	8.0	9.5	79	4.0
France	2.5	(2.5)	7.0	7.9	73	3.6
Belgium	1.8	(1.9)	5.0	3.9	58	5.7
Italy	1.2	(1.5)	3.5	4.5	83	2.3
Japan	0.5	(0.6)	1.5	2.5	108	1.8
Austria	0.5	(0.5)	1.5	NA	75	NA
Spain	0.4	(0.4)	1.0	NA	97	NA

Source: as Table 7.1, pp. 23, 26, 42 and 48 and Swiss Tourism in Figures 1989, p. 7.

Kingdom, Italy and France. Significantly, 92 per cent of US visitor-nights are spent in hotels, compared with 76 and 71 per cent for visitors from Italy and the United Kingdom, but only 43 per cent for those from the Federal Republic of Germany. Consequently, the fall in their number in 1988, probably due to alarm over terrorist attacks on transatlantic air routes, was a blow for Swiss tourism. Billet (1984) has analysed the accommodation and seasonal preferences of foreign visitors to Switzerland and has found that non-Europeans stay almost entirely in hotels, compared to a fifty-fifty breakdown for Europeans in hotels and apartments respectively. Seasonally, the summer season is most popular with Americans (74.7 per cent) and the British and Dutch (66 per cent) while the West Germans and French have weaker preferences (54 and 50 per cent, respectively) for this season.

Seasonally, the summer is still the peak season, with July and August accounting for nearly 23 million of the 74 million annual bed-nights, while the two peak winter-sports months—February and March—only account for 16 million nights (Table 7.4). Within the accommodation sectors hotels have a fairly even seasonal rhythm with 10 of the 12 months being near to the monthly average of 3 million bed-nights. In contrast, self-catering shows wild swings around the mean of 3.2 million bed-nights, with peaks of 7.5 million and 5.0 million in August and February, yet with three months—May, November and December—falling below 850,000 nights. Another difference between the two sectors emerges in the mean length of stay, with apartments registering 9.8 nights and hotels only 3.0 nights (Office Fédéral de la Statistique Suisse (OFSS) 1986a, p. 26).

The structure of the accommodation industry also provides some interesting contrasts. In the hotel-type sector, 7,167 establishments existed in 1985, with 4,122 hotels, 2,928 guesthouses and 117 motels with a mean number of beds of 57, 11 and 61 respectively. Since 1960 the number of beds in hotels has risen by around 35 per cent and the mean number of beds per hotel by nearly 40 per cent. However, the number of hotels, after rising by 10 per cent by the mid-1970s, has since fallen to only 97 per cent of the 1960 level. At the same time the quality of accommodation has been improved, with the number of rooms

Table 7.4   Seasonal pattern of bed-nights in Switzerland, 1985 (millions)

Month	Hotel	Self-catering	Total
January	2.49	4.07	6.56
February	3.11	5.03	8.14
March	3.39	4.43	7.82
April	2.66	3.34	6.00
May	2.45	0.85	3.30
June	3.26	1.70	4.96
July	4.32	6.44	10.76
August	4.45	7.50	11.95
September	3.80	2.70	6.50
October	2.73	1.86	4.59
November	1.40	0.24	1.64
December	1.94	0.55	2.49

Source: as Table 7.1, p. 25

with bath or shower quadrupling during the period 1960–85; even so, in 1985 only 82 per cent and 60 per cent, respectively, of rooms in the two most expensive price bands (over 90 francs and between 70 and 89.50 francs) had baths in 1985.

The decline in the number of Swiss hotels is partly accounted for by a growing tendency for the Swiss to own or use a second home for Swiss holidays but to take a hotel-based holiday abroad. In 1985, for example, 6.3 million foreign trips were made by the Swiss, up 5 per cent from 1984, with 60 per cent travelling to the Mediterranean and 28 per cent to the rest of Europe (OFSS 1986b, pp. 8–9). Another reason is the perception by foreigners that Switzerland is an expensive country to visit, and this appears to be true when the falling value of the pound sterling against the franc is considered; for example, from around 10 francs to the pound in 1970, to around 3.20 in the early 1980s, 2.70 in the mid-1980s, and only 2.40 in 1987. To some extent this is ameliorated by the fact that inflation in Switzerland has been significantly lower than in the United Kingdom and the Federal Republic of Germany, two of the main sources of visitors.

Although Switzerland is a small country, it embraces five types of tourist area within its borders: first, the lakeside resorts of the Alpine fringe, for example Interlaken and Locarno; second, the Alpine resorts based on winter sports and summer activities, for example St Moritz and Zermatt; third, the big cities of Berne, Geneva and Zurich; fourth, the Jura, with mainly Swiss-based winter sports; and fifth, the central lowland or Mittelland which is mainly a transit area but includes some major tourist destinations such as Gruyère. The next section analyses the regional pattern of Swiss tourism in more detail.

7.3   The regional pattern of Swiss tourism

There are significant regional variations in the supply of all beds for tourism (Figure 7.2). First, the most important areas are the two mountain cantons of Valais and Graubünden, closely followed by the lakeside/mountain canton of

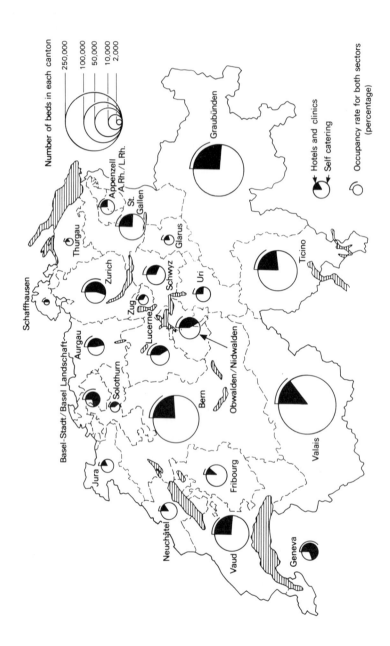

Fig. 7.2 Supply of tourist accommodation in Switzerland, by canton and type of accommodation

Source: Office Fédéral de la Statistique Suisse (1986c, insert leaflet)

Berne, and then by the lakeside cantons of Vaud and Ticino. The only other significant areas are the two big cities of Zurich and Geneva and the small cantons in the Swiss heartland around Schwyz and Lucerne. Second, hotel beds are in the majority only in three cantons—Basel, Zurich and Geneva—reflecting the business nature of accommodation in these areas. Hotels are also significant in older resort areas like Lucerne and Obwalden/Nidwalden but, in most of the main areas, self-catering accommodation dominates, notably in the large modern resorts in canton Valais, such as Crans-Montana and Verbier. Third, occupancy rates are high in the main city areas and in a few lakeside areas, for example, Lucerne, but occupancy rates are very low—20–40 per cent—in the main mountainous areas.

Another important feature is that many hotels do not actually open—for example, in canton Valais only 662 of the 805 hotels in the canton were open in 1985 (OFSS 1986c)—and in terms of beds only 74.6 per cent of the potential capacity were actually available in 1985. The regional distribution of all beds is hard to estimate, since the number of beds in apartments and other forms of self-catering may be available only on an adventitious basis. However, the OFSS has conducted two surveys of tourist accommodation in Switzerland in 1978–9 and 1986, sending out questionnaires to each of the 2,678 political communes to ask them to record the number of tourist beds available. The results for each commune have been published (OFSS 1986c) and, in essence, show major concentrations in Graubünden and Valais. Economically, the most interesting feature of these two cantons is that Valais has an estimated 178,000 second homes, of which only 87,000 are let. This represents a major under-use of fixed capital and a positive misuse of the resources of land and public services.

The supply of tourist beds is of course only half of the tourist equation, for Figure 7.2 has already shown that occupancy rates vary widely across Switzerland. More details about the regional demand for tourist beds are shown in Figure 7.3. First, the pattern of demand is dominated by the four cantons of Graubünden, Valais, Berne and Ticino. Second, hotel bed-nights are much more important than the supply of hotel beds in Figure 7.2 implies. Of the major cantons, only in Valais are self-catering bed-nights more than half of the total; in the other big three, the share is almost half. Third, the percentage of Swiss amongst the tourists varies widely but without any simple pattern, dominating in the less spectacular but pleasant landscapes of the Jura and north-east Switzerland, but falling to a tiny share in Zurich and Geneva. Fourth, summer tourism is now dominant only in the lake and mountain regions, notably Berne and Ticino. Fifth, and finally, three countries dominate the influx of tourists from abroad, namely the Federal Republic of Germany, the United States and the United Kingdom but the two large neighbouring countries, France and Italy, send surprisingly few tourists.

In terms of the regional evolution, the position of mountain resorts as the main provider of hotel bed-nights has been further strengthened since 1970 with the shares of both lakeside and large-city hotels falling behind. By 1986 mountain resorts claimed 39.0 per cent of all hotel bed-nights compared with 21.7 and 18.1 per cent respectively in lakesides and the big cities (OFSS 1987). In 1950, the mountain resorts claimed 34.0 per cent and the lakesides and the large cities 26.0 and 20.3 respectively (OFSS 1986c).

The growing importance of the mountain resorts and, in particular, the Bernese Oberland, Valais and Graubünden was recognised as long ago as 1976

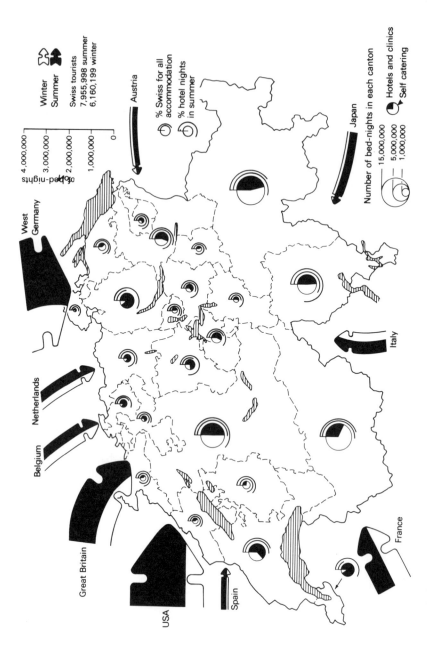

Fig. 7.3 Demand for tourist accommodation in Switzerland by canton and type of accommodation, by season, and by nationality

Source: Office Fédéral de la Statistique Suisse (1986c, insert leaflet and pp. 67 and 73)

by Rougier (1976) who attributed their growth to the increased demand for winter sports holidays. This conclusion has been supported by Baumgartner (1983) who has shown how Valais, Graubünden and the Bernese Oberland had become the most visited regions in 1983, compared with 1955, with visits to Valais and Graubünden growing by factors of ten and eight respectively. These changes can be attributed to the development of modern, high-altitude, purpose-built resorts in Valais and in Graubünden, where the capacity for skiing has grown by a factor of around ten, compared with a factor of only three in the lower altitude resorts of the Oberland. Hannss and Schröder (1985) have visibly demonstrated this regional shift to the south-east and south-west by mapping out the capacity of ski lifts in each resort. On their map, Crans-Montana, Verbier and Zermatt in the south-west, stand out as larger resorts than the traditional Oberland resorts, as do Laax, Lenzerheide, Davos and St Moritz in the south-east. Of these large resorts, Crans-Montana, Verbier, Laax and Lenzerheide are relatively new resorts, reflecting the regional shift of winter tourism away from the Oberland. In terms of major regions, Graubünden leads with 29.6 per cent of capacity. Valais follows close with 28.7 per cent and the Oberland is next with only 14.7 per cent.

All this growth in the high Alpine regions contrasts starkly with the experience of one of Switzerland's neglected tourist areas, the Jura. In this region Rumley (1983) has found very low winter occupancy rates of between 8.9 and 28.4 per cent, a low length of stay (between 2.4 and 3.5 days), and a high percentage of Swiss tourists (between 63.2 and 86.4 per cent). The summer figures are only marginally and not consistently better, with occupation rates ranging from 12.5 to 40.3 per cent, and a lower length of stay (from 1.8 to 2.7 days), reflecting the transit nature of tourism in the area.

The experiences of the Jura and the Oberland show that tourism in Switzerland does not always lead to population growth and economic prosperity. Even in those regions where tourism has expanded rapidly in recent years (Boesch 1983), there have been growing doubts about its overbearing importance and fears have been expressed about the dangers of a monostructural economy. For example, Elsasser and Leibundgut (1982) have identified ten regions centred on Crans-Montana, Zermatt, Saas Fee, and Grindelwald which are dangerously dependent on tourism. One measure they use to identify overdependence is the ratio of yearly tourist nights to local people, as shown below:

Tourist Cantons		*Tourist resorts*		
Switzerland	12:1	Ascona	157:1	(lakeside resort)
Ticino	28:1	St Moritz	210:1	(winter sports)
Valais	58:1	Grindelwald	267:1	(all year round)
Grisons	85:1	Arosa	347:1	(winter sports)
		Saas Fee	800:1	(winter sports)

The remainder of the chapter examines briefly the economic and social impact of tourism on Switzerland, before considering in more detail these impacts by using two major studies of Swiss tourism, the 1979 'Concepts' report and the 1987 Krippendorf report.

Table 7.5   Changes in the Swiss balance of trade in tourism, 1975–85
(millions of francs)

	Receipts	Expenditure	Balance
1975	5,380	2,870	2,510
1977	6,070	3,330	2,740
1979	5,640	4,160	1,480
1981	7,840	5,260	2,580
1983	8,630	5,940	2,690
1985	10,120	7,280	2,840

Source: Office Fédéral de la Statistique Suisse, (1986a, p. 10)

7.4   The economic and social impact of tourism in Switzerland: some introductory remarks

Tourism is very important to the Swiss economy. In summary, it is the third most important export, provides 170,000 jobs directly and, with indirect employment, accounts for 14 per cent of the working population, while it contributes 8 per cent of the Swiss national income (Watson and Watson 1983). Receipts from tourism accounted for 10.12 billion francs in 1984, against expenditure of 7.28 billion francs, giving a surplus of 2.84 billion francs, or 435 francs for every Swiss national (OFSS 1986d). However, this balance of trade did not really grow between 1975 and 1985 and, indeed, as in the late 1970s (Table 7.5) when Swiss tourism was hit by the world recession and by the high value of the franc, the late 1980s has seen a similar reverse. For example, in 1988 receipts were 10.3 billion francs and expenditure was 8.8 billion francs, giving a surplus of only 2.5 billion (Fédération Suisse 1989). None the less, tourist receipts did grow between 1975 and 1985 at the same pro rata rate as the first and second Swiss export sectors, engineering and chemicals.

Within the tourism sector, hotels and international transport are by far the most important earners. Self-catering accounted for less than 10 per cent of receipts in 1985. It is not surprising that Switzerland, in its position at the crossroads of Europe, should cater for considerable transit traffic and thus derive over 13 per cent of tourism receipts in 1985 from this sector. In this respect, Switzerland has always been in something of a cleft stick: if it fails to build enough facilities to prevent holdups, then travellers will bypass the country, but if it improves its transport facilities, travellers can speed through the country in only a couple of hours, spending little if any money.

Even when foreigners do spend a night in Switzerland, their rate of expenditure is very much dependent on their type of accommodation, for, as Table 7.6 shows, hotels only account for 59 per cent of bed-nights but for a massive 82 per cent of expenditure with an average expenditure per night of 194 francs (OFSS 1986d). By contrast, self-caterers account for 29 per cent of bed-nights but for only 13 per cent of expenditure, spending on average 65 francs per night. The lowest spenders, not surprisingly, are campers and caravanners, and youth hostellers.

Turning to employment, it is not surprising that hotels should be a major employer in Switzerland. For example, in 1985 the hotel sector employed 67,343 men and 35,000 women (OFSS 1986a). When the restaurant sector is

Table 7.6 Breakdown of foreign visitors' expenditure in Switzerland by type of accommodation, 1985

Type of Accommodation	Bed-nights (thousands)	Expenditure (millions of francs)	Expenditure per night (francs)
Hotels	20,686	4,007	194
Self-catering apartments	10,065	652	65
Group lodgings	1,912	94	49
Camping and caravanning	2,045	91	45
Youth hostels	475	18	39

Source: As Table 7.5, p. 17.

added the total rises to 174,600 (OFSS 1986e). However, although tourism is a major employer, it can also be said to be a major contributor to three of the four labour market problems of the Swiss mountain economy, as defined by Elsasser and Leibundgut (1983): branch-line factories; a high ratio of foreign workers; a high ratio of women workers; and seasonality. Of these, clearly the last three could be due to tourism. First, foreign workers account for one worker in three in the hotel and restaurant sectors (Table 7.7). This is largely because few Swiss want to work in jobs which are seen as poorly paid and offering poor career status, and also because Switzerland has a very low unemployment rate.

Turning to the number of female workers, women account for just over half of all hotel workers, and this proportion is remarkably consistent across the regions, across the three main areas of Switzerland, and also across the three main types of resort (Table 7.8). From these figures the proportion of women workers in tourism does not seem to pose any problem of imbalance in any Swiss labour market area, except in the context of the rather conservative Swiss society in which a proportion of over 50 per cent of women workers is perceived as a problem *per se*. In terms of seasonality, just taking into account foreign workers, only 34 per cent were employed on a permanent basis in 1984, but 57 per cent were either employed on a temporary or a seasonal basis.

Table 7.7 Employment in Swiss hotels and restaurants, 1979 and 1984

Nationality and type of work	1979		1984	
	Number	(%)	Number	(%)
Swiss	113,100	68	106,600	61
Foreigners	53,700	32	68,000	39
Permanent jobs	19,000	11	23,300	13
Temporary	15,300	9	17,500	10
Seasonal	15,900	9	21,100	12
Daily commuters	3,500	2	6,100	3
Total	166,800	100	174,600	100

Source: as Table 7.1, p. 3.

Table 7.8   Employment in Swiss hotels, by gender and by area, 1985

Area	Total	Women Number	Women (%)
Switzerland	67,343	35,039	52
Grisons	9,276	4,737	51
Bernese Oberland	6,115	3,279	54
Central Switzerland	7,304	4,162	57
Ticino	5,096	2,545	50
Valais	5,179	2,791	54
Lake Geneva	10,009	4,252	42
Mittelland and Zurich	10,261	5,135	50
Jura and North-West	8,410	4,731	56
Eastern Switzerland	5,695	3,430	60
Alps	34,674	18,302	53
Mittelland	27,705	14,046	51
Jura	4,965	2,712	55
Mountain resorts	16,699	10,093	60
Lakeside	14,753	7,536	51
Big cities	12,127	5,301	44

Source: As Table 7.1, p. 69

The geographical simile of seasonality is regional or local overdependence on tourism. Examples are provided by canton Valais and Grindelwald in canton Berne. In canton Valais (Bertrisey 1981) the share of the primary sector in employment fell from nearly 80 per cent in 1888 to under 10 per cent in 1975, while the share of the tertiary sector rose from 10 per cent to 50 per cent during the same period. In the meantime, the share of the secondary sector had also grown from 10 per cent to 40 per cent. By 1980 industry employed 12,395 men and 2,701 women, a very different male:female ratio to the figures for tourism (see Table 7.8). In contrast, tourism in 1979 employed 9,976 directly, 15,738 indirectly, and 6,053 partially; half of these were women. This gives a figure of 31 per cent of the working population of Valais being totally dependent on tourism, even when the 6,053 who are partially dependent on tourism are left out.

It has been calculated that the resort of Grindelwald as a whole is 57 per cent totally dependent on tourism, 35 per cent indirectly dependent, and only 8 per cent independent of tourism (Krippendorf 1987). Services provide the biggest income to the resort, with just over 55 million francs, and about 40 per cent of this comes directly from tourism. Hotels provide just over 50 million francs in income, with nearly 100 per cent being derived from tourism. The next biggest earner is building, with nearly 30 million francs, of which 20 million francs is indirectly dependent on tourism. Transport, self-catering, and administration each bring in between 11 million and 18 million francs, most of which is directly or indirectly dependent on tourism. Agriculture only brings in less than 5 million francs, but this is mostly independent of tourism.

In a study of Crans-Montana, a major resort in canton Valais, it has been emphasised that tourism may divide generations (Darbellay 1979). As Table 7.9a shows, Crans-Montana, like other resorts in canton Valais, grew rapidly via the medium of self-catering apartments with a twelvefold increase in self-catering beds between 1950 and 1974, compared to a mere doubling of hotel beds. Table 7.9b shows that this has led to a dual economy for farmers, with half their income coming from secondary activities. However, farming only accounted for 10 per cent of all income in the canton and, although tourism only accounted for 17 per cent of income on a crude division, Crans-Montana is dependent on tourism for probably three-quarters of its income when direct and indirect effects are taken into account. Finally, Table 7.9c shows major age differences between employment sectors. Young people have been the main beneficiaries of the tourist boom in terms of employment, although it must not be forgotten that many farmers have cashed in by selling their land at very high prices (for example, at 400 francs per square metre in the resort centre, compared to 3–5 francs for good meadowland).

The impact of tourism on local farm communities is therefore hard to assess and tends to be erratic, depending on whether the farm is near a resort centre and, even then, on whether the farmer has been able to develop or sell his land for tourism. In either case, tourism has usually destroyed local culture and values (White 1974) and it is not surprising that farmers outside the resort centres have shown a great reluctance to offer their buildings for farm tourism. For example, Leimgruber (1985) reports that Reider could find only 171 farms offering farmhouse holidays in Switzerland compared with over 26,000 in Austria, while letting a chalet only ranked fourth as a source of non-farm income and only accounted for 4 per cent of total income. This was despite the fact that only 13–15 weeks were needed to cover basic overheads and interest, and that the gross margin of letting three fully furnished flats for 19 weeks compared equally to that from keeping either 125 pigs or 20 beef cattle for a year.

7.5   Evaluation of the Swiss tourist industry

The analysis of the role of tourism in the Swiss economy, past and present measures to guide its future pattern, and tourism's wider impacts on Switzerland relies heavily on two recent reports on Swiss tourism: first, the so-called 'Concepts' report produced on behalf of the government in 1979, and second, the so-called 'Krippendorf' report produced by an eminent academic in 1987. Both reports pose serious questions about the desirability of past tourism trends and even more serious questions about its future.

Switzerland has always been a country reluctant to adopt governmental, especially central government, measures even to guide let alone direct its economy. To do so is anathema to the Swiss view of federalism, local political power and free enterprise. The development of measures to shape the pattern of Swiss tourism has therefore been slow (Commission Consultative Fédérale pour le Tourisme (CCFT) 1979).

The first measures were attempts to protect hotels from the effects of the First World War in 1915. These led quickly to a vote to allow the Confederation to use state finances to publicise Swiss tourism, and the Swiss National Tourist Office was set up for this purpose in 1917. In 1922 the Confederation voted to help pay for the repair of hotels, and in 1933 it took over the collection of tourism statistics from the private sector. Faced with a dramatic drop in visitor numbers during the Second World War (see Table 7.1), in 1947 the

Table 7.9   Some features of economic and social life in Crans-Montana, Canton Valais

(a)   Changes in accommodation 1950–74 (number of tourist beds)

Year	Hotel	Other	Total
1950	2,200	2,200	4,400
1960	3,300	9,500	12,800
1970	4,000	14,000	18,000
1974	4,500	25,500	30,000

(b)   Source of income by economic sector (millions of francs)

Sector	Main Income	Second Income	Total	(%)
Agriculture	3.2	3.0	6.2	10
Construction	12.5	0.3	12.8	22
Industry	4.3	0.1	4.4	7
Commerce, banking	9.8	0.2	10.0	17
Tourism	9.9	0.4	10.3	17
Administration	14.8	0.3	15.1	26
Other	0.1	0.1	0.2	1
Total	54.6	4.4	59.0	100

(c)   Employment by age and by economic sector (per cent)

Age	Primary	Secondary	Tertiary	Total
20–29	1	39	60	100
30–39	4	44	52	100
40–60	16	36	48	100
60+	37	23	40	100

Source: Darbellay, C. (1979, pp. 488, 491 and 493)

Confederation gave itself powers to assist sectors of the economy, including tourism, mainly through loans and rarely through subsidies. These economic aids were increased in the 1970s.

This principle is central to the first of the modern measures for aiding tourism, the introduction in 1974 of LIM regional aid (the Loi Fédérale sur L'Aide en Matière d'Investissements dans les Régions de Montagne). Under this measure regions throughout the Alps and the Jura (see Gilg 1985) can qualify for a regional development investment loan to develop their infra-structure. Such a loan can cover a new road to a ski resort, or a new ski lift, and thus can indirectly benefit tourism. By the end of 1985, fifty-two regional development programmes had been approved, and within this framework 2,209 individual community projects had been financed with funds totalling 612 million francs (OECD 1987). The 80.6 million francs spent in 1985 were allocated as follows: tourist transport 20.6 million; sports facilities 42.4 million; swimming pools 9.2 million; museums 7.5 million; and conference centres 0.9 million. Tourism was clearly the main beneficiary of the aid.

The LIM measure was the first official response to a growing crisis in Swiss tourism in the mid-1970s as the number of bed-nights became static (see Figure 7.1 and Table 7.1) as a result of the oil crisis, competition from Mediterranean tourism, modern and often cheaper ski resorts in France and Italy, and the strength of the Swiss franc. In response to this crisis, the Confederation set up a Federal Consultative Commission on Tourism in 1973 (CCFT 1979), doubled federal funds for aiding tourism between 1969 and 1977, and admitted that the encouragement of tourism was a Federal task which served the interests of the whole country and not just the tourist regions, an essential move in a country where intercantonal jealousies can often wreck any attempt to introduce new national policies.

7.5.1 The 'Concepts' report

One of the main tasks of the Commission was to produce a report for the Confederation on the role of tourism and to propose policy measures. Their 128 page report (CCFT 1979), the 'Concepts' report, is divided into six major sections: an analysis of the present; perspectives for the future; problems; principles and objectives; strategies; and political measures for the confederation.

In their analysis the Commission set out the reasons for the growth in tourism, which included increased income, more cars, more urbanisation (and thus a need to escape stress) and a growing passion for skiing. This had resulted in the rapid construction of hotels, second homes and ski lifts in the 1960s. However, in the early to mid-1970s the first falls in demand were noted, especially in the number of foreigners. The Commission attributed Swtizerland's success up to the mid-1970s crisis to five factors: first, the slogan of The Swiss Tourist Office 'Switzerland works'; second, a safe, liberal and stable country; third, Switzerland's position at the crossroads of Europe; fourth, tradition; and fifth, Switzerland's beauty. The Commission also noted some adverse factors, notably, the decreasing amount of land left for development, the strong franc, a moderate climate, and a reluctance amongst Swiss people to work in tourism.

In spite of these adverse factors, the Commission found that most experts still forecast a doubling of tourism between 1975–2000, with self-catering leading the way. However, the growing pressure of such rapid development on the environment was also recognised and it was forecast that some resorts would have to stop growing by 1990 while new areas would have to be developed. Another problem was said to be the declining attraction of the older resorts in terms of their facilities.

With regard to current problems, the Commission pointed to the issues of seasonality, the high rate of spare capacity, the role of foreign workers, and structural problems within the industry. For example, they pointed out that hotel employment had fluctuated between 71,000 and 45,000 in 1977, and that, out of the total of 90,000 foreign workers in the country in 1977, no less than 41,000 were employed in tourism. In terms of the use of capacity, the report noted that while industry was running at 80 per cent, hotels only used 40 per cent, and *téléphériques* a miserable 23 per cent. The report also pointed out the poor social image of tourist work for the Swiss, and that skiing was degrading some mountain pastures, while there were many conflicts between agriculture and tourism. Finally, the report noted the large number of small hotels (80 per cent had fewer than fifty beds) and, conversely, an over-concentration into a

Table 7.10   Factors providing justification for a Swiss tourist policy

Overall	(a)	Without relaxation and tourism no healthy society can exist
Social	(b)	Recreation makes the daily round more productive.
	(c)	Tourism integrates society and nations.
	(d)	Improves the quality of life in the tourist area.
Economic	(e)	Provides an economic motive to preserve the countryside
	(f)	Integral part of the Swiss economy.
	(g)	Important to balance of payments.
	(h)	170,000 direct employees (5.6% of work force).
	(i)	240,000 indirect employees.
	(j)	When combined this makes 15% of work-force.
	(k)	The only alternative to agriculture in the mountains.
Environment	(l)	Tourism depends on a good environment.
	(m)	Tourism depends on beauty and spiritual value of monuments.
	(n)	So tourism must in the end respect the environment.

Source: Commission Consultative Fédérale pour le Tourisme (1979)

few large resorts (60 per cent of hotel nights were in the twenty largest resorts).

On the basis of these introductory findings, the report offered guiding principles and objectives. The overriding principle was that tourism is a vital attribute of a healthy and sane society. Within this overall principle, the importance of tourism was justified under the headings of social, economic and environmental factors, as shown in Table 7.10. These three linked partial objectives break down to twenty-nine intermediate and partial objectives, as shown in Table 7.11, and into forty possible detailed strategies and 114 recommendations for the future of Swiss tourism.

Finally, the report outlines the powers the Confédération already has and the measures already in force. Although there is no specific legal basis for tourism aid or development in Switzerland, tourism can be encouraged by the Confederation under Article 31 of the Constitution, which allows the encouragement of certain economic activities and the protection of areas whose economy is threatened. Using this Article, the Confederation spent 59 million francs on tourism development in 1977: the most important expenditures were on repayable grants to develop tourist facilities (19.6 million francs) and publicity in Switzerland and abroad (17 million francs). In addition to direct economic aid, the Confederation also promotes tourism through a range of social, economic and environmental measures (see Table 7.12), which are seen as overlapping and complementary. Indeed, the Confederation tends to see its role as co-ordinating the policies of the cantons and the communes, and the policies of individual ministries. This is important for certain parts of the tourism industry where responsibility lies with several subdepartments in various ministries, though in the 1970s the main department in charge of tourism was the *Service du Tourisme* in the Federal Department of Transport, Communications and Energy.

Table 7.11 Objectives for Swiss tourism

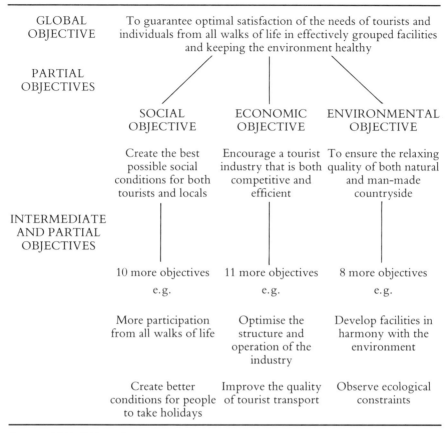

GLOBAL OBJECTIVE — To guarantee optimal satisfaction of the needs of tourists and individuals from all walks of life in effectively grouped facilities and keeping the environment healthy

PARTIAL OBJECTIVES

SOCIAL OBJECTIVE — Create the best possible social conditions for both tourists and locals

ECONOMIC OBJECTIVE — Encourage a tourist industry that is both competitive and efficient

ENVIRONMENTAL OBJECTIVE — To ensure the relaxing quality of both natural and man-made countryside

INTERMEDIATE AND PARTIAL OBJECTIVES

10 more objectives e.g.

11 more objectives e.g.

8 more objectives e.g.

More participation from all walks of life

Optimise the structure and operation of the industry

Develop facilities in harmony with the environment

Create better conditions for people to take holidays

Improve the quality of tourist transport

Observe ecological constraints

Source: as Table 7.10, p. 60

The result of the Commission's report was a list of thirty measures, of which three were urgent, two were supplementary measures in the field of planning, and the remaining twenty-five were measures for the medium term.

7.5.2 *Events in the 1980s following the 1979 'Concepts' report*

In 1981 the Confederation asked government departments and ministries to take due account of the recommendations when dealing with tourism (OECD 1982) and in June 1981 they invited the cantons to co-operate in a similar fashion, especially in the preparation of their detailed plans, the *Plans Directeurs* or Cantonal Land Use Plans (see Gilg 1985).

Elsewhere, as part of long-term research on Swiss tourism, a survey of over 10,000 tourists in 1982–3 discovered considerable loyalty to Switzerland among tourists, with 60 per cent of those surveyed being on at least their fourth visit. Many respondents cited the consistently high quality/price ratio as the main appeal of Switzerland (OECD 1984). Furthermore, in 1984 the

Table 7.12   Summary of the overlapping measures taken by the Swiss Confederation with regard to tourism

SOCIAL	DIRECT	ECONOMIC
	Publicity	
Infrastructure		*Labour market*
Aid for rail, post, roads and other infrastructure	Advice, finance and approval of regional development programmes	Maintaining supply of seasonal workers
	Aid for regional infrastructure for tourism (LIM)	Encouraging the retraining of workers
International		
Relaxation of boundary formalities	Renovation, construction and aid for the purchase of hotels and village facilities	Encourage professional associations
	Collection of tourism statistics	
Promoting the image of Switzerland	Encouragement of tourism planning and research	*Encourage regional economy*
	Concessions for foreigners to buy land	*Campaigns*
		Limitation of excessive growth

ENVIRONMENTAL
Encouraging good land use planning
Protecting the environment

Source: as Table 7.10, p. 113

development fund for mountain infrastructure was increased to 300 million francs, after 73.4 million francs had been spent specifically on tourism projects between 1975 and 1984 (OECD 1985).

The main change in 1984 was, however, the relocation of the Tourism Service into the Federal Economic Department so that measures directly linked with tourism could be concentrated in the single office of the Federal Office of Industry, Arts and Crafts and Labour within that Department (OECD 1985). The new organisation was given the following responsibilities:

1. to formulate tourism policy for the Confederation;
2. to promote tourism via the Swiss National Tourist Office;
3. to supervise and fund hotel loans via the Société Suisse de Crédit Hotelier (SSCH, Swiss Hotel Credit Society);
4. to give financial aid for tourism projects;
5. to contribute to tourism planning;
6. to fund vocational training;
7. to act on the tourism labour market; and
8. to service the CCFT (the authors of the 'Concepts' report) and the 100-strong parliamentary group on tourism in administrative matters.

Finally, with regard to measure no. 7 of the 1979 'Concepts' report, the Confederation voted to increase the annual funding of the Swiss National Tourist Office from 21 million to 27 million francs between 1988 and 1990, and to 31 million francs for the years 1991 and 1992 (Conseil Fédéral 1986). This was in recognition of the need to expand the work of the office in the four key areas of researching potential supply; attracting foreigners to Switzerland; publicising Switzerland; and co-ordinating the supply of tourist facilities. Swiss tourism was also promoted to the tune of some 200 million francs in 1985 by the cantons, communes, and businesses, and by a further 60 million francs spent by local tourist offices. This expenditure, combined with the 10 million francs spent on promotion by the Swiss National Tourist Office, brought total spending on tourism promotion in Switzerland to 270 million francs against receipts of 16,500 million francs (Conseil Fédéral 1986).

Other measures to promote tourism include a scheme run by the Caisse Suisse de Voyage (a co-operative founded in 1939) which gives special cheques to some lower-income families providing an average discount of 16 per cent on the cost of holidays. In 1985, 37,764 people spent a total of 405,930 nights in either the 584 accommodation units belonging to the co-operative in Switzerland, or its 85 units abroad (OECD 1986).

Another organisation, the SSCH makes loans for modernising hotels and resorts, constructing new hotels and purchasing hotels; 16.5 million francs were loaned for these purposes in 1985 (OECD 1986). The SSCH also guarantees loans for these purposes, amounting to another 16.3 million francs in 1985; in turn, 75 per cent of this amount was guaranteed by the Confederation.

Swiss tourism is promoted by a variety of organisations and, in addition to those already mentioned, the tourist section in the OFSS publishes monthly, seasonal, annual and occasional reports on all aspects of tourism, often in great detail and sometimes down to the commune level (Anon. 1983). Swiss tourism is thus very well served by accurate, up-to-date and highly disaggregated tourism data. Also important are the Swiss Travel Service, the Swiss Federation of Tourism, the Institute of Tourism and Travel in the University at St Gallen, and the Institute for Tourism and Leisure at the University of Berne.

Indeed, the most recent report on the state of Swiss tourism was produced by Jost Krippendorf at the Institute in Berne. This report provides an excellent way of concluding the analysis of Swiss tourism.

7.5.3 *The Krippendorf report*

The Krippendorf report (Krippendorf 1987) is a summary of a series of research projects conducted on behalf of the Man and Biosphere programme of Unesco and is based on the Pays d'Enhaut, Aletsch, Grindelwald and Davos. It identifies seven possible benefits of tourism:

1. Tourism can stop the exodus of people from the mountains. However, the Mittelland grew by 60 per cent between 1940 and 1980, compared to 49 per cent for Switzerland as a whole and only 20 per cent for the mountain areas. Moreover, within the mountains some areas experienced rapid growth while others declined rapidly. For example, Zermatt and Crans-

Montana grew by 209 and 78 per cent respectively, while Pays d'Enhaut and Val de Travers declined by 15 and 18 per cent respectively.

2. Tourism can create employment, which in 1985 was estimated at 350,000.
3. Tourism can create revenue as the balance sheet below clearly shows (figures in billions of francs):

Expenditure of foreign tourists	10.1
Expenditure of Swiss tourists	6.4
Total expenditure	16.5
Less taxes, imports and interest	approx 3.0
Net tourist revenue	approx 13.5
Expenditure on new tourist facilities	approx 4.0
Total revenue from tourism	approx 17.5

4. Tourism can finance infrastructure through a positive chain reaction.
5. Tourism can improve an area's facilities.
6. Tourism can help to support agriculture and contributes to the management of the countryside.
7. Tourism maintains the character and customs of mountain areas and people.

These possible benefits are countered by seven possible dangers of tourism:

1. Tourism can lead to a fragile monostructural economy.
2. Tourism can develop in an uncoordinated way, can undermine the real economy and may only use 20 per cent of its capacity. It is a poor economic use of land compared to industry.
3. Tourism can waste land, and 1 square metre of cultivable land is lost to tourism every second. In addition, a hotel bed requires five times less land (30 square metres) and is used three times as often as an apartment bed (160 square metres).
4. Tourism can spoil the countryside; for example ski pistes reduce forage yields by 4–18 per cent, floral diversity by 15–18 per cent, and can lead to avalanches.
5. Tourism can lead to overdependence on foreign investment, with decisions being taken abroad. This is anathema to the Swiss with their fierce local pride in their commune.
6. Tourism can undermine the authenticity of local culture, and replaces it with 'commercial folklore'. There is also a growing problem of alcoholism among young people with nothing to do between seasons in tourist resorts.
7. Tourism can generate social tensions and accentuate disparities of wealth, both locally and regionally.

The report tries to produce a balance sheet of the benefits and the dangers. It emphasises that it is not a case of all or nothing. Instead, the choice is one of adjusting the costs and benefits to produce a balanced tourism, and to stop growth at the point at which tourism yields diminishing returns. In a devolved political economy it is, of course, difficult for small communal councils to prevent the goose from laying one too many golden eggs, but Krippendorf notes that there are signs that local populations are beginning to think in terms of a self-sustaining rather than a continuously developing tourism.

Krippendorf then addresses the future pattern of tourism and, following one of the themes of the 1979 'Concepts' report, he advocates that tourism be based on the growth of quality rather than quantity. In this scenario tourism is increased by extending the season; offering new types of tourist experience; limiting tourist traffic, notably low-spending day-trippers; aiding local suppliers of self-catering apartments and hotel rooms; stressing the quality of life in the resort; introducing new services for conferences; offering training schemes for tourists in rural skills and crafts; widening employment opportunities through the use of electronics and by combining jobs between sectors; and finally by aiding agriculture. These provide some of the major challenges to be faced by Swiss tourism in the future, and it remains to be seen if Krippendorf's self-sustaining, qualitative tourism with higher added value can be realised.

7.6   Concluding remarks

Swiss tourism has had a long and successful history, and has adapted its product and its geography to changing demands. However, the last section has shown that the Swiss have been aware of a large number of danger signals since the mid-1970s when the post-war era of expansion first faltered. For example, Watson and Watson (1983, p. 15) in their comparison of Swiss and Scottish tourism concluded that: 'Many Swiss experts in tourism and planning . . . now see tourism as an industry with an inherent tendency to overdevelop and become self-destructive, and also destructive of the local community if not firmly controlled.' In a different argument Grafton (1984), in a study of growth centres in Switzerland, said that tourism should not be seen as a panacea for development—even though most local economic plans advocate that it should be the main focus for development—because of its low multiplier, its reliance on foreign and seasonal workers, and its limited spread effects. These problems are also confirmed by Swiss authors, and, for example, de Hanni (1984) notes the problems of one-sided labour markets; rising land costs; continual fluctuation of the population; and threats to the continuation of mountain farming. He argues that the quality and quantity of tourist development must be controlled in the interests of regional development. However, he also notes a lack of political will in the communes to curtail further development and concludes that 'the chances for an effective control of tourist development are not likely to improve significantly in the near future' (p. 668).

Future developments will be crucial, for not only do the local communes have a stake in the future of Swiss tourism, but so does the population of the world, since the Alps are a world-wide resource. In this respect, their future use is of widespread concern, not least to those of us who are addicted skiers (like the author, who is a minor if frequent element in the statistics used in this chapter). However, the future looks bleak. The potential for the further expansion of winter sports is enormous for, as Barbier (1978) has shown, the number of skiers is still small; for example, 5 million West Germans (8.0 per cent of the population), 2.5 million French (4.7 per cent), 2.0 million Italians (3.6 per cent), and only 400,000 British (0.7 per cent). However, even given such low participation rates, resorts are already crowded, lift queues are long, and rarely does the skier find the 800 square metres of space around him which, according to psychologists, are necessary to create the feeling of well-being from skiing (Sinnhuber 1978). In the late 1980s the impact of several poor snow seasons, possibly brought on by the 'greenhouse' effect, and a rapidly growing 'green' movement have brought about a general antipathy to further tourism development. This has led to a virtual moratorium on further ski resort development, the construction of second homes or the installation of snow-making machinery.

The route proposed by Krippendorf therefore appears to be the one being espoused by the Swiss, namely an expansion of quality at the expense of quantity, even if this means that many people have to join a long waiting-list for a holiday in Switzerland in the years to come. The alternative is a long-term destruction of the resource itself, from which nobody would gain.

Note

1. This represents about 10 per cent of Swiss national revenue and about 10 per cent of foreign revenue in the balance of payments.

8 Austria: contrasting tourist seasons and contrasting regions

Friedrich Zimmermann

8.1 National tourist trends

8.1.1 The framework of the social environment

Important changes in the social and demographic composition of potential visitors have caused a demand in Austria which is significantly different from the generally positive development of international tourism. This section outlines some of the essential social features which provide the framework for the dynamics of the tourist market, as outlined below. These have had a considerable influence on the problems of the industry at all levels.

A number of elements have been identified in the literature on social change (Agricola 1982, Eggeling 1981, Krippendorf 1984, Opaschowski 1982, Österreichische Raumordnungskonferenz 1985, Papson 1979; Prognos 1982; Stamm 1984). These include:

1. The move to shorter working hours;
2. dynamic development of the right to holidays;
3. a high level of private transport;
4. improvements in real income, with the creation of a 'new middle class';
5. a tendency to saturation in the consumer sector;
6. manifold employment problems;
7. new mediums of communication; and
8. a number of related social changes.

All these developments, which are associated with post-industrial society, have had a lasting effect on the structure of tourism in Austria, but several specific characteristics should be emphasised. First, the emergence of unemployment has mainly affected those social classes which are predominant in Austrian summer tourism, that is, the lower (to middle) classes. Unemployment, low wages, reduced overtime, etc. have had a lasting effect on their family budgets and, consequently, on the resources available for holidays.

Second, in demographic terms, the visitors are likely to include fewer young people, more single households, and not only more but also more active senior citizens. These processes have had a strong negative effect on summer tourism in Austria. The last two groups, in particular, have a considerable degree of independence and flexibility in holiday-making. They have relatively low travel expenses, compared with those incurred by a household consisting of several persons, and there is, therefore, a tendency to travel by air to more distant holiday regions, thereby bypassing Austria. Language is not really a barrier any longer, not even for the elderly, because the level of travel experience has risen considerably. Furthermore, destinations in southern Europe guarantee better weather and are more likely to provide settings which comply with young people's cravings for freedom and adventure. In this respect, Austria has quite a poor image amongst young people.

Third, other social changes — which may be summed up by such phrases as 'greater demands on quality', 'a higher body consciousness', 'more thirst for adventure, entertainment and club atmosphere' and 'stronger environmental consciousness' — have also had a negative effect on the traditional structure of Austrian tourism. Many of these changes result from increasing saturation of general household consumption. Increased surplus income has become available for purposes such as travelling, but aspirations have also risen with respect to the standards of living expected when on holiday. This results in increasing demands for quality, and the tourist trade — which has lagged behind these general developments — has suffered losses in terms of both image and of demand.

A similar situation arises where greater demands for adventure need to be satisfied or where increased 'body consciousness' requires a particular supply response; tourist areas need to develop adventure experiences for sports or for fitness purposes if they are to check the 'overflow' of tourists to competing areas. Austrian tourist resorts have sometimes been slow to respond to such challenges.

Finally, a word is necessary about ecological consciousness. As a clear expression of changes in values and standards, increasing attention will have to be paid to the environment. One may expect that in future the quality of the environment will be a (or even *the*) essential criterion for tourists when they take decisions on where to spend their holidays. Thus far, only a small beginning has been made in the process of reorientation which is necessary in the field of tourism supply. There is still a need for a shift from current preoccupations with short-sighted profit-maximising considerations to greater ecological consciousness in planning and development.

8.1.2   *Foreign demand as a dynamic component*

Among international destination countries, Austria has a very distinctive market profile, in terms of the origins of its tourists.[1] Austria's special position in the international market stems from two particular features. One is the extremely high share — 76 per cent — of foreigners in the total of about 115 million overnight stays per year. By comparison, the proportion in Spain is 66 per cent, in Switzerland 46 per cent and in Italy 29 per cent. Second, there is a very high level of dependency on guests from a single country of origin, that is, the Federal Republic of Germany, which accounts for two-thirds of all foreign overnight stays in Austria. In Spain, Switzerland and Italy the comparable values are around 40 per cent.

What are the consequences of this exceptional level of foreign dependency? The very high percentage of foreigners, which has a positive effect on both the tourist trade and the national budget, is not a problem as long as there are no major difficulties in the world economy, such as the sectoral or the regional

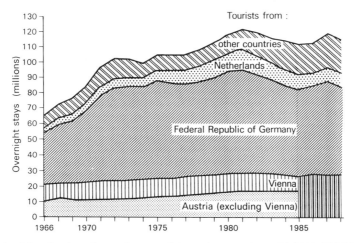

Fig. 8.1   The foreign dependency of Austrian tourism, 1965/6–1988/9

incidence of recession and employment. In other words, as long as the values, standards, incentives, and so on, of this very significant element of the market do not change, there are few problems for the Austrian industry. However, any developments of this nature could very considerably affect Austrian tourism.

Even during the early 1970s, foreigners in Austria were referred to as the 'dynamic variable in the system of mass tourism' (Figure 8.1) (Lichtenberger 1976). Nowadays, this assertion is only partly true. Total foreign demand has not only declined more in Austria than in the rest of Western Europe, but the losses have also been discernible at an earlier stage than in other countries (Smeral 1985).

The central problem of the structural changes in demand has been a shift to shorter stays—and, therefore, an essential loss of overnight stays—by guests from the Federal Republic of Germany. Although this group overcame the effects of the 1973–4 oil shock relatively well, they were adversely affected by the general economic and social changes outlined earlier. Until the mid-1980s, there were considerable losses of demand from this group; between 1981 and 1985 the number of overnight stays of guests from the Federal Republic of Germany fell by more than 10 million, although numbers have stabilised since 1986. Above all, there are fewer guests from the large urban centres of north and central Germany (Hamburg, Berlin, etc.) and less summer tourism. However, the net balance is somewhat improved by increasing winter tourism, and growing numbers of tourists from southern Germany visit Austria for short-stay holidays.

There is a similar situation with tourists from the Benelux countries. Whereas the sales strategies initially proved successful in these countries, the effects of recession on the traditional branches of manufacturing have resulted in problems in the labour market, as well as falling real incomes, with a resulting reduction in travel intensity. This has especially affected the social classes with lower incomes, which are a very important element in Austrian summer tourism.

The percentages of tourists from the United Kingdom and France have more than doubled and this is also the case with tourists from the United States; the American share in the tourist market increased mainly after the dollar rose in value in the early 1980s. However, the fall in the dollar exchange rate at the end of 1985 (engineered so as to reduce the deficit on the balance of trade of goods and services), together with the effects of economic recession, as well as fear of terrorism and the impact of Chernobyl, resulted in considerable losses of demand all over Europe in 1986. The number of American visitors to Austria was almost cut in half. Between 1985 and 1989 a new trend is visible: in winter Austria is becoming more frequented by Germans, while in summer increasing numbers from Italy, the United States and Japan are visiting the major cities, especially Vienna and Salzburg.

Domestic demand cannot be ignored in this analysis. In view of the fact that Austria is a small country with a population of only 7.5 million, there is only limited endogeneous demand potential. Furthermore, this is characterised by a very low travel intensity of less than 40 per cent, compared with Switzerland, with 76 per cent, the Scandinavian countries with more than 70 per cent, the United Kingdom and the Netherlands with about 60 per cent and the Federal Republic of Germany with about 55 per cent (Österreichische Raumordnungs-konferenz 1985). In addition, Austrian nationals also have a very strong propensity to travel to foreign countries (involving more than half of all Austrian travellers annually). The Mediterranean regions are preferred, Italy receiving 30 per cent of Austrians, Yugoslavia 22 per cent and Greece 10 per cent (Skolarz 1985).

Summing up it can be said that domestic demand, originating mainly from Vienna, dominates the east of Austria. The share of Austrian guests in the eastern provinces is more than 60 per cent, but in the western region is less than 10 per cent. With a total share of 25 per cent, domestic visitors are not capable of contributing significantly to tourism and certainly cannot compensate for the fluctuations arising from the loss of foreign tourists.

8.1.3   The seasonal rhythm of tourist demand

The Alpine regions have virtually no real competition for winter tourist activities. Together with a growing number of second and third holidays, as well as short trips, and the development of the middle class, this resulted in a continuous growth of demand in winter, with increases of almost 12 per cent per annum between 1966 and 1981. The winter season seemed to have its own development dynamism. Subsequently, the increases slowed to a rate of little more than 1 per cent. This tendency to stagnation, as well as an unprecedented decline of demand in the winter of 1982–3, suggests that the development of the winter season has reached its limits; the mature phase of 'winter sports tourism' seems to have been reached.

In contrast to winter tourism, the summer season, with all its long traditions, has been characterised by strong fluctuations since the beginning of the 1970s. During recent years there have been dramatic recessions (Table 8.1). While up to 1972 there were annual rates of increase of around 7 per cent, subsequently there were losses up to 1978, followed by a short but vigorous phase of recovery. A peak of overnight stays of more than 78 million was attained in the summer of 1981. Thereafter, the following years were characterised by substantial decline, with a resulting decrease in income;

Table 8.1 The seasonal development of tourism in Austria, 1950/1–1988/9

Year	Overnight stays in total (millions)	Percentage share of summer	winter
1950–51	19.22	75	25
1955–56	31.65	78	22
1960–61	50.77	78	22
1965–66	70.15	78	22
1970–71	96.49	76	24
1975–76	105.00	69	31
1980–81	121.30	64	36
1985–86	113.34	59	41
1988–89	122.56	59	41

serious problems followed for the summer tourist industry in Austria. In 1986 overnight summer stays reached only 67 million and, since 1981, they have dropped to a level comparable to 1970. This reversal has had a number of consequences. The tourist product 'summer in the Alps' in its traditional form, no longer seems to be sufficiently attractive given prevailing socio-economic, demographic and social changes; moreover, it is subject to considerable international competition (cf. Baier 1985, Müller 1985, Tschurtschenthaler 1985). This can essentially be generalised for the summer tourism industry throughout the Alpine regions of Switzerland, Bavaria and South Tyrol.

Special attention must also be paid to the problems of these structural seasonal differences because summer season losses are not just restricted to the single-season regions near the lakes. Thus, the region around the Wörthersee lost more than 320,000 overnight stays between 1981 and 1985, the region of the Millstätter See more than 400,000; these figures are equivalent to around one fifth of their maximum number of visitors. The losses also increasingly involve the so-called 'mountain summer' areas in the western provinces. Beside the factors already mentioned, there are other reasons for the negative developments in summer tourism. For example, there has been a loss of attractive countryside for summer activities due to the building of large hotels, cableways, ski slopes, second homes, roads and so on. All kinds of resources (investment, subsidies, publicity, etc.) have been reallocated to the winter season, while the summer season has been increasingly neglected. Even so, there has been some stabilisation of the summer season since 1986 as a result of new marketing ideas and positive environmental effects. The ecological problems of the Adriatic Sea also brought Austria's summer season a renaissance in 1988. With 122.6 million overnights in 1988/9, Austria achieved its best result of the post-war period.

8.1.4 *Modern recreational trends and short-term tourism*

In addition to the seasonal rhythm of the demand peaks of long-term tourism there are also short-term tourism rhythms. This is linked to the growth of day trips and short-term tourism. While this offers some advantages for the winter season, it requires more flexibility in the provision of accommodation and some regions are increasingly faced with the problem of utilisation conflicts.

There is a definite stagnation of travel intensity in the case of the main holidays; main summer holidays are being spent at more distant destinations (mostly on package tours). However, there is also a strong tendency to taking several shorter journeys, and short holidays, especially in winter, frequently are spent in the Alps. Nevertheless, Austria has lost much of its importance as a destination for main holidays; while in 1980 it was still the favourite destination for tourists from the Federal Republic of Germany, by 1985 Austria ranked fourth behind Italy, Spain and Bavaria (Studienkreis für Tourismus 1987a).

It is expected that the future development of short-term tourism in Austria will involve a quantitative increase in the number of day trips and short holidays. Of greatest interest is the development of demand from the Federal Republic of Germany (see also Ruppert and Maier 1970, Ruppert *et al.* 1986; Zimmermann 1985b; 1986a). The industry needs to pay special attention to this fact, especially where there is a danger of utilisation conflicts with long-term tourism. The most significant negative aspects of overlap between short and long-term tourism are summarised below (cf. Röck 1977; Haimayer 1984):

1. High traffic intensity at week-ends, with much noise and exhaust pollution, and lack of parking-spaces for long-term tourists.
2. Damage to the environment caused by visitors who do not identify with the region.
3. On days when tourist numbers reach a maximum, the basic and tourist infrastructures are overloaded (with, for example, long queues at cable-ways, overcrowded restaurants, problems with garbage, etc.).
4. Trying to extend the infrastructure to cope with maximum tourist demand causes economic problems because of the enormous maintenance costs involved and long periods during which the facilities are not fully utilised.
5. Excessive exploitation of the landscape for sports activities, and for construction (for example, to build second homes).
6. Special problems due to second homes and their pressure on the local real estate market.

In spite of some positive aspects, such as a better use of recreational facilities and, thus, higher profitability, it would seem to be advantageous to plan for a development which would separate long-term and short-term tourism. This would reduce the problems for both the people and the landscape, and would help to preserve the quality of recreation of guests, and of the environment for the resident population.

8.2   Regional trends

8.2.1   *A lop-sided distribution*

The distribution of tourism in Austria is extremely lop-sided (Figure 8.2). The majority of guests visit the western provinces; thus the Tyrol, Salzburg and Vorarlberg have 66 per cent of all overnight stays (1986). This concentration has been increasing constantly, from 42 per cent in 1952, through 50 per cent

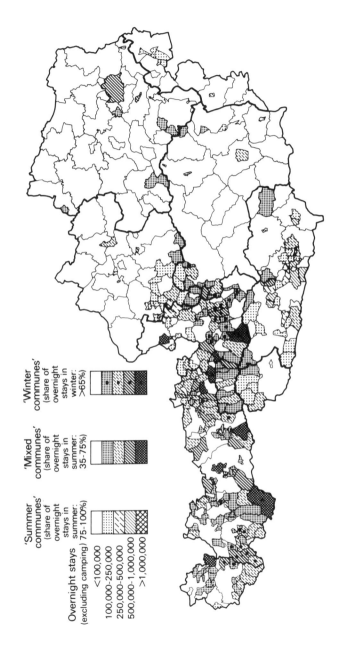

Fig. 8.2 The regional and seasonal distribution of tourism in Austria in 1988–9

in 1962, 55 per cent in 1972 and 60 per cent in 1982. There has been a correspondingly large reduction in the importance of the eastern provinces; they registered half of all overnight stays in 1952, but barely 25 per cent in the mid-1980s. The main areas of demand can be classified into five major types.

The first of these are the *cities*, which includes not only those specially favoured by business or congress tourism, but also those which offer either important cultural activities and sights (Vienna, Salzburg, etc.) or have been able to enhance their image by hosting international sporting events (Innsbruck). These cities, despite the aggregate decline, show very large rates of increase. Vienna ranks fourth in the league table of European city tourism after London, Paris and Rome; it registered about 6.75 million overnight stays in 1989, which represented a rise of more than 5 per cent per annum since 1981. These rates of increase are due to a polystructured demand and world-wide expansion of congress tourism and city tours.

The second main area of demand are the *spas*, which have survived the different phases of tourism development by adapting their very specialist facilities to modern circumstances. They include communities in northern and eastern Austria which are monofunctional spas, visited mainly for health reasons, mainly by Austrian guests (Bad Schallerbach, Bad Hall, Bad Tatzmannsdorf, Bad Gleichenberg). In the Salzkammergut, the Gastein Valley or in Carinthia there is a very strong overlap between, on the one hand, the cure function (with recreation in summer) and, on the other hand, winter sports and a considerably higher proportion of foreign visitors. Examples include Bad Ischl, Bad Aussee, Bad Mitterndorf, Badgastein, Bad Hofgastein and Bad Kleinkirchheim. In these places short-term tourism is also more important.

Lake communities, located in the areas of the Carinthian Lakes and the Salzkammergut, are the third main area. They have long traditions, which makes it difficult to respond to the new structures of demand because of the effects of inertia. The region around the Neusiedler See is a rather special case due to the scenic attraction of the Pannonic-Continental lowland; this is unique in Austria and is suitable for further development.

The fourth main area of demand are the *mountain communities*, which represent the favoured places in the western parts of Austria, characterised by a combination of summer and winter tourism, by a preponderance of foreign tourists, and important demand from short-term tourists. Monofunctional winter-regions are only found in the areas of Arlberg, the Paznaun and the Radstätter Tauern.

The fifth and final main area of demand are the *recreation communities*, which mostly lie either close to the major tourist centres and take advantage of their infrastructure, or they offer alternative, 'small scale', additional supplies. Sometimes they take the initiative in local development, and can generate an important level of demand. Examples include Lungau and Eastern Tyrol.

Besides these there are many mixed types such as transit communities, holiday resorts, administrative and economic centres, and places of pilgrimage. Today these mostly overlap with other tourism functions.

8.2.2   *Regional trends*

The Alpine West

A major consequence of the changing structure of the industry and of trends in free time has been increasing concentration of demand in the west of Austria, together with a strong gradient from the west to the east. In particular, there has been considerable dynamism in regions suitable for winter sports, although this has again diminished over the past few years.

Winter demand has strongly characterised these provinces over the past ten years, and virtually all suitable regions have been affected, although with differing degrees of intensity. Consequently, most locations seem to have been involved in tourist developments and in the future preference should be given to quality improvement rather than to opening up new (winter sports) areas. More immediately, however, an important new trend is that both the Tyrol and Vorarlberg, as well as Salzburg, show large losses of summer demand. This leads to problems in the accommodation sector because the lack of demand in the summer season undermines the profitability of such high-quality supply. Development seems to be shifting in the direction of single-season, winter utilisation, which has negative consequences for the regional economic structure.

The lake regions

The lake regions, which concentrate on the summer season, have been characterised by economic difficulties for many years because the two high-frequency months yield only small net profits. Their situation can be outlined as follows. There are heavy losses of summer demand and, therefore, there is little utilisation of tourist establishments and facilities. This leads to an increasing lack of private funds and there is less investment for improving structures, for restructuring and for innovation, even though the present tourist market (with its short cycles of innovation) requires constant adaptation to new conditions. In consequence, the standards of buildings often lag behind modern requirements, there is a low percentage of rooms with *en suite* amenities, and there are low utilisation rates in the accommodation sector. Furthermore, there is a great shortage of building sites available at attractive locations and this makes adaptation even more difficult, leading to serious supply gaps and preventing the creation of an adequate marketing mix. This again deters many potential tourists and, as a result, the negative cycle is reinforced.

These tendencies in the field of supply have virtually led to immobility. Given the dynamic nature of the competition—in terms of both quantity and quality—this suggests that the future of the single-season lake regions will be fraught with difficulties and it may become increasingly distanced from the international level of tourist supply. Some measures could be taken to improve the product such as improving the marketing organisation, giving more publicity to the clean bathing waters and the environment, and extending the season by means of short-term tourism. Only in this way will it be possible to realise the innovations and investments which are essential to improve the quality of the industry and of tourist infrastructure.

The eastern regions

Stagnation tendencies are particularly conspicuous in eastern Austria, and often these began as early as the 1960s. They are due to a lack of facilities for winter sports, a low share of foreign guests, the increasing importance of day trips, and the growth of second homes. These developments have mostly affected the former holiday destinations of the Viennese (such as Semmering and Wechsel), and the places which attracted the urban population during the summer (for example, Weinviertel). Nowadays, they are experiencing a certain revival as areas for day trips and short holidays. The tendencies to stagnation in eastern Austria have often been accentuated by lack of tourist initiatives, not least because there are a number of alternative sources of income and thus less motivation for the local population to foster the development of tourism. Nevertheless, there are a number of isolated instances of innovation which have been favourable for small-scale developments in peripheral locations.

One aspect which should be given special emphasis is the extremely difficult situation in peripheral regions, which have few income alternatives to agriculture. In these regions tourism development is very often considered to be one possible strategy for reducing disparities. This is often a false assumption as there is frequently a lack of adequate conditions for development and site prerequisites; the consequences are misdirected investments in those tourist infra and suprastructures which are supposed to 'improve' the regional structure (see Zimmermann 1985a).

8.3   The economic importance of the industry

The economic importance of tourism in Austria can be summed up by the following facts: Austria is visited by about 18 million foreign tourists, who spend 95 million nights there each year. It holds sixth place among the world's tourist countries, only being surpassed by France, the United States, Spain, the United Kingdom and Italy. The receipts from international tourism in Austria are about $10 billion per year. This compares with $11 billion in the United Kingdom, $13.8 billion in France, $12.4 billion in Italy, $18.4 billion in the United States, and $16.7 billion in Spain (OECD 1988).

Domestic tourism comprises about 5.5 million guests who also make an important contribution to the total receipts of the tourist industry; Austrians account for 28 million overnight stays per year. More significant is Austria's position within the international market for tourism and also the economic importance of the industry when looked at in terms of average tourist receipts per inhabitant. In 1988 Austria was the leader with $1200 per season, clearly ahead of Switzerland ($800), Spain ($380), Italy ($230) and Greece ($210).

What is the role of tourism in the labour market? In all kinds of accommodation and restaurants there are about 140,000 employees, 63 per cent of whom are female. In winter the level of employment is about 10,000 persons lower than in summer. The share of foreign workers amounts to more than 10 per cent. There is less empirical information available on the impact that tourist expenditure has on other economic sectors. Based on international comparisons, total employment in tourism-related industries is estimated at about 14 per cent of global employment. On this basis, the share in Austria is approximately 18 per cent, which is equivalent to more than 500,000 employees (Papadopoulos 1987). In this respect, 'direct' employees seem to account for only a quarter of all employees in tourism-related sectors.

Finally, the role of tourism in regional economies can be noted. Investments, carried out by tourist enterprises, mainly benefit other firms within the immediate locality. Some 57 per cent of the total capital expenditure is spent within a distance of 20 km, 34 per cent between 20 and 100 km, and only 9 per cent is paid to enterprises at a distance of more than 100 km. The multiplier effects of tourism are therefore highly localised.

8.4   The economic organisation of the industry

The organisation of the tourism industry in Austria can be characterised as small to medium-scale, while the sources of capital are mostly private and family enterprises are dominant. There has been only limited multinational investment, and venture capital is of little importance within Austrian tourism. The supply of accommodation has developed in response to strong demand pressures dating back to the early 1960s. From an initial number of approximately 200,000 guest beds in 1950, supply increased to about 1.25 million by the late-1980s.

This development is not evenly distributed in respect of either the seasons or the individual types of establishment. While high-quality establishments (five and four-star hotels), with about 135,000 beds in 1989, have developed considerably, and three-star establishments (with 225,000 beds) have experienced a minimal increase, two and one-star establishments, which are predominant in Austria's commercial supply with 320,000 beds, have declined in importance. The letting of private rooms is highly significant in Austria and this is in contrast to Switzerland, where it is of little importance (see Chapter 7). Instead, the supply of accommodation in the latter is based more on traditional hotels, and therefore Switzerland has a better image in some respects. In Austria private establishments have contributed to the diffusion of tourism to peripheral regions and function as an important reserve of accommodation for the peak periods in tourism. It is precisely the letting of private rooms which has been most affected by the losses in the industry. Development, which had been expansive up to the mid-1970s, reached a peak in the summer of 1976 with a total of 470,000 beds and a 40 per cent share of total bed potential. This compares with a share of 25 per cent at the present and the decline, of course, is due to greater demand for quality and rapid development of holiday apartments. The competitive pressure of apartments has caused an adaptation of the existing structure, with units being created out of several rooms, and quality being improved, but it has also caused the elimination of many private rooms from the fierce competitive struggle.

The utilisation rates of the supply of accommodation present an interesting pattern. The rhythmic nature of the level of demand, and the dynamism of winter demand and short holidays, have exercised strong pressures on the adaptation of supply structures. This has led to shorter cycles of innovation, with which the existing stability of the restaurant and accommodation trade can cope only to a limited extent. Figure 8.3 shows a tendency towards better-quality supply, as is inherent in recessive phases while at the same time poorly-equipped establishments have suffered heavy losses. Therefore, the higher-category trade establishments show clear profits, with increases of just under 10 per cent during the winter season.

Developments in the summer season show only slight increases in demand, even in the case of high-quality establishments (around 3 per cent). In contrast, there are large losses in the case of two and one-star establishments, as well as in the number of private rooms. Demand for the latter has changed dramatically and is now little more than one half of what it had been ten years earlier: there were 25 million overnight stays in the summer of 1975 compared to 12 million spaces in the summer of 1989.

This leads to the question of utilisation of bed spaces and, thus, to the profitability of establishments (Figure 8.4). The major feature is that the utilisation of beds in winter, at an average of 44 days or 24 per cent, is still lower than utilisation during the summer season, at 53 days or 29 per cent. Nevertheless there has been a noticeable increase in the winter season, for utilisation in 1975 was only an average of 37 days. By comparison, in the summer season utilisation was much higher in the mid-1970s, with an average of 64 days of full utilisation.

The differentiation according to types of accommodation and standards of quality further emphasises the developments outlined so far (see Figure 8.4). In winter when, as a rule, only the better-quality rooms (those with heating, etc.) are offered, all categories, including private rooms, have experienced increasing utilisation rates of between 5 per cent in five and four-star hotels and 2 per cent

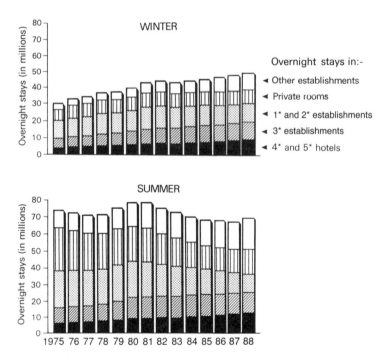

Fig. 8.3 Overnight stays in Austria by type of accommodation and by season, 1975–1988

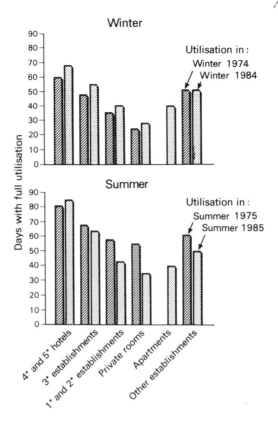

Fig. 8.4 Utilisation of bed-spaces in Austria, by type of accommodation and by season, 1974/5 and 1984/5

in private rooms. In summer, only hotels in the top categories have experienced increased levels of utilisation, at around 2 per cent. With decreasing quality, utilisation rates have declined progressively: by 2 per cent in the three-star category, by 8 per cent in two and one-star hotels, and by 11 per cent in private rooms.

These developments show how the present economic structure has evolved. The profitability of establishments has held up if their quality is adequate and if there is the possibility of two seasons. However, profit margins have decreased elsewhere, and the constant need to innovate to maintain standards requires continual reinvestment. The situation is worse in establishments which do not have a high level of amenities and in tourist regions which have one season only; here, incomes are too low to maintain or to achieve the necessary quality and standards. There is a negative spiral, given that only better quality guarantees an adequate level of demand in modern tourism. As a result there are clear tendencies towards qualification, commercialisation and centralisation.

8.5   Impact on local social structures

In addition to the processes outlined with respect to demand, there have also
been important social changes related to the supply structure in recent years. In
the Alpine area, the development of modern society, with its diverse activities,
has overlapped with Alpine farming and society (Lichtenberger 1979). As a
result, young people, growing up in the context of an assured existence and
having constant contacts with guests, have become very familiar with new
ways and styles of life. Consequently, they are no longer prepared to deny
themselves leisure time and recreation, and to be tied to the traditional ways of
family life and of the village community. Extremely high workloads and
lower net profits have reduced the attractiveness of taking over a family
business in the restaurant or accommodation trade. In some ways, the
situation in the tourist industry in the mid-1980s is similar to that of farming a
few decades ago. An increasing number of low-quality establishments face the
problem of not having anyone willing to take over; for this reason, the owners
of such businesses are often elderly, and consequently have little initiative to
innovate. Loss of quality leads to reduced utilisation and net profits and thus to
even less attractive conditions for working in tourism. Young people go
elsewhere to work, and the native population identifies less and less with
tourism and the guests.

The consequences for the local housing market are of essential importance.
There are significant connections between quality and the perceived image of a
tourist place, and real estate prices. Typically, the average price level of real
estate is extremely high; for example, at Kitzbühel, Mayrhofen in the Zillertal,
Lech and St Anton am Arlberg there were top-price levels of about £250 to
£300 per square metre in 1986. The average price level in leading winter
tourism communes is between £60 and £120, whereas the price of real estate in
less touristic communes lies between £20 and £40. This is the result of the
enormous pressures that seond homes exercise in the local real estate market
and it results in many problems for the young, native population in tourist
regions. In practice they have little chance of being able to buy real estate and
of staying in their home areas. The consequence is that these regions become
overwhelmed with foreign influences (the owners of second homes, seasonal
employees, etc.) which do not identify with the region and the local culture;
there is a real danger that the residents will increasingly lose their regional
identity.

8.6   Policies

8.6.1   *Official tourism policy in Austria*

Under the Austrian Constitution, tourism is the responsibility of the provinces
(*Länder*) which, with the Federal government, shape the framework of tourism
policy. The main objectives are:

1.   to encourage patriotism and regional identity;
2.   to make people more aware of environmental problems;
3.   to ensure that tourism gives guests positive emotional feelings;
4.   to take advantage of old and new segments of the tourist market;

5. to intensify promotional activities; and
6. to improve marketing.

In 1981, the Österreichische Raumordnungskonferenz (Austrian Regional Development Conference), an institution which was founded at the beginning of the 1970s by the Federation, the provinces and the communes (Union of Austrian Communes, Union of Austrian Towns), published the *Österreichisches Raumordnungskonzept* (Austrian Land-Use Concept). This will be phased in over a period of ten years and covers the following aspects of tourism:

1. further improvements in the quality of accommodation;
2. development of special packages to prolong the seasons;
3. special development strategies for peripheral regions;
4. conservation of the environment and local culture, and improved presentation of the cultural heritage;
5. restoration of environmental damage (e.g. recultivation of ski slopes);
6. development of tourism supply without technical infrastructure, the so-called 'gentle tourism', which is more ecologically conscious and pays more attention to the living space and life styles of the native population (Hasslacher 1984; Commission Internationale pour la Protection des Régions Alpines 1985).

Besides this publication, there are further expert opinions on special problems, and on tourist trends and developments, which form the basis for tourism-related political decision; for example, Österreichische Raumordnungskonferenz (1985; 1987a; 1987b).

 Another institution which establishes tourism policy in Austria is the Österreichische Fremdenverkehrstag (Austrian Tourism Congress), which takes place every four years. This is organised by the Ministerium für Wirtschaftliche Angelegenheiten (Ministry for Economic Affairs) and Kuratorium des Österreichischen Fremdenverkehrs (the Board of Trustees of Austrian Tourism), an institution which has the task of discussing and co-ordinating decision-making for Austrian tourism policy. The last meeting was in Baden in 1989 and subcommittees discussed tourism and the environment; man and tourism; education, training and information; the tourism economy; tourist infrastructure; tourist supply; traffic and communications; public relations and marketing special offers; future trends; tourism and culture. For the first time a committee discussed future trends in tourism in Austria (see 8.6.2).

 It is very difficult to estimate the effectiveness of tourism policy in Austria because the influence of the Federal government is very limited compared with the provinces, which operate very different frameworks for assisting the industry. Therefore, much depends on individual effort. Nevertheless, in general terms, increased emphasis has been given to policy in recent years, not least because of growing concern about the selective decline in demand. More promoters and entrepreneurs are making an attempt to take into account official tourism policies and plans in their projects—not least to ensure that they receive official sanctions for these.

8.6.2   Future tourism trends in Austria

In order to provide perspectives on future tourism trends, 168 top experts drawn from all parts of Austria were questioned on the topic: 14 per cent had influential positions either at the federal or the provincial level, 25 per cent were hotel-owners or managers of leading tourist centres, while 17 per cent were professionals or others who were active on a freelance basis; the remainder were qualified personnel in travel agencies, principals of Schools of Tourism, etc. The questioning of the experts was carried out in three stages via anonymous written surveys. The results (statistical evaluations, arguments, counter-arguments) of the previous round were made known at each stage. The advantage of such iterative group-questioning is that the experts are able to reassess their opinions in the light of other views and arguments. The results of the third round yield an optimised estimation of future trends, based on sustained discussion; their introduction at the political and planning levels can influence development in a positive way. The results were presented and discussed at the Austrian Tourism Congress in 1989.

8.6.2.1   The weaknesses and strengths of Austrian tourism

The advantages are seen as:

1. A central location in Europe (close to markets).
2. Varied natural features, a countryside which is still intact, and a healthy climate.
3. Rich in cultural and educational activities.
4. A general understanding of tourism and of the consequences of rising standards of living.
5. Organically-evolved structures with long experience and tradition of tourism.
6. A reasonable size distribution of establishment.
7. Varied supply, high standards, family-run businesses and a lack of tourist ghettos.
8. Positive prerequisites for winter tourism.

The disadvantages are considered to be:

1. A supply with little free-space, and too many regulations and constraints.
2. Too many laws which are hostile to tourism such as taxation, labour regulations, social legislation, the opening hours of shops, hard currency policy, etc. These impede the international competitivity of the industry and excessively burden the relation of price to service.
3. An antiquated supply side which is too conservative, too imitative, lacking in innovation, unspecialised, marketed unprofessionally, and has too many substandard rooms and too many establishments which lack self-financing capacity.
4. Inadequate services for guests and a lack of target-group orientation. Regional and supraregional tourism-marketing has little influence on the presentation of the product (packages, price, quality etc).
5. Careless attitudes to nature with too much scattered building, excessive development and too much traffic.

6. The growth of hostility towards tourism due to excessive exploitation of nature and the social environment, the selling-off of the countryside (homeland), land price increases, damage to village communities because of competitive attitudes and cultural overloading.
7. A negative image due to scandals, political controversy and media treatment.
8. Too little material and immaterial support of tourism by public funds, an indifference to and even hostility towards tourism by federal and, to some extent, provincial political parties.

8.6.2.2   Arguments for continuing (qualitative) growth:

1. The potential of increased leisure-time and of growing numbers of people participating in tourism (e.g., more active elderly persons).
2. Growth possibilities in the winter season, due to an increase in short holidays and the opening-up of new regions.
3. Improvement in marketing (internationalisation, and a policy of filling market gaps).
4. Support of target-group orientated activities (health, culture, education).
5. Restructuring to improve quality, rationalise antiquated structures, and appeal to the intellect.
6. Consciousness of the environment will bring about advantages, as against the disadvantages of competition
7. Growth will increase, and make tourist products more sophisticated and richer in substance.
8. More 'flexible' guests will make an extension of the season necessary, if they are to be properly catered for.

8.6.2.3   The main problems of ecology in Austria are seen as:

1. Exploitation of nature by tourist infra and superstructures, especially winter sports resorts coming to the end of their loading capacity. This has already led to a change in the politicians' views. For example, the province of Voralbert ended the development of new cableways in their Alpine regions in 1978. The most important winter province, the Tyrol, ordered a 'meditation phase' of three years to evaluate the ecological and social problems and costs of tourism.
2. The spoilation of the countryside and land speculation are leading to an expansion of the settlement area into potentially dangerous zones, and to the necessity to regulate the channels and flows of streams and rivers.
3. In this way the potentially disastrous consequences of elemental forces (floods, landslips, avalanches etc.) have increased. Additional factors are the careless exploitation of natural resources, e.g. clearing of woodland, devastation of protective forests, soil damage, opening-up of glaciers for winter sports activities and road-building.
4. The decline of agriculture and, in consequence, a failure to preserve the landscape has impaired the natural scenery which is so important for the summer season. Furthermore, agriculture is losing its function as a stabilising factor in rural social structure, while the harmonious appearances

of villages are being disrupted by non-local structures and architectural styles. Traditional cultures and ways of life are also giving way to a 'Lederhosen-mentality'.

5.   The woodlands are threatened by utilisation conflicts and by the increasing space required by tourism. The decline of the forests is making improved protective measures essential; otherwise their leisure function will be lost in the future.

6.   Waste separation, avoidance and utilisation will be a central problem in the future because refuse pits are meeting with increasingly fierce resistance from local populations.

7.   Transit traffic is a problem within the Alpine area. In several regions the endurance breaking-point has already been reached or passed.

8.   Electricity power-supply companies will have to rethink their policies. The rivalry between ecology-reorientated tourism and the construction of power-stations, the transfer of water from several Alpine valleys to one huge power-station, and the disfigurement of the landscape by high-tension lines are only a few examples of the negative effects which have to be addressed.

The main ecological problems of Austria will have to be solved through legislation, financial support, training measures, the creation of environmental models and co-operation concepts, especially by investment in 'human capital' in the form of consultation to find individual solutions to problems. This is essential because in the year 2000 nature and environment will be the main factors in high-quality tourism.

8.6.2.4   The visitor in Austria in 2000

The new trends in international tourism indicate some of the more important characteristics of the 'visitor 2000'. He or she

1.   compares, is critical, has a marked sense of quality, is cultured, and is predominantly aware of price and service;
2.   has an environmental awareness and buys a life-style rather than a product;
3.   is health-conscious at all levels of life, is a more conscious consumer, prefers light food and natural and dietary products, and is 'more culture- and environment- and less alcohol-orientated'.

There is therefore a polarisation of market segments: on the one hand there are critical and higher-class guests with initiative, and on the other there are passive, 'average-type' guests who need to be entertained.

8.6.2.5   The 'new identity of Austria'

The 'visitor 2000', as well as the international competitive set-up, will require a new identity for Austria. The focal points are outlined below. They are all based on ecological and environmental consciousness, as the bases of future tourism in Austria.

1. Art and Culture: As a land of culture in the centre of Europe, Austria has a high status in the tourism of culture and education. This offers good future opportunities, especially in view of the saturation of lower quality tourism services, and the increasing demand for non-material goods.

2. Nostalgia and Tradition: Greater future orientation to foreign markets, as well as to mega-events such as 'World Exhibition Vienna–Budapest 1995', could turn the disadvantages of traditional tourism structures into advantages. However, qualitative hardware and software will have to be linked with tradition to provide this 'nostalgia-package'.

3. Health: With an increase in the elderly population, health tourism will be stimulated by growing demand for prophylactic measures and other health activities. At the same time, the new health trends will also be boosted by rising environmental awareness and by body consciousness amongst younger generations.

4. Sports: Sporting activities will become more important as a part of the new health consciousness. Given the potential of the 'young seniors' market, growth is likely in 'soft and gentle' activities (cross-country skiing, hiking, cycling, horse-riding etc.), with an emphasis on the enjoyment of nature.

5. Adventure and attractions: There will be a policy of filling market gaps through aiming at adventurous and dangerous sports (mountain–climbing, paragliding, rafting etc.), and this promises dynamic development. At the same time, attractions with a high-quality base and professional know-how (e.g., recreation centre packages with special topics) are also definite future investments. They could help protect nature by controlling the streams of visitors.

A reorientation towards the new tourism identity of Austria will require large-scale specialisation of supply, as well as adaptation to the holiday styles of segmented target-groups. The packages must provide holidays which are as varied as possible, are innovative and sociable and, above all, present a life-style.

Note

1. The most important and most detailed data available concerning tourism in Austria, based on information covering all types of accommodation, are submitted to the Österreichisches Statistisches Zentralamt (Austrian Statistical Central Office). The first level provides data on the development of accommodation and bed-spaces with respect to both quantity and quality, in both the commercial and private sectors. The second level gives information on tourist flows, that is, numbers of tourists differentiated by country of origin, and numbers of nights spent in several types of accommodation. Aggregate-level data are published annually for communities and provinces, along with a survey of development as a whole (latest publication: Österreichisches Statistisches Zentralamt 1988). In addition to the published data, it is possible to get further, more detailed information from the data bank of the Austrian Statistical Central Office.
   Every three years (since 1969) a microcensus surveys the travel habits of the Austrian population, with respect to the travel intensity of main holidays, day trips, short-term tourism and business trips, differentiated by destination, time (month) and length of stay, and type of accommodation used, etc. (the results of

the 1984 survey have been published in Österreichisches Statistisches Zentralamt 1987).

Further detailed information on accommodation establishments (enterprises, employees, etc.) is published by the Austrian Statistical Central Office in different surveys as part of the Austrian census of 1981. The latest detailed and specialised collection of data on commercial tourist establishments (including restaurants and campsites) was undertaken in 1983, with information on employees, turnover, profit, operating costs, taxes and investments, etc. (Österreichisches Statistisches Zentralamt 1986).

Beside the official information sources, there are several individual publications of data available on particular aspects, mainly collected by regional, provincial, federal and scientific departments.

9 The United Kingdom: market responses and public policy

Gareth Shaw, Justin Greenwood
and Allan M. Williams

9.1 Tourism and the UK economy

The significance of tourism to the UK economy is considerable and takes a variety of forms, ranging from its contribution to the balance of payments through to its role in the creation of jobs. It is estimated that the tourist industry has an annual turnover exceeding £10 billion, with foreign exchange earnings of at least £4.1 billion. Both these figures, moreover, compare favourably with the turnover and foreign exchange earnings of major manufacturing sectors such as the UK car industry. In addition, studies by the British Tourist Authority and the Confederation of British Industry have estimated that between 1974 and 1984 the number of jobs primarily dependent on tourism and leisure spending rose from 1 million to 1.2 million (HMSO 1985). This trend is made all the more significant given the sharp downturn in the UK economy since 1979, affecting not only most areas of manufacturing but also jobs within parts of the service sector. In the latter case employment peaked in 1980, after which it experienced a fairly rapid decline with a loss of about 330,000 jobs in two and a half years; however, by 1985 a recovery had restored job numbers back to the their 1980 level (English Tourist Board 1986). Employment has continued to increase during the late 1980s.

It is against this background of wealth and job creation that successive UK governments have developed public policy towards tourism. The early initiatives during the 1960s culminated in the most significant legisation to date, the Development of Tourism Act 1969. This established the British Tourist Authority, together with the three national tourist boards in England, Scotland and Wales. In Northern Ireland a tourist board had been established much earlier through the Development of Tourism Act 1948 (Smyth 1986).

The economic importance of tourism was reiterated in 1974 with ministerial guidelines being issued which stressed tourism's role both in the country's balance of payments and as an aid in promoting regional development. Emphasis was placed on concentrating financial aid in economically fragile areas with untapped tourism potential (English Tourist Board 1978). This regional dimension of tourism policy was further strengthened in England with the introduction in 1974 of tourism growth projects (Heeley 1981).

Further reviews of the tourist industry have stressed not only its potential in regional development, but have also given more weight to its role in job creation. Indeed, during the 1980s the tourist industry has taken on a far more significant role in an economy faced with massive job losses through the restructuring of manufacturing activities. This has led the government to lay considerable emphasis on the employment creation of tourist activities in such publications as *Pleasure, leisure and jobs* (HMSO 1985), and *Jobs in tourism and leisure* (English Tourist Board 1986).

While there is considerable enthusiasm to reap the political and economic benefits offered by tourism, any such strategies face numerous problems. Thus, many changes tend to be induced by factors outside the direct control of the industry, for example, the value of sterling, the cost of oil, political and industrial unrest, and variations in the weather. Furthermore, government policy is also strongly conditioned by the fact that much of the tourist industry is under the direct control of private enterprise. Consequently, the relationship between public concern and commercial activity is at best one of loose co-operation between, on the one hand, the tourist boards and, on the other hand, private operators.

This chapter seeks to explore some of these factors by considering three broad and interrelated themes. The first draws on a wide range of published statistics and presents an analysis of changing trends in the tourist industry. This is followed by an examination of market responses to changed levels of demand and competition. The chapter concludes by considering the role of public policy.

9.2   General trends

9.2.1   *Domestic and foreign tourism*

Historically, domestic tourism received its first real stimulus from the government with the passing of the Holiday Pay Act in 1935, which gave workers one week's paid holiday every year. The subsequent growth to two, and then three weeks' paid holiday saw the annual seaside break become a national institution during the 1950s. By 1970, some 20 per cent of workmen had four weeks' paid holiday per annum, and by 1980 80 per cent of working men enjoyed this amount, while 55 per cent of all workers received up to five weeks. Given this clear trend of increasing leisure time and, in many cases, associated disposable income, it can be argued that the British domestic tourist industry has not benefited to the extent that might have been expected.

There is general agreement that a number of factors have led to complex changes in the British holiday market during the last 25 years. Of particular importance has been the growth of foreign package holidays, partly at the expense of traditional domestic seaside holidays. The domestic market has also increased in complexity because of the development of self-catering holiday accommodation and an increase in the frequency of holiday breaks. This latter trend is related to changes in the duration of breaks but not, as is often supposed, in the direction of a 'boom' in the short-break market. Another significant change is the increase in so-called business tourism, part of which is related to conference travel. Law (1985b) estimated that in 1984 there were around 14,000 international conferences and that the United Kingdom attracted a majority of these. Such trends are also important in contributing to the increasing number of arrivals in Britain of foreign visitors, a fairly buoyant market which has bolstered some sectors of the domestic tourism industry.

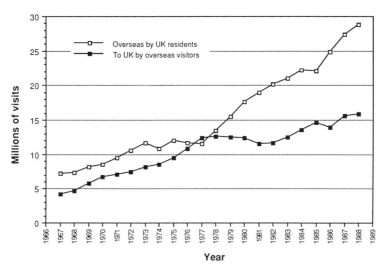

Fig. 9.1   The number of visits to and from the UK, 1967–88

According to many commentators, the United Kingdom's position in relation to international tourism is the most crucial and influential factor in the development of tourism at present (Key Note Report 1986). The United Kingdom is currently a net sender of international visitors rather than a net recipient, a position that has prevailed during the last 20 years (Figure 9.1). The year 1977 marks an interesting exception to this trend; partly because it was Silver Jubilee year, which re-emphasised the importance of cultural tourism, and also because the previous summer was the hottest on record, with 1977 also being a good summer. This stresses the importance of the weather to domestic tourism, a feature which was confirmed in research conducted in the early 1980s among those who had taken a holiday abroad; significantly, more than half agreed with the statement that 'the main reason I go abroad for holidays is the weather in Britain' (Mintel 1985a, p. 83).

The weather does not appear to be a factor influencing foreign tourists visiting the United Kingdom, with the main motivations being cultural and historical experiences, and the attractiveness of the British countryside. Foreign visitors to the United Kingdom have been on the increase and their tourist spending accounts for 50 per cent of United Kingdom receipts (British Tourist Authority 1985). To holiday in the United Kingdom accounts for the purpose of visit of just under half of all foreign visitors, with business visits and visits to friends and relatives accounting for one-fifth each (Mintel 1985b). In terms of the UK position in the international tourism market, the fastest period of growth as a recipient of foreign tourists came in the years 1975–7 (Figure 9.1). Current BTA forecasts predict a growth up to 20 million visits by 1992 (British Tourist Authority 1986).

Visits by UK residents to overseas destinations also rose sharply during the 1970s, an expression of the dramatic increase in leisure and holiday time afforded to the majority of the UK working population. Throughout the 1980s — despite the recession — the result of these trends has been a net deficit on the balance sheet of UK tourism. Although the BTA forecasts some

Table 9.1 Seasonality of foreign visits to the UK and visits abroad by UK residents, 1986 (millions)

Month	Foreign visits to the UK (A)	Visits abroad by UK residents (B)	Ratio B/A
January	920	1,137	1,236
February	726	1,012	1,394
March	914	1,586	1,735
April	1,025	1,623	1,583
May	1,123	2,139	1,905
June	1,164	2,647	2,274
July	1,677	2,896	1,727
August	2,043	3,777	1,849
September	1,134	3,353	2,954
October	1,170	2,300	1,966
November	910	1,400	1,538
December (1985)	811	1,022	1,260

Source: Department of Trade (International Passenger Survey)

reversals of this trend up to 1992, it is unlikely that reality in the medium term will match expectations, despite the emphasis given to the expansion of the foreign visitor market in the United Kingdom.

As Table 9.1 shows, there are some positive seasonality aspects to foreign visits to the United Kingdom, in that they are far less concentrated than visits by UK residents abroad. Furthermore, recent years have witnessed a trend towards a less seasonal pattern of foreign visitors. On the debit side, however, the highest ratios of Britons going abroad to foreign visits to the UK occur in the months of June and September, potentially vital months for the domestic industry. This in turn raises questions about the failure of the UK tourist industry to appeal to its domestic market in these important months, and also highlights the relative failure of domestic tourism policy to persuade UK residents to holiday at home.

9.2.2 Changes in the domestic market

Since the early 1970s there have been striking changes in the domestic market in terms of trips, nights and spend. Figure 9.2 reveals that holiday tourism declined as a proportion of all tourist spend in the United Kingdom from 62 per cent in 1972 to 32 per cent in 1988; over the same period business tourism increased its share from 17 to 25 per cent. Similarly, tourism classified as visits to friends and relatives increased from 5 per cent to 10 per cent, perhaps as a reflection of the increase in the number of people unemployed (British Tourist Authority 1986). It seems that, despite an increase in leisure time and a general rise in disposable income, the UK domestic holiday market is in decline.

Domestic tourism in the early 1970s was characterised by young people and those in skilled manual occupations. By the mid-1980s it still patronised in the main by younger people, but members of professional classes had become more important, partly reflecting the upturn in business tourism. Significantly,

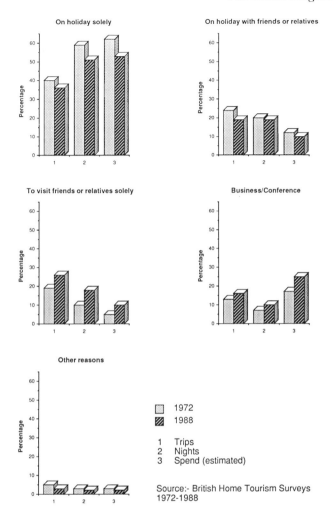

Fig. 9.2   Domestic tourism in Britain: purpose of visits, 1972–88

the increasing representation over time of the 25–34 age group in domestic tourism may have very positive implications for the industry, given the well-documented spending patterns of this group (British Tourist Authority 1986).

The decline in holiday tourism and the growth of business tourism also have important geographical implications via the distribution of tourism in different parts of the United Kingdom. One of the most notable trends since the early 1970s has been the decline of tourism trips, nights and spend in the West Country and Wales (Figure 9.3). Other traditional holiday areas, such as the coastal resorts of north-west England, have also experienced a decline, though not as marked as that of the West Country. The reasons for this are related to broad changes in holiday and business tourism, as well as to the competition from foreign tourism. This latter factor hit the West Country particularly hard since the South-East experienced a massive 12 per cent increase in people

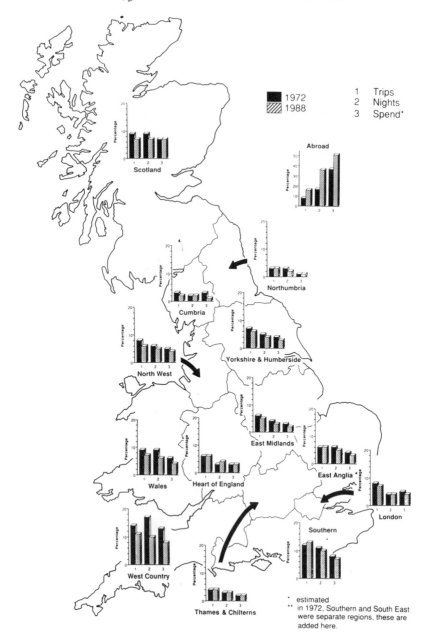

Fig. 9.3   Regional destinations of British tourists, 1972–88

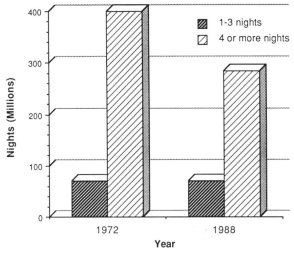

Fig. 9.4　Domestic holiday tourism nights in Britain, 1972–88

taking foreign holidays while this region had traditionally been the origin of most tourists to Cornwall and Devon. The traditional holiday regions have also been vulnerable to economic recession, particularly in the mid-1970s and early 1980s. As Figure 9.4 shows, the longer domestic holidays of four or more nights have shown the greatest decline, compared with more modest changes in short-term holidays. This also serves to highlight the fact that talk of a 'boom' in the short-break holiday market may be misleading. Indeed, 1985 saw this sector of the market decline in volume by 13 per cent to a level little different from that of the mid-1970s.

The short break is mainly centred on the large towns, often involving visits to friends or relatives, despite increased pressure from the commercial sector. It is a market with a high socio-economic profile, reflecting the influence of business tourism, and one where, typically, the average distance travelled is 208 km (*Financial Times* 14 January 1986). Since some 38 per cent of UK adults report taking more than one holiday per year, it may be that the short-break market, centred on the United Kingdom, is ripe for some growth—although, as emphasised, talk of a current 'boom' seems somewhat premature. An important segment of this market is based on urban areas, particularly London, York, Chester and Bath. These towns have more recently been joined by a new group, including Bradford (with its industrial heritage and new museum), Stoke (with its garden festival), and Glasgow (with its 'miles better' campaign).

A further growth area has been in so-called 'conference tourism' which, in 1985, was worth about £1,775 million to the UK market. Of particular importance are international conferences and exhibitions, since visitors to these spend two-and-a-half to three times as much as the average tourist. Such prospects have encouraged widespread investment in conference facilities and, between 1976 and 1986, thirty-two new conference centres were built or refurbished, together with some twenty new exhibition centres (English Tourist Board 1984; Law 1987).

Holiday tourism has been characterised by some limited success in diminishing seasonality from the peak months of July and August. Beneficiaries of this trend—however slight—have been May and, interestingly, December. The latter may represent a different concept, that of a second UK holiday in winter for those whose main summer holiday may have been abroad.

9.2.3 The structure of the tourism accommodation sector

The holiday accommodation sector accounts for well over one-third of all tourist expenditure in the UK. However, as Table 9.2 shows, the accommodation sector is very diverse and has undergone changes during the last decade or so. Over time the licensed hotel has experienced an increase in its share of the market, while the guest house has declined both in terms of the proportion of nights and of expenditure (Table 9.2). This part of the accommodation sector is highly polarised, a trend that is increasing as the market share of larger hotels is growing. Such a trend is long established: between 1951 and 1971 there was a 5–10 per cent increase in the number of hotel bedrooms in the United Kingdom, but a 40–50 per cent reduction in hotels and guest houses (Stallinbrass 1980). As a result, while over 90 per cent of hotels are still relatively small and independently owned, 20 per cent of beds are in hotels which belong to larger groups (Stallinbrass 1980).

The nature of large-scale hotel-ownership is shown in Table 9.3, which also emphasises the diverse range of other activities that these groups are involved in. For example, Trusthouse Forte not only owns the largest number of hotels, but also controls restaurants, through such chains as Little Chef and Kardomah, and has a role in contract catering for British Airways. Grand Metropolitan is another major group with diverse interests including the International hotel chain, Warner Centre holiday camps, Travelscene travel agents, Horizon holiday tours and Berni Inns. Such large organisations have considerable competitive advantages, with identifiable brand images and the benefits of economies of scale in purchasing and marketing. In addition, they are favourably positioned to gain access to capital from bank loans or rights issues.

Table 9.2 Holiday tourism in Britain by accommodation type, 1973 and 1988 (per cent)

| | 1973 | | 1988 | |
	Nights	Spend	Nights	Spend
Licensed hotel	9	22	14	36
Unlicensed hotel or guest house	9	14	6	9
Holiday camp	6	7	5	5
Camping	6	4	4	3
Towed caravan	6	3	3	2
Fixed caravan	13	10	10	7
Rented	10	10	10	10
Paying guest	3	2	2	2
Friend/relative	37	26	43	23
Second home	1	1	2	1

Source: British Home Tourism Surveys, 1972 and 1988

Table 9.3   Major hotel chains in the UK, 1984 (ranked by number of rooms)

Chain and parent	UK hotels	UK rooms	Ownership/interests of parent
Trusthouse Forte	200+	21,200	International hotels; leisure and catering
Ladbroke/Comfort (Ladbroke Group)	50+	6,200	International hotels; leisure and catering
Crest (Bass)	60+	5,700	International hotels; leisure and catering
Thistle (Scottish) & Newcastle	37	5,000	Brewery linked
Mount Charlotte	42	4,600	Hotel specialist
Queens Moat Houses	57	4,500	Hotel specialist
Grand Metropolitan	20+	4,500	International hotels; leisure and catering
Holiday Inn (USA)	15	3,500	International hotel group
Swallow (Vaux)	32	3,000	Brewery linked
Embassy (Allied Lyons)	42	2,600	Brewery linked and foods
Virani	19	2,200	Hotel specialist
Metropole	7	2,200	Hotel specialist
Reo Stakis	30	2,100	Hotel specialist
Rank Hotels	5	1,900	International hotels; leisure and catering
Imperial London	6	1,700	Hotel specialist
Sarova	8	1,500	Hotel specialist
De Vere (Greenall Whitley)	14	1,500	Brewery linked
Anchor Inns (Imperial group)	29	1,300	International hotels; brewery linked
Rowton	5	1,300	Hotel specialist
Hilton (USA)	3	1,100	International hotels
Sheraton (USA)	4	1,100	International hotels
Skean Dhu	5	1,033	Hotel specialist

Source: Key Note Report, 1986

Other significant changes in the accommodation sector relate to self-catering. This expanded rapidly in the 1970s, and in 1973 camping, caravan holidays and rented accommodation accounted for 27 per cent of tourism spend (Table 9.2). The indications are that this important sector is now reaching saturation point and its share of the market is likely to level off at about a third of all holiday nights. Such general trends do, however, conceal important changes within the self-catering sector, particularly the growth of time-share holidays in the United Kingdom.

The fragmented nature of the accommodation sector, together with an inadequate system of data collection, make it impossible to gain exact figures on the number of units. Estimates suggest that there are about 33,600 hotels and nearly 500,000 bedrooms; and that in England alone there are some 240,500 self-catering units or pitches (Pannell Kerr Forster Associates 1986).

Their regional distribution is highly uneven and London dominates with 20 per cent of hotel bed-spaces, followed by the major long-stay holiday region, the West Country, with 18.6 per cent of bed-spaces and up to one-third of all

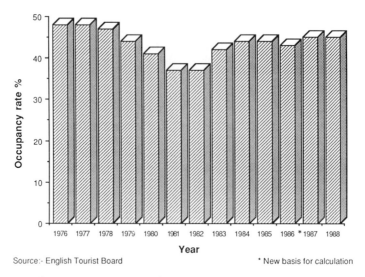

Source:- English Tourist Board   * New basis for calculation

Fig. 9.5   Bed–space occupancy in hotels in Britain, 1976–88

self–catering establishments (Mintel 1985a; 1985b). In addition, the occupancy levels of holiday accommodation vary over time. Within any one year, hotel bed–space occupancy rates are estimated to average around 40 per cent, with a peak of 60 per cent in August and a trough of 23 per cent in January. As Figure 9.5 shows, occupancy levels also vary over longer time periods, and the domestic holiday industry is highly vulnerable to recession, as witnessed between 1979 and 1983.

9.3   Market responses and public policy

9.3.1   *Market forces and responses*

Moving from the general UK situation to a closer examination of the individual sectors of the tourism industry and of particular resorts is problematic, largely because official statistics are extremely generalised, both spatially and in terms of specific activities. As an alternative, use must be made of the results of individual surveys, which, though relatively numerous, often have different aims and methodologies.

It is also worthwhile to highlight the various types of holiday environment within the United Kingdom, albeit in a fairly generalised fashion. At one end of the scale are large traditional seaside resorts such as Blackpool and Scarborough. These remain firmly wedded to serviced accommodation; for example, 76 per cent of holidaymakers in Blackpool stay in hotels and guest houses (English Tourist Board 1973). A subset of this category are those smaller–scale resorts found particularly in south–west England and along the south coast which have lower levels of serviced accommodation and attract more middle–income holiday–makers. In addition, in many of these resorts, especially in south Devon, the holiday industry is now competing with the retirement industry for accommodation and sites. There has also been a declining base of holiday-makers in these types of resorts.

A second major grouping are inland centres, either countryside-based centres often focused on old spa towns, or established historic centres such as York or Chester. Added to this group are new tourist centres based around industrial heritage themes as in Bradford and Glasgow (Law 1985a). Following on the successes of these places, many other towns and cities have initiated studies of the potential for tourism (for example, Manchester Polytechnic n.d.). In many cases success depends on an identification of the centre's potential, an ability to market the facilities, and funding to develop fully the attractions. In Greater Manchester, for example, the English Tourist Board has helped financially with grants of £45,000 and £50,000 to the Museum of Science and Industry. Most tourist developments are, however, funded by a mixture of public and private investment. The industrial centres have been responding to selective growth of short-break holidays, particularly out-of-season trips. These types of development show the response of the tourist industry to changing market trends and also illustrate the role of tourism agencies and public policy.

9.3.2   Public policy

It is an oft-repeated dictum that government policy towards tourism in the United Kingdom is at best nebulous, in the sense that little official policy actually exists save to emphasise that tourism is a 'good thing'. Effective policy-making in UK tourism is left to sub-state agencies which, in other fields, would only be charged with the task of policy implementation. Given, however, that 'policy is frequently made during the implementation process', it may well be that policy-making in tourism is little different from that in other, supposedly rational, policy fields (Ham and Hill 1985).

The most significant legislation to date is the Department of Tourism Act 1969, which established the British Tourist Authority and the three national tourist boards of England, Scotland and Wales (Figure 9.6). It was an exercise more incrementalist than innovatory, given that the Northern Ireland Tourist Board had been established some 21 years previously. Given that almost all tourism enterprise is currently in the private sector, and that most public sector tourism policy is delegated to sub-state agencies such as the British Tourist Authority, UK tourism initiatives tend to be distinctly corporatist in nature. Tourism policy analysis, then, is highly amenable to the three-dimensional model of policy analysis suggested by Ham and Hill (1985), in the sense of consideration of the micro-level of decision-making within organisations, the middle range analysis of policy formulation, and the macro-analysis of political systems.

The authors have argued elsewhere that the relationship between public concern and commercial activity is, at best, one of a loose co-operation between, on the one hand, the tourist boards and, on the other, private operators (Shaw *et al.* 1987). At a local level, the result is often one of conflict between the demands of private capital accumulation and the contingencies of the requirements of local authorities to discharge their statutory duties in environmental, social and economic terms. In addition, when the policy model is readjusted to interpret the British Tourist Authority as 'the state' for

The Tourist Board framework

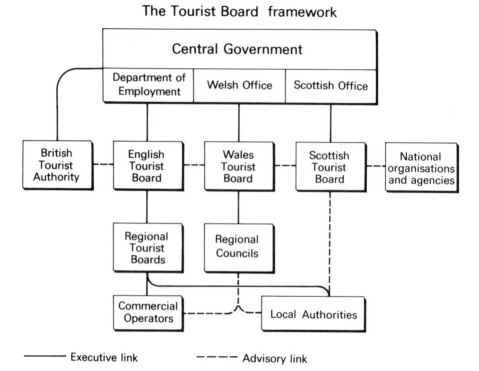

Fig. 9.6   The administrative framework of British tourism planning

the purposes of public tourism policy, conflict further arises out of frustration of the failure of policy outcomes to match the desires of policy initiatives; a frustration which is often vented by policy officials towards 'street-level bureaucrats', that is, the small, private sector operator who is the characteristic figure of the UK tourism industry. Such frustration arises largely from a failure to consider policy initiatives in terms which take account of the contingencies of these operators; for instance, it has long been the policy of national and regional tourist boards to extend the tourist season, particularly into the 'shoulder months' of early and late season. As Table 9.1 shows, such policy has not been successful, largely because the fragmented nature of the industry militates against co-ordinated initiatives divorced from the interests

Table 9.4   Economic considerations leading to public sector involvement in tourism in the UK

1.   Improve the balance of payments
2.   Foster regional development
3.   Diversification of the national economy
4.   Increase public revenue
5.   Improve income levels
6.   Create new employment

of other agencies; if the accommodation units in a resort, for instance, close in October, little encouragement exists for the shopkeepers in that resort to remain open throughout the winter months.

Public sector involvement in tourism stems from a variety of economic factors, which are listed in Table 9.4. Corporatist elements of tourism policy-making are highlighted by considering these in the light of the joint initiative in the 1970s by the English Tourist Board and the Trades Union Congress (TUC) to stress the importance of holidays to disadvantaged and low-income groups. In addition, policy initiatives contain environmental motivations in the sense of the need to protect and conserve a whole range of environments.

A 1974 review of tourism policy by the Department of Trade further stressed the economic component of the goals which influence tourism policy. It reaffirmed that the development of tourist trade could fulfil two aims: to ease balance-of-payment problems and aid regional policy. Incremental initiatives followed with the identification of 'tourism growth points'. Although these were not successful—largely for political reasons—they helped develop a series of initiatives designed to assist capital accumulation in tourism (and therefore in the national economy) through the provision of Tourist Development Grants which formally introduced widespread discretionary measures into the policy process. Currently, attempts are being made to plan and integrate these through a series of Tourism Development Action Programmes (TDAPs), involving integrated schemes of between 1 and 3 years duration.

The agenda for tourism is largely covert in the sense that it is made at sub-governmental level and implemented by private sector operators largely divorced from these structures. Policy was further controlled and restricted by the last review of tourism, which reported in 1985. The review reflected pressures for a more traditional, rationally modelled approach to policy-making for tourism and it attracted widespread criticism for its limited scope in considering only the burdens and obstacles to the industry. The most publicised change was that of a shift in departmental responsibilities from the Department of Trade and Industry to the Department of Employment, which reflected the hopes invested in tourism as one solution to UK employment needs. Such moves further highlight the neo-corporatist element of tourism policy which is guided through the Department of the Employment, with public sector strategies joining private sector establishments, aimed at creating employment, often directed towards regional needs.

9.3.3   The role of the tourist boards

The British Tourist Authority is mainly concerned with general strategic planning for tourism in Great Britain and as such advises central government directly. It is particularly charged with the role of developing foreign tourism to Britain, and consequently a considerable amount of its effort goes into overseas marketing. In addition, the British Tourist Authority undertakes a variety of survey work on the activities, numbers and forecasts of foreign tourists. It provides tourism data from the Department of Industry's International Passenger Survey as well as collecting information on British tourism for the British National Travel Survey. Finally, the British Tourist Authority also serves as an outlet for central government's economic and regional policy,

Table 9.5   Major long-term objectives of the English Tourist Board[1]

1.	The encouragement of the general, long term economic performance of England's tourist industry.
2.	To increase public understanding of the social, economic and cultural value of tourism.
3.	To maintain a correct balance between tourism growth and the capacity and types of tourist facilities.
4.	To extend the tourist season and spread the economic benefits of tourism, as appropriate, throughout the country.
5.	To raise the standard of information, accommodation, catering and other services for tourists.

Note: 1. Not ranked in any order of priority

by promoting particular regions and their tourist facilities to foreign markets.

The English Tourist Board (ETB) focuses the broad strategy of central government's response to tourism upon the situation in England, and since its creation, the ETB has embraced a number of long-term objectives, as shown in Table 9.5. These aims are pursued by the Board through three major strategies: marketing, the provision of information and advice, and financial assistance.

Under the first of these the ETB has mounted a number of major marketing campaigns aimed at extending the holiday season. The ETB has also undertaken special national promotions, such as 'The English Garden' between 1979 and 1981, and 'Maritime England' during the period 1982–5. Apart from the obvious benefits from increased tourist potential created by such schemes, they also serve to stimulate the development of tourist resources. Associated with these aims, there have been more specific marketing campaigns to promote tourism in 'development areas'. For example, recent efforts have been made to encourage holidaymakers to visit the Cumbria coast, Merseyside and north Devon.

The Board's information-related strategies cover both the supply and demand sides of the industry. On the demand side the ETB, together with the regional tourist boards, provides an increasingly well-developed network of tourist information centres. In terms of the provision of facilities, the ETB seeks to improve the situation through its advisory services. These include meetings with potential investors and the identification of investment opportunities in tourism as, for example, in the case of self-catering (English Tourist Board 1981a). It also published, in 1979–80, a series of development opportunity portfolios in conjunction with the regional tourist boards.

Financial assistance is the final strategy of the ETB; under the 1969 Act it may give financial help to any project which 'will provide or improve tourist amenities and facilities in England' (English Tourist Board 1981b, p. 51). The amounts of money vary according to the scheme, but no project can receive more than 50 per cent of total costs. In this area, however, the ETB's activities and overall strategy are limited compared with the demand for support and the costs of major new projects. For Assisted Areas, further finance can be made available, since the ETB is the European Investment Bank's agent for tourism in England.

Many of the broad aims of the English Tourist Board are placed in specific area frameworks by the activities of regional tourist boards. Despite the strong policy links between the ETB and the regional boards, the latter are, in effect, autonomous, administrative bodies. They draw their funds and members from the local authorities and commercial tourist operators within their area. There are twelve such regional boards throughout England and they vary considerably in their area of coverage, constitutions and internal organisations (Figure 9.3). In general terms, however, the regional boards mirror the strategies used by the ETB and also serve to administer the financial aid scheme.

One of the most significant roles of the regional tourist boards is to offer advice both to commercial operators and local authorities on tourism planning. It is within this important area of activity that conflict emerges between national aims and local priorities, a point that is explored later in this chapter. In order to meet these planning responsibilities, the regional tourist boards had a series of regional tourist studies commissioned on their behalf by the ETB during the 1970s. These studies collected detailed information on tourism, and have been used to draw up regional tourist strategies.

9.3.4   *A regional tourist strategy: an example from the West Country*

All the regional tourist boards are empowered to produce policy statements to help shape tourism development within their areas. The example of the West Country Tourist Board (WCTB) is taken since it presents the case of a fairly diversified region (Figure 9.3) and also covers some of the major tourist areas in the United Kingdom. The region's strategy was published in 1980 following consultations with the ETB and regional organisations and used the findings of *A Tourism Study for the West Country Board, 1979* (West Country Tourist Board 1980). This research highlighted a number of significant characteristics of the region's tourist industry. It showed, for example, that the industry is fragmented into mainly small, independent units. The emphasis is on summer holidays, peaking in July and August, with a traditional dependence on the domestic holiday market. Finally, the impact of tourism varied greatly throughout the region, with two-thirds of the total number of tourist nights concentrated in Devon and Cornwall. It was against this background that the policy strategy had to be developed.

The two broad aims of tourism policy in the West Country are 'to maintain and improve the economic and social benefits derived from tourism in the region', and 'to preserve the relationship between tourism and conservation' (WCTB 1980). Both of these contain some degree of conflict when considered within the specific context of local areas in the region. For example, tourism and conservation are often in sharp conflict in parts of the region's National Parks and Areas of Outstanding Natural Beauty. Similarly, the economic benefits of tourism to the low-wage economy of Cornwall and parts of Devon are often difficult to reconcile.

Leaving aside for the moment such potential difficulties, let us examine the strategy and policies adopted by the WCTB. It is worthwhile pointing out at the outset that, like all regional boards, the WCTB sees itself in a central position with regard to public policy-making. Thus, its policies are designed not only to reflect national thinking (for example, the aims of the English Tourist Board) but they are also aimed at influencing national level policies. In addition, the shaping of tourist policies also takes place at a local level through the influence on structure and local plans.

Table 9.6   The broad themes of the West Country Tourist Board's strategy

AIMS
1. To maintain and improve the economic and social benefits derived from tourism in the region
2. To preserve the relationship between tourism and conservation.

Broad themes (no priorities indicated)
1. To help the established holiday areas maintain their competitive position.
2. To encourage, where appropriate, the promotion of new products and the continued growth of existing tourism from home and abroad.
3. To encourage continued investment in the existing tourism capacity to raise standards in order to meet the rising expectations of holiday makers.
4. To attract new investment in areas where there is potential and the local residents' willingness to receive it.
5. To help extend the season to make the best use of existing and any newly developed capacity, and to encourage the availability of existing capacity for longer periods of the year.
6. To ensure that the value of tourism is recognised within the region.
7. To ensure that tourism is taken into full and proper account in the planning of all forms of land use, communications, infrastructure and the economy in the region's future.
8. To encourage a more co-ordinated and increasingly professional approach to the marketing, development and management of the industry, so as to ensure that the region can continue to succeed in an increasingly competitive market.
9. To make better use of existing tourism resources through visitor services.
10. To help relieve pressures arising from tourism, particularly in peak season, in environmentally sensitive areas, areas of historic, architectural or scientific interest, and localities where the infrastructure is vulnerable.
11. To encourage facilities and attractions which are in harmony with the environment and which help to explain and interpret the unique qualities of an area.

Source: West Country Tourist Board (1980)

Returning to the tourist strategy of the WCTB, its policy document identified a number of broad 'themes' associated with the two main aims. As Table 9.6 illustrates, many of these are very closely related and, taken together, form a series of secondary aims that structure themselves around the WCTB's three main functions: marketing, advice-giving and financial assistance. They may also be compared with the aims of the English Tourist Board as outlined in Table 9.5.

At the regional level these broad aims are, of necessity, sharpened by a series of more specific policies. This may be illustrated by taking the aim of promoting new products and the continued growth of existing tourism from home and abroad (aim B in Table 9.6). The WCTB strategy outlines eight policies to support this particular aim. These range from projecting an image of 'uniqueness' for the West Country, through to attracting more business and conference tourism and encouraging the market for country-house hotels (Table 9.7). Obviously, in themselves, these promotional or marketing-type policies can do little to stimulate overall change in tourist provision, which is only brought about through financial investment, the activities of developers and local authorities. In the case of both national and regional tourist boards the implementation of tourism strategies relies to a considerable extent on the

Table 9.7   An example of the marketing aims and related policies of a regional tourist board

---

Policy aim

To encourage, where appropriate, the promotion of new products and the continued growth of existing tourism from home and abroad.

Supporting 'policies'
1.   To increase overseas visitors.
2.   To increase short holidays and bargain breaks.
3.   To attract more business and conference tourism.
4.   To project the image of 'uniqueness'.
5.   To promote tourists' awareness of the region.
6.   To encourage the market for the country-house hotels.
7.   To encourage the role of historic towns/cities as short-stay centres.
8.   To encourage the growth of activity and theme holidays.

---

efforts of commercial operators, local authorities and other statutory and semi-public bodies.

The reality of the situation is that tourism is a commercial sector, and the total amount of grant aid available from government via the tourist boards is extremely small compared with private investment. For example, Cornwall (including the Isles of Scilly) received in 1984–5 some £620,000 of grant aid from the WCTB for forty tourist projects. This figure is obviously insignificant compared with the vast levels of commercial investment in tourism throughout the county. In this type of environment the implementation of the tourist board's strategy can only be achieved with the co-operation of commercial operators, and their participation in joint marketing schemes, as for example, in the 'Bargain Breaks' campaign.

The implementation of the WCTB's strategy is further complicated by the administrative fragmentation of other statutory bodies involved in tourism. In terms of the provision of tourist facilities and attractions, the number of interested organisations is extremely diverse. Furthermore, some of the bodies, such as the National Trust or the South West Arts Council, are also involved in marketing sections of tourist facilities contained within the region. Such marketing activities also bring in British Rail ('Golden Rail Holidays'), the National Bus Company and other travel operators.

An extremely complex interlinkage of organisations therefore exists, with the whole scene fragmented along economic and administrative lines. Under such conditions there is considerable scope for conflict and confrontation to occur. It therefore falls to the lot of the regional tourist board to smooth out the differences, but in attempting to do so it often has to make its aims and policies far too general.

This problem of conflict arising out of a fragmented tourist industry is, if anything, increasing, a feature noted by Gunn (1977) in her analysis of tourism planning. One response is to create a central government department of tourism, although in Britain the hierarchy of tourist boards bears most of the strain.

9.4   Conclusions

The UK tourism scene is one which, in common with many other European countries, has changed a great deal in the past twenty-five years. The basic package to the overseas visitor appears an attractive one and there is scope for optimism that, given political backing and a concentration of resources, this sector of the market will continue to do well. In contrast, the domestic market is far more problematic and the future for many traditional holiday regions remains uncertain. Structural changes in tourism demand and the competition from foreign package tours have taken a heavy toll on many UK resorts. The rise of specialist holiday centres based on short breaks and an increase in conference-based trips has stimulated the domestic market. However, in many cases such trends have only served to emphasise the plight of the traditional seaside resorts, which have tended to miss out on such opportunities. In this sense this geography of UK tourism is undergoing profound changes.

In the rush to cater for the opportunities which the overseas visitor market present, the tourist industry would do well not to forget the pressing problems of the domestic market. These are essentially related to an outdated market, geared to historic patterns of holiday-taking based on resorts which lack high-level investment in new facilities. Furthermore, despite a framework of tourism policy and planning agencies, there has been a general inability of public policy to formulate workable solutions.

10 France: the changing character of a key industry

John Tuppen

10.1 Introduction

Thirty years ago tourism had little impact on the French economy, yet now it has become a major 'industry', with an annual turnover exceeding 360 billion francs (Py 1986). Growth was particularly vigorous in the 1960s and 1970s (Boyer 1982; Mesplier 1986), as the number of French people going on holiday each year increased rapidly, the majority choosing to remain in France. Simultaneously the inflow of foreign tourists rose sharply, so that by the 1980s the income earned from this source substantially exceeded the amount spent by French tourists abroad (Commissariat Général du Plan 1983). Family spending on leisure and recreation was also increasing, with these items currently accounting for over 6 per cent of total household expenditure, a proportion similar to that devoted to clothing (INSEE 1987a).

Tourism, therefore, could be seen to have become a key sector of the economy, not least as other traditional branches of activity, notably those linked to manufacturing, have been affected adversely by prolonged recession. The tourist industry is important for the jobs and income which are generated and for its far-reaching multiplier effects. Consequently it is of little surprise that the promotion of tourism should often have become a significant element in regional development strategies. At the same time the character of the tourist industry has changed; new branches of tourism have emerged, new resort areas have been developed and the structure and organisation of the industry have altered. Over recent years, however, the dynamism of tourism has diminished. The number of French people taking a holiday each year has stabilised, while the average length of stay has tended to decline, emphasising that even tourism has not been immune to the negative effects of economic depression.

It has also become clear that just as tourism brings benefits, so it may produce certain costs. The expansion of tourism has not always been welcomed by local communities, nor has it always produced the anticipated results. Problems of congestion and over-use have become features of many Mediterranean resorts and the more fashionable skiing centres, while, at the other extreme, ill-conceived tourist complexes in remote rural areas have often failed to generate the anticipated jobs and income, instead becoming a burden on local authority budgets. The impact of tourism on the environment has also come under closer scrutiny, with the recognition that in the past too little attention was often paid to this aspect of development.

10.2   General characteristics of French tourism

Accurate measurement of tourist activity is often difficult due to the incomplete or unreliable nature of the data. Such problems apply in France (Cazes 1986), although a relatively clear pattern of French holiday-making emerges from the biannual surveys carried out by INSEE. Even these have certain limitations, however, relating principally to the definition of the term 'holiday'; this is taken to consist of at least four consecutive days' absence from a person's normal place of residence for reasons other than business, study or health (Flament 1984). This definition makes international comparisons difficult and also tends to underestimate the volume of tourism, for it ignores the increasingly popular 'short break' (Lefol 1987).

Despite such shortcomings, it is still possible to obtain a clear picture of the nature and recent growth of tourism in France and, indeed, considerable detail exists concerning this. Currently just under 60 per cent of the country's population go away on holiday on at least one occasion each year. This proportion has risen steadily since the mid-1960s (when surveys were first taken) although little change in the rate has occurred since the early 1980s (Figure 10.1). Not surprisingly, it is the summer season that attracts most tourists, with over 55 per cent of the population taking a holiday in this period. Fewer people go away in winter, although the proportion of the population

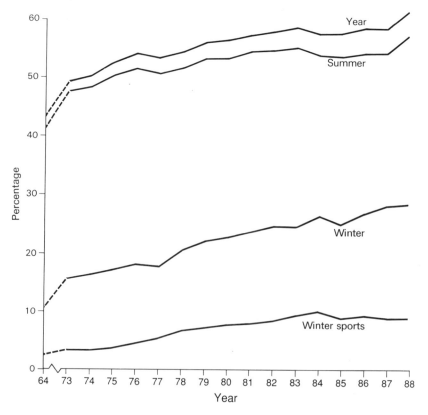

Fig. 10.1   Proportion of French population taking a holiday, 1964–88

holidaying at this season has risen sharply since the early 1970s, largely reflecting considerable growth in the popularity of winter sports. Little change has been observed in the average number of days that people spend on holiday, which has remained at approximately 30 days a year since the late 1960s, although there are some indications that this mean has tended to decrease recently (Christine and Samy 1987).

Less information is available concerning the flows of tourists in and out of France, although the same general pattern of strong growth is evident until the late 1970s, followed by a period of more modest expansion (Cazes 1986; 1984). Movement in both directions is considerable. It is estimated that in 1987 foreign visitors made over 37 million stays in France, while the corresponding figure for French people travelling abroad was 10.3 million (Conseil Economique et Social 1988). The origins and destinations of these visitors are essentially European and Mediterranean. Italy and Spain are the most preferred venues for French tourists abroad, while the Federal Republic of Germany, the Benelux countries and Great Britain are the sources of the largest contingents of foreign visitors to France.

10.2.1   Growth factors

Two key variables appear to underlie the development of tourism—an increase in leisure time and the rise in personal well-being. A shorter working week, longer holidays and substantial increases in real income have underlain the post-war tourism explosion in France; indeed these influences have been brought together by a progressive increase in the minimum legal entitlement to paid holidays, which was raised most recently to five weeks by the Socialist government in 1982. Of these two variables, income might be seen as the more influential, for the recent stagnation in holiday activity has coincided with cuts in spending power stemming from the Socialists' deflationary policies in the early 1980s. Indeed, despite the addition of a fifth week's paid holiday, recent trends show a general shortening of the holiday period (Mirloup 1984).

Other factors have also influenced tourist activity (Tuppen 1983). The substantial growth of tourism in the early post-war period corresponded with a rapid increase in the country's population, while more recently the lowering of the retirement age has offered one section of the population more leisure time. Greater personal mobility has further encouraged people to go on holiday, as have various government inspired initiatives such as the *chèque-vacances*; this is a form of voucher to pay for holidays to which employers as well as employees contribute and it is aimed essentially at the less well-off. Changing attitudes have also played a role, as people have shown a willingness to devote greater proportions of their income and leisure time to tourist pursuits. In part this reflects changes which have occurred in the nature of the tourist 'products' on offer. Better and reasonably priced accommodation, cheaper air travel, new resorts and, although not as popular as in Britain, the extension of 'package holidays' have all been influential.

Table 10.1   The proportion of French people taking holidays, for selected socio-economic groups, 1987 (per cent)

The professions, upper management	87.2
Middle managment	80.4
Other white-collar workers	68.0
Manual workers	54.7
Farmers and farm workers	26.8

Source: INSEE, *Annuaire Statistique de la France*, Paris, 1988.

10.2.2   Unequal access

Although more than 31 million French people now take a holiday at least once a year, this opportunity is not spread equally throughout the population. On the contrary, marked inequalities exist between different social groups, related to a range of socio-economic variables such as income, occupation, age and place of residence; of these, income is generally considered to be the most significant (Cazes 1986). Fewer than 30 per cent of families where the annual income is under 45,000 francs go on holiday whereas, for those earning more than 240,000 francs, the corresponding rate is over 90 per cent (Cazes 1986). Similar contrasts exist between manual and white-collar workers (Table 10.1). Residents in the major cities are also more frequent holiday-makers than those people living in small or medium-sized towns or rural areas. In part this contrast relates to the lack of opportunities for conventional forms of tourism in the former areas, although it can also be a reflection of income differentials. As far as age is concerned, people aged between 25 and 40, and children below the age of 14 are the most frequent holiday-makers; for other age groups, rates decline consistently with increasing age (Christine 1987).

These basic characteristics have remained remarkably consistent over time (Cazes 1986), but certain changes can still be detected. Over the last twenty years, the growth in holiday-making has been greater amongst the less well-off than amongst the more affluent, suggesting some success for the efforts to develop low-cost or subsidised (social) tourism. This would appear confirmed by the growing number of residents from rural areas going on holiday. However, such interpretations should be treated cautiously for, in the latter case, it is often the redistribution of city-dwellers (with different life-styles and incomes) to semi-rural locations that is reflected in the data (Flament 1984).

10.2.3   Tourist locations

The destinations of French holiday-makers are diverse, varying in relation to factors such as age and income, and with the different seasons. Seaside locations remain universally popular as holiday venues, accounting for more than 40 per cent of the total days spent by French people on holiday (Table 10.2). They are followed by rural and then mountainous regions, but whereas the former areas have become generally less popular over the last twenty years, the latter have gained considerably in importance (Cazes 1986). As might be expected, upland areas prove a more popular holiday choice in winter than in summer (the reverse is true of coastal areas), largely due to the influence of

Table 10.2   Major holiday destinations of the French, 1987

Holiday type/location	Percentage of total days spent on holiday		
	Summer	Winter	Overall
Seaside	46.5	20.8	42.8
Rural areas	25.7	27.8	27.4
Mountainous areas	15.8	33.3	18.5
Urban areas	6.7	16.5	7.6
Touring	5.3	1.6	3.7

Source: INSEE, *Annuaire Statistique de la France*, Paris, 1988

winter sports, and it is in relation to this activity that contrasts in behaviour are most evident between social groups. Skiing holidays are expensive so that there is a sharp divide between the life-styles of senior executives and manual workers—nearly 30 per cent of the former go on winter sports holidays compared with only 5 per cent of the latter (Christine and Samy 1986).

Similar contrasts exist in the choice of accommodation (Table 10.3). Around 30 per cent of all holidays are spent in the home or second home of parents and friends, while campsites, personally owned second homes and rented flats and houses each take approximately 15 per cent of the market. Finally, hotels account for only 5 per cent of all accommodation. Not surprisingly, hotel accommodation is more popular in the winter season and campsites in the summer.

Patterns of accommodation have remained relatively stable over time, although a gradual transformation of tourists' preferences is discernible. The last decade has produced a growing disaffection with hotels, largely due to their high cost (Flament 1984), with a corresponding growth in demand for lower-cost options; this was first seen on a large scale with the boom in camping and caravanning holidays in the 1960s and 1970s. Growth in this sector has eased since then, however, partly due to 'natural' saturation of the market and partly to the increased cost of sites and equipment as this holiday formula has tended to move up-market (Flament 1984).

Of the other types of accommodation, modestly priced rented apartments, often purpose-built in resorts, and second homes have gradually become more popular. France has long been renowned for the importance of its second homes; indeed if holiday stays are evaluated in terms of the total number of

Table 10.3   The relative importance of different forms of holiday accommodation in France, 1987 (percentage of total stays)

Home of parents or friends	30.4
Hotel	5.3
Rented property	15.2
Tent or caravan	15.7
Second home	15.5
Second home of parents or friends	9.9
Other	8.0

Source: INSEE, *Annuaire Statistique de la France*, Paris, 1988.

days spent in different forms of accommodation, then second homes (whether owned, borrowed or rented) represent the single most important category (Renucci 1984). The 1982 census revealed that there were more than 2.2 million second homes in France, the number having increased fivefold since 1954. By 1985 it was estimated that over 12 per cent of French households either owned, rented on a long-term basis or were loaned a second home (Christine 1987). These *résidences secondaires* are not equally spread throughout the country but are concentrated in the main tourist areas, principally in south-eastern France and Brittany. In the former case there is a particular preference for the Mediterranean coast, notably in the *départements* of Alpes-Maritimes and Var. Inheritance, a ready supply of rural property following the strong rural-urban shift of population in the 1950s and 1960s, and new flat and villa developments in the main resort areas, all help to explain the high level of second home ownership. But the desirability of this trend remains contentious. Does such development in the most sought-after areas cause unwanted speculation and ultimately produce little by way of positive spinoffs, at the same time necessitating expensive investment in new infrastructure? Or does this breathe new life into remote rural areas, bringing jobs and services, and leading to a substantial injection of income into the community? The debate continues although, overall, the balance sheet has been adjudged favourable (Renucci 1984).

10.2.4   *Concentration in time and space*

Tourist activity is far from evenly spread throughout the country and several aspects of this might be noted. First, there is considerable spatial variation in holiday participation rates. Flament (1984) depicts three broad, contrasting regions where rates differ, highlighting the considerable difference which exists between remote, rural areas (such as are found in the region of Limousin) where only a modest proportion of the population takes a holiday, and the highly urbanised area of Ile-de-France (Paris) where nearly 80 per cent of the inhabitants are holiday-makers. High income levels, the absence of local holiday venues, and the strain and exhaustion of living in the French capital help explain the elevated rate in this latter region.

The destinations of tourists also exhibit a high degree of areal concentration. In summer the coast is the principal attraction, but not all coastlines and resorts have the same appeal. The Mediterranean beaches are easily the most popular, followed by the Atlantic and Brittany coasts, but there are contrasts even within these areas. While certain sections of the Côte d'Azur are completely saturated, resulting in a relative stagnation of tourist numbers, growth continues unabated along the Languedoc and Roussillon coastal fringe. Elsewhere there are even signs of decline, as in some of the Normandy and Channel coast resorts.

There is also considerable spatial concentration in the winter season largely due to the impact of winter sports and the resulting polarisation of holidays on the main mountainous regions. But the spread between such areas is unequal, with the majority of winter sports holidays being based in the Alps, particularly in the northern part of this region. The best snow conditions are found here as well as the most challenging runs, and the major and most prestigious resorts.

French tourism movements have a broad North–South pattern. Regions in the North experience a net outflow of holiday-makers, whereas there is a net inflow of visitors in the South, especially in those areas backing the Mediterranean or the northern Alps. The annual *transhumance* of French people has a number of important consequences. These range from a substantial transfer of spending power during the holiday season, to the considerable strain placed on the main communication arteries, especially the road network, (the car being by far the preferred mode of transport used by holiday-makers). The A6/A7 motorway route to the south has become infamous for the continuous series of traffic jams along its length, particularly to the north and south of Lyon, which have become a regular feature in July and August. Substantial costs result from these holiday movements, but substantial benefits also accrue to a limited number of resort areas.

Such congestion is made considerably worse by the extent to which holidays remain highly concentrated within a limited period of the year. More than 50 per cent of the holiday stays of French people fall within the two months of July and August (Figure 10.2), a proportion which rises to over 80 per cent when holidaying is measured in terms of the total number of days spent away (Flament 1984); few other countries display such extreme concentration (Cazes 1986). Two other comparatively minor peaks are discernible; the first in December corresponds with the Christmas holidays and the second, straddling February and March, is related to school holidays at this period and their popularity for skiing trips.

The undesirable consequences of the extremely uneven and concentrated character of the tourist season have long been recognised. The summer peak, in particular, places unwanted strain on transport systems, causes unpleasant congestion in resorts (not to mention exhorbitant prices!) and results in lost production with the closure of factories and offices. Efforts have been made to encourage employers to stagger holidays and for schools to modify their calendar, but despite some changes, the impact of these measures appears limited. In part this is explained by intertia; surveys show that despite the extra costs and inconvenience of going away in the high season, few people seem to want to change their holiday routine (Cazes 1986). A more ruthless approach

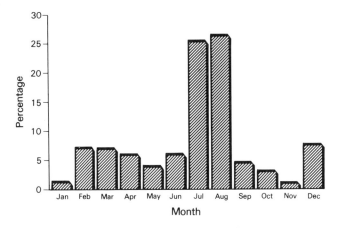

Fig. 10.2   Seasonal distribution of holidays taken in France during 1985

may be required, involving a substantial remodelling of the school year to avoid the long summer break from the end of June to early September.

10.2.5   Other forms of tourism

Thus far the term 'tourism' has been used mainly to refer to summer and winter holidays, focusing principally on coastal, mountainous or rural locations. Yet there are other forms of tourist activity, sometimes affecting other localities, which form an integral part of the wider tourist industry. Within this group might be included visits to historic monuments or sites and museums, visits to festivals and other similar events, coach touring holidays and health cures.

Business tourism represents a further, although somewhat different branch of activity in that the emphasis is primarily on work rather than pleasure. Business meetings and attendance at conferences, trade fairs and exhibitions are the basis of this market sector and can be seen as particularly significant due to their past record of growth (Lanquar *et al*. 1980). Evidence of this is provided by the scale of recent investment in new conference and exhibition centres (Tuppen 1988), while overall this branch of tourism is estimated to offer over 270,000 permanent jobs (Commissariat Général du Plan 1983).

France plays a leading role in the world conference market, taking second place to the United States in terms of the number of international meetings organised each year (Labasse 1984). The actual conference centre rarely makes a profit, but this has not deterred cities such as Nice, Lille, Toulouse and Montpellier from investing heavily in new facilities; the Acropolis convention centre opened in Nice in 1985 is a model of this type (Tuppen 1985). The interest in such development relates primarily to the spinoff for other branches of the urban economy, for a conference brings business to hotels, restaurants and bars, shops and transport operators. It is estimated that a conference delegate spends approximately twice as much as an average tourist, making him or her a particularly sought-after client (Commissariat Général du Plan 1983).

Reliance on conferences carries certain risks. While it is clear that the demand for conference facilities is increasing (Labasse 1984), so too is the competition, and not just from within France. Equipping and running a conference centre is also expensive, particularly if the number of events held in any year is limited. Reasons of prestige and a desire to participate in what can be an extremely lucrative market have pushed municipal authorities to continue to invest in this activity, but economic realism has dictated a number of new approaches—more versatile conference halls, a keener interest in location within the urban area to offer maximum access to accommodation or recreational and cultural facilities, and more careful planning of related hotels capacity.

One city which has undoubtedly benefited from business tourism is Paris, with its extensive conference facilities, including a major complex at the Porte Maillot, and a wide range of exhibition halls offering more than 520,000 square metres of covered floorspace. The exhibition complexes include the Parc International des Expositions at Villepinte in the northern suburbs (not far from Roissy airport), which was originally opened in 1982 and has already been enlarged to provide 117,000 square metres of display space. Paris is a world leader as an exhibition centre and the spinoff from this is calculated to bring the capital around 7 billion francs of business a year (Kern 1986). It is also the world's premier conference venue, heading the rankings with 274 international events in 1985 (*Le Monde* 1986); this activity is estimated to attract over 650,000 people to the French capital each year (Ambroise-Rendu 1986).

Paris's role as a tourist centre is far wider than that of playing host to conferences and trade fairs. The appeal of its museums, art galleries, theatres, historic monuments and educational establishments, and its reputation for entertainment and night life draw a vast inflow of tourists. In 1984 Ile-de-France attracted an estimated 20 million visitors, of whom approximately half were foreigners (Lagadec and Starkman 1986): one-third of all foreign visitors to France stay in Paris (Ragu 1985). Hotels play a key role in accommodating these people. Paris alone has 1,300 classified hotels, offering 64,000 rooms (substantially more than London), which in 1984 welcomed over 11 million people (60 per cent of them foreigners). They have an occupancy rate averaging 70 per cent over the year, helping to explain the dynamism of this sector which, over the last decade, has seen a substantial increase in capacity through both new construction and renovation (Lagadec and Starkman 1986). This situation contrasts sharply with the net deficit recorded by the Paris region in terms of the holiday movements of French people, offering a more realistic picture of the impact of tourism on the capital.

10.3   The role of tourism in the economy

Precise measurement of the economic impact of tourism, particularly at a national level, is notoriously difficult, largely due to the absence or inadequacy of appropriate statistical information (Cazes 1986). However, certain generalisations may still be made. In 1984 tourism is estimated to have contributed just over 8 per cent of French Gross Domestic Product (Py 1986). The weight of this sector in the economy is therefore considerably greater than that of other major branches of activity, such as agriculture and the car industry. Furthermore, the importance of tourism has been increasing over recent years (Cazes 1986).

Tourism is also an important 'exporting' industry. In part this results from the numerous tourist-related services and products sold abroad. These range from skiing and camping equipment to shipping and air services, and the hotel-building industry: it is estimated that such activities represent 3 per cent of the value of French exports (Nancy 1987). Tourism also earns a considerable income from foreign visitors to France. Since the late 1960s there has been a continuous positive balance on foreign tourist expenditure, with French tourists abroad spending considerably less than their counterparts coming to France (Direction du Tourisme 1986; Py 1986). Despite the recession, this surplus increased substantially in the late 1970s and early 1980s, rising to over 30 billion francs in 1985. As a result tourism produced a net gain for the French economy similar to that generated by either the agricultural and food sector or by the motor-vehicle industry. However, in 1986 and 1987 the surplus fell to little more than 20 billion francs, illustrating the vulnerability of tourist activities to factors such as currency exchange rates, as the dollar depreciated considerably against the franc, and to external events; in this latter case, the terrorist attacks in Paris were held to have reduced the number of foreign visitors (Pasgrimaud 1987). Similar arguments have been used to explain the increase in tourist earnings in the early 1980s, as a weak franc helped bring more foreign tourists to France, while the French were limited in their travel abroad by foreign currency control measures introduced in 1983 as part of an economic austerity package (Tuppen 1985).

At a time of high unemployment and slow employment growth, one of the principal attractions of tourism has been its ability to continue to generate jobs in relatively large numbers. Whereas employment in the economy as a whole stagnated or even declined during the early 1980s, jobs in tourism continued to rise at a substantial rate, estimated to have averaged around 15 per cent per annum 1978–88 (Conseil Economique et Social 1988). Tourism is a major employer, although precise measurement is made difficult by the diverse character of this activity (Py 1986). Nevertheless, it is widely accepted that this sector currently provides employment for approximately 600,000 people; when indirect employment in related manufacturing and service activities is taken into account the total rises to approximately 1.6 million, representing nearly 8 per cent of the total employed population (Pasgrimaud 1987).

While tourism is undeniably an important generator of employment, this generalisation needs to be qualified. Many jobs require few skills or qualifications, and are correspondingly poorly paid; many are also of a seasonal or part-time nature, although this might not always be a disadvantage. In mountainous regions it is the availability of just this type of employment that has helped retain the indigenous rural population through the supplement it offers to the relatively meagre incomes earned in other, more traditional activities such as farming or forestry. But whatever benefits tourism brings in the form of jobs, these are again limited to relatively few areas of the country.

10.3.1   The regional impact

A number of studies have tried to assess the nature and impact of tourist activity at a local level. Not surprisingly, considerable attention has been focused on the more popular areas such as the Mediterranean coast, where tourism is seen as a vital element in the regional economy. It is not just the jobs and revenue generated within the tourist industry itself which are important, but also such indirect effects as the stimulus provided for the building and property industries (Wolkowitsch 1984; Langevin 1981).

The scale of the tourist economy is evident in the region of Provence-Alpes-Côte d'Azur. In this one area are located nearly 4 per cent of French hotel rooms, 13 per cent of second homes and 12 per cent of all campsite places (INSEE 1987b). Summer is the main season, with over 70 per cent of tourist nights spent in the region concentrated in the months of July and August; in 1985 over 7 million people visited the area during this short period, three-quarters of whom were French (INSEE 1987b).

Tourism is highly concentrated along the coastal fringe, with the two *départements* of Var and Alpes-Maritimes alone accounting for nearly 60 per cent of the total number of nights spent by summer tourists in this region. A recent survey (Bras 1985) based on a sample of visitors to the resorts of the Var department (strung out along the coast between Bandol and St Raphaël), provides a useful indication of the character of tourism along the Côte d'Azur. In 1984 the typical visitor was French, with a white-collar job, staying in a rented apartment or villa, or on a campsite; average per capita holiday expenditure was 1,475 francs, excluding transport costs. A quarter of French holiday-makers originate from the Paris region alone (Figure 10.3). Foreign tourists only represent approximately 20 per cent of the visitors, the majority coming from Britain, Belgium and the Federal Republic of Germany. For all visitors the principal attraction is the sea, with other possible 'pull' factors, such as cultural events or sightseeing, proving of little significance. Yet there is a price to be paid for this appeal—inflated land and house prices, severe congestion along the main coastal roads, with associated delays, difficulties in parking, noise and beaches which become dirty and impossibly crowded.

Such problems are not new and, indeed, one of the factors behind the decision taken in the early 1960s to develop the considerable potential for tourism of the neighbouring coastline of Languedoc-Roussillon, was to help relieve this type of pressure. Since that time, as is well documented (Cazes *et al.* 1980; Ferras *et al.* 1979; Pearce 1981; Thompson 1975), seven new resort complexes have been built, transforming this 180 kilometre long, previously inhospitable coastline. The costs and benefits of such development have been much debated (Tuppen 1983) but, from a purely economic standpoint, the effects might be seen as largely positive. Whereas only 500,000 tourists visited this coastal area in 1964, the total had risen to over 3 million in 1982 and is currently estimated at more than 3.5 million; in excess of 3 billion francs is spent in the resorts during the summer season (Racine 1983). In a wider sense more than 6 billion francs of state investment along this coastal strip has proved an effective lever for bringing in further private capital, and over the period 1965–80 it is estimated that tourist development was responsible for around 30,000 new jobs in the region (Pommier 1985).

The economic impact of tourism might be considered even more dramatic in certain Alpine communities. Although France's mountainous regions still receive more visitors in summer than in winter, it is the vast increase in winter sports holidays (with the building of new resorts and the extension of existing centres) which has transformed many parts of such areas. Twelve years ago just under 5 per cent of French people went on a skiing holiday (Christine and Samy 1986); that proportion has since doubled, with the country's resorts being visited by an estimated 6 million skiers each year, including up to 800,000 foreigners (d'Erceville 1986). Such vigorous growth has now eased (Tuppen 1988), but the effects of past expansion are readily evident, nowhere more so than in the northern Alps.

Change is apparent in the human landscape—new chalets, apartments, ski-lifts, shops and restaurants have mushroomed—and this area is covered by a series of modern, purpose-built, high-altitude resorts such as les Arcs or les Deux-Alpes. But the demographic, economic and social structures of village life have also been profoundly transformed. In the main resort areas the exodus of population has been arrested and, in many cases, the current has been reversed, as populations are now rising again (Préau 1983). Agriculture has largely disappeared as a full-time occupation, as the majority of the inhabitants in work now have tertiary sector jobs—shopkeepers, waitresses and ski instructors are just some of the new options. The gap between generations has widened, as the young show far greater readiness to exploit the opportunities offered by tourism; and new strains have been created in families where the traditionally conservative values of parents have been challenged by the enterprising ideas of their children (Préau 1984). Tourism has therefore been at the root of a fundamental change in society.

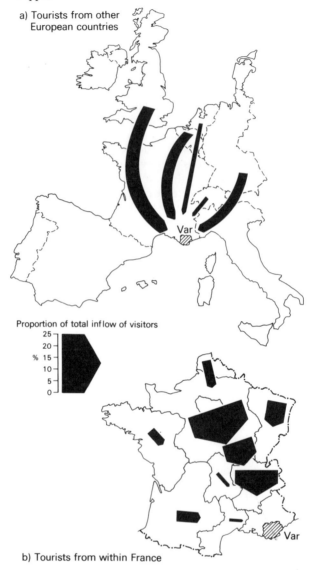

Fig. 10.3 The principal origins of tourists staying in the department of Var, July–August 1984

Source: Bras (1985)

The success of tourism in many Alpine regions in creating employment, generating income and reviving population growth, has encouraged many other rural communes to seek to benefit from the same growth process (Mallon 1985). Generally, change in such areas has been modest, relying largely on individual enterprise to improve hotels and develop campsites or other forms of low-cost accommodation, such as bed and breakfast and *gîtes ruraux*. These changes have often been facilitated by government grants, made available either to individuals or, more generally, to communes to help improve their tourist facilities. In the latter case this has occurred increasingly through the negotiation of a contract either with the state or, more recently with the regional council, frequently as part of a general programme of rural development (Cazes 1986; Robert 1986). Other joint initiatives have also been undertaken. In the Massif Central, for example, voluntary hotel chains have developed, grouping a series of small hotels seeking to develop their own identity and offering new types of holiday such as 'fishing breaks' or 'gastronomic stays' (Varenne 1986).

But the development of tourism in many rural regions still faces difficulties. These may relate to the often indifferent quality of the tourist attractions and accommodation, or to problems of access. The season is generally short, for few areas attract many visitors outside the months of July and August. Amongst the local population, particularly the older generations, there still exists a certain apathy to change and a reluctance to invest in new facilities (Fel and Bouet 1983). Local councils also face difficult decisions over new investment. Béteille (1981) highlights their dilemma with reference to swimming-pools; failure to invest in such a key facility may reduce considerably the appeal of an area for tourists; yet if a pool is provided, its cost is likely to exceed the direct return in revenue, placing an impossible burden on the commune's finances.

10.4 The organisation of the tourist industry and the role of government

10.4.1 *Ownership and concentration*

Tourism may form a significant branch of the economy, but its structure remains highly diversified and its organisation is characterised by the continued importance of a host of small businesses. It has been estimated, for example, that in the hotel and restaurant trade there are as many as 145,000 outlets, providing jobs for 400,000 workers (Conseil Economique et Social 1984). Furthermore, 70 per cent of the country's hotels have less than five employees, reflecting the extent to which family businesses are still dominant (Py 1986). The preponderance of small firms might also be seen to result from the fragmented nature of the industry and the specialised character of related business concerns, typified by the independent restaurant, hotel, travel agent, coach operator or ski-lift company.

In recent years, these traditional structures have undergone substantial modification. The key process has been concentration, as large firms have come to play a more dominant role in the organisation of tourist activities. In part this has been brought about by the increasingly competitive nature of the industry, and the need for substantially greater investment to develop new 'products'. But it has also been a means by which companies have been able to expand their businesses particularly in international markets.

This trend has been marked in the hotel sector (Py 1986), where it has been accompanied by a parallel movement of modernisation and upgrading. It has led to the formation of a series of large multinational companies, epitomised by the Accor group, now Europe's leading hotel chain, controlling 713 hotels (1987) under such names as Novotel, Ibis and Sofitel. Accor's interests are in fact much wider, including restaurant chains and travel agencies, while the group's operations are world-wide, covering sixty-four countries. Substantial investment, coupled with new forms of management and ownership, have thus given France a leading position in the European hotel industry. But there are other sectors of the tourist market where the potential for development remains considerable. In the past, for example, the individualistic Frenchman has tended to shun the use of travel agencies and to show little enthusiasm for the package tour, certainly by British standards. Attitudes are changing as tour operators reorganise their activities and improve their marketing. However, on a European scale Club Méditerranée—France's leading company in this field—still only transports roughly one-third of the holiday-makers handled by Britain's Thomson travel group (Pourquery 1987).

One other distinctive feature of French tourism is the substantial role played by non-profit-making clubs and associations in the provision and organisation of holidays (Cazes 1986). Estimates of the importance of this sector vary, but it represents somewhere between 10 and 15 per cent of all holiday accommodation in France. One of the largest such organisations is Villages-Vacances-Familles (VVF) which alone provided holidays for 500,000 people in 1985 (Cazes 1986). These associations have diverse origins, but many are concerned with providing holidays or holiday accommodation for the less well-off, as a form of 'social tourism' (Lanquar and Raynouard 1981). Considerable interest has been shown in developing this market, but in recent years increasing difficulties have been encountered. In part social tourism became a victim of the recession, as demand slackened and firms were less inclined to help subsidise what could be seen as non-essential activities. Some associations have also been adjudged at fault, lacking clear development goals and displaying insufficient rigour in their management (Py 1986).

10.4.2   Government policies

The attitude of the French government to tourist development is somewhat ambivalent. The fact that over time the minister responsible for tourism has been frequently moved from one ministry to another might indicate the relatively low priority accorded to this activity. Cazes (1986) suggests further that the resources allocated to tourism have been inadequate and too widely dispersed between different ministries and funding bodies, and that there has been a lack of clear and consistent policy direction.

Despite such shortcomings, the government has still been active in promoting tourism. It first intervened in a significant way in the early 1960s at a time of rapid economic growth in France, when some form of central planning and control over tourist development was considered desirable. To this end three special study and planning services were set up, covering mountainous, coastal and rural areas. During the same period, special development companies were created to oversee ambitious plans to expand tourism along the Languedoc-Roussillon and Aquitaine coasts, and in Corsica (Py 1986). More general intervention to encourage tourism has occurred through the regional planning initiatives of the Délégation à l'Aménagement du Territoire et à l'Action Régionale (DATAR) while some ministries—such as those of Agriculture and Transport—have long devoted part of their spending to tourist-related activities. Government grants and loans have also been made available to assist development, notably to help modernise small, family-owned hotels, especially in rural areas.

10.4.3 The environment

Over time government attitudes to the expansion of tourist facilities have altered. While the economic motives for developing tourism have long been recognised, more recently it has been accepted that these have to be balanced against other interests, such as the environment (Lozato-Giotart 1987; Michaud 1983). In the 1960s and early 1970s the prevailing philosophy appeared to be one of development at any price, an approach typified by the construction of new resorts along the Languedoc coast and in the French Alps; in the latter case this represented part of the response to the government's ambitious *plan neige*, launched in 1970, to increase substantially the skiing capacity of the country's mountainous regions (Knafou 1978).

The grandiose scale of these schemes, and the apparent lack of concern for wider environmental consequences have been widely criticised. Increased opposition has been expressed at the seemingly endless 'concrete walls', stretched out along the coastlines of the popular seaside resorts; at the rapid increase in marinas, further restricting access to the coast for all but the most affluent (Michaud 1983); and at the huge out-of-place apartment blocks, the *Sarcelles-sur-neige* (named after a once infamous *grand-ensemble* in the Paris region) which became a feature of many of the ski resorts developed in the 1960s and 1970s. Tourism has led to other forms of environmental damage — pollution of beaches and the sea (notably along the Mediterranean coast); the destruction of vegetation through forest fires (now virtually an endemic feature of the Midi), or through the development of new ski runs, or simply through the over-use of an area, and the disappearance of associated animal life.

In recent years there has been much greater, if belated, official recognition of the need for a more careful and integrated approach to tourist development, particularly in the more heavily used areas. Competition between different forms of land use is often intense, while the needs of the farmer, small businessman or local resident have to be balanced against those of the property dealer or developer. After lengthy discussion, such awareness has been embodied in new legislation designed to regulate development in mountainous and coastal areas — *la loi montagne*, 1985 and *la loi du littoral*, 1986 (Dufau 1986; Knafou 1985). Whether this offers an effective means by which to resolve the many conflicts associated with the use and exploitation of these areas, and the potentially detrimental effect on the environment, has yet to be determined.

10.4.4 Decentralisation

A rather different aspect of change in government policy concerns the redistribution of certain decision-making powers. While tourist policy is still largely controlled and financed from Paris, the enhanced powers given to local authorities under the 1982 Decentralisation Act (Tuppen 1988) are producing an increasing number of local initiatives. Regional councils, whose role in economic development planning was strengthened by the above legislation, are taking a far more active part in promoting tourism, aided by their considerably enlarged budgets. Action may range from contributing to the running costs of Regional Parks, to providing subsidies for improving hotel accommodation or developing *gîtes*. In some regions investment in tourism has also been one of the priorities featuring in regional plans which were first formulated for the period 1984–8, and in most cases have formed the basis of a contractual arrangement with the state, each partner being committed to a fixed proportion of total investment (Tuppen 1988). In total nearly 2000 million francs were invested in tourist related activities over these five years (Conseil Economique et Social 1988).

Further examples of decentralisation exist. Municipal councils now have increased powers to sanction (or refuse) tourist-related building projects and in the major mountainous regions local committees advise on the desirability of new resort development (Knafou 1985). This might be seen as an important vote in favour of local democracy, enabling councils to resist more strongly unwanted expansion. But, while it is true that local authorities have a greater say in such matters, resisting development when jobs and a substantial local tax income are at stake may prove far harder than it would be for a Paris-based civil servant.

10.5   Conclusion—the way ahead

For much of the post-war period the French tourist industry has experienced continuous growth, bringing substantial benefits to the economy and to selected regions of the country, although the changes accompanying this development have not always gone unchallenged. Currently, growth has slowed, although longer-term estimates indicate that tourism is likely to remain a significant area of expansion within the economy, not least as leisure time continues to increase. However, if the French tourist industry is to retain its dynamism, it is essential that it resists increasing foreign competition and adapts to constantly changing patterns of demand.

Certainly there is evidence of the tourist industry responding to this challenge. A continuing series of mergers and looser forms of association between firms is producing a more effective and coherent management structure. The government, for its part, has given priority to improving the image of French tourism and encouraging the provision of a better standard of welcome and accommodation. New products are appearing, ranging from holidays based around some form of activity (such as tennis or golf) to leisure complexes and theme parks, the latter epitomised by the Disneyland planned to open at Marne-la-Vallée (to the east of Paris) in 1992. However, almost inevitably, much of the new investment is occurring in areas which already possess a strong tourism tradition, serving not only further to enhance their appeal, but also to pose even greater problems of managing demand and protecting the environment. Herein lies part of a wider problem which has long faced the French tourist industry and which remains a major challenge for the future—the need to reduce the excessive spatial and temporal concentration of holiday-making in France.

11 The Federal Republic of Germany: a growing international deficit?

Peter Schnell

11.1 Introduction

Since the mid-1970s West Germans have secured the reputation of being 'the world champions of travelling': this refers not only to the high ratios of Germans taking their holidays within the Federal Republic or abroad, but also to the broader economic features of this travel. In 1986 nearly two-thirds of all holidays of 5 or more days had foreign destinations, and German tourists spent DM 44.9 billion abroad. This sum corresponds to about 4 per cent of private consumption and to about 20 per cent of the total travel expenditures of industrialised Western countries (Commerzbank 1987, p. 4).

The Federal Republic and its tourist regions also represent a tourist destination. The number of beds offered by commercial accommodation enterprises increased by about 300 per cent between 1954 and 1985, and during the same period the number of visitor arrivals and nights grew by about 200 per cent. Although the share of foreign visitors to the Federal Republic has increased recently, the receipts amounted to 'only' DM 17.0 billion, so that tourism is a source of economic deficit for the Federal Republic. Furthermore, on a regional basis, tourism development reveals regional differences which cause problems for local and regional tourist organisations and enterprises.

This chapter considers the major features of national tourist trends in terms of the spatial distribution of West German tourist flows, the development and regional structure of tourism in the Federal Republic, and the impact of tourism and tourism policies.

11.2 National tourism trends

National tourism trends are summarised in Table 11.1. Travel intensity, that is the percentage of the West German population aged over 14 taking one or more holidays of 5 or more days per year, has increased rapidly since the mid-1950s. At that time, not even a quarter of the West German population undertook holiday travel, although there is no information about shorter holidays in that period. By 1980, travel intensity had reached a peak of 57.7 per cent, then dropped to 54.4 per cent in 1983, but subsequently increased to 57.1 per cent in 1985. Since the early 1970s there has also been a growing trend for short breaks (2–4 days), and by 1985 one-third of the population aged over 14 partook in these.

Table 11.1   Development and structure of West German tourism, 1954–85
(per cent)

	1954	1960	1970	1975	1980	1985
Travel intensity (5 days and more)	24	28	42	56	58	57
Short-term travel intensity (2–4 days)				21	26	33
Travel destinations						
Domestic	85	69	47	46	40	34
Abroad	15	31	53	54	60	66
Organisation						
Individually organised travel	87[1]		83	82	74	66
All-inclusive package tour	13[1]		17	18	26	34
Means of transport						
Car	19	38	61	61	59	60
Aeroplane	–	1	8	12	16	18
Train	56	42	24	19	16	11
Bus	17	16	7	7	8	10
Other	8	3	–	1	1	1
Duration						
5–8 days		22	8	9	8	10
9–15 days		35	35	38	40	43
16–22 days		27	39	37	35	34
23 days or longer		16	18	16	17	13
Travel expenses per person						
up to DM 600		57	72	46	22	22
DM 600 to DM 1,000		26	20	27	26	23
DM 1,000 to DM 1,500		11	8	15	25	23
DM 1,500+		–	–	8	24	26
No response		6	–	4	3	6
Type of accommodation						
Hotel/inn/boarding-house	29	24[2]	42	46	48	46
Cottage/bungalow/apartment	–	–	7	9	10	14
Private room (rented)	17	35[2]	20	16	11	10
Relatives/friends	43	23[2]	17	13	12	10
Camping/caravanning	5	9[2]	9	8	10	10
Other	6	11[2]	5	8	9	10
Type of holidays						
Rest/pleasure				83	82	71
Visiting relatives/friends				10	9	9
Sightseeing/study/education				2	4	7
Health				3	2	6
Sporting				2	3	5

Sources: Studienkreis für Tourismus (1986); Koch (1959); Statistisches Bundesamt (1965)
Notes: 1. 1958
    2. 1961–2

There has also been a major shift in the preferences for destinations. While only 15 per cent of all West German holiday travel involved foreign destinations in 1954, this share had increased to 66 per cent in 1985. This development not only caused problems for the tourist regions in West Germany, but also meant there was a growing outflow of West German currency. In 1960 DM 2.8 billion was spent abroad and DM 2.0 billion received from foreign visitors to the Federal Republic. However, by 1986, as pointed out above, DM 44.9

billion was spent abroad and only DM 17.0 billion received from foreign tourists, so that the gap between expenditures and receipts is considerable (Statistisches Bundesamt 1965; Commerzbank 1987, p. 1).

In 1958 only 13 per cent of all holiday travel was booked as package tours, but this has since increased to 34 per cent. This development and a shift in holiday destinations has led to changes in the means of transport. In the 1950s and the early 1960s car-ownership levels were relatively low and the railway was the most important mode of transport, but later the car took the lead, accounting for 60 per cent of holiday travel, though this level has stagnated in recent years. The latest trend—which has to be seen in relation to the increase of foreign package tours—is that the share of air transport is increasing.

Most holidays last between 9 and 15 days, but longer holidays are also common. However, shorter (5–8 days) and longer (over 23 days) holidays are not taken relatively as often as in 1960. Although the data seem to indicate an increase in travel duration, and despite the rise of paid holidays, the average duration has slightly fallen in recent years from 18.8 days in 1977 to 17.3 days in 1985 (Zucker 1986, p. 54). This decrease is explained by the growing number of West Germans who undertake a second or third holiday and who participate in short breaks, thereby shortening their main holidays.

The types of accommodation preferred by most West German holiday-makers are hotels, inns and boarding-houses, and this has changed little since 1970. Staying with relatives or friends has become less popular, dropping from 43 per cent in 1954 to 23 per cent in 1960, and is rather unimportant today. In the 1960s the renting of private rooms—another type of inexpensive accommodation— took the lead, but this has lost prominence since 1970, when foreign destinations became important. A relatively new trend is the growth of self-catering accommodation. The increasing demand for cottages, bungalows and apartments can be explained by the preference for independence, the wish not to be confined to one or two rooms, and a desire to economise. The percentage of those booking such accommodation has tripled in the past fifteen years (Commerzbank 1987, p. 3). Camping and caravanning have also become more popular for partly the same reasons, reinforced by the demands of locational independence and social mixing. The rapidly growing stock of caravans and mobile homes indicates the strength of this trend (Table 11.2).

Travel expenses per capita have risen considerably since 1960. There are two reasons for this: first, the general increase in the cost of living; and second, the growing share of transport costs, given the shift in destination preferences.

Table 11.2   Numbers of caravans and motor-homes in the Federal Republic of Germany, 1960–1985/6

	Caravans	Motor-homes
1960	19,000	—
1965	55,000	—
1970	150,000	6,242
1975	300,000	16,288
1980	418,000	65,486
1985/6	630,000	143,054

Sources: Fisk (1984, p. 6); Deutscher Bundestag (1986a, p. 16); Commerzbank (1987, p. 1)

Table 11.3 Opinions in the Federal Republic of Germany about different
types of holiday, 1986

Type of holiday	Favoured % of population	Rank	Not favoured % of population	Rank
Beach/bathing/summer holidays	55.2	1	7.1	24
Snow holidays (winter)	55.1	2	9.0	23
Rest holidays	47.1	3	13.9	19
Health holidays	46.9	4	15.7	17
Pleasure holidays	44.4	5	12.5	21
Long-distance travel	44.2	6	12.8	20
Sporting holidays (summer)	43.9	7	12.0	22
Cruising holidays	41.2	8	17.4	15
Mountain holidays	40.5	9	16.1	16
Caravanning holidays (caravan/motor-home)	38.4	10	19.4	13
Activity holidays	37.9	11	15.1	18
Camping holidays	36.7	12	25.3	6
Medical treatment holidays (*Kururlaub*)	35.1	13	23.9	7
Adventure holidays (e.g., safari)	34.0	14	18.2	14
City travel	31.0	15	21.2	12
Farmhouse holidays	30.3	16	27.1	5
Club holidays (e.g., Club Méditerranée)	29.7	17.5	21.7	11
Study travel	29.7	17.5	23.0	9
Holidays in a holiday centre/holiday park	28.3	19	22.5	10
Holidays with a group	26.1	20	23.5	8
Nudist holidays	22.5	21	32.7	2
Visiting relatives/friends	19.8	22	35.1	1
Hobby holidays (e.g., painting, pottering)	18.1	23	30.3	3
Advanced learning holidays (e.g., language courses)	17.6	24	28.7	4

Source: Studienkreis für Tourismus (1987a, p. 13)

The average holiday cost DM 365 in 1969 (domestic DM 280; abroad DM 490)
and DM 795 in 1979–80 (domestic DM 553; abroad DM 977) (Statistisches
Bundesamt 1970, pp. 624–5; 1981, p. 869).

Relaxation and pleasure have been the predominant aims of holiday-makers,
although these have decreased in importance since 1980. In contrast, sightseeing, study and educational holidays as well as health and sport-oriented
holidays are of increasing importance. According to Studienkreis für
Tourismus (1987a) further changes can be expected which will influence the
choice of destinations (Table 11.3). Although the survey represents a
'snapshot' of German opinion concerning holidays, Table 11.3 confirms the
general trend towards activity-oriented holidays.

Finally, the seasonal aspect of holidays has to be considered. Data
concerning the seasonal distribution of travel were deliberately not included in
Table 11.1 because there have not been any significant changes during the past
thirty years. It is a characteristic feature of West German tourist flows that
more than 50 per cent of all holiday travel takes place in July and August with

about another 30 per cent in May, June and September. This concentration is largely conditioned by the prevailing systems of school and works holidays. Indeed, in 1975 nearly 50 per cent of all holiday-makers had to adjust their holiday plans to these kinds of constraint (Fornfeist 1976, p. 15). The summer season (May to October) is clearly predominant but since a growing number of West Germans undertake a second or third holiday in the winter, the ratio between summer and winter travel had fallen to 89:11 in the tourist year 1984–5 (Zucker 1986, p. 53).

The growth of winter holidays will almost certainly continue because the increase of tourist arrivals and nights in the ski resorts continued undisturbed after the energy crisis of the 1970s and the economic depression of the early 1980s, in contrast to the experiences of the summer resorts. The reason for this is the differences in the socio-economic profile of winter tourists, as compared with summer tourists.

11.3   The exodus to the sun

11.3.1   Foreign destinations

More than 50 per cent of West German holiday-makers were travelling abroad as early as 1970 (Table 11.1). By 1985 more than 50 per cent of all holidays spent abroad had their destinations in Mediterranean countries (Table 11.4 and Figure 11.1). In the early phase of international travel, however, Austria—essentially the Alps—was the country most favoured by West German tourists. At that time more than one-third of all cross-border travel was to Austria, and the joint share of the Mediterranean countries was only 4 per cent larger than Austria's share. At the level of individual states, Austria at that time held top position, but in 1970, its share already had declined by about 10 per cent over the previous decade. Since then, this trend has continued so that in 1985 Austria was the destination of only 14.5 per cent of all West Germans

Table 11.4   Foreign holiday destinations of West Germans, 1958–85 (per cent)

	1957–8	1962	1970	1975	1980	1985
Austria	36.0	37.0	27.8	27.9	20.9	14.6
Italy	24.0	27.0	22.2	16.2	15.9	18.4
Spain	4.0	5.6	9.3	15.7	14.8	17.3
Yugoslavia	4.0	2.5	3.7	6.6	6.9	9.2
France	8.0	4.3	3.7	6.8	6.9	8.2
Greece	0.0	0.9	3.7	2.6	3.5	5.0
Scandinavian countries	0.0	4.0	–	5.0	5.8	6.0
Other European countries	–	–	25.9	10.2	10.5	9.2
Eastern Europe (without GDR)	24.0	18.7	–	4.4	3.4	4.4
Non-European countries			1.9	4.4	8.5	7.7
Number of holidays (millions)	3.1	5.8	10.0	13.6	16.8	18.5
Percentage of all holidays	25.0	38.7	53.0	54.2	60.4	65.9

Source: Koch (1959); Statistisches Bundesamt (1965); Studienkreis für Tourismus (1986)

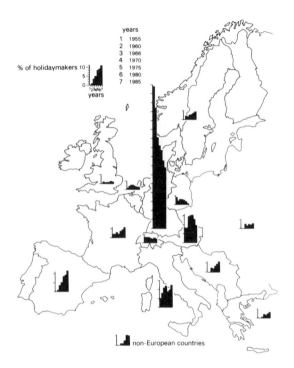

Fig. 11.1   The destinations of German tourists, 1955–85
Source: Jurczek (1986b, p. 76)

travelling abroad. The Mediterranean countries, on the other hand, were the definite winners in this process, for Spain, Yugoslavia, France and Greece had growing market shares; the only exception is Italy, for its share has more or less stagnated. The joint share of the Mediterranean countries is in fact even higher, for Turkey, Malta and the North African countries are not identified separately in Table 11.4. The greatest increase has been in Spain which was visited by more than 3 million West Germans (over 14 years of age) in 1985 while, in 1986, 1 million spent their holidays on Majorca alone (Commerzbank 1987, p. 5).

The reasons for the changes in destinations are several. There are, of course, climatic differences between the Federal Republic and the Mediterranean countries. Unstable weather conditions in the Federal Republic (air and water temperatures, sunshine, etc.) have caused many West Germans to seek holiday destinations with guaranteed fine weather. Italy became popular at an early stage for this reason, although cultural tourism also has always been important in this case. A second reason is the preference for a total change of scenery, and this not only refers to the climate, but also to the physical and cultural landscape. A third reason lies in the nature of mass tourism with its innovations such as mass accommodation, charter flights and all-inclusive package tours. The fourth reason is the favourable movement of currency exchange rates for German tourists, though these differ between destination countries from year to year. This last reason not only caused many West Germans to spend their holidays in the Mediterranean countries but also, where possible, to acquire second homes there.

Finally, long-distance travel has become increasingly important since the mid-1970s. The reasons for this boom are virtually the same as those for the popularity of the Mediterranean countries. In addition, however, the economic prosperity of a large part of the West German population plays an important role since transport costs are a much larger share of total travel costs than is the case with Mediterranean holidays.

11.3.2 Structural aspects of international tourism

The structural features of West Germans' international tourism can best be demonstrated by comparing domestic and cross-border travel (Table 11.5). The results of the surveys of 1962 and 1979–80 show that, in the early phase of cross-border holiday travel, the car was the dominant means of transport. Its share subsequently has remained stable, but transport by train has decreased by 20 per cent, with air travel taking over second place. To some extent, the importance of the railway in 1962 is explained by the prevalence, at that time, of neighbouring countries (over 50 per cent of tourists going to Austria, Switzerland and the Netherlands) as destinations. Moreover, access to

Table 11.5 Structural features of West German domestic and cross-border tourism, 1962 and 1979–80

	1962 Domestic	Cross-border	1979–80 Domestic	Cross-border
Means of transport (%)				
Car	41.9	59.2	67.1	60.3
Train	48.1	29.3	23.0	9.2
Bus	7.7	7.8	7.1	6.9
Aeroplane	0.3	1.8	0.7	21.0
Other	2.0	1.9	2.2	2.7
Type of accommodation (%)				
Hotel/inn/boarding-house	15.0	34.0	25.3	43.1
Cottage/bungalow/apartment	–	–	10.4	14.5
Private room (without paying)	33.0	8.7	27.9	14.0
Private room (rented)	34.0	37.0	17.5	12.4
Camping/caravanning	4.8	15.0	5.8	9.0
Other	13.2	5.3	13.1	6.9
Length of stay (%)				
Up to one week	34.0	28.0	19.5	10.8
Up to two weeks			41.5	40.5
Up to three weeks	37.0	40.0	25.7	31.9
More than three weeks	29.0	32.0	13.2	16.7
Cost per tourist (DM)	425	661	553	977
Number of tourists (thousands)	9,156	5,819	16,482	22,473

Source: Statistisches Bundesamt (1965, p. 41; 1981, p. 869)

private motor vehicles was still limited while mass tourism had only just begun to develop.

With the rise of mass tourism and the rapid growth of new resorts on, for example, the Spanish and Yugoslav coasts, these and other countries offering similar accommodation and infrastructure became increasingly popular with West German holiday-makers. Air transport also developed rapidly in order to reduce travelling time, and since most holidays in the Mediterranean countries are booked as package tours (90 per cent of the air passengers to Spain booked all-inclusive packages in 1986; Commerzbank 1987, p. 5), charter flights are of particular importance. In 1985, 13.5 per cent of the 18.2 per cent of travel undertaken by air involved charter flights (Zucker 1986, p. 49). The greater the distance to the destination country, the higher the share of all-inclusive package tours. Thus, in 1985, only 18.6 per cent of all holidays in Austria were booked as package tours (of which only 12.6 per cent were all-inclusive tours), while 80.9 per cent of all holidays in Greece were package tours (with 79.8 per cent being all-inclusive tours) (Zucker 1986, p. 47).

West Germans taking holidays abroad are more likely to stay in hotels, inns or boarding-houses, or in cottages, bungalows and apartments, as well as on campsites, than are those travelling within the Federal Republic, where private rooms, whether rented or provided by relatives or friends, are more popular. Privately rented rooms had taken a much higher share of foreign holidays in 1962, reflecting the importance as destinations at that time of neighbouring countries which had an accommodation structure which was similar to that of the Federal Republic. Moreover, in 1962 many West Germans spending their holidays abroad could not yet afford to stay in more expensive types of accommodation.

Over time there has been a shift to shorter holidays, but in 1979–80 foreign holidays tended to be longer than domestic ones. The mean cost of travel has also increased more for those travelling abroad. This is due to the changes in transport mentioned previously and to the fact that the distances travelled are generally longer than in 1962. Despite the higher travel costs, a large and increasing number of people are able and willing to meet these, for the growth of cross-border travelling is continuing, although the rate of increase is slackening.

11.4   Tourism in the Federal Republic of Germany

11.4.1   General trends

Although only 34 per cent of tourists take holidays within the Federal Republic, they still number more than 9 million. Together with foreign visitors, with West Germans spending a short break or a second or third holiday, and those on business travel, they recorded more than 210 million overnights. Even this figure is an underestimate because after 1981, as a result of a new tourist registration law, only those enterprises with more than eight beds had to record visitor arrivals and nights. Thus there are no data concerning private rooms being rented on a cash basis, even though these accounted for 28 per cent of accommodation capacity in 1980 and for 19.3 per cent (47.9 million) of tourist nights, in 1979–80. The consequences of this change in registration procedure are even greater at a disaggregated spatial scale: in the province of Schleswig-Holstein, for instance, there are no data for 51.5 per cent of all beds (1980). If it is assumed that the increase in tourist nights in private lodgings between 1974–5 and 1979–80 has continued at a linear rate, then the total number of tourist nights in 1984–5 was probably 269 millions.

Despite the continuous decline of interest amongst West Germans in domestic tourist destinations, domestic accommodation capacity as well as the number of tourist arrivals and nights have increased considerably (Table 11.6). At the national level, the accommodation capacity almost quadrupled between 1954 and 1985, even though private rooms are excluded from the analysis. The only accommodation category with below-average rates of increase are the hotels, inns and boarding-houses. As a result, the larger cities display a rather slow rate of increase in bed capacity. The highest growth rates of commercially and privately offered beds are typical of the seaside resorts, which, of course, underlines their attractiveness. Above-average increases are also typical of the spas, which have special tourist characteristics. In most cases the decision to stay in a spa is not voluntary but results from an illness, or a physical deficiency and, to a large extent, the stay is paid for by a health insurance company sickness fund. Apart from this, spa tourists usually cannot choose the dates of their stays so that the spas tend to attain very high and evenly distributed utilisation rates for their bed capacities.

Tourist arrivals increased from about 20 million in 1954–5 to 58 million in 1984–5 (190 per cent), and the share of foreign tourists from 16.2 to 21.4 per cent. Arrivals of West German tourists rose more slowly than those of foreign visitors. However, tourist nights and mean length of stay are better indicators of tourism development. The number of nights increased from about 70 to more than 210 million (201 per cent) between 1954–5 and 1984–5. Although the share of foreign tourists increased from 9.1 to 13.0 per cent, this is much lower than their share of arrivals, for foreign visitors do not holiday as long in West Germany as domestic tourists do. The sudden jump in the rate of increase from 354 to 429 per cent between 1979–80 and 1984–5 is due to the change in the registration law, for nearly one-third of all tourist nights spent in the large cities were accounted for by foreign guests in 1979–80. Since the absolute number of foreign visitors to the large cities has not decreased since then, and tourist arrivals and nights in private lodgings are not recorded any longer, the percentage of the tourist nights accounted for by foreigners is somewhat exaggerated.

Differentiation of the tourist nights according to types of tourist community again shows that the seaside resorts have the highest growth rates. With respect to foreign visitors, the predominance of the big cities is striking. Finally, in terms of the seasonal distribution of tourist nights, it can be observed that the winter season (34.2 per cent of the total in 1984–5) does not play a very important part in West German tourism, although it is slowly increasing in importance.

11.4.2   *Tourist regions and the distribution of tourists in the Federal Republic*

The official tourism statistics present data for ninety-one tourist regions of varying size and attractiveness. Most popular are the seaside resorts on the islands and the coast of the North Sea and the Baltic Sea, and the Alps.

Table 11.6 Development and structure of tourism in the Federal Republic of Germany, 1954/5–1984/5 (1954-5 = 100)

	1954–55	1959–60	1969–70	1974–75	1979–80	1984–85
Accommodation capacity						
Type of accommodation						
Hotels/inns/boarding-houses	100	167	236	269	290	337
Rest centres/holiday centres	100	165	297	366	430	1,108
Sanatoriums/spa hospitals	100	180	286	369	383	415
Private rooms	100	195	285	366	382	–
Total (excluding private rooms)	100	154	224	283	323	395
Type of tourist community						
Spas	100	164	238	314	357	354
Health resorts	100	175	235	259	288	320
Seaside resorts	100	212	349	425	474	479
Large cities	100	156	235	283	299	337
Unclassified resorts	100	150	210	291	325	337
Total	100	164	239	303	337	395
Tourist arrivals and nights						
Arrivals	100	147	195	220	267	290
Germans	100	146	192	224	266	277
Foreigners	100	166	233	223	297	383
Foreigners (%)	16.2	18.3	19.3	16.4	18.0	21.4
Nights	100	178	260	321	353	301
Germans	100	179	260	328	353	289
Foreigners	100	175	252	250	354	429
Foreigners (%)	9.1	9.0	8.9	7.1	9.1	13.0
Length of stay (days)	3.5	4.2	4.6	5.1	4.6	3.6
Germans	3.8	4.7	5.2	5.6	4.1	4.0
Foreigners	2.0	2.1	2.1	2.2	2.3	2.2

Type of tourist community						
Spas	100	173	237	308	330	362
Health resorts	100	156	216	250	269	181
Seaside resorts	100	216	446	533	561	366
Large cities	100	148	217	303	341	294
Unclassified resorts	100	131	187	183	219	
Percentage of foreigners (nights)						
Spas	4.5	3.4	2.6	2.2	3.1	5.1
Health resorts	4.9	6.2	5.3	3.7	6.0	8.1
Seaside resorts	3.4	1.8	0.9	0.7	0.7	0.7
Large cities	18.2	27.3	29.0	27.6	30.5	21.0
Unclassified resorts	8.3	9.2	10.4	8.5	10.7	
Length of stay (days)						
Spas		11.3	11.5	11.5	9.7	7.9
Health resorts		7.2	7.4	8.0	6.7	5.3
Seaside resorts		10.7	11.4	11.1	10.0	8.8
Cities		2.0	2.0	2.0	2.0	2.4
Unclassified resorts		2.7	3.1	3.6	3.4	
Percentage of winter season	28.8	28.5	28.8	29.6	31.6	34.2

Sources: Statistisches Bundesamt, *Jahrbuch für die Bundesrepublik Deutschland, Wiesbaden*, 1955, 1956, 1961, 1971, 1976, 1981, 1986

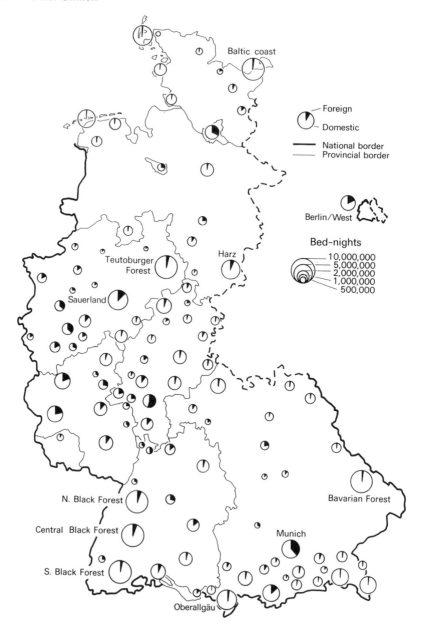

Fig. 11.2 Total number of tourist nights and share of foreign tourists in the Federal Republic of Germany, 1980: for regions and larger cities (with over 250,000 nights)

Source: Becker (1984a, p.3)

Figure 11.2 shows the absolute number of nights and the percentage of nights accounted for by foreigners in the tourist year 1979–80. The Federal Republic is clearly divided into three large tourist regions: the coast and its hinterland in the North; the midland region (e.g. the Harz, Eifel, Rhön and Black Forest) which stretches into the far South-West and South-East; and the South, mainly east of Lake Constance, and the Alps and their foothills (Allgäu). While the coast and the Alps increased their share of tourist nights from 17.4 to 23.7 per cent and from 23.8 to 24.3 per cent, respectively, between 1966 and 1979–80, the share of the midland region dropped from 58.8 to 52.0 per cent during the same period: the sub-regions most affected were north of the rivers Main and Nahe (Uthoff 1982, p. 299). Tourism development in the midland area shows regional differences and there is a clear shift of demand amongst these regions. The northern part of the midlands has suffered a relative loss of demand while the southern midlands have gained from an above-average increase of demand (Uthoff 1982, p. 304). At the provincial level, above-average rates of increase in the number of tourist nights, between 1954–5 and 1984–5, are characteristic of the provinces of Schleswig-Holstein (410 per cent), Lower Saxony (470 per cent) and the Saar (403 per cent). The same holds true also for West Berlin (451 per cent).

Foreigners visiting the Federal Republic concentrate on urban destinations such as Hamburg, Bremen, Hannover, Düsseldorf, Cologne, Bonn, Heidelberg, Stuttgart and Munich. The maximum share of tourist nights accounted for by foreigners is reached in Frankfurt because of its international airport (cf. Figure 11.2). (Becker 1984a, p. 5; Wolf and Jurczek 1986, p. 101). Foreign tourism is particularly conspicuous in those cities which have important roles as political (Bonn and the provincial capitals) and/or fair, exhibition and congress centres (for example, Hannover, Hamburg, Düsseldorf, Cologne, Stuttgart, Munich). Cultural and historical motives are especially important in the case of Heidelberg. However, Roth (1984, pp. 160–2) has shown considerable variations in motives for visiting West Germany, and in the spatial travel patterns of foreigners. Accessibility and the attractiveness of the landscape contribute to the popularity of some midland regions for foreign tourists. Thus in Sauerland — located south of the Ruhr district — there are communities in which more than 90 per cent of all foreign tourist nights, between 1974–5 and 1979–80, fell to visitors from the Netherlands, Belgium and Luxembourg (Schnell 1983, pp. 148–9, 1986, p. 10 and Map 2.3).

West German tourists have always preferred destinations in southern Germany. According to the micro-census of 1962 the destinations of 14.4 per cent of all domestic travellers were in the Alps and their foothills (Voralpen), while 7.4 per cent visited the seaside resorts of the North Sea and the Baltic Sea; in the survey of 1979–80 these percentages had changed to 17.7 and 17.8, respectively (Koch 1986, p. 11). The same trend emerges from the 'Travel Analysis' surveys of 1970 and 1985, for in the former year 26.1 per cent of all domestic holiday travel fell to Bavaria and 23.8 per cent to Schleswig-Holstein and Lower Saxony; however, in the latter year, Bavaria's share had increased to 31.8 per cent and Schleswig-Holstein and Lower Saxony's to 31.8 per cent (Studienkreis für Tourismus 1986, Table 5). Despite the decreasing relative interest of domestic holiday-makers in West German destinations, the number of main holidays spent within West Germany increased from 8.5 million in 1970 to 9.3 million in 1985, mainly because of a rise in travel intensity (Studienkreis für Tourismus 1986, Table 4).

11.5   The impact of tourism and tourism policies

11.5.1   *The economic impact*

The increasing gap between the expenditures of West German tourists abroad and receipts from tourists to the Federal Republic has already been mentioned. The Federal government has not considered taking measures to reduce the travel-expenditure deficit; it is argued that the destination countries will use the receipts from West German tourists to buy West German products, so that, ultimately, the West German economy does profit from tourism (Deutscher Bundestag 1986b, p. 8).

The economic impact of tourism in the Federal Republic has not been analysed systematically at the national or provincial level. There are, however, several studies of particular areas which give an indication of the economic impact of tourism. Priebe (1971, p. 27), in a regional study of eastern Bavaria, concluded that tourism, at most, generates 20 per cent of the regional income. Becker and Klemm (1978, p. 70) emphasise the three secondary effects of tourism on the local and regional economy: the employees of tourism enterprises spend most of their incomes in their respective regions; tourists not only pay for accommodation but also spend money on other items; while the maintenance and the services required by tourism enterprises creates additional jobs in the region. Taking into account these secondary effects, tourism enterprises have a regional multiplier of 1.43, which is much lower than was previously assumed (Becker and Klemm 1978, p. 75).

A rule of thumb has been developed by economists to determine the regional income effects of tourism: 4 tourist nights per inhabitant of a region or a community are considered to represent a contribution of 1 per cent to average per-capita incomes (Koch 1986, quoted in Deutsche Gesellschaft für Freizeit 1986, p. 129). The direct job-creation effects can be determined by means of indices, such as the number of full-time employees per bed in the various types of accommodation enterprise (Koch 1986, p. 16). The overall economic effect of tourism can be estimated from the following formula:

$$\frac{\text{net income per tourist night} \times \text{tourism intensity}}{\text{per-capita income}}$$

If, for instance, there is a tourism intensity of 1,000 (i.e. 1,000 tourist nights per 100 inhabitants), the net income per tourist night is DM 50, and the per-capita income amounts to DM 20,000 per year, then the contribution of tourism to regional income amounts to 2.5 per cent (Koch 1986, p. 17).

It has been estimated that in 1986 about 1.5 million jobs depended on tourism, some 6 per cent of all gainful employment (Commerzbank 1987, p. 1). In addition, a study of day trips and short-term tourism has analysed the structure of tourist expenditures, while calculating the effects on job creation (Billion and Flückiger 1978, pp. 44–56). In general, there is still a lack of studies about the economic impact of tourism, especially at the provincial and national level, and the data currently available are inadequate for economic impact studies.

11.5.2   The social impact

The impact of tourism on the social structures of tourist communities can be positive, but there are also negative consequences to be taken into account. Among the positive effects are improvements in infrastructure which also benefit the local population, improved income and employment prospects, and higher returns for local retailers. The result is improvements in standards of living which allow people to obtain goods and services formerly out of their reach. However, it has also been argued that tourism, especially mass tourism, disturbs or destroys traditional local and/or regional value systems. Moreover, since many tourist places are located in attractive landscape settings, the demand for real estate rises. Thus, in 1978, real estate prices in the Alps and their foothills were as high as in Munich and its surroundings, while the population had increased at above-average rates between 1974 and 1978 (Bayerisches Staatsministerium für Landesentwicklung und Umweltfragen 1980, Maps 3 and 4). In Mittenwald, a Bavarian tourist resort in the Alps, the price per square metre of land in 1974 was five times higher than the Bavarian average, and such prices excluded more than one-third of the local population not owning real estate from having plans to build their own houses (Alpeninstitut 1978, pp. 31–2).

Other negative impacts involve the physiognomy of the settlements and the landscape. The most attractive parts of the recreation landscape are most favoured as real estate, so that, for instance, lake fronts are no longer accessible to the public. The outward appearance of settlements has also changed under the influence of tourism, because large functional and urban buildings are often superimposed on traditional architectural and building styles. There can also be negative traffic effects. Thus, more than 50 per cent of the inhabitants surveyed in a study of Garmisch-Partenkirchen and Mittenwald (Alps), Meersburg (Lake Constance), Hinterzarten and Titisee (Black Forest) and Heiligenhafen (Baltic Sea) complained about frequent traffic congestion during the main season (Alpeninstitut 1978, p. 41).

Finally, it is to be expected that tourism has an effect on the demographic structure of tourist resorts, not least because many have attracted large numbers of older people. Initially, they may have become familiar with the tourist resort from a holiday visit, and then may have acquired a second home there, to which they have moved after retirement. This tendency to demographic imbalance has been noted in a number of case studies (Alpeninstitut 1978, p. 45).

11.5.3   Tourism policies and tourist innovations

Because of the growing number of West Germans who spend their holidays abroad, special efforts have been made to support tourism development in the Federal Republic. There is no national tourism policy, given the federal structure of the Republic, but at the national level, tourism is the responsibility of two ministries, those for Economics, and Regional Planning and Urban Affairs. The Ministry of Economics is responsible for a programme developed in 1969 to improve the economic structure of less-developed regions, but the execution of this programme is the responsibility of the provinces. In 1975, 12.6 per cent of the programme funds were spent on tourism projects (Becker and Klemm 1978, p. 27; Schnell 1975, p. 78; 1979, pp. 93–8). By 1987 this percentage had dropped to 8 per cent, of which 5 per cent was spent on the creation of new and the protection of existing jobs, with 3 per cent allocated for public tourism facilities (Deutscher Bundestag 1986c, p. 179).

The new holiday centres and holiday parks are impressive examples of the application of this programme: Becker (1984b, pp. 164–85) has analysed 137 of these centres and parks, which are highly concentrated along the line of the historic West German–East German border and German–Czech border (Figure 11.3), where special financial and taxation advantages are available in addition to the tourism programme, and in well-known tourist regions such as the North Sea coast and the Black Forest. The map also reveals that many dwellings—some 31 per cent in 1984—are used as second homes on a private basis (Becker 1984b, p. 170). The construction of these holiday centres and parks represented an innovation in West German tourism; the growing domestic demand for self-catering accommodation was taken up by the planners who were able to attract private investors for these schemes because of the taxation advantages they offered, supported by the tourism programme. It emerged later that the level of demand had been overestimated by some investors; therefore a number of dwellings were sold to private owners or converted to alternative uses, so that, for example, in the Baltic region in 1984 only 49 per cent of the 9,355 dwelling units were available for renting to tourists (Becker 1984b, p. 170).

Farm holidays were advocated in the early 1970s as an alternative to vacations in far-away, noisy and congested places. It was argued that the advantage of holidays in rural areas lay in the contrast they provided to 'normal' tourist centres (Klöpper 1973, p. 5). The share of farm holidays amounted to 4.1 per cent of all domestic holidays in 1972, increased to 5.2 per cent in 1978–9, and has since stagnated (4.9 per cent in 1981–2) (Martin 1986, p. 23). The people taking farm holidays are mostly younger families with children who live in urban areas. The main attraction for the farmers is the additional income which tourism generates. The federal government supports the 'holidays on a farm programme' and the Deutsche Zentrale für Tourismus (German National Tourist Board) advertises it abroad (Deutscher Bundestag 1986b, p. 20). The 'holidays on a farm' idea is of particular importance because it is linked to the concept of 'simple' or 'soft' tourism—that is, a kind of tourism that does not require a sophisticated infrastructure, and which therefore does not substantially alter the landscape and the settlement structure, and thus does not interfere with the ecological balance. It is argued that this kind of tourism will help to avoid social and ecological conflicts (cf. Bundesforschungsanstalt für Landeskunde und Raumordnung 1983).

Urban tourism has been promoted in the larger cities, especially in regions which lag behind in terms of economic development. There has been little research on this type of tourism and its variants (day visitors, business visitors, congress and exhibition visitors) but it is potentially important for the urban economy (Becker and Hensel 1982, pp. 174–82). Cultural and historical motives are also important in urban tourism (Jurczek 1986a).

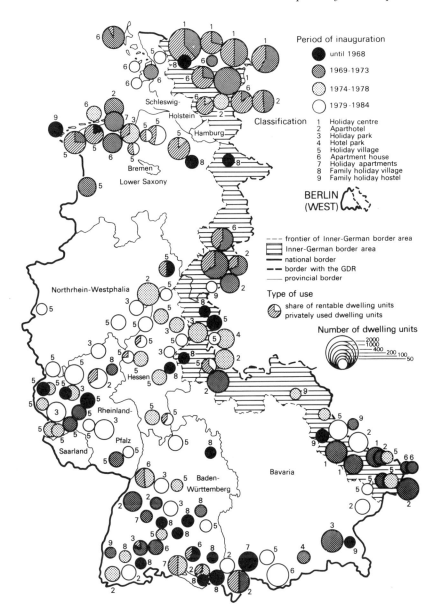

Fig. 11.3 Holiday centres and holiday parks in the Federal Republic of Germany, 1984

Source: Becker (1984b)

11.6   Conclusions

The situation, problems and prospects of West German tourism are summarised in a recent report (Commerzbank 1987, p. 1). The wet summer of 1987 has caused a boom in travel agency bookings and for promoters of foreign holidays. Furthermore, as a result of the strength of the Deutschmark, holidays in the classical holiday regions such as the Alps and the Mediterranean, as well as in 'new' destinations such as the United States, are considerably cheaper than in the preceding season. This is not seen as a cause of grave concern. The Federal government takes a sanguine view of the future of tourism: the basic economic determinants of tourist demand—increased net income and leisure time—will effectively remain unchanged, while there is no apparent reason why the West Germans should cease spending a disproportionate amount of their incomes on travelling (Deutscher Bundestag 1986b, p. 8). The trend to preferring foreign destinations to those within the Federal Republic will continue. However, there are opportunities to improve domestic tourism because of the increasing participation in short-term travel, and developments such as urban tourism will continue to be important. Nevertheless, it has been recognised that further research is necessary into how domestic demand for holidays within West Germany can be increased (Deutscher Bundestag 1986b, p. 23).

12 The Netherlands: tourist development in a crowded society

David Pinder

12.1 Introduction

Economic success and the absence of uplands in their country have for many years ensured that the majority of Dutch holiday-makers go abroad. In the winter of 1986–7 2.2 million did so, as did 5.8 million the following summer; this was 54 per cent of the total. Skiing—both cross-country and Alpine—dominates winter vacations; in summer, upland areas—especially the Alps, the Pyrenees and the Massif Central—compete with the Mediterranean for the Dutch market. Yet, although foreign destinations are important to the Dutch, the Netherlands' 14.5 million inhabitants are not a dominant component in total European tourism. Moreover, the international dimension of Dutch holiday-making has eclipsed the fact that tourism within the Netherlands—by foreigners as well as by the Dutch—is far from negligible (Ashworth and Bergsma 1987). To compensate for this neglect, and to emphasise that tourist-deficit countries may still have significant tourist industries, this chapter concentrates on the domestic tourist industry. Its primary aims are to provide a factual overview of this underresearched activity; to establish its spatial dimensions; and to consider the spatial strategies favoured by planners in this crowded country. Background geographical information is provided by Figure 12.1.

12.2 Accommodation structures

Tourist accommodation, as in many other countries, has traditionally been provided by hotels and guest houses. This sector is still substantial: in 1986 hotels had a total capacity of 93,000 beds. Although it remains significant, however, the hotel industry has recently experienced distinct structural changes. Between 1975 and 1984 the number of hotels fell by 27 per cent, while many of the surviving businesses invested in capacity expansion. This investment compensated almost exactly for capacity losses caused by closure, leading to a marked increase in average hotel size—from 29 beds in 1964 to 50 in 1984. More recently the number of hotels has increased (by 4 per cent between 1984 and 1986) while the average size has continued to rise (to 51.5 beds in 1986). Restructuring and expansion have sometimes entailed new construction, but in many instances change has been brought about by the restructuring and acquisition of existing properties. In individual hotels

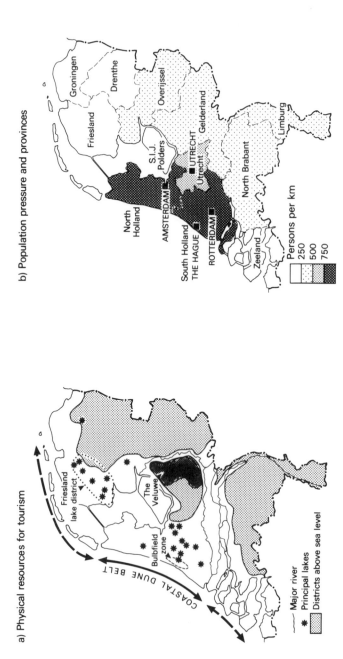

Fig. 12.1 The physical and human background for tourism in the Netherlands

growth has often been associated with the provision of new facilities (especially private toilet facilities), but concern to improve the quality of accommodation has not been restricted to hotels undergoing expansion. Meanwhile guest houses, unable to emulate these scale increases, have declined dramatically: no less than 60 per cent left the register between 1975 and 1986. By then, total guest house capacity was only 8 per cent of hotel capacity, compared with 21 per cent in 1975. Although hotels and guest houses remain significant, they are overshadowed by the campsite sector. Following impressive expansion since the 1950s, almost 3,000 sites now provide 93 per cent of all land-based tourist accommodation and can absorb 1.6 million people at a time, this is more than 10 per cent of the Dutch population. Campsites frequently have chalets available for hire, and specialist chalet parks are growing in importance (see p. 219). But, nation-wide, almost 90 per cent of campsite accommodation comprises tent and caravan pitches. This substantial provision, is, however, deceptive because by no means all the capacity is available to touring holiday-makers. Almost two-thirds of the pitches are rented on long leases and, although they may also have a holiday function, they frequently serve as weekend retreats in a country where second-home costs are high (Thissen 1978).

Given the abundance of water in the Netherlands, marina development must also be considered. Three points are particularly relevant. First, because demand has risen substantially, in the summer months the number of Dutch people using this type of accommodation for weekend breaks probably exceeds the number staying in hotels and guest houses. Second, satisfaction of this demand has led to the proliferation of marinas: between 1967 and 1981 the average number opened annually was 31, and by 1981 883 were operational. Finally, as in the hotel industry, investors have placed increasing emphasis on scale economies. In 1967 the average number of rented berths per marina was 90, compared with 127 in 1981. Moreover, these averages conceal the importance of exceptionally large schemes: developments able to accommodate more than 350 boats account for only one-tenth of all marinas, yet house one-third of the berths. One advantage of these major developments is that scale economies aoften make feasible the provision of high-quality facilities that are increasingly demanded by water sports enthusiasts.

12.3 Tourist behaviour

Analysis of behaviour requires consideration of three principal variables: tourists' origins; their length of stay; and their demands on accommodation detailed above. Origins are best considered in terms of Dutch and foreign tourism, and other variables will be examined under both these headings. While the discussion focuses on residential tourism, the country's small size — and its accessibility from Belgium and the Federal Republic of Germany — dictate that day visitors should not be overlooked, even though data are far from satisfactory.

12.3.1 *Dutch tourist preferences*

The definition of day visitors is very broad, and the number of trips enumerated is consequently high. The largest single category of excursion —

Table 12.1   Short breaks in the Netherlands (excluding those with family or friends), by accommodation type, summer period, 1975–85 (per cent)

	1975	1980	1985
Hotels or guest houses	7	9	9
Chalets etc.	13	11	11
Tents	9	11	16
Caravans or trailer tents	52	50	44
Boats	11	9	9
Youth hostels etc.	4	6	7
Other	4	4	4

Source: Centraal Bureau voor de Statistiek, *Jaarcijfers voor Nederland*, 1986, p. 124

almost 40 per cent of the total—entails visits to relatives or friends, and is therefore of little significance in placing pressure on tourist facilities or rural areas. But outdoor recreation ranks second in terms of trip motivation, is responsible for 20 per cent of all journeys and is substantially more important than sport (13 per cent). In round terms demand is equivalent to one trip per inhabitant every 2 weeks. It is, of course, divided between urban parks and rural areas, but in a country with restricted public open space and no rights of access to farmland, it cannot be considered negligible (see p. 237).

Short stays, requiring accommodation for up to 3 nights, are numerous but, perhaps surprisingly, are not a growth sector for the industry. Since the mid-1970s up to 500,000 people per week have taken short breaks in summer, falling to 125,000 in winter. A second significant feature is that breaks are not generated primarily by a hotel sector offering bargain terms for off-peak visits. In 1985 hotels accounted for only 9 per cent of all short breaks—no more than those taken on boats and far less than the 60 per cent taken on campsites (Table 12.1). While this pattern certainly reflects cost factors, the use of campsites for weekend retreats should not be overlooked (see p. 227). In addition, in many areas perceived to be desirable for recreation—including large parts of the southern and eastern Netherlands—the supply of hotels suitable for weekend breaks is far from plentiful (Figure 12.2).

As the introduction has indicated, despite the expansion of the foreign market, holidays in the Netherlands remain popular and of central importance for the home tourist industry. In 1987, 5.3 million Dutch people took their main annual break in the country, chiefly in the brief late June to mid-August season. This was 48 per cent of all holidays that year, and was 800,000 more than in 1975. Moreover, summer holidays taken in the Netherlands still last on average 14 days, and when economies on travel time are considered, are comparable with those taken abroad (17 days). Also, the domestic tourist industry benefits in times of national economic recession as fewer holiday-makers choose to go abroad. Between 1980 and 1983 average unemployment rose from 6.1 per cent to 17.3 per cent, while foreign holidays fell by 700,000 and those taken in the Netherlands rose by 800,000.

As with short breaks, however, buoyant demand for holidays in the Netherlands has not greatly benefited the hotel and guest house sector although—largely because of the popularity of bed and breakfast—an upturn

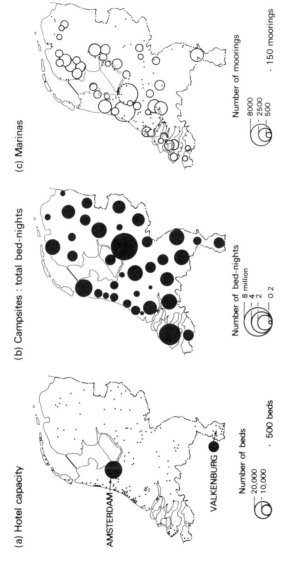

(a) Hotel capacity

(b) Campsites : total bed-nights

(c) Marinas

Fig. 12.2 Hotels, campsites and marina facilities in the Netherlands

Table 12.2   Holidays[1] in the Netherlands, by accommodation type, 1975–87
(per cent)

	1975	1980	1985	1987
Hotels or guest houses	11	10	7	12
Chalets etc	29	32	33	31
Tents	16	14	15	11
Caravans or trailer tents	28	30	32	34
Boats	7	6	6	6
Youth hostels etc.	5	4	4	3
Self-catering apartments	3	4	2	1
Other	2	1	1	2

Sources: Centraal Bureau voor de Statistiek, *Jaacijfers voor Nederland*, 1986, p. 127; Centraal Bureau voor de Statistiek, *Statistisch Zakboek*, 1986, p. 144 and 1988, p. 144.
Notes: 1. Breaks of more than 3 days.

in the figures for these types of accommodation has recently occurred (Table 12.2). Much more popular forms of accommodation are camp and chalet sites. Tents and caravans are used for more than 40 per cent of all holidays, and—in keeping with short-break accommodation preferences—the large majority of these stays are in caravans. Rented chalets, meanwhile are also proving increasingly popular. In 1987 they accounted for almost one-third of all holidays and were the most important single type of accommodation used. Because of the attractions of space and comfort during long stays, chalets are much more important for holiday-makers than for those taking short breaks. Specialist chalet parks are now to be found in all areas where camping is popular (Stoelers and Karssen 1986, pp. 7–9) and innovative operators in this field are investing heavily to maintain growth. The market leader is Center Parcs, a firm now operating seven sites in the Netherlands and two in Belgium. These feature high-quality self-catering accommodation, and a range of all-weather recreational facilities designed to ensure that sites are attractive throughout the year. The firm's success—1.5 million visitors were attracted to the nine centres in 1986—clearly demonstrates that there is a place for innovative, high-quality tourist products in this part of Europe.

12.3.2   *Foreign tourist preferences*

The accommodation preferences of foreign visitors contrast sharply with those of the Dutch. The essence of this contrast lies in the low level of campsite usage by foreign tourists. Although foreign campers number 1.2 million, their share of total nights spent on campsites is little more than 10 per cent. Campsite facilities are therefore a central element of the national—rather than the international—tourist infrastructure.

Hotels, conversely, are closely geared to the demands of foreign leisure and business tourism. In 1985 hotel stays by foreigners reached 3.4 million, 1 million of whom were visitors on business. Altogether, there were three times as many foreign hotel guests as foreign campers. As in other countries, the Netherlands' international catchment area for hotel visitors has evolved as tourism has grown. In 1964 more than half came from neighbouring countries

Table 12.3   International catchment area of the hotel sector in the
Netherlands, 1964–87 (per cent)

	1964	1985	1987
FRG	30.6	18.2	19.4
Belgium and Luxembourg	5.6	3.9	4.3
Denmark	1.9	1.8	3.0
UK and Ireland	14.1	18.6	18.4
Sub-total	52.2	42.5	45.1
Other European countries	24.5	23.2	26.1
United States and Canada	16.8	20.8	15.8
Asia, Oceania and Australia	3.6	9.2	9.6
Other countries	2.9	4.3	3.4
Total foreign guests (millions)[1]	1.705	3.361	3.111
Total bed-nights (millions)	4.320	6.788	6.485
Average length of stay (days)	2.5	2.0	2.1

Sources: Centraal bureau voor de Statistiek, *Jaarcijfers voor Nederland*, 1969, p. 101; Centraal Bureau voor de Statistiek, *Statistisch Zakboek*, 1986, p. 146 and 1988, p. 146.
Note: 1. Excluding Allied military personnel.

(including Britain) and almost a quarter from elsewhere in Europe (Table 12.3). By 1985, the neighbouring countries' share had fallen to 45 per cent—due largely to the changing preferences of West German tourists—while the combined share of the United States, Canada, Asia and Australasia had risen from 20 to 25 per cent. Yet the broadening catchment area has not altered a very striking feature of foreign hotel tourism: visits are brief and have become briefer. While the average stay in 1964 was 2.5 nights, in 1987 it was only 2.1.

Data published by the city of Amsterdam initially suggest that short stays reflect high accommodation costs. Between 1963–6 and 1976–9 the occupancy rate for first-class hotels fell from 65 per cent to 42 per cent, while class 2 hotels maintained a stable rate of 51 per cent (Stad van Amsterdam 1980, p. 293). But other evidence indicates that cost factors should not be overemphasised. First, the declining occupancy rate for first-class hotels arose because first-class facilities expanded faster than the growth of tourists. Second, occupancy rates for much cheaper hotels (classes 3 and 5) also declined (from 43 to 32 per cent). Third, the average length of stay does not vary greatly according to the grade of accommodation. Visitors in first-class hotels stayed 2.0 nights in 1979, compared with 2.2 nights for those staying in *pensions*. Factors other than cost must therefore be included in any explanation of the hotel sector's dependence on brief visits. Here perception is a central consideration. Because foreigners do not generally perceive the Netherlands to be a scenic country, its main attractions are specific features—historic towns, museums, art galleries, the bulbfields, windmills, and the few remaining communities where traditional costume can still be seen. Many of these attractions are conveniently concentrated in and around the Randstad cities of the western Netherlands, and it is possible to experience most of them—if only perfunctorily—in a stay of only two or three days. The practical implication of this, especially in the west, is that the hotel industry must constantly adjust to fast turnover and maintain a marketing system capable of sustaining rapid throughput. Equally important—but outside the industry's direct control—is the necessity of maintaining the appeal of attractions, an issue closely associated with urban conservation policies (Voorden 1981; Whysall 1982).

12.4   Macro-economic impact

Economic data are less numerous and less comprehensive than those detailing the industry's structure, growth and development. In addition, comparability problems complicate the task of interrelating data sets. Day tourism expenditure cannot be calculated, but using assumptions concerning length of stay and seasonality, estimates of short-break and holiday expenditure can be made. In Table 12.4 these estimates are presented as minimum and maximum expenditure scenarios (variants A and B respectively). For Dutch tourism the estimates are that expenditure in 1984 was between approximately 2.5 billion and 2.8 billion guilders. Between a quarter and a third of this was probably generated by short breaks spread throughout the year, with the majority being concentrated into the restricted summer holiday season. Foreign tourists, meanwhile, probably injected between 1.9 billion and 3.0 billion guilders into the economy, a figure that could be raised by 0.6 billion guilders if foreign business visitors were included in the analysis. The estimate for total leisure-oriented expenditure ranges from 4.3 billion to 5.8 billion guilders with the industry's income being derived almost equally from Dutch and foreign tourists.

The scale of this expenditure can be measured against consumption and trade, although the results are initially unimpressive. For example, estimated expenditure is equivalent to less than 3 per cent of total national consumption. Similarly, foreign tourist earnings amount to less than 2 per cent of visible exports. On the other hand, turnover is comparable to Dutch expenditure on

Table 12.4   Estimated tourist expenditure in the Netherlands 1984 (billions of guilders)

	Variant A	Variant B
Dutch expenditure[1]: short-break summer	0.400	0.600
short-break winter (1984/5)	0.220	0.330
holidays	1.830	1.830
Total Dutch expenditure	2.450	2.760
Foreign expenditure[2]: total short breaks and holidays	1.860	2.980
Total Dutch foreign expenditure	4.310	5.750
Dutch as % of total expenditure	57	48

Sources: Centraal Bureau voor de Statistiek, *Statistisch Zakboek*, 1986, G.7, G.8, G.9, G.11, G.13, G.14, Q.2

Notes: 1. Variant A assumes short-break stays average one night; Variant B assumes short breaks average two nights.

2. Variant A assumes short-break and holiday earnings fall by 75% during October–March compared with April–September. Variant B assumes that the proportional importance of short-break and holiday earnings is constant throughout the year.

the output of several traditional industries, such as market gardening and dairy products. Relative to the public sector, it equals between half and three-quarters of law-and-order expenditure. But the most significant indicators are those relating earnings to the balance of payments. First, expenditure by foreign tourists reduces by between a quarter and a third the outflow caused by the Dutch holidaying abroad (6.8 billion guilders in 1984). Second, foreign tourist income in the early 1980s—when visible exports were in recession—greatly ameliorated balance-of-trade deficits. In 1984, estimated tourist earnings were between an eighth and a fifth of the country's total balance-of-payments surplus.

The industry's impact is also significant in terms of employment. Although employment data are generalised, information is available for three leisure-related activities: hotels, restaurants and cafés (HORECA); cultural and sociocultural facilities; and sport and recreation. These cover the employment opportunities most closely associated with residential and day tourism. Employment in these activities was 172,000 in 1985, or 3.9 per cent of total national employment. This was considerably larger than the labour forces of several traditional and advanced industries, such as food processing (152,000) and electrotechnical production (112,000). Growth rates over the last decade have exceeded 2 per cent per year, demand for male and female labour is almost evenly balanced, and unemployment statistics suggest that seasonality is no more severe than in the economy as a whole. Despite these positive features, however, two notes of caution must be sounded, particularly with respect to the HORECA sector. First, part-time employment is widespread: at least one-fifth of all HORECA employees work less than fifteen hours a week, and it is possible that the true proportion of part-timers is much higher. While part-time work suits the requirements of individuals for whom full-time employment is impractical, there may be many employees requiring a full-time position but unable to obtain one. Second, there is a large reservoir of surplus HORECA labour which, despite recent national economic recovery, shows little sign of diminishing. In July 1987, HORECA unemployment accounted for 6 per cent of total national employment, compared with 3.4 per cent in the mid-1970s. Moreover, between July 1985 and July 1987 national unemployment decreased by 8.9 per cent, while HORECA unemployment fell by only 0.7 per cent. The prospects for those attempting to enter the catering and accommodation industries are therefore worse than those of almost any other group of unemployed workers.

12.5 Spatial impact

Data problems seriously hinder the analysis of day tourism, important though it is. For foreign day visitors—essentially from the Federal Republic of Germany and Belgium—geographical preferences and, by implication, spatial expenditure patterns are known. But figures for the Dutch are mingled with data for almost 1 billion short-distance journeys. This section, therefore, focuses on the geographical dimensions of foreign and Dutch residential tourism.

12.5.1   Foreign tourism and impact concentration

The discussion has already implied that the economic benefits of foreign tourism are concentrated in the western Netherlands as a result of the centripetal effects of specific attractions. For business tourism, a western focus is dictated by the leader-region status enjoyed by the provinces of North Holland, South Holland and Utrecht. The strength of these centripetal forces is demonstrated by the national distribution of hotel accommodation (Figure 12.2). Amsterdam dominates the industry, and close by lie most of the subsidiary clusters of accommodation, particularly in coastal towns and cities. Outside the western provinces there is only one significant hotel concentration, around Valkenburg in south Limburg. With rolling farming landscapes reaching up to 250 metres above sea level, south Limburg has been somewhat grandly marketed as the Netherlands' 'Little Switzerland', yet even here the industry's development must be placed in perspective. Lacking attractions other than its landscape, the district draws in only 3 or 4 per cent of foreign hotel guests. In sharp contrast, 75 per cent of all bed-nights are spent in the western provinces of North and South Holland, with Amsterdam alone accounting for 47 per cent of the national total. Even concentration on this scale, however, is not linked with tourist domination of local or regional economies. For example, the leisure-related employment discussed above—employment that is not simply based on tourism—accounts for less than 6 per cent of Amsterdam's labour force. This point is also relevant to other popular tourist areas identified below. Leisure-related employment is significant in all of them, but this benefit is not developed to the point of overdependence (Table 12.5).

Foreign campers spend as many nights in the Netherlands as do foreign hotel guests. They display similar, but not identical, regional preferences (Table 12.6). The western bias is muted (North Holland and South Holland together account for 28 per cent) and outlying provinces are of correspondingly greater importance. Limburg and Gelderland each attract 10 per cent, Gelderland

Table 12.5   Leisure-related employment in leading tourist areas[1] in the Netherlands, 1985 (thousands)

		% of local employment
Western provinces (North Holland, South Holland and Utrecht)	89.2	4.1
including North Holland	42.2	5.3
Amsterdam	17.5	5.5
South Limburg	6.1	3.5
South-West Friesland	1.0	4.8
The Veluwe	6.8	4.3
Zeeland	3.3	3.4
Southern Ijsselmeer polders	1.3	5.4

Sources: Centraal Bureau voor de Statistiek, *Statistiek Werkzamen Personnen*, 1985, Table 1.3
Note: 1. Including SICs 67 (hotels, restaurants and cafes), 95 (cultural and socio-cultural facilities) and 96 (sport and recreation).

Table 12.6 Nights spent on campsites in the Netherlands: provincial
distribution, 1986 (per cent)

	Foreign visitors	Dutch visitors	Share of woodland, nature and recreation areas
Northern provinces			
Groningen	0.6	1.2	2.0
Friesland	12.1	5.9	7.4
Drenthe	1.5	7.6	8.1
Eastern provinces			
Overijssel	1.5	8.6	10.4
Gelderland	10.8	20.0	23.6
Western provinces			
Utrecht	0.7	4.1	2.4
North Holland	16.6	8.4	7.8
South Holland	11.1	7.3	6.4
South-West			
Zeeland	27.3	9.3	2.8
Southern provinces			
North Bradbant	3.7	15.2	17.5
Limburg	10.5	10.1	7.5
Southern Ijsselmeer polders	3.6	2.3	4.1
Nights spent (millions)	6.605	52.438	

Source: Centraal Bureau voor de Statistiek, *Regionaal Statistisch Zakboek*, 1986, p. 94

being popular for the outstanding Veluwe district (see Figure 12.1 and below). Friesland, distinctive for its culture and a landscape dominated by low-lying pastures and extensive lakes, attracts 12 per cent. And, impressively, the deltaic province of Zeeland is the destination for more than a quarter. Coastal scenery and improved transportation lie at the heart of the delta's popularity. Until the 1960s communications, and the economy, were poor (Pinder 1983). Today this former backwater is the natural terminus of motorways leading westwards from the Ruhr; is skirted by the Stockholm–Amsterdam–Paris axis; and is the destination for a major North Sea ferry crossing (Sheerness–Vlissingen). Improvements have also made the delta accessible to foreign day visitors from Belgium and the Federal Republic of Germany. One and a half million, almost a quarter of the country's total, are drawn to the delta each year.

12.5.2 Dutch tourism and impact dispersion

Hotel-based breaks and holidays account for only about a tenth of Dutch residential tourism (Tables 12.1 and 12.2). Geographical data are unavailable, but it is likely that Dutch hotel guests are less heavily biased towards Amsterdam than are foreign tourists, largely because of the city's accessibility to day visitors from the regions. The distinction between the regional preferences of Dutch and foreign tourists emerges more clearly when other forms of accommodation are considered. One one-fifth of the Dutch choose campsites in North Holland, South Holland or Utrecht, despite the region's extensive coastline (Figure 12.2 and Table 12.6). Similarly, deltaic Zeeland attracts only 9 per cent. Meanwhile one-sixth of the Dutch opt for the northern and eastern provinces of Drenthe and Overijssel, another one-fifth for Gelderland and 15 per cent for North Brabant, south of the river district. These areas' shares of foreign camping are 3 per cent, 11 per cent and 4 per cent respectively.

Dutch interest in eastern and southern districts partly reflects push factors. Forty-four per cent of the population live in the west, mainly in the crowded Randstad cities, from the pressures of which there is an understandable desire to escape (Figure 12.1). This desire is often strengthened by familiarity with the west's main recreation areas, along the coast and in the delta. The west is also unappealing to many tourists from outlying regions because of its high level of urbanisation. But the geography of Dutch camping preferences reflects positive, as well as negative, forces. Central to the positive influences is the fact that, unlike most foreigners, the Dutch do not perceive their country to be monotonously uniform.

Three valued landscapes outside the west (south Limburg, the Friesian lake district and the Veluwe) have already been noted (Figure 12.1). Of these the Veluwe requires discussion since it provides the key to understanding the popularity of many parts of the east and south, as well as of the area itself. The Veluwe's distinctiveness derives from its origin as an extensive tract (45 km by 25km) of glacial sands forming low hills (up to 30 m above sea-level) that have not required reclamation from the sea. Vegetated initially by heathland and natural woodland, since the mid-nineteenth century the landscape has evolved rapidly. Farming has extended, especially around the periphery; in these agricultural districts a diverse landscape of small farms and woodland has emerged. Elsewhere the *Staatsbosbeheer* has established 40,000 hectares of coniferous plantations. And, amongst the farming and forestry, some 60,000 ha of heathland and 1,100 ha of open sand dunes have survived (Hanekamp, 1979). Although these heath and sand residuals are small compared with their mid-nineteenth century extent (600,000 ha and 15,000 ha respectively), they are highly attractive for recreation. This attraction is enhanced by the presence of two of the country's three national parks, the Hoge Veluwe and the Veluwezoom. Pedestrian and cyclist access to many woodland areas is also important. And, although there are no access rights to farmland, additional visual appeal is undoubtedly provided by the contrast between the Veluwe's small-scale agricultural landscapes and the wide pasture landscapes of reclaimed areas in the west.

The same factors underlie the attractions of many other areas in the north, east and south. Where glacial outwash predominates, the landscape has undergone conversion from heath and woodland. Conversion has generally progressed further than on the Veluwe, yet it has produced an attractive mixture of small-scale farming landscapes, studded by areas of heath and wood with substantial recreational potential. This is well documented by the *Atlas van de Nederlandse Landschappen* (Morzer Bruijns and Bentham 1979) and is evaluated by the *Atlas van Nederland* (sheet V1–S–5). Against this background it can be demonstrated that the regional distribution of camping by the Dutch is well adjusted to the occurrence of recreational land, nature areas and woodland (Table 12.5). The correlation coefficient for these variables is 0.900 (r^2 = 81 per cent), implying—at least on the provincial scale—a very close relationship between an area's environmental attractions and its ability to benefit from expenditure generated by the Dutch enthusiasm for camping.

Brief mention must finally be made of water sports and, in particular, of marina development. Naturally enough, marina facilities are primarily found in western and northern districts lying below sea-level (Figure 12.2). In the north development concentrates on the Friesland lake district; in the west, lake areas around Amsterdam and the waters around and south of Rotterdam provide foci. Thus, in contrast to the camping sector, marina development is localised. Despite this localisation, however, the areas in question do not make large financial gains as a result of expenditure by visitors from other parts of the country or, indeed, from abroad. Even in sparsely populated Friesland, more than 50 oper cent of the craft are owned by residents of the province; in the west the local proportion exceeds 75 per cent (*Atlas van Nederland*, Sheet X1–16–5). In general, therefore, the sailing fraternity circulates finance within regional economies, rather than generating major interregional financial flows.

12.6   Spatial strategies and planning

The Netherlands is renowned for its planning systems (Dutt and Costa 1985) yet, as Ashworth and Bergsma (1987) have stressed, there is no long-standing strategy guiding tourist development. The industry's growth has been moulded largely by market forces encouraged or constrained by individual strategic decisions and by local planning authorities. But since the early 1970s planners have increasingly favoured the adoption of a spatial strategy designed to accommodate the pressures generated by a prosperous, leisure-conscious society (Ministerie van Volkshuisvesting en Ruimtelijke Ordening 1977, pp. 39–41; Ministerie van Cultuur, Recreatie en Maatschappelijk Werk 1981a; Ministerie van Landbouw en Visserij 1981, pp. 56–65; Rijksplanologische Dienst 1986, pp. 104–13). Also, in the economically difficult 1980s, politicians have advocated stimulation of tourism to attract more foreign visitors and curtail Dutch tourism abroad. Instruments for implementing this policy have yet to be devised (Ashworth and Bergsma 1987, p. 154), but progress has been made towards a national spatial strategy. This chapter therefore concludes by reviewing the main elements of spatial planning. These focus on day tourism, on residential tourism in rural areas and on water sports development.

Public investment to promote day and residential tourism takes two forms, providing extensive and intensive recreational opportunities. A major problem for extensive recreation is that many rural areas are visually appealing, yet, because of property rights, are inaccessible to visitors. Policy therefore aims at achieving joint use of the countryside, by local farmers and by tourists, through an opening-up process. While this may be achieved by individual negotiation, significant opportunities are offered by the national programme of land consolidation. Although this mainly aims to improve agricultural efficiency, the comprehensive rural redevelopment schemes that are undertaken allow relatively easy provision of footpaths, cycle paths, bridle paths, picnic sites and similar facilities. Investment for these purposes is now typical of land-consolidation projects.

In sharp contrast to this policy of joint countryside use, public investment in intensive facilities generally entails the complete conversion of areas from agricultural to leisure purposes. This has clear social ramifications because of the displacement of farming families. It is also expensive: farmland must be purchased outright and must be transformed into an attractive recreational environment. The techniques of conversion are, however, highly developed. Aided by fast-growing species, projects mature quickly, the typical environment created being one of woods, footpaths and lakes fringed by sunbathing and picnic areas. Between 1978 and 1985 the area of completed recreation projects increased from 11,700 ha to 23,300 ha. In 1981 the target was to complete projects covering another 18,000 ha by 1995 and 28,000 ha by 2005 (Ministerie van Cultuur, Recreatie en Maatschappelijk Werk 1981b). Planned projects are invariably close to substantial towns and cities, with a strong bias towards the western Netherlands. Of the 18,000 ha planned before 1995, three-quarters lie in the urbanised Randstad and 60 per cent are associated with Amsterdam, Rotterdam, The Hague and Utrecht (Figure 12.3). This emphasises that, above all, policy aims to provide day-tourist facilities within easy reach of congested centres. To date it appears successful: an estimated 44 million visits were made to these projects in 1985, a 70 per cent increase compared with 1978.

Camping expansion plans are also partly urban-oriented. By 1995 at least 400 ha are to be made available for the popular long-lease camping opportunities noted in Section 12.2. Most of this growth will be either within or close to the Randstad, but it will be outstripped by the expansion of touring facilities and chalet parks. At least 1,400 ha are to be released for these, giving capacity growth of between 15 and 20 per cent. For this sector of the industry the strategy is to restrict development in most of the more popular camping regions. Thus permited capacity growth is likely to be less than 3 per cent in Overijssel and North Brabant. In Gelderland, including the Veluwe, it will be little more than 1 per cent. Conversely, 25 per cent of the expansion has been allocated to the north (Groningen, Friesland and Drenthe) where capacity may increase by up to 8 per cent. And in the southern IJsselmeer polders capacity growth of 60 per cent is envisaged, a proposal closely linked to the belief that multi-purpose planning is now appropriate for this expensively reclaimed land (Dutt *et al.* 1985). Figure 13.3 specifies planning preferences in more detail, identifying major areas where containment rather than expansion is preferred. In many instances, particularly in the east and south, these containment areas coincide with districts earmarked for designation as 'national landscapes' (Ministerie van Cultuur, Recreatie en Maatschappelijk Werk 1981c). The largest of these is the Veluwe. But control is also a priority in many popular districts with less highly valued landscapes, particularly in the coastal zone and the delta.

The protection of areas under pressure is also a goal of water sports planning. When environmental factors are considered, most leading areas in Friesland and around the Randstad cities are now subject to excessive use. Moreover, the nature of this pressure is changing as water sports develop: dinghies and sailboards are proliferating, yet are difficult to control because they require few facilities. Even though lakes are included in many of the new recreation projects, water areas cannot be created on a scale that will solve problems of excess demand. Protection therefore aims to divert demand into areas currently under-used, and it is argued that effective planning is most

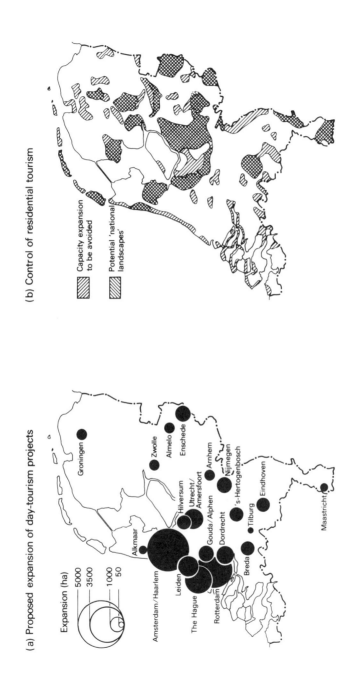

(a) Proposed expansion of day-tourism projects

(b) Control of residential tourism

Fig. 12.3 Planned day-tourism projects and restrictions on residential tourism in the Netherlands

likely to be achieved by the regulation of marina facilities. Construction of up to 40,000 additional berths before 1995 has been proposed, with two-thirds being allocated to just two areas: the lakes separating the IJsselmeer polders from the mainland (42 per cent) and the delta (25 per cent). The priority given to the IJsselmeer lakes reflects their proximity to the Randstad, and underlines once more the belief that IJsselmeer reclamation has created opportunities extending well beyond agriculture. Selection of the delta is more controversial. On the one hand the region's sheltered waters are temptingly extensive, but on the other it is argued that the delta already experiences excessive pressure from day visitors, campers and water sports enthusiasts. This concern is evident in camping policy (which seeks to divert growth from most coastal districts, see Figure 12.3) and it is also reflected in marina proposals. Marina construction in the Oosterschelde estuary—saved by environmentalists from closure by a sea-defence dam—is to be severely restricted, even though the estuary is much larger than any other water area in the region.

Finally, it is appropriate to examine the future sketched for tourism by the Netherlands' latest national planning document, the Fourth Report on Physical Planning, which establishes a framework for development until 2015 (Ministerie van Volkshuisvesting, Ruimtelijke Ordening en Milieubeheer, 1988). This envisages that the maintenance of a successful tourist industry will be closely related to efforts to maintain or improve environmental quality. Based on this principle, a number of specific initiatives are proposed. In eastern and southern parts of the country, opportunities are identified to repair damage done to small-scale agricultural landscapes as the result of the adoption of intensive, relatively large-scale agricultural practices between the 1950s and the 1980s. Similarly, against the background of the European Community's agricultural surpluses, it is proposed that the extensification of agriculture should allow diversification of rural environments and, most particularly, lead to a more intricate mixture of farms, nature areas and woodland. In a rather different vein, the provision of attractions and accommodation to stimulate recreation and tourism is considered to be one goal of urban renewal, particularly in a number of outmoded port areas in Amsterdam and Rotterdam and on the coast near The Hague.

In broader terms, the Fourth Plan's most extensive proposals for tourism are concerned with the effective use of the country's water resources. The Netherlands is characterised in the Report as 'Waterland', and to underline the principle that a healthy tourism industry will require high environmental standards, current water pollution is identified as a major threat to future development. Emphasis is therefore placed on the need for a national programme of water quality improvement, with priority being given to existing foci of water-based recreation, most particularly the lakes separating the IJsselmeer polders from the mainland. Part of this programme will of necessity be the provision of improved water-treatment facilities, but investment in these cannot be a complete solution, not least because much pollution enters the Netherlands via the Rijn and the Maas. In response, the Report advocates the adoption of more innovative control measures, such as the creation of marshlands to exploit their natural purification qualities and simultaneously extend the stock of nature areas.

In addition to its general emphasis on water quality, the Fourth Report proposes a spatial structure for the development of water-oriented tourism, a structure primarily comprising two axes. The first extends from the Friesland

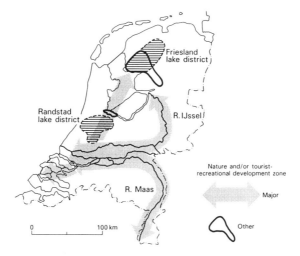

Fig. 12.4   Tourism—recreational zones proposed by the Fourth Report on Physical Planning

lake district in the northern Netherlands, through the IJsselmeer and the lakes of the western provinces to the delta. The second crosses the country from the delta, passing through the river district to the German border, where it bifurcates to follow the rivers Maas and IJssel (Figure 12.4). This structure has the merit of conceptual clarity, but it may be argued that in practice it is likely to pose major challenges for physical planners in the coming decades. To a degree, the basis of these challenges is that, as indicated above, parts of the axes are already under intense recreational pressure. But, beyond this, potential difficulties lie in the fact that the axes are not simply conceived as zones for water-oriented tourism development. Instead, following the argument that sound tourism will be attracted by quality environments, the current strategy envisages that the axes will also become nature development zones. Although positive action is proposed to strengthen and extend existing nature reserves throughout the axes, it is evident that careful implementation of the strategy will be required in order to ensure that tourism pressure does not frustrate nature conservation and, ultimately, impair the attractions of tourism in the river valleys and lake districts.

12.7   Conclusion

Tourism in the Netherlands is underresearched, but it is a diverse and important activity. Despite the industry's own balance-of-payments deficit, expenditure in the country by foreign tourists makes a significant contribution to the nation's overall trade surplus. Foreign visitors are particularly important for the prosperity of the hotel sector, even though visits are typically brief. The Dutch, meanwhile, are major generators of holiday, short-break and day-tourist demand. They have a strong preference for accommodation on campsites and in chalet parks, plus a particular need for water sports facilities. This structural contrast between foreign and Dutch tourism is echoed in the western provinces including, for campers, the delta. The Dutch often avoid the west, except for day recreation and water sports, but they perceive and exploit recreational opportunities throughout the remainder of the country. Given the high level of urbanisation, this extensive use of rural areas for recreational purposes is essential. Yet available space is restricted, and in the most popular districts demand is an acknowledged threat to both the landscape and the environment. National planning strategies to contain this threat have been devised, albeit belatedly. In theory these strategies should be effectively implemented, since environmental awareness is now extremely high in Dutch society (Pinder 1981). However, two considerations suggest that success cannot be taken for granted. First, it is questionable whether the strategies are sufficiently far-reaching. For example, should planners envisage *any* expansion of sailing in Friesland or of camping around the Veluwe? Second, planning is now a contentious activity in the Netherlands (Faludi and de Ruijter 1985). Much decision-making power rests at the local level, and great scope exists for divergence between national plans and local reality. Looking to the future, therefore, the goals and achievements of tourism and recreation planning offer important opportunities for further research.

13 Scandinavia: challenging nature in Norway

Knut S. Brinchmann and Morten Huse

13.1 Norway as a part of Scandinavia

13.1.1 Introduction: at the top of Europe

'New Scandinavia, the top of Europe'. Located at the very top of Europe with a beautiful natural environment, purity, tradition and reliability is the new Scandinavia. This is the way the five Scandinavian countries like to introduce themselves. The Nordic countries consist of Norway, Sweden, Denmark, Finland and Iceland. According to traditional definitions, Scandinavia is defined as Norway, Sweden and Denmark. Efforts are now being made to eliminate the concept of the Nordic countries and to introduce the term Scandinavia for all five. Their nature and beauty can be marketed in a stressed world, where population and progress limit the availability of beautiful and untouched natural areas. Fresh air, deep fjords, clean lakes and rivers, the midnight sun and the northern lights. These are all qualities that the Scandinavian countries can use in their profiling.

Even if there are efforts to market the new Scandinavia collectively, there will be considerable differences between countries in their approaches. Denmark, unlike the other countries, is a member of the EC, whilst its geography is also very distinctive. Therefore, instead of reviewing all the Scandinavian countries, we have chosen to focus mainly on Norway. Norway is, possibly to a greater degree than the other countries, characterised by the special 'Scandinavian' qualities. For most people it is still an undiscovered tourist destination. Reference will also be made to Sweden and Finland, countries which, as tourist destinations, are similar in many ways to Norway. The detailed examples are mainly drawn from northern Norway.

This chapter begins with a general survey of essential demographic, geographic and economic trends. It will then review the structure of the tourism industry and the markets of tourism.

13.1.2 Scandinavia: demography and geography

The total area of Norway, Sweden and Finland is 1,142,000 square kilometres. In addition, the area of the Norwegian islands Svalbard (Spitsbergen) and Jan Mayen (situated in the Arctic Ocean between Greenland and Norway) is 62,000 square kilometres. The area of the three countries is about equal to that

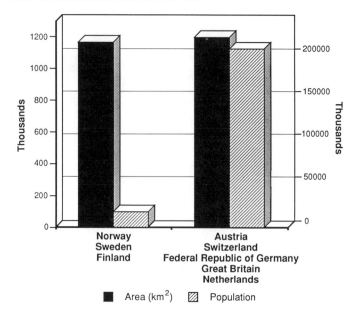

Fig. 13.1   Area and population in Norway, Sweden and Finland compared with other Western European states

of Great Britain, the Federal Republic of Germany, France, Netherlands, Austria and Switzerland together. The population, however, is only 17.5 million (1986). This is about 9 per cent of the total for the above-mentioned countries. The population density in Norway (excluding Svalbard and Jan Mayen) is 13 persons per square kilometre, while in Sweden and Finland it is 19 and 15 respectively. Nordkalotten, the area north of, or intersected by, the Arctic Circle, constitutes about one-third of the total area of these countries. The population north of the Arctic Circle is approximately 900,000 inhabitants. This implies a population density of about 2 persons per square kilometre.

Figure 13.2 shows the administrative divisions within Norway, Sweden, Finland and Denmark. In Norway there are 19 counties and 448 districts or municipalities. Finland has 12 counties and 464 districts, and Sweden has 24 counties and 284 districts. Denmark has 12 counties and 277 districts. In Norway, Finland and Sweden, respectively, about 7 per cent, 10 per cent and 5 per cent of the economically active population are in agriculture, forestry and fishing. In mining, manufacturing and electricity the figures are 25 per cent, 24 per cent and 22 per cent.

13.1.3   Tourism and the national economy: the creation of value and employment

According to the national accounts, tourism contributes about 1.7 per cent of the Norwegian gross national product. More than 70 per cent of the sales comes from restaurants. The costs of the products used (food and beverages) are about half of the total sales. In some counties and districts, tourism is much more important than the national level data indicate. Norway, Sweden and

Fig. 13.2 Major administrative divisions (countries) in Scandinavia

Finland are all facing considerably higher expenditure by their nationals on foreign holiday tourism than their export income from tourism. This can be seen in Table 13.1. In Norway, Sweden and Finland the expenditures connected with travelling abroad constitute a larger part of the gross domestic product than the OECD average. However, the income received from foreigners is a smaller part of the gross domestic product than the OECD average. According to the Yearbook of Nordic Statistics 1988, Scandinavians spend abroad approximately double what these countries receive as corresponding income. The differences are largest in Norway. Sweden is the country receiving most of the travel expenditures from both Norway and Finland. Sweden receives about 25 per cent of total Norwegian travel expenditures abroad and 20 per cent of the Finnish. The United States receives most of the Swedish foreign travel expenditures.

Internationally there has been an increase in total tourist income during the past few years. Measured in fixed prices, the international tourist income for

Table 13.1   Share of travel account expenditure in imports and export of goods and services in Finland, Sweden and Norway, 1985–7

Imports	1985	1986	1987
		(percentages)	
Finland	4.6	5.3	6.0
Sweden	5.1	6.2	6.8
Norway	7.1	8.1	8.9
OECD	4.4	5.0	5.3
Exports	1985	1986	1987
Finland	3.0	3.1	3.5
Sweden	3.1	3.3	3.7
Norway	2.6	3.7	3.9
OECD	4.4	4.7	4.9

Source: OECD (1989)

Norway increased in 1984–6, before decreasing later. By 1989 it was at the level of 1984. During the same period, tourism in Sweden achieved constant growth; in 1989 the tourist income was 132 per cent of the 1984 level. During the early years in this period, Finland faced a decrease, followed by a sound recovery. In 1989, tourist income in Finland was 115 per cent of the 1984 level. Of the Scandinavian countries, only Sweden managed to achieve a development rate corresponding to the OECD average.

These figures indicate how sensitive to economic conditions the tourism industry is in Scandinavia, especially in Norway. They also show how Norway, in the late 1980s, did not manage to take its share of the growth of the international tourism industry. The economic downturn in Norway during the same period also reduced Norwegians' purchases of tourist services in other countries. In 1989, for example, this figure was 12.5 per cent lower, in fixed Norwegian crowns, than in the previous year.

The investments and the number of employees in the industry increased considerably in the 1980s. In 1988 the number of employees in Norwegian tourism was estimated at 90,000, with about 55,000 working in hotels and restaurants. In the hotel and restaurant industry this represented an increase of 12,500 since 1980. According to NORTRA (Nortravel Marketing), there is the possibility of creating a further 35,000 jobs over a five-year period. The numbers of employees in hotels and restaurants in Norway, Sweden and Finland are shown in Table 13.2.

Another important feature is the number of female employees in the tourist industry. In Finland 78 per cent of employees are female. The figures in Norway and Sweden are 71 per cent and 64 per cent respectively. In comparison, the average female activity rates across all industries are 44 per cent in Norway, 48 per cent in Sweden and 48 per cent in Finland. In all three countries investment in tourism is deliberately used to maintain settlements in the rural districts. Creating jobs for women has been particularly important in this.

Table 13.2   Employees in tourism in Norway, Sweden and Finland in 1987

	Norway	Sweden (thousands)	Finland	Total
Female employees in restaurants and hotels	39	54	50	143
Male employees in restaurants and hotels	16	30	14	60
Employees, total, in restaurants and hotels	55	84	64	203
Percentages of all employees	2.58%	1.94%	2.64%	2.31%

Source: Central Bureau of Statistics of Norway; *Yearbook of Nordic Statistics* (1988). ISIC industry classification is used.

13.1.4   *Important tourist products/areas*

Many of the characteristic Scandinavian tourist features are found in Norway. However, the other countries have, to a greater extent, exploited existing attractions and created new tourist events and attractions.

Norway is characterised by the combination of sea and mountains, manifested in the famous fjords. The northernmost parts of the country also contain two of the Scandinavian countries' greatest attractions, the North Cape and the Lofoten Islands, which offer fishing holidays in fishermen's shanties, whale-watching and other nature-based attractions. The Coastal Line, a coastal steamship service, is also a famous Norwegian attraction, combining local traffic and tourism, and is a unique part of the local culture. The Coastal Line makes daily calls along the coast from Bergen in the south to Kirkenes in the north. According to Norwegian officials, this is one of the areas to be given priority for development. At the same time, the Ministry of Transport and Communications, which is formally responsible for the Coastal Line, has recently (1990) suggested drastic reductions in its annual subsidies, from 200 million Norwegian crowns in 1990 to 64 million in 1995. The future of the Coastal Line is thus very uncertain.

Sweden and Finland do not have the same nature-based attractions as Norway. These countries, however, compensate through having better organisation and co-ordination of tourism. Their infrastructure is also generally better developed. for example, wildlife tourism has been developed more in Sweden and in Finland than in Norway. These countries also have more liberal regulations concerning motorised traffic in wilderness areas. Sweden and Finland also have, to a higher degree than Norway, created tourist attractions of their own. 'Santa Claus' country', Lapland in Finland, is an excellent example of such attractions. Finnish national authorities are making determined efforts to incorporate Santa Claus as a part of the national identity.

In addition, Sweden and Finland make use of the famous attractions of the Lofoten Islands and the North Cape in their national marketing. Most of the charter traffic to these destinations is organised by Sweden and Finland, rather than by Norway. The tourists live, eat, sleep and spend most of their money in Sweden or Finland, while the Lofoten Islands and/or the North Cape are included as a part of the total package. Usually a one to two-day excursion is arranged during the package in order to visit one of the Norwegian attractions. The Finns have even invested in a large airport in Karigasniemi, close to the border with Norway and the entrance to the North Cape. This airport will be able to receive Concorde planes carrying wealthy foreigners on day trips to the North Cape.

13.2   The structure of the tourist industry

The visitor's total experience of a tourist destination is influenced by a number of different factors. In general, everything within the area will contribute to the total tourist product. In this section we focus on the importance of the political authorities and the tourist organisations, both of which influence the external working conditions of tourism-related activities.

13.2.1   The role of the authorities

The tourist industry in Norway is formally subject to the Ministry of Industry. Other ministries are also, directly or indirectly, involved in tourism. The Ministry of Transport and Communications, for example, is responsible for the Coastal Line, one of the greatest tourist attractions in Norway. However, the decisions made in this Ministry are based only on political considerations related to the communications sector.

The national authorities can influence tourism both through offering finance and grants and by controlling arrangements and regulations. There are several different means available to support and develop the tourist industry in Norway. The Norwegian Tourist Board has prepared an outline of loans, guarantees, grants and subsidies which can be used by the industry. The Regional Development Fund offers subsidised loans and investment aid, starting-up aid, grants for research and planning, education, marketing and for development projects. In addition, the Ministry of Municipal Affairs and Labour has a separate enterprise and development programme for the private sector in the districts, as well as municipal organisational arrangements and regional development programmes. The Norwegian Industrial Fund offers liable loans, loans for product development, currency loans, grants for loans, mergers and transportation, as well as grants for business programmes.

Tourism-related enterprises may also receive loans from the Norwegian Bank of Industry, and grants from the Export Council of Norway and from NORTRA. The Guarantee Institute of Export Credit (GIEK) offers grants on certain occasions. It is also possible to obtain government grants to avoid losses due to exchange rate fluctuations. The State Office of Sobriety disposes a fund for hotels and restaurants which do not serve alcohol. The Development Fund for Agriculture may offer establishment support and grants for projects related to countryside tourism. The Agriculture Bank supplies loans and grants to cabin and chalet investors, while the Ministry of Agriculture provides loans for development and protection of remote areas. The Ministry of the Environment may give grants to finance development of outdoor areas, and the Nordic Investment Bank can support projects involving two or more Nordic countries.

It is useful to make comparisons with the European Community, where most European structural instruments can be used to promote tourism. Subsidies and grants may be obtained through the European Regional Development Fund, the European Social Fund and the Agricultural Fund. The European Investment Bank may also participate in financing tourist projects. The grant rates seem to be higher, especially in the development regions, than those in Norway. In addition, the spectrum of undertakings within the EC covers both infrastructure and the experience aspect of the tourist product. The Common Market will also support regional equalisation, and protection of the environment programmes. Direct operational support, such as that which exists in Finland, is not permitted, except in the regional development areas.

In Finland, the tourist industry in the most underdeveloped parts of the country may receive up to 45 per cent investment aid. This is considerably higher than in Norway. The Norwegian Regional Fund (DU) offers a maximum of 15 per cent investment aid (and another maximum loan of 35 per cent) of the total investment. The Finns may, in addition, receive start-up aid of up to 50 per cent in the first operating year and 45 per cent in the second year, while they can also benefit from development aid of 25–75 per cent. None of these means of financial support is found in Norway.

The organisation and financing of the industry show how priorities vary in the three Nordkalott countries. The national tourism organisations are integrated parts of the political system in both Sweden and Finland, subject to the Ministry of Commerce and Industry (Finland) and the Ministry of Industry (Sweden). In general, the Finnish authorities and, to a certain extent the Swedish have national economic perspectives in their development of tourism policy. This is far more significant than in Norway.

13.2.2   *The organisation of the tourist industry*

In Norway, tourism is organised by two agencies: the Norwegian Tourist Board (NR) and NORTRA (Nortravel Marketing). The NR is the tourism industry's political agency, while NORTRA is the operative agency responsible for marketing the country. The Norwegian Tourist Board is the agency for the organisations, institutions and companies related to the tourism sector. Membership may be offered to:

1. Regional tourist organisations with rules approved by the NR.
2. Institutions, organisations and companies of nation-wide coverage or of major importance.
3. Local tourism groups (Reiselivslag) with rules approved by NR, in regions with no regional organisation.
4. Organisations, institutions and businesses that do not belong to local/ regional organisations.

The Norwegian Tourist Board consists of local and regional subdivisions. At the local level, the most common model is the tourist group (Reiselivslag). The members of these Reiselivslags are, traditionally, tourism companies, municipalities and others involved in tourism. The local groups are gathered into tourist boards (Reiselivsråd) at a regional level.

NORTRA is the operative marketing agency of tourism in Norway and abroad. The organisation was established as a foundation by the state and the Norwegian Tourist Board in 1984. The foundation is represented by foreign offices in a number of different countries, and these are under the Ministry of Foreign Affairs. The total NORTRA budget almost doubled from 1988 to 1990, from 70 million Norwegian crowns to 122.6 million. Half of this amount, however, has to be supplied by the industry itself, as NORTRA requires the tourism industry to 'match', crown for crown, the amount offered by the organisation. In other words, the tourist industry in Norway has to supply some 61.3 million crowns, corresponding to the state grant of 61.3 millions provided through NORTRA (1990).

This organisational and financial principle of the tourism industry has been exposed to strong criticism from several directions. Today, the different tourist groups and boards often serve merely as membership organisations, where all municipalities and companies can participate in development decisions. For this reason it has often proved to be impossible to set priorities and to carry out desirable development projects.

There have been suggestions that the Norwegian Tourist Board should be closed down. Alternative solutions are presently (1990) under consideration. One of the proposals is to close down the national organisation, leaving the regional organisations totally independent of central administration and co-ordination. This is very close to the Swedish model, where regional tourism organisations are totally independent of the Swedish Tourist Office, a purely political agency subject to the Ministry of Industry. Another option is to gather both the development of products and marketing/sales under NORTRA. Yet another possibility is to establish a separate company, with major tourism companies as owners/shareholders.

There have also been criticisms of NORTRA's principle that companies 'match' the governmental contribution to NORTRA's marketing and profiling campaigns. This method of financing national marketing is unique in Europe. In Norway only the larger and more profitable enterprises have been able to make use of this channel. NORTRA's 50/50 principle has been criticised by the board of the Norwegian Tourist Board. They have emphasised the need for 'matching free' means to finance improved national promotion activity.

Criticism of the existing organisation model has further resulted in reorganisation of several regional tourist boards. Some of these have been replaced or supplemented by new organisations run according to pure economic principles. Examples of this new model can be found in Finnmark, Troms and Telemark.

A commercial organisation for marketing and selling tourism services in Northern Norway was established in 1990. This company will sell the travel products of Nordland, Troms and Finnmark. It will be the first company of this kind in Norway, with formalised co-operation across regional boundaries. As for the future, it is probable that more and more regional and local organisations will base their management on commercial principles.

In Sweden, tourism is directly subject to the Ministry of Industry, via the Swedish Tourist Board, a purely political organisation. A separate commercial unit has also been established, offering different services to the regional organisations. The national budget for 1990 is about 123 million Swedish crowns, of which some 83 million are grants from the government. The public sector share of the budget is 67 per cent, compared with 50 per cent in

Norway. The separate regional tourism organisations are completely independent of the central organisations. There are several types of models, ranging from purely commercial organisations to foundations and membership organisations corresponding to the Norwegian tourist boards. At the local level, the situation is also similar to that in Norway, with pure membership organisations being dominant. However, commercial companies are also active at this level: for example, 'Destination Kiruna Inc.' has been established recently in Kiruna.

Finland is characterised by a still higher degree of public administration and financing of the tourist industry. The national organisation is the Finnish Tourist Board. As in Sweden, this organisation is directly subject to political authorities as part of the Ministry of Industry and Commerce. Of a collective budget of about 120 million Norwegian crowns for 1990, the authorities are responsible for 105 million or 87.5 per cent.

13.2.3   *The hotels: capacity, size and chains*

Analysis of the tourist industry shows that hotels and restaurants have the same problems as small and medium-sized companies in other economic sectors. Profitability and equity ratios are too low for them to have a sufficient degree of freedom to act efficiently. In Norway, average labour costs in 1988 amounted to 37 per cent of the hotels' operating revenues. The city hotels have the best results in this respect. This industry is very sensitive to changes in the general economic situation.

In 1987, according to the Yearbook of Nordic Statistics, there were 1,118 hotels in Norway, 918 hotels in Finland and 2,300 hotels in Sweden. The average number of beds per hotel in the respective countries was 93, 86 and 92. The characteristic company structure of predominantly small and medium-sized units has made it difficult to obtain economies of scale. In consequence, there have been attempts to establish voluntary chains for co-operation in many sectors, which seems to have been successful. With the large numbers of small and weaker units, the organisations of the industry, together with the contribution of a few chains, are of great importance.

The main chains in Norway are Best Western (42 hotels/5,975 beds), InterNor (32/7,045), NM-hotels (32/2,350) and Kilde (15/3,131). These chains are all working on a franchise-type basis. Kilde and InterNor are about to merge. The major Norwegian-owned hotel concerns are Rica (24 hotels/5,000 beds) and Thon (14/2,943). During the last few years, the major Swedish chains have moved into the Norwegian market. The most important Swedish hotel chains in the Norwegian market are Reso (5 hotels/2,800 beds), Scandic, Sara and Home. SAS International Hotels have 10 hotels in Norway: four of these are tourist hotels in Finnmark. SAS also has central ownership and management interests in the tourist centre at North Cape.

In Norway there are two main service and interest organisations for the hotel and restaurant industry. These are the Norwegian Hotel and Restaurant Association (NHRF) and the Association for Lodging and Food Establishments (FOS). NHRF has traditionally attended to the interests of the largest companies in the industry; it has about 600 members. FOS has about 1,600 member companies, including camping-grounds and snackbars.

13.2.4   Special features

During the last few years there has been a considerable increase in the variety of activities and experiences within Scandinavian tourism. Different kinds of experiences have become an essential part of the tourist industry's product. Market needs, to a lesser degree than in earlier years, seem to be connected with the services offered by hotels and restaurants. Instead, there has been a great demand from tourists for specific activities. In Norway the investment in such activities has resulted in a extensive development of alpine areas for the winter season, and of playgrounds and holiday parks for the summer season. This development is illustrated by the fact that, in the period 1975–84, only fifteen new ski-lifts per year were built, while the average since 1985 has been close to seventy-five. The speed of development has been influenced considerably by public national financing arrangements (White Paper 14/ 1986). A well-developed transport network within, and to, Scandinavia is a condition for making tourist products available. Foreign tourists mostly use private cars, buses and ferries to travel to and from Norway.

There are a number of limitations to tourism in Norway. Among the most important are high prices and costs, as well as long distances to major markets. Wages and salaries are especially high, which is particularly important in an industry characterised by personal service. Norway also has restrictive alcohol legislation, unrelated to tourism. There are strict laws governing where to buy alcoholic beverages, while high taxes have made drinking prohibitively expensive for foreign tourists.

Regulations within the communication sector are primarily decided with regard to the needs of local populations and business travellers. In addition, Norway has a number of rules that complicate and increase the costs of different undertakings. Demands on the working environment and working hours, closing times, health and safety laws, maintenance of the rights of minorities, preservation and conservation measures for the environment, and building rules, etc. have to be considered. So far there has been no VAT on housing and other services in Norway. In 1990 this was imposed in Sweden. The higher price level caused by this tax might result in some displacement of tourism from Sweden to Norway. Partly due to the process of adaption to EC norms, the levying of VAT on housing in Norway is currently under consideration, although it will probably be at a lower rate than in Sweden.

13.3   The markets

In this section we discuss some essential features of the development of tourist markets and visitor patterns in Norway. In the first section we present the main tourist flows in Scandinavia. The second section deals with the development of the holiday habits of Norwegians. We shall discuss the development nationally with a focus on northern Norway. We shall also, to a certain degree, compare holiday habits in Norway with corresponding figures for Sweden and Finland. The following section will discuss international market segments in Norway and northern Norway. The last section presents the most important means of travel in northern Norway.

Table 13.3 Tourist flows in Scandinavia in 1988: relative market shares of the total number of nights spent in hotels and similar establishments

	Denmark	Finland	Norway	Sweden
Total 1988 (thousands)	4,377	2,298	3,356	3,191
% change from 1987:	−2.3	4.1	−13.2	−1.6
Relative share:		(percentage market share)		
Denmark	NA	3.0	19.2	6.4
Finland	2.6	NA	3.1	11.3
Norway	15.5	5.3	NA	19.5
Sweden	24.1	24.3	17.2	NA
France	1.7	2.9	3.6	2.8
Germany	21.2	14.0	16.1	14.9
Italy	2.4	3.6	NA	3.0
Netherlands	2.3	2.0	3.2	2.2
Switzerland	NA	3.2	NA	1.9
UK	6.6	5.7	9.9	7.5
Canada	NA	1.3	NA	0.7
United States	8.6[1]	8.8	10.4	10.2
Japan	2.5	2.4	2.0	2.3
Total OECD countries	87.5	79.9	91.5	82.8
Non-OECD countries	12.5	20.1	8.5	17.2

Source: OECD (1989)
Note: 1. Including Canada.

13.3.1 Tourist flows in Scandinavia

None of the Scandinavian countries collects data concerning the total number of foreign visitors at frontiers. Furthermore, there are no data available for Norway and Finland on the total number of nights spent by foreigners in all types of accommodation. As a consequence, the best estimate of tourist flows to and between the countries is the statistics provided by hotels and similar establishments (see Table 13.3). The data for foreigners in all means of accommodation in Denmark and Sweden show totals of foreign bed-nights, which are around twice as large as the statistics for hotels only. These are for Denmark, 8.0 million foreign bed-nights (4.4 million in hotels), and for Sweden, 7.1 million foreign bed-nights (3.2 million in hotels). The picture is probably much the same in Finland and Norway.

As can be seen from Table 13.3, local markets in the neighbouring countries are important to all four countries. In Denmark, the Scandinavian segment is 42.2 per cent of the total. Tourists from Sweden (24.1 per cent) and Norway (15.5 per cent) are together contributing close to 40 per cent of the total market. In Finland, the three other countries make up 32.6 per cent of the total. The Swedes are by far the most important, taking 24.3 per cent of the foreign bed-nights in the hotels. In addition, due to historical relations, eastern countries contribute 12.9 per cent of the total. The USSR alone accounts for 9.3 per cent. In Norway, the share of the other Scandinavian countries is 39.5 per cent. The Danes contribute 19.2 per cent of the total, while the Swedish segment is 17.2 per cent. In Sweden, the Danes (6.4 per cent), the Finns (11.3 per cent) and the Norwegians (19.5 per cent) together take 47.2 per cent of the total bed-nights spent in hotels.

The Germans are by far the most important non-Scandinavian segment in the Scandinavian countries, contributing 21.2 per cent of the total in Denmark, 14.0 per cent in Finland, 16.1 per cent in Norway and 14.9 per cent in Sweden. Other major tourist markets are the United States and the United Kingdom.

13.3.2   Holiday habits of the Norwegians

The Central Bureau of Statistics in Norway has recently published two reports on the holiday habits of Norwegians: 'Norwegian holidays habits in a regional perspective' (87/19) and 'Who spend their holidays at home?' (88/8). Tourism activity varies regionally in Norway. Residents of the counties of Oslo and Akershus are the most widely travelled. Only 11 per cent did not take a holiday in 1985/6. while 38 per cent had at least three holiday trips. On average, Norwegians had 2.3 holiday trips per year, lasting a total of 17.2 days. In 1986/7, 22 per cent of the Norwegian adult population did not take a holiday. The corresponding figures for Sweden, Finland and Denmark are 18 per cent, 50 per cent and 40 per cent. In Scandinavia, it is older people who tend not to take holidays. Residents living in densely-populated areas go on vacation more frequently than people from sparsely-populated areas.

The Central Bureau of Statistics in Norway prepares annual surveys of Norwegians' holiday habits. These surveys show the distribution of holidays in the longest vacation, and the second-longest vacation, as well as the seasonal variations of vacations. The percentage of Norwegians going on a long holiday trip increased from 55 per cent to 68 per cent in the period 1970–85. However, this development has stagnated during the last decade, as the proportion of such holiday trips decreased from 71 per cent in 1978 to 68 per cent in 1985. The national segment (Norwegians taking holidays in Norway) increased from 48 per cent to 54 per cent from 1970 to 1978, and has thereafter shown a decline, levelling off at 41 per cent in 1985. The other Scandinavian countries increased their share of the Norwegian tourist market from 4 per cent to 13 per cent, while other countries increased their share from 3 per cent to 14 per cent. There is now a growing tendency amongst Norwegians to take their holidays in Norway.

The number of second-longest holiday trips also shows a considerable increase between 1970 and 1985. The percentage of shorter holiday trips shows a clear increase to all destinations, from 10 per cent to 17 per cent for holidays in Norway, from 1 per cent to 3 per cent for holidays in the other Scandinavian countries, and from 1 per cent to 2 per cent for holidays in other foreign countries.

13.3.3   Foreign tourists in Norway

This section examines the most important foreign market segments in Norway. Special circumstances in northern Norway are related to developments in two of Norway's central tourist counties, Oppland and Sogn og Fjordane. Oppland is a typical mountain and winter sports county, while Sogn

Hotels in Norway

Changes in guest nights according to nationality

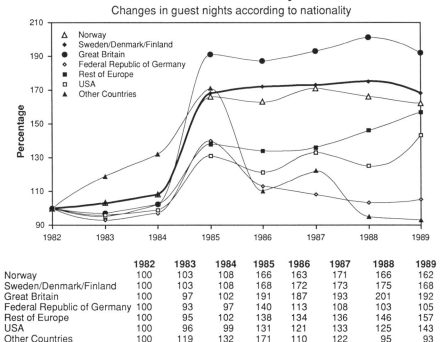

	1982	1983	1984	1985	1986	1987	1988	1989
Norway	100	103	108	166	163	171	166	162
Sweden/Denmark/Finland	100	103	108	168	172	173	175	168
Great Britain	100	97	102	191	187	193	201	192
Federal Republic of Germany	100	93	97	140	113	108	103	105
Rest of Europe	100	95	102	138	134	136	146	157
USA	100	96	99	131	121	133	125	143
Other Countries	100	119	132	171	110	122	95	93

Fig. 13.3   Hotel guest-nights in Norway, by market share, 1982–9

og Fjordane is particularly known for its magnificent fjords. Similarities with, and contrasts to, northern Sweden and northern Finland are also highlighted.

Developments in foreign market sectors in Norway are illustrated by the overnight stays in hotels and other lodgings during 1982–9 (Figure 13.3). The total number of overnight stays in Norway shows an increase of about 62 per cent for this period. However, there is a negative trend during recent years, with a decline of 9 per cent from 12,272,000 overnight stays during the peak year 1987 to 11,624,000 overnight stays in 1989.

Further disaggregation of the statistics reveals a particularly strong growth of tourists from Denmark. The number of Danish tourists in Norway in 1989 was 648,000, and this was 277 per cent of the 1982 level. Corresponding figures for some of the other countries are: Federal Republic of Germany, 581,000 (93 per cent); United Kingdom, 337,000 (105 per cent); France, 140,000 (157 per cent); Netherlands, 118,000 (101 per cent); and Finland, 99,000 (150 per cent). For 'other countries in Europe' there were 265,000 overnight stays in 1989, which was 164 per cent of the 1982 level. In countries outside Europe (except for the United States), the figures were 377,000 (192 per cent).

When it comes to volume, however, the Norwegian market is the most important. During this period, the Norwegian had about 70 per cent of the total number of overnight stays in Norway. In comparison, the next largest sector, the Danes, had only about 5.5 per cent of the overnight stays. Then

Table 13.4   Guest–nights in Norway, 1988

	Norway	Oppland	Sogn & Fj	Nordland	Troms	Finnmark
HOTELS						
The whole year:						
Guest-nights	11853	1613	555	533	316	251
Foreigners (%)	28%	27%	33%	24%	19%	35%
Summer (May–September):						
Guest-nights	5926	758	381	282	160	160
Foreigners (%)	35%	25%	46%	36%	31%	53%
July:						
Guest-nights	1634	244	114	83	39	55
Foreigners (%)	42%	32%	54%	57%	54%	77%
Foreigners:	(% share of total foreign market)					
Denmark	19%	37%	2%	3%	5%	3%
Finland	3%	2%	2%	8%	7%	7%
Sweden	17%	18%	4%	14%	12%	8%
France	4%	2%	8%	4%	3%	6%
The Netherlands	3%	4%	5%	12%	3%	1%
United Kingdom	10%	8%	14%	6%	7%	2%
West Germany	16%	17%	32%	29%	32%	42%
Rest of Europe	7%	2%	5%	9%	16%	18%
USA	10%	6%	17%	9%	10%	4%
Japan	2%	0%	7%	0%	1%	1%
Others	9%	3%	6%	5%	4%	9%
CAMPING						
Camping-grounds (nos)	764	115	67	83	36	33
Nights spent ('000s)	3430	505	279	288	122	128
Foreigners (%)	42%	31%	58%	55%	49%	65%
	(% share of total foreign market)					
Denmark	10%	15%	7%	5%	5%	7%
Finland	8%	5%	4%	15%	31%	31%
Sweden	18%	22%	8%	23%	16%	11%
France	6%	3%	6%	5%	5%	4%
The Netherlands	11%	18%	15%	5%	5%	4%
United Kingdom	3%	2%	4%	2%	2%	2%
West Germany	36%	31%	47%	34%	27%	31%
Rest of Europe	6%	4%	5%	7%	9%	9%
Others	3%	1%	4%	5%	2%	1%

Source: Central Bureau of Statistics (1989)

come the Federal Republic of Germany (5 per cent) and Sweden (4.5 per cent), while the United States, the United Kingdom and the group of 'other countries' each had about 3 per cent.

In northern Norway, there are interesting deviations from the national picture. The foreign share of overnight stays is 77 per cent for Finnmark, in connection with North Cape tourism in July (Table 13.4). Table 13.4 further compares the figures from northern Norway with figures from two other counties, Oppland in eastern Norway and Sogn og Fjordane in western Norway. The figures show that the Danes constitute the largest category of foreigners for Oppland, where Danes and Swedes together account for 55 per cent of total overnight stays. A large number of these Danes and Swedes come for short skiing vacations. The Americans are primarily fjord tourists, and constitute 17 per cent of overnight guests in Sogn og Fjordane. In northern Norway, the West Germans are the largest group. In addition, there is a large increase in the number of Italians who visit Finnmark and the North Cape.

Holiday trips can vary from a one-day excursion to a much longer trip. There are considerable differences between the visitor patterns in northern Norway and those in other counties. Most vacations spent in the tourist counties of Oppland and Telemark are weekend trips and short holidays. The tourists are mostly people from Oslo and other densely-populated areas. Short holidays and weekend trips from Denmark and Sweden also have noticeable effects on the visitor statistics, especially in winter.

Northern Norway, which lies far from central population areas, has a totally different visitor structure. Long-distance tourists represent, especially in summer, the most important visitors to northern Norway. In the future, long-distance travellers on shorter holiday trips outside the summer season, together with people on incentive tours, may be of increased importance for this part of the country.

As the hotel statistics reflect, to a considerable degree, group tourists, the figures indicate foreign and Norwegian tour operators' engagements and priorities concerning traditional package tours to northern Norway (and Nordkalotten). The camping statistics, on the other hand, give an interesting hint of the travel patterns of the individual travellers who visit Norway, primarily by car. This survey shows that many West Germans and Dutch visitors do not go further north than Sogn og Fjordane. The travel pattern to Norway via Sweden and Finland is obscure. North Cape and the Lofoten Islands contribute to extending the Germans' (and others) stays in Finnmark and Nordland. Finns and Swedes are also enthusiastic camping tourists in northern Norway.

The camping statistics from the Central Bureau of Statistics have suffered from poor reporting from the camping-grounds. The real figures are probably much higher than those in the statistics. To obtain a more accurate picture of camping in this part of the country, free camping outside the official camping-ground must be taken into account. Estimates indicate (Viken and Sletvold 1988) that this free camping is twice as large as registered camping.

Market partitioning according to nationality, however, only provides a rough division of tourists visiting Norway. Even if the visitors who come to Norway have very different backgrounds, it is possible to discern some general characteristics of the 'typical' tourist in Norway. The results from an investigation amongst potential French tourists (Freitag 1989), show that the following factors are weighted most heavily in the choice of northern Norway as a holiday destination:

1.   Beautiful scenery (96 per cent of people questioned)
2.   No mass tourism (88 per cent)
3.   Solitude (52 per cent)

In order to market Norway as a tourist destination, it is important to know and understand the country's profile among potential groups of customers. Norway in general, and northern Norway in particular, are characterised by long distances to central markets. The climatic conditions are also one reason why the tourist season is very short, while there are some hectic summer weeks from June to August. However, the tourist industry does hope to extend the season. New activities and experiences are being created during the autumn, winter and spring. For the time being, however, international tourism will remain connected mainly with the summer season. As the local market base is limited, the busiest period for the tourist industry is therefore short and busy. This tendency is strengthened the further north that people travel, which can be explained both by climatic conditions and increasing distances to the markets.

An important consequence of this visitor pattern is the great variation in the capacity utilisation of hotels. The average occupancy rate of hotel rooms in Norway in 1988, according to the Central Bureau of Statistics, was 38 per cent. Oppland is one of Norway's central areas for winter tourism. Accordingly the county experiences two seasonal visitor peaks: one during the winter season with capacity utilisation of 52.4 per cent and 51.5 per cent in February and March, respectively; and one in July with capacity utilisation of 54.2 per cent. On an annual basis, the capacity utilisation was 39.1 per cent. The figures for Finnmark and Sogn og Fjordane show that capacity utilisation in the two counties follows the same pattern, with a peak in June–July. This is particularly the case for Finnmark, where the capacity utilisation was as low as 29.7 per cent on an annual basis. During the busiest period in July, the figure was 62.7 per cent, while in December and January it was below 20 per cent. The percentage of foreign overnight stays increases during the summer season. Again this is most noticeable for northern Norway. In July 77 per cent of the overnight stays in Finnmark are made by foreigners, mostly through to North Cape Tourism.

Corresponding figures from the other Nordkalott countries show a rather different visiting pattern in northern Finland (Lapland) from that of northern Norway and northern Sweden. Historically, it has not been considered especially fashionable for Norwegians to spend their vacation in northern Norway (nor for the Swedes in northern Sweden). In Finland, on the other hand, a holiday in Lapland is considered to be fashionable. The national sector is thus far more important to the tourist industry in Finland than the corresponding Norwegian sector is in northern Norway. The number of foreign nights spent in Finnish Lapland only constitutes 18 per cent of the total, while the figure in Finnmark is almost double at 35 per cent. The national sector is thus far more important in Finnish Lapland than in Finnmark: 82 per cent and 65 per cent respectively.

Generally the holiday tourist market constitutes 65 per cent of the total visitor market in Lapland, but only 45 per cent in Finnmark. The total market was 1.03 million bed-nights in Finnish Lapland in 1988, and 0.25 million in Finnmark. While the tourist industry in Lapland contributes 11 per cent of the total national number of bed-nights in Finland, Finnmark's share of the Norwegian total amounts to only 2.1 per cent (Viken 1989). A more loyal and stable local market in Northern Finland also increases the profitability potential on a year-round basis.

In northern Sweden (Norrbottens Län) the visitor pattern closely resembles that of northern Norway: Swedes 70 per cent, Norwegians 17 per cent, Germans 5 per cent, Finns 2 per cent and 'others' 6 per cent. Therefore, the national share of the market is similar to that in northern Norway, being about 70 per cent of the total (Tourist Board of Norrbotten, 1989).

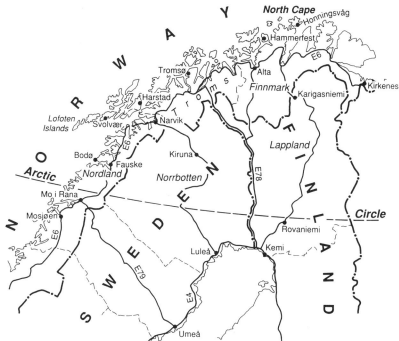

Fig. 13.4 Nordkalotten

13.3.4 Means of travel

Most foreign tourists come to Norway as individual travellers in their own cars. The final destination for their travels is often North Cape or the Lofoten Islands. However, in order to reach their destinations, most of the tourists drive through Sweden or Finland. These countries, in general, offer better roads than northern Norway. In this section we will discuss the most important ways of travelling for foreign tourists visiting northern Norway: by car, charter bus, the Coastal Line, cruising, railway and aircraft.

The mainstream of tourists in northern Norway use E6 and Highway 95 to North Cape (see Figure 13.4). A considerable part of the traffic, however, passes through Finland and Sweden, especially on E78, Highway 93 through Alta, and Highway 96 through Lakselv, together with E79 to Mo in Rana. In addition, a constantly increasing number of tourists arrive on Highway 70 from Sweden, via Narvik, bound for the Lofoten Islands. For the tourists heading for the Lofoten Islands, the ferry service between Skutvik and Svolvær is essential. Highway 19 through the Lofoten Islands is one of the most important tourist routes.

The central traffic arteries constitute a starting-point for different tourist-related enterprises. During the summer season, most of the nights spent in hotels located close to the major highways in northern Norway involve organised bus groups. This sector includes both tourists arriving by bus directly from foreign countries, and local round-trips as a part of an organised package within the area. The most important markets for bus tourism directly from abroad are Sweden, Finland and the Federal Republic of Germany.

Most of the tourists travelling by the Coastal Line are round-trip passengers who usually do not leave the ship. Many of the tourists chose to sail parts of the route after making separate travel arrangements. The round-trip passengers on the Coastal Line have a longer season than the usual holiday period (about 20 June–20 August), and the demand for round-trips in connection with Christmas and New Year is steadily increasing. The cruise ships visit places with particular attractions in northern Norway such as North Cape, Hammerfest, Ramsund, Raftsund, Svolvær and Tromsø. These ships have relatively limited economic importance for this part of the country, but are nevertheless important from a promotional point of view.

The largest group of train tourists to the northern part of Norway are inter-railers to Fauske and Bodø, possibly via Kiruna/Narvik. Most of these tourists continue their visit in northern Norway as hitch-hikers. They spend the nights at camping-grounds, as free campers, or at youth hostels. If the Norwegian States Railways (NSB) is to increase the number of tourists on Nordlandsbanen (the railway to northern Norway), there is a need for better organisation, co-operation and marketing.

A relatively small number of tourists come to northern Norway by scheduled flights. They primarily belong to groups with higher incomes, demanding high-quality products at high prices. Bodø, Tromsø, Evenes and Alta are the towns with major airports most suitable for this kind of tourism. In addition, there are a large number of short-runway airports in this part of the country. By using combinations of transport modes, these tourists can easily reach the famous attractions of northern Norway. Routes with fast local boats, minor air routes and bus routes contribute to distributing the flow of tourists in the northern part of the country. The development of a permanent air link between Tromsø–Luleå–Oulo, and between Bodø–Luleå could also be important in bringing tourists to the area.

13.4   Future prospects

Tourism in Norway, Sweden and Finland has played a central part in the local districts' politics, especially in Nordkalotten. It is also of importance that the female share of employees in tourism is about 70 per cent, as it is a national objective to create more job opportunities for women in the districts.

The importance of tourism in Norway, represented by restaurants and hotels, is 1.7 per cent of the total value added and 2.6 per cent of the labour force. The tourist industry has great potential, both in value creation and providing new job opportunities. In Norway, the official policy is to concentrate investment in order to develop a few large tourist centres. The government wants to give priority to undertakings in the northernmost parts of Norway to help stem depopulation.

The holiday markets in Western Europe have experienced explosive growth during the last twenty years. In relation to nights spent in hotels, cabins and camping-grounds, Norway has not managed to secure a part of this explosive growth. There are, however, indications that this negative trend is about to change. Norway has a very low capacity utilisation that might be regarded as a resource with increased marketing investment.

During the last decade, the Norwegian tourist industry has based product development and market adjustments on totally or partly protected markets.

The promotion has mainly been directed towards the holiday markets in Norway, Sweden and Denmark. Active product or market adjustment has, for the most part, concentrated on the winter product. The rest of the holiday market has not been developed systematically. To a great extent, it has been turned over to foreign tour operators. Northern Norway has, to a very limited extent, been promoted internationally by Norwegians, while Sweden and Finland use destinations in northern Norway as a basis for much of their own marketing campaigns.

As a tourist destination, Norway has a number of major weaknesses:

1. Product development has lagged behind the development of markets.
2. Distribution channels for Norwegian tourist products are inefficient both at home and abroad.
3. The marketing of Norwegian tourist products is limited.
4. Cost levels in Norway are perceived to be high.
5. The lack of thorough knowledge about markets limits the development of products and of market planning.
6. The degree of internationalisation of the industry is too low.

The strength of the tourist industry is associated with the following features:

1. Conditions provided from nature are important, while the demand for nature-based activities is expected to increase strongly in the future. Attitudes and life styles are changing. This may increase the demand for Norwegian tourist products.
2. The physical standard of and the variation within the housing sector and transport are generally good.
3. There is a clear understanding of strengths and weaknesses within the industry, together with the motivation and ability to make changes.
4. The quality of transportation to Norway is steadily improving.

Based on NORTRA's Programme 90, a market analysis programme, a product development programme and a marketing programme have been started. Concerning product development, NORTRA considers the following to be important:

1. Organisation of good and cheap transport from abroad to Norway and internally in Norway. Initiatives will be taken to organise more competitive air flights, especially to northern Norway.
2. Organisation of information from product to market via new technological channels. It is important that Norwegian tourist products are included in foreign distributors' sales brochures.

In Norway, several interesting projects are planned to increase tourism:

1. Destination 'Nordkalotten' (northern Norway). How could northern Norway be developed into an exotic holiday destination?
2. Organisation, arrangement and marketing of the Norwegian camping product.
3. The 'road of experience' (creating a rounded travel product) intended for individual visitors in cars, including experiences of mountains, culture and cities.

4. Destination Lillehammer. Utilisation of the investments in and the attention that Lillehammer has received and will receive as Olympic city. Lillehammer will be developed into an international skiing-centre.
5. Wildlife holidays.

In addition to these products, primarily directed toward traditional western markets, there are opportunities in Eastern Europe. In Russia, close to the Norwegian border, there are several million inhabitants with Norway and Finland as their closest western neighbours.

Beyond the domestic market, the Norwegian high priority markets are currently Sweden, Denmark, Germany and North America. Other markets given high priority are Finland, Netherlands, Belgium, France, the United Kingdom and Japan. Switzerland, Austria, Italy, Spain and other overseas markets are given lower priority. The recent developments in Eastern Europe may also open up new markets, but they might also become competitors threatening tourism in Scandinavia. NORTRA thinks that the high priority markets ought to be the starting point for 3–7 per cent per annum growth of hotels, camping-grounds and cabins. Growth of 3–5 per cent should also be obtainable within the groups given medium priority.

14 Tourism policies in a changing economic environment

Allan M. Williams and Gareth Shaw

14.1 Introduction: the requirement for interventionism

Most tourism policies have been designed to expand the tourist industry—whether in a relatively infant stage, as in Spain in the 1950s, or in a more mature stage, as in the United Kingdom in the 1980s. However, the very nature of tourism—with its heavy spatial and seasonal polarisation—usually requires some form of interventionism. Furthermore, the tourist product has a determinate life cycle, and ageing resorts in decline are a problem of increasing importance. Examples touched upon in this book include the spa towns of Portugal and the lakes region of Austria. In essence, however, the aim of policy has to be to influence the number of visitors that are attracted and to modify their quality (spending capacity and range of activities), the timing of their visits and their specific destinations or, indeed, some combination of these.

The study of policy formation is made more complex because the aims of the local state may diverge from those of the central state. The local state is likely to be concerned with the needs of the local community as a whole. Therefore, the economic benefits of tourism are likely to be evaluated against the requirements of other economic sectors and the interests of local residents. Consequently, social and environmental concerns may be prioritised and tourism development may not always be encouraged. In contrast, the objectives of the central state are usually those of economic maximisation: they include the improvement of the balance of payments, diversification of the national economic base, increasing incomes, raising state revenues and creating new jobs (Pearce 1981). Increasingly, however, as has been shown in this volume, state policy is also likely to incorporate, at least nominally, the aims of regional equity, environmental concern and social improvement.

According to the OECD (1974, p. 3), post-1945 tourism policies can be divided into three distinct phases: in the late 1940s and 1950s 'there was a need to dismantle and streamline the many police, currency, health and customs regulations which were the legacy of a war and immediate post-war situation'; in the 1950s governments moved more into promotion as they 'became aware of the "dollar gap" and hence the need to increase their earnings of both dollars and any other hard currency'; while, latterly, governments have become concerned with the problems of tourism supply and with the link between this and regional development. By the 1970s and early 1980s broader social and environmental issues had become the dominant issues in the tourism policies,

Table 14.1   The principal issues in the tourism policies of Belgium, France, the Federal Republic of Germany, Italy, the Netherlands and the UK, 1972–82 (by frequency of mention)

---

1. Regional development
2. Seasonality
3. Consumer protection
4. Balance of payments
5. Social tourism
6. Rural/green tourism
7. Environmental protection

Source: Airey (1983)

at least of northern Europe, according to Airey (1983) (see Table 14.1). However, it is doubtful whether the reality of tourism policy — as measured by state expenditure — corresponds to the emphases given to these issues on paper. Instead, most of the contributors in this book have highlighted the continuing preoccupation of most governments with increasing or redistributing demand.

The prime attraction of tourism for national policy-makers is as an agent of economic change and, especially in the face of global recession in the 1980s, as a source of employment creation. Furthermore, tourism may be prioritised because of the rapidity with which economic growth can be generated, even — or especially — in previously, virtually uncommercialised regions, such as the South of Tenerife or particular Greek islands. As a minimum, the development of tourism has only two prerequisites: the generation of demand, and the provision of food and accommodation for tourists. Beyond this, investment may be necessary to create or open up particular attractions; examples are the provision of ski lifts or the construction of beaches and/or swimming-pools. Much of the post-war boom in mass tourism has been based on such minimalist provision. In this context, and bearing in mind the mixed economies prevalent in Western Europe, the lead role in the development of tourism has been taken by the private sector. The role of the state has mainly been that of providing a regulatory framework or, in particular instances, providing investment (such as in leisure centres or airports) where the private sector has been unable to guarantee the minimalist provisions. Therefore, although state intervention is relatively limited in scope, it is often highly influential in the development of tourism.

14.2   The international framework for tourism services

There is very little in the way of supranational regulation of tourism services, except for the major controls which exist over air transport. Tourism — along with the service sector in general — has rarely been prominent in the discussions of the General Agreement on Trade and Tariffs (GATT) and has only recently attracted the attention of the European Community, as the move to a single market gains pace. This was highlighted in a position paper by the Commission of the European Community (1982, p. 5):

Article 2 of the Treaty of Rome assigns to the European Community the task of promoting closer relations between the States which belong to it. Tourism can assist the Community to achieve this goal and, by bringing the people of Europe into contact, it buttresses the edifice of European integration.

Tourism is also an important economic activity in the spirit of Article 2 of the Treaty. It provides jobs for 4 million people in the Community and its indirect effect on employment is considerably greater. It contributes to balance-of-payments stability between the northern European countries and those of the south and assists in the development of the poorest regions of the Community. Special attention should therefore be paid to promoting its harmonious development throughout the Community.

A further measure of the importance of tourism to the Community is the large number of Community policies which, directly or indirectly, have a bearing on it. These range from the free movement of persons and the freedom to provide tourist services, through passenger transport to regional development and the protection of the environment. To give further stimulation to tourism within the Community, a 'tourist dimension' should be given to these so that the needs of tourism are taken into account when decisions are taken and Community actions implemented.

In practice, European Community policy for tourism has had little impact, precisely because it is located in an area of very weak common policy, that is, the production and delivery of services. Tourist-related policies can be broadly subdivided into five categories (see Table 14.2). The first of these is freedom of movement and the protection of EC tourists. Only in 1986 have any real advances been made in this and, even then, they have been minimal. They include guidance on classification of hotels and standard EC signs (but not procedures!) at international frontiers. A second area of EC policy covers working conditions, but, other than small-scale training and Social Fund expenditures, these have also been of limited importance. However, the free movement of labour required by the Treaty of Rome has influenced the supply of labour for the tourist industry. Transport, which is the third area, presents an equally dismal picture. This is probably the least developed of all the 'common' policies specified in the Treaty of Rome. The only real progress, apart from some harmonisation of international motorway construction, has been the attempt by the Commission during 1986–7 to deregulate and liberalise air traffic, which is likely to lead to some reduction in air fares. Similarly, measures to promote the environment have had more symbolic than real effects on tourism.

Probably the most significant contribution of the EC to tourism has been through expenditure by two of its 'structural' funds, the European Regional Development Fund (ERDF) and the European Agricultural Guidance and Guarantee Fund (EAGGF). ERDF expenditure is divided between quota (for individual countries) and non-quota funds. Under the quota scheme the EC contributed some 69 million ECU in 1975–81 to tourist projects jointly financed with member states, having a total value of 481 million ECU. Under its operating rules the EC provides up to 20 per cent of the costs of new or modernised accommodation (subject to not exceeding 50 per cent of the aid provided by the national government), and up to 30 per cent of the costs of infrastructure projects. In practice most (59 millioin ECU) resources have been granted to infrastructural development. Non-quota funds have largely been channelled into a few selected projects, especially in the frontier region between Ireland and Northern Ireland, in Aquitaine, Rousillon-Languedoc, Midi-Pyrénées and the Mezzogiorno. Although ERDF grants have been

Table 14.2   The European Community policy framework for tourism

---

(a) Freedom of movement and the protection of EC tourists
    (i)   easing customs checks
    (ii)   reduction of police checks at frontiers
    (iii)   social security provisions for tourists
    (iv)   assistance for tourists and regulation of car insurance
    (v)   protection of tourists' interests, e.g. in complaints about the shortcomings of tourist services

(b) Working conditions for those engaged in tourism
    (i)   right of establishment and freedom to provide tourist services
    (ii)   vocational training grants and mutual recognition of qualifications
    (iii)   aid from the European Social Fund
    (iv)   promotion of staggered holidays
    (v)   harmonisation of taxation
    (vi)   promotion of energy efficiency

(c) Common Transport Policy and tourism

(d) Safeguarding the European heritage and tourism
    (i)   environmental protection
    (ii)   art heritage

(e) Regional development and tourism
    (i)   ERDF assistance
    (ii)   EAGGF assistance

Source: based on Commission of the European Communities (1985)

important to particular projects and regions, tourism still has a very low priority within this fund. For example, Pearce (1988) estimates that tourism received only 1.4 per cent of all ERDF expenditures, 1975–84. EAGGF funds have mainly been used to train farmers for tourist-related jobs, and to promote farm tourism and rural craft industries. Compared with the funds provided for other EC expenditure, tourism still appears marginal to the central interests of Community policy.

Awareness of the importance of tourism in the EC continues to grow. 1990 was declared to be European Tourism Year, with the following objectives:

1. preparation for '1992' and the Single Market;
2. promoting greater knowledge of cultures and life-styles;
3. stressing the economic importance of tourism;
4. improving the spatial and temporal distribution of tourism;
5. increasing awareness of the need for a high-quality environment for tourism;
6. promoting greater freedom of travel within the EC.

Most of these activities are concerned with the general promotion of tourism, and the EC still has a very limited role in either investment in or regulation of the industry.

While there has been relatively little supranational regulation of tourism, national governments have placed a number of constraints on the internationalisation of tourism services. These include exchange controls, customs regulations, and travel documentation requirements for travellers, and limits on profits remittances and local equity participation for firms (Ascher 1983; see also pp. 23–4). However, national policies have mostly been concerned with the development and promotion of the tourist industry rather than with regulation.

14.3   National tourism policies

14.3.1   *National context*

Not all states have equal interests in tourism. This depends on their capacity for developing tourism, the current state of the industry (whether it is perceived as prospering or struggling), and the dictates of wider economic considerations, such as the pressure to create jobs in times of recession. With respect to the capacity for developing tourism, Wolfson (1964) recognises four main types of country: where tourism is limited and is likely to remain so; it has limited possibilities of being developed; it exists and, with proper handling, could become a very important factor in the national economy; it is highly advanced and the problem is how to maintain the industry. In Western Europe all countries (if not all regions) fall into the last two categories. Indeed, as the case studies in this volume have shown, most countries are faced with the need for policies both to help traditional tourist regions and to develop new regions. The precise form of the policies, however, depends on a number of broader considerations, including the division of power and finance among the national, regional and local levels. Thus federal Switzerland and the Federal Republic of Germany have quite different tourism policy structures from those which have evolved in more centralised France or Portugal. Even so, the general shift to local economic initiatives as part of a broader emphasis on self-reliance and indigenous resources in development strategies (Bassand *et al.* 1986), has meant that increasing numbers of municipal authorities have become involved in tourism policies. Virtually every rural region has a strategy for rural tourism, while all major (and most minor) cities have urban tourism projects. While the domestic and foreign market segments are still distinctive in many respects, the growing internationalisation of tourism means that, increasingly, all local areas are tending to compete for the same limited (if expanding) market.

National policies for the development of tourism are broadly similar, even if these vary considerably in detail. They are considered here under the following headings: promotion; direct investment; subsidies; labour market intervention; and regulation.

14.3.2   *The promotion of tourism*

The promotion of tourism, especially in foreign markets, has been favoured by virtually every national tourist board. One of the first ventures in this field was the establishment of the Travel Association of Great Britain and Northern Ireland in the 1920s to attract foreign visitors. There has been a rapid expansion in the number of tourist boards subsequently, and according to

Ascher (1983), more than 170 governments have foreign travel promotion offices. This is but the tip of the iceberg, for most regions and tourist resorts have their own tourism promotion services. There are two main ways in which the tourist industry of any one country can be promoted: encouraging foreign tourism, and redirecting the holidays of nationals from foreign to domestic destinations.

The promotion of tourism in foreign markets is mainly based on advertising campaigns aimed either directly at the public or at travel agents and tour companies. These campaigns can take a variety of forms, including advertisements in general newspapers or public spaces, free distribution of brochures, and representation at trade or holiday exhibitions. National tourist boards may either seek to promote the whole country or specific regions. Spain provides notable examples of both approaches in its 'Everything under the sun' and 'So you think you know Spain' campaigns. Balancing diverse regional interests poses particular problems for any national tourist board: for example, the British Tourist Authority is frequently criticised for giving too much emphasis to London in its campaigns. This is a particularly difficult problem which can be resolved into two separate questions: how best to attract foreign visitors initially; and how, subsequently, to ensure that there is some geographical spread in their visits and spending. Another major consideration is the identification of the market segments to be targeted in the promotion campaign. Most tourist authorities are aware of the advantages of higher-income tourism and, indeed, some tourist boards have strategies to attract the higher spenders. However, in other cases—such as Spain—the existence of large numbers of hotels in mass tourist resorts makes it difficult to achieve any significant shift from mass to élite tourism.

The domestic tourist industry can also be assisted by measures aimed at reducing the numbers of foreign holidays taken by nationals. This may involve restrictions on foreign travel, such as the exchange controls in operation in the United Kingdom in 1966–70, and in France in 1983. Alternatively, the attractions of domestic tourism can be promoted. Recent examples include Belgium's '*Vacances au pays*' campaign and Finland's 'Ski cheaply' campaign (OECD 1986). Many such domestic campaigns emphasise the neglected cultural heritage and landscape beauty of the home country in contrast to the discomfort of foreign travel and the grosser attributes of (foreign) mass tourist resorts. A related aspect of domestic promotion campaigns has been the attempt to extend the tourist season and reduce the considerable seasonal peaking in demand (see Chapter 2, Section 2.2.4). This may involve the promotion of 'shoulder-season' or 'out-of-season' lower-cost short breaks, or it may involve attempts to stagger holidays. For example, in France the tourist authorities grant *Aménagement du temps* prizes to the projects which have been most successful in this respect.

Domestic tourism can also be assisted through measures to assist social tourism, that is, tourism for economically weak groups, such as single-parent families or handicapped persons. The assistance, which may be provided by the state or by voluntary bodies, can involve either payments of grants (which will probably be spent on domestic tourism) or provision of free or subsidised accommodation or holiday packages. Social tourism has long roots and one of the earliest organisations was the Co-operative Holidays Association founded in the United Kingdom in 1893. At present, the state-financed Swiss Travel Saving Fund is one of the more highly developed forms of social tourism

(Teuscher 1983). It secures price reductions in holidays, helps low-income families to save and publicises details of low-price holidays. In addition, individuals may be granted a 'tourism cheque' to be used—as they wish—to purchase a holiday (see Chapter 7, Section 7.5). Social tourism is a more recent innovation in other countries but even in Greece, where such schemes only date from 1982, some 400,000 individuals (especially the disabled, the unemployed and pensioners) had been assisted in taking vacations by 1985 (OECD 1986; see also Chapter 5, Section 5.5.2).

14.3.3 State investment in tourism: direct and indirect devalorisation of capital

State investment has become widespread in most modern economies, as a means to support the private sector. This may involve state subsidies to the private sector or direct state investment where there are market gaps which are not filled by the private sector. Such a process has been labelled 'the devalorisation of capital' (Damette 1980), whereby the state socialises part of the cost of production; examples include subsidies for hotel construction, investment in infrastructure or investment in tourist attractions. The reasons for such state interventionism were outlined earlier (see pp. 263–4). In recent years there has been a tendency for the tourist industry to become more capital-intensive—with the requirement for new airports, marinas, theme parks, hotel swimming-pools, etc.—and this has increased the pressure on government intervention.

Infrastructural investment usually depends on the state and this can be crucial in opening up regions to tourism. For example, the construction of the M5 motorway greatly assisted the continuing development of tourism in south-west England, while the construction of Málaga airport was critical in opening up Spain's Costa del Sol. In addition, the development of greenfield sites or substantial (non-incremental) additions to existing resorts will require large-scale investment in water and energy supplies and sewage and waste disposal. It is, invariably, the state which takes the lead role in such investments. In addition, the state may invest in tourist attractions such as conferences centres or the conservation of historic sites, as non-profit-making poles of attraction; a notable example is the Vienna Conference Centre (see p. 20).

The accommodation sector has not usually been the object of direct state investment. There are examples of this, notably the *pousadas* of Portugal and the *paradores* of Spain which were designed to attract tourists away from the seaside resorts: however, these are the exceptions and most government intervention has been limited to providing subsidies to the accommodation sector. Examples include the English Tourist Board grants for upgrading hotel rooms, and the low-cost loans made by Spain's Industrial Credit Bank and by Greece's Organisation for the Financing of Economic Development for hotel construction. This system of subsidies can be critical both in opening up new tourist zones (as in parts of the Algarve in the 1960s) and in assisting hotels in existing resorts to upgrade their facilities in line with rising consumer expectations (as in the United Kingdom in the 1980s).

State investment in tourism may often be linked to particular regional development strategies. For example, tourism featured in the development programmes of Italy's Cassa per il Mezzogiorno and 7–10 per cent of its

Table 14.3   Tourism teaching and training at the national level, 1983

	Numbers of establishments	Diplomas awarded in Tourism	Hotel studies
Austria	5	5	3
Belgium	13	10	6
Finland	11	5	7
France	22	23	5
FRG	5	5	0
Greece	8	5	6
Ireland	1	0	1
Italy	28	6	24
Netherlands	4	4	2
Norway	5	3	2
Portugal	2	1	2
Spain	28	27	5
Sweden	4	2	1
Switzerland	11	10	8
UK	37	29	12

Source: World Tourism Organisation (1986)

budget was spent on this in the 1960s (White 1976; See also Chapter 4, section 4.5.3). Other examples include France's regional plan to open up the Languedoc-Roussillon area to tourism, and the 1973 Swiss plan to spend 500 million francs opening up the mountain regions to tourism. While tourism does offer some advantages for regional development strategies, it is appropriate to repeat Middleton's (1977, paragraph 11.2) view on this: 'Unfortunately, in the current state of knowledge one must conclude that tourism, in practice, is a rather blunt instrument for achieving regional objectives and carries with it dangers arising from the difficulties of control.'

14.3.4   *Labour-market intervention*

There is far less specific state intervention in tourism labour markets than in the provision of capital. This is not to say that tourism is unaffected by the general regulation of labour markets. Minimum wages, hours and conditions of work regulations, and restrictions on immigration, all affect the supply of and the price of labour. For example, Switzerland's immigrant labour laws contribute to the existence of a cheap, flexible and seasonal labour force for tourism. However, these are secondary effects from legislation which usually has not been primarily or specifically designed for the tourist industry.

Most direct intervention is limited to specific minimum wages regulations for the accommodation and catering sectors, and to the provision of training courses. Most European countries provide some training courses either in tourism in general or in specific skills such as catering or hotel work (see Table 14.3). In some countries training is relatively well organised: in France, for example, all firms with more than ten employees have to pay 1.1 per cent of their wage bill as a training levy. However, as most surveys of tourist firms have shown (for example, Shaw, Williams and Greenwood 1987), the majority of employers and employees have had little formal training. Most have only a minimal amount of on-the-job training or learn to run their businesses from practice. This tends to reinforce the casual nature and the rapid turnover which is characteristic of tourism labour markets.

14.3.5   *Environmental regulation*

Large-scale tourist developments produce considerable pressures on the environment and on the local population. These include destruction of the traditional landscape, congestion in the transport system, and air, land and water pollution. Such problems are usually most acute in the rapidly developed mass tourist resorts. In contrast, rural tourism, business tourism and élite tourism tend to be more incremental in nature and the tourists are more easily integrated within existing economic, social and built-environment structures. This is linked to the concept of 'the capacity to absorb tourism' (see Getz 1983) but it is clear that this can be evaluated from several different perspectives. Different sectors of the local community—depending on their economic interests and precise place of residence—may be affected in strongly contrasting ways by tourism development. Furthermore, while municipal authorities may decide to limit further tourist development for social or environmental reasons, this may bring them into conflict with the economic interests of central or regional governments wishing to promote tourism. Ultimately, environmental controls have to be enforced, otherwise uncontrolled tourist development may lead to the attraction of the tourist area being severely reduced.

All municipal authorities in areas of large-scale tourism are likely to come under pressure to limit tourism development for environmental reasons. Their ability to do so depends on the precise distribution of powers between central, regional and local government in each country. In the United Kingdom, for example, development-control powers give local authorities considerable scope to refuse planning permission for new tourist developments but little power to modify existing tourist activities. The Netherlands has an even stronger system of land use regulation (see Chapter 12, section 12.6). There are also strong controls at the commune level in Switzerland but the considerable degree of decentralisation means that neighbouring municipalities may pursue conflicting tourism policies (see Chapter 7, section 7.5). Environmental regulation is least developed in southern Europe (see Wynn 1984) because of the traditions of centralism and the weakness of municipal finances in these countries. As these are also the countries where the rate of tourist development has been greatest in recent decades, they tend to have experienced the greatest amount of environmental degradation as a result of tourism development (see Chapters 3, 5 and 6). In contrast, all provinces in the Netherlands have to produce a Tourism and Recreation Development Plan which provides both an inventory of existing facilities and an assessment of the potential for future development. By the late 1980s most European countries had begun to discuss the ways in which tourism development could be harmoniously integrated with environmental conservation; for example, this was the specific aim of France's 1985 'Mountain Act'. However, in most countries, this still remains an elusive goal rather than common practice.

14.4   Tourism and development: an uneasy relationship

The diverse range of experiences reported in this volume underline the central fact that tourism does not offer a single model for development. Consequently, it is neither a curse nor a blessing in itself. Any evaluation of the role of tourism — and of the jobs, income and value added which it produces — must depend on particular national and local circumstances. Tourism can bring jobs and can revive stagnating local economies, but it can also be detrimental to other economic activities, destroy the environment and contribute to the informalisation of labour markets. There is a need, therefore, to look not just at tourism but at the opportunity costs of its development, and the alternative strategies which could be pursued by a region or community. As de Kadt (1979, p. 21) emphasised, over a decade ago:

tourism projects are often developed without being tested within the framework of a sectoral plan, while their costs and benefits may not even be compared with those of alternative projects in the same sector. Most seriously, although the sectoral plan should establish the place of tourism within the development strategy for the whole economy, in many cases such a plan is nonexistent or not decisively implemented.

The increased emphasis by almost all European governments on tourism development as a source of jobs in the 1980s, makes it imperative that this fuller evaluation of tourism is not neglected.

Tourism does offer economic benefits, but the total market for tourism is still limited, if expanding. Most communities, therefore, can only hope for small-scale economic advantages and in such areas tourism can be no more than one element in a wider development strategy. However, some areas may attract or generate large-scale developments, for there is no reason why the mass tourist resorts of the present will continue to dominate in the future. As tastes, incomes and mobility change, new European resorts may emerge, and with the likely shift away from minimalist provision, these may create new types of jobs and investment. However, the greatest challenge for decision-makers in the future concerns the renewal of the mass tourist resorts of the post-war period. As the product cycle reaches maturity and their facilities age, potentially they will present enormous redevelopment problems. If they do not attract new rounds of investments in tourist facilities, how is the built environment to be maintained and what will be the impact on local labour markets? It is not inconceivable that in future decades some tourist resorts will replace steel or textile communities as the major concern of regional economic policies.

Bibliography

Agricola, S. (1982), 'Freizeit—Kurzdarstellung', *Deutsche Gesellschaft für Freizeit e. V.*, *vol. 49*.

Airey, D. (1983), 'European government approaches to tourism', *Tourism Management*, vol. 4, pp. 234–44.

Alcaide, A. (1984), 'La importancia de nuestra economía turística', *Situación*, 1984/1, pp. 26–49.

Alexandrakis, N.E. (1973), *Tourism as a leading sector in economic development: a case study of Greece*, Ann Arbor, MI: University Microfilms.

Alhaique, C. (1975), 'Appunti per una "Manuale di patologia turistica del Mezzogiorno" (gli impianti ricettivi)', *Realtà del Mezzogiorno*, vol. 15, pp. 627–64.

Allcock, J.B. (1983), 'Tourism and social change in Dalmatia', *Journal of Development Studies*, vol. 20, pp. 34–55.

Alpeninstitut für Umweltforschung und Entwicklungsplanung (1978), *Belastete Fremdenverkehrsgebiete*, Bonn: Der Bundesminister für Raumordnung, Bauwesen und Städtebau.

Ambroise-Rendu, M. (1986), 'Le tourisme d'affaires, première industrie de la capitale', *Le Monde*, 3–4 August.

Andronicou, A. (1979), 'Tourism in Cyprus' in E. de Kadt (ed.), *Tourism: passport to development?*, Oxford: Oxford University Press.

Anon (1983), 'Bundesbehörden und Tourismus', *Geographica Helvetica*, vol. 38, pp. 88–96.

Arcangeli, F., Borzaga, C. and Goglio, S. (1980), 'Patterns of peripheral development in the Italian regions 1964–77', *Papers of the Regional Science Association*, vol. 44, pp. 19–34.

Archer, B.H. (1977), *Tourism multipliers: the state of the art*, Cardiff: Bangor Occasional Papers in Economics II, University of Wales Press.

Archer, B.H. (1982), 'The value of multipliers and their policy implications', *Tourism Management*, vol. 3, pp. 236–41.

Ariza, M.J. and Villegas, F. (1984), 'La actividad turística en la Estación de Esquí Solynieve, Sierra Nevada (Granada)' in *Aportación Española al XXV Congreso Internacional de Geografía*, Paris.

Ascher, B. (1983), 'Obstacles to international travel and tourism', *Journal of Travel Research*, vol. 22, pp. 2–16.

Ashworth, G.J. and Bergsma, J.R. (1987), 'New policies for tourism: opportunities and problems', *Tijdschrift voor Economische en Sociale Geografie*, vol. 78, pp. 151–3.

Atlas van Nederland, 's-Gravenhage: Stichting Wetenschappelijke Atlas van Nederland, Staatsuitgeverij'.

Baier, S. (1985), 'Der alpine Sommertourismus aus der Sicht der Fremdenverkehrswirtschaft', *Problem Sommerfremdenverkehr in den Alpen*, Referate zum 2. Hochschulkurs für Fremdenverkehr in Neustift/Brixen, Institut für Verkehr und Tourismus, Schriftenreihe B 14, Innsbruck, 41–45.

Barbaza, Y. (1966), *Le paysage humain de la Costa Brava*, Paris: Librairie Armand Colin.

Barbier, B. (1978), 'Ski et stations de sports d'hiver dans le monde', *Wiener Geographische Schriften*, vol. 51–2, pp. 130–48.

Baretje, R. (1982), 'Tourism's external account and the balance of payments', *Annals of Tourism Research*, vol. 9, pp. 57–67.

Barker, M.L. (1982), 'Traditional landscape and mass tourism in the Alps', *Geographical Review*, vol. 72, pp. 395–415.

Baron, R.R. (1983), 'The necessity for an international system of tourism statistics', *International Tourism Quarterly*, vol. 4, pp. 39–51.

Barucci, P. (ed.) (1984), *Primo rapporto sul turismo italiano*, Rome: Ministero del Turismo e dello Spettacolo.

Bassand, M., Brugger, E.A., Bryden, J.M., Friedmann, J. and Stuckey, B. (1986), *Self-reliant development in Europe: theory, problems, actions*, Aldershot: Gower.

Baumgartner, F. (1983), 'Zur raumplanerischen Beurteilung touristischer Transportan-langen', *Aménagement du Territoire: Bulletin d'Information*, vol. 3, pp. 7–9.

Bayerisches Staatsministerium für Landesentwicklung und Umweltfragen (ed.) (1980), *Landesplanung in Bayern—Erholungslandschaft Alpen*, Munich.

Becheri, E. (1986), 'I mutamenti del turismo' in *Secondo rappoto sul turismo italiano*, Rome: Ministero del Turismo e dello Spettacolo.

Becker, Ch. (1984a), 'Der Ausländertourismus und seine räumliche Verteilung in der Bundesrepublik Deutschland', *Zeitschrift für Wirtschaftsgeographie*, vol. 1, pp. 1–10.

Becker, Ch. (1984b), 'Neue Entwicklungen bei den Feriengrossprojekten in der Bundesrepublik Deutschland—Diffusion und Probleme einer noch wachsenden Betriebsform', *Zeitschrift für Wirtschaftsgeographie*, vol. 3–4, pp. 164–85.

Becker, Ch. and Hensel, H. (1982), 'Struktur- und Entwicklungsprobleme des Städtetourismus—analysiert am Beispiel von 19 Städten, in *Städtetourismus: Analysen und Fallstudien aus Hessen, Rheinland-Pflaz und Saarland*, Hannover: Akademie für Raumforschung und Landesplanung, pp. 167–83.

Becker, Ch. and Klemm, K. (1978), *Raumwirksame Instrumente des Bundes im Bereich Freizeit*, Bonn: Der Bundesminister für Raumordnung, Bauwesen und Städtebau.

Bell, D. (1974), *The coming of post-industrial society*, London: Heinemann.

Bennett, R.J. (1986), 'Social and economic transition: a case study in Portugal's Western Algarve', *Journal of Rural Studies*, vol. 2, pp. 91–102.

Bernal, A.M., Fourneau, F., Heran, F., Lacroix, J., Lecordier, P., Martin Vicente, A., Menanteau, L., Mignon, C., Roax, B., Zoido Naranjo, F. (1979), *Tourisme et développment regional en Andalusie*, Paris: Editions E.de Boccard.

Bertrisey, G. (1981), *Valais 2000: Réflexions sur le devenir économique d'un canton*, Sion: Crédit Suisse.

Béteille, R. (1976), 'Le tourisme en milieu rural en France', *Information Géographique*, vol. 40, pp. 174–90.

Béteille, R. (1981), *La France du vide*, Paris: Litec.

Billet, J. (1984), 'Le tourisme en Suisse: Une activité en adaptation constante' in B. Barbier *et al.* (eds), *Les Alpes: 25 Congrès International de Géographie*, Caen: Comité International d'Organisation.

Billion, F. and Flückiger, B. (1978), 'Bedarfsanalyse Naherholung und Kurzzeit-tourismus', research report prepared for Bremen: the Bundesminister für Wirtschaft, Bonn.

Boesch, M. (1983), 'Raumentwicklung und Fremdenverkehr im Kanton Graubünden', *Geographica Helvetica*, vol. 38, pp. 63–8.

Boissevain, J. and Inglott, P.S. (1979), 'Tourism in Malta' in E. de Kadt (ed.), *Tourism: passport to development?*, Oxford: Oxford University Press.

Bonapace, U. (1968), 'Il turismo della neve in Italfia e i suoi aspetti geografici', *Rivista Geografica Italiana*, vol. 75, pp. 157–86, 322–59.

Bosch, R. (1987), 'Turismo de masas' in *Turismo: horizonte 1990*, Barcelona: Editur.

Bote, V. (1985), 'Plan de acción para la conservación y desarrollo de los recursos turísticos de la Comarca de la Vera (Caceres)', *Estudios Turísticos*, vol. 88, pp. 51–64.

Bouquet, M. (1982), 'Production and reproduction of family farms in South-West England', *Sociologia Ruralis*, vol. 22, pp. 227–49.

Boyer, M. (1982), *Le tourisme*, Paris: Seuil, 2nd edn.

Bras, M. (1985), 'Juillet-août 1984: près de deux millions de touristes dan lac Var', *Sud Information Economique*, no. 62, pp. 19–24.

Brinchmann, K.S. and Jensen, Ø. (1990), 'Turistproduktet Nord-Norge', NF working paper 1055/90, Nordland Research Institute.

British Tourist Authority (1985), *British tourism survey — monthly*, London.

British Tourist Authority (1986), *Tourism forecasts and trends*, London.

Brunetta, R. (1976), 'Turismo sociale e territorio', *Nord e Sud*, vol. 23, pp. 31–50.

Brusco, S. (1982), 'The Emilian model: productive decentralisation and social integration', *Cambridge Journal of Economics*, vol. 6, pp. 167–84.

Bryden, J.M. (1973), *Tourism and development: a case study of the Commonwealth Caribbean*, Cambridge: Cambridge University Press.

Buckley, P.J. and Papadopoulos, S.I. (1986), 'Marketing Greek tourism — the planning process', *Tourism Management*, vol. 7, pp. 86–100.

Bundesforschungsanstalt für Landeskunde und Raumordnung (ed.) (1983), 'Neue Entwicklungen im Fremdenverkehr', *Informationen zur Raumentwicklung*, vol. 1, pp. 1–92.

Cabildo Insular de Tenerife (1983), *Economía y turismo en Tenerife*, Tenerife: Aula de Cultura.

Calatrava, J. (1984), 'Análisis de la potencialidad del turismo rural como elemento generador de rentas complementarias en zonas en depresión socioeconómica: el caso de las Alpujarras granadinas' in *Coloquio Hispano-Francés sobre Espacios Rurales*, Madrid: Ministerio de Agricultura, Servicio de Publicaciones.

Cals, J. (1974), *Turismo y política turística en España: una aproximación*, Barcelona: Ariel.

Cals, J. (1983), 'El modelo turístico español', *Estudios Turísticos*, vol. 80, pp. 15–21.

Campagnoli-Ciaccio, C. (1979), 'The organisation of tourism in Sicily', *Wiener Geographische Schriften*, vol. 53–54, pp. 132–42.

Canto, C. (1983), 'Presente y futuro de las residencias secundarias en España, *Anales de Geografia de la Universidad Computense de Madrid*, vol. 3, pp. 83–103.

Castagnari, G. (1975), 'La campagna come investimento', *Nord e Sud*, vol. 22, pp. 151–60.

Castles, S., Booth, H. and Wallace, T. (1984), *Here for good: Western Europe's new ethnic minorities*, London: Pluto Press.

Cavaco, C. (1979), *O turismo em Portugal: aspectos evolutivos e espaciais*, Lisbon: University of Lisbon, Estudos de Geografia Humana e Regional.

Cavaco, C. (1980), *Turismo e demografia no Algarve*, Lisbon: Editorial Progresso Social e Democracia.

Cavaco, C. (1981), *A Costa do Estoril*, vols 1 and 2, Lisbon: University of Lisbon, Centro de Estudos Geográficos, Estudos de Geografia Humana e Regional.

Cazes, G. (1984), 'Le tourisme français vers l'étranger', *Revue de Géographie de Lyon*, vol. 59, pp. 95–102.

Cazes, G. (1986), *Le tourisme en France*, Paris: Presses Universitaires de France, Paris, 2nd edn.

Cazes, G. et al (1980), *L'aménagement touristique*, Paris: Presses Universitaires de France.

Central Bureau of Statistics of Norway (various), *Monthly Reports and Statistical Yearbooks*.

Chib, S.N. (1977), 'Measurement of tourism', *Journal of Travel Research*, vol. 16, pp. 22–5.

Christine, M. (1987), 'Les vacances' in *Données Sociales*, Paris: INSEE.

Christine, M. and Samy, C. (1986), 'Les vacances de la saison d'hiver 1985–1986', *Premiers Résultats* (INSEE), no. 74.

Christine, M. and Samy, C. (1987), 'Les départs en vacances de l'été 1986', *Premiers Résultats* (INSEE), no. 96.

Clement, H.G. (1967), 'The impact of tourism expenditures', *Development digest*, vol.

5, pp. 70–81.

Cohen, E. (1974), 'Who is a tourist? A conceptual clarification', *Sociological Review*, vol. 22, pp. 527–55.

Cole, J.P. (1968), *Italy*, London: Chatto and Windus.

Commerzbank (1987), *Branchen-Bericht: Hochstimmung in der Touristikbranche*, Frankfurt.

Commissariat Général du Plan (1983), *Tourisme et loisirs*, Paris: La Documentation Française.

Commission Consultative Fédéral pour le Tourisme (1979), *Conception Suisse du tourisme*, Berne: Office Central Fédéral des Imprimés.

Commission Internationale pour la Protection des Régions Alpines (CIPRA) (ed.) (1985), '*Sanfter Tourismus: Schlagwort oder Chance für den Alpenraum?*', Vaduz.

Commission of the European Communities (1982), *A Community policy on tourism*, Brussels.

Commission of the European Communities (1985), *Tourism and the European Community*, European File 11/85, Brussels.

Commission of the European Communities (1986), *Community action in the field of tourism*, Documents, com. (86) 32 final, Brussels.

Commission of the European Communities (1987), *Europeans and their holidays*, VII/165/87–EN, Brussels.

Comunidades Europeas (1986), 'Acción comunitaria en el sector del turismo', *Boletín de las Comunidades Europeas*, 4/86, pp. 10–11.

Conseil Economique et Social (1984), *Les aspects économiques de l'industrie du tourisme*, Paris: Conseil Economique et Social.

Conseil Economique et Social (1988), *Pour une industrie touristique plus compétitive*, Paris, Conseil Economique et Social.

Conseil Fédéral Suisse (1986), *Message concernant une modification de l'arrêté fédéral sur l'office national suisse du tourisme*, Berne.

Cooper, G. (1952), *Your holiday in Spain and Portugal*, London: Alvin Redman.

CPER (Centre of Planning and Economic Research) (1972), *Plan for model long-term development of Greece*, Athens (in Greek).

CPER (1976), *Programme for development 1976–80: tourism*, Athens (in Greek).

CPER (1987), *Reports for the programme 1983–87: tourism*, Athens (in Greek).

CPER (1988), *Five year plan for social and economic development 1988–92*, Athens, first draft of final text (mimeo, in Greek).

Cuadrado, J.R. and Aurioles, J. (1986), 'Las actividades turísticas dentro de la estructura económica de Andalucía', *Revista de Estudios Regionales*, vol. 6, pp. 41–64.

Cunha, L. (1986), 'Turismo' in M. Silva (ed.), *Portugal contemporâneo: Problemas e perspectivas*, Lisbon: Instituto Nacional de Administração.

Damette, F. (1980), 'The regional framework of monopoly exploitation: new problems and trends' in J. Carney, R. Hudson and J.R. Lewis (eds), *Regions in crisis*, London: Croom Helm.

Darbellay, C. (1979), 'Peri-urban agriculture of the Crans–Montana region' in Organisation for Economic Cooperation and Development, *Agriculture in the planning and management of peri-urban areas: Volume II*, Paris.

Demarinis, F. (1972), 'Tourism in Italy on the eve of the expansion of the EEC', *Banco di Roma Review of Economic Conditions in Italy*, vol. 26, pp. 379–96.

Demarinis, F. (1979), 'Geografia economica e turismo', in *Atti del convegno sulla funzione della geografia economica nella formazione economica e profesionale*, Rome: Università di Roma Istituto di Geografia Economica (special issue of *Notiziario di Geografia Economica*, vol. 10. pp. 153–7).

Dematteis, G. (1979), 'Repeuplement et revalorisation des espaces périphériques: le cas de l'Italie', *Revue de Géographie des Pyrénées et du Sud-Ouest*, vol. 53, pp. 129–43.

Denia, A. and Pedreño, A. (1986), 'Problemas de la actividad turística en la Comunidad Valenciana' in *Papeles de Economía Española, Economía de las Comunidades Autónomas, Comunidad Valenciana*.

Dernoi, L.A. (1983), 'Farm tourism in Europe', *Tourism Management*, vol. 4, pp. 155–66.

Desplanques, H. (1973), 'Une nouvelle utilisation de l'espace rural en Italie: l'agritourisme', *Annales de Géographie*, vol. 82, pp. 151–64.

Deutsche Gesellschaft für Freizeit (ed.) (1986), *Freizeit-Lexikon*, Ostfildern: Schriftenreihe der Deutschen Gesellschaft für Freizeit no. 059.

Deutscher Bundestag (ed.) (1986a), *Fremdenverkehr. Antwort der Bundesregierung*, document no. 10/5454, Bonn, 9 May.

Deutscher Bundestag (ed.) (1986b), *Fremdenverkehrspolitik. Antwort der Bundesregierung*, document no. 10/5455, Bonn, 9 May.

Deutscher Bundestag (ed.) (1986c), *Fünfzehnter Rahmenplan der Gemeinschaftsaufgabe 'Verbesserung der regionalen Wirtschaftsstruktur'. Unterrichtung durch die Bundesregierung*, document no. 10/5910, Bonn, 5 August.

Dicken, P. (1986), *Global shift*, London: Harper and Row.

Diem, A. (1980), 'Valley renaissance in the high Alps', *Geographical Magazine*, vol. 52, pp. 492–7.

Di Majo, L. (1982), 'Per una politica del turismo nel Mezzogiorno', *Nord e Sud*, vol. 29, pp. 153–67.

Diputación Provincial de Valencia (1983), *Urbanismo y medio rural: la vivienda ilegal de segunda residencia*, Valencia: Art. Gráf. Soler.

Direcção Geral do Turismo (1984), *O turismo estrangeiro em Portugal: inquérito 84*, Lisbon: Direcção Geral do Turismo, Gabinete de Estatística e Inquéritos.

Direcção Geral do Turismo (1986), *O turismo em 1983/1984*, Lisbon: Direcção Geral do Turismo, Gabinete de Estatísticas e Inquéritos.

Direcção Geral do Turismo (1988), *O turismo em 1987*, Lisbon: Direcção Geral do Turismo, Gabinete de Estatísticas e Inqueritos.

Direction du Tourisme (1986), *Mémento du tourisme*, Paris: Sécretariat au Tourisme.

Doxiadis Assoc. (1974), *National regional plan of Greece*, Athens: Ministry of Co-ordination (in Greek).

Dufau, J. (1986), 'Le littoral sera mieux protégé, *Le Moniteur*, 7 February.

Duffield, B.S. (1977), *Tourism: a tool for regional development*, Edinburgh: Tourism and Recreation Research Unit.

Duffield, B.S. (1982), 'Tourism: the measurement of economic and social impact', *Tourism Management*, vol. 3, pp. 248–55.

Dutt, A.K. and Costa, F.J. (eds) (1985), *Public planning in the Netherlands*, Oxford: Oxford University Press.

Dutt, A.K., Costa, F.J., van der Waal, C. and Lutz, W. (1985), 'Evolution of land uses and settlement policies in Zuiderzee project planning' in A.K. Dutt and F.J. Costa (eds), *Public planning in the Netherlands*, Oxford: Oxford University Press.

Edwards, A. (1981), *Leisure spending in the European Community—forecasts to 1990*, London: Economist Intelligence Unit.

Eggeling, V.-T. (1981), 'Freizeit und Massentourismus. Freie Zeit und Freizeitraum als Gegenstand politischer Bildung' in H.-J. Wenzel (ed.), *Studienreihe Geographie/ Gemeinschaftskunde*, vol. 2, Stuttgart: Metzler.

Elsasser, H. and Leibundgut, H. (1982), 'Touristische Monostrukturen—Probleme im schweizerischen Berggebiet', *Geographische Rundschau*, vol. 34, pp. 228–34.

Elsasser, H. and Leibundgut, H. (1983), 'Wirtschaftgeographische. Probleme des touristischen Arbeitsmarktes in der Schweiz', *Geographica Helvetica*, vol. 38, pp. 83–8.

English Tourist Board (1973), *Blackpool visitirs and tourism survey*, London.

English Tourist Board (1978), *Bude to Wadebridge: A new growth point for tourism*, London.

English Tourist Board (1981a), *Prospects for self-catering development*, London.

English Tourist Board (1981b), *Planning for tourism in England: Planning Advisory Note 1*, London.

English Tourist Board (1984), *The UK conference market: Providing for the future*, London.

English Tourist Board (1986), *Jobs in tourism and leisure: An occupational review*, London.

EOT (National Tourist Organization of Greece) (1979), *Sample survey of mobility of tourists in Greek space*, Athens: EOT, Division A of Research and Development (in Greek).

EOT (1985), *Tourism 1985*, Athens: EOT, Division A of Research and Development (in Greek).

d'Erceville, I. (1986), 'Premières neiges au salon', *Le Monde*, 18 October.

Esteban, J. and Pedreño, A. (1985), *Estimación de la renta familiar disponible a nivel municipal en la Comunidad Valenciana*, Alicante: Caja de Ahorros de Alicante y Murcia.

Esteve, R. (1986), 'El turismo deportivo en Andalucía', *Revista de Estudios Regionales*, vol. 6, pp. 239–66.

European Travel Commission (1986), *Annual report 1985*, Dublin: European Travel Commission.

Faisca, S. (1985), *Desenvolvimento turístico do nordeste Algarvio*, Faro: Commissão do Coordenação da Região do Algarve.

Faludi, A. and de Ruijter, P. (1985), 'Not match for the present crisis? the theoretical and institutional framework for Dutch planning' in A.K. Dutt and F.J. Costa (eds), *Public planning in the Netherlands*, Oxford: Oxford University Press.

Fédération Suisse du Tourisme (1989), *Swiss tourism in figures*, Bern: La Fédération.

Fel, A. and Bouet, G. (1983), *Atlas et géographie du Massif Central*, Paris: Flammarion.

Ferrão, J.M. (1985), 'Regional variations in the rate of profit' in R. Hudson and J.R. Lewis (eds), *Uneven development in southern Europe*, London: Methuen.

Ferras, A. *et al.* (1979), *Atlas et géographie du Languedoc et du Roussillon*, Paris: Flammarion.

Figuerola, M. (1983), 'Importancia del turismo en la economía española', *Estudios Turísticos*, vol. 80, pp. 21–31.

Figuerola, M. (1986), 'Tendencias y problemas del turismo actual', *Revista de Estudios Regionales*, vol. 6, pp. 17–40.

Fisk, W. (1984), 'Der Campingtourismus—ein Bestandteil des Fremdenverkehrs', *Jahrbuch für Fremdenverkehr, 1982/83*, pp. 1–37.

Flament, E. (1984), 'Les vacances des français', *Revue de Géographie de Lyon*, vol. 59, pp. 7–14.

Fornfeist, D. (1976), *Urlaubsreisen 1975, Einige Ergebnisse der Reiseanalyse 1975, Kurzfassung*, Starnberg: Studienkreis für Tourismus.

Fourneau, F. (1979), 'La Costa de la Luz de Huelva' in *Tourisme et Développment Régional*, Paris: Editions E. de Boccard.

Fragakis, I. (1987), 'The average length of stay of foreign tourists in Greece is 14 days', *Tourism and Economy*, vol. 2, pp. 127–8 (in Greek).

Fraser, R. (1974), *The pueblo: a mountain village on the Costa del Sol*, London: Allen Lane.

Freitag, R. (1989), 'The Norwegian/Scandinavian tourist product from a French point of view', presentation at the Tourism Congress in Harstad, 1 June 1989.

de Freitas, J.A. (1984), *Madeira: construir o futuro hoje*, Lisbon: Editorial Caminho.

Fuà, G. (1983), 'Rural industrialisation in later developed countries: the case of north-east and central Italy', *Banca Nazionale del Lavoro Quarterly Review*, vol. 147, pp. 351–78.

Fuscà, F. (1983), 'Luci ed ombre della "Legge Quadro" sud turismo', *Rassegna di Studi Turistici*, vol. 18, pp. 197–220.

Gambino, R. (1978), *Turismo e sviluppo del Mezzogiorno*, Rome: SVIMEZ.

Gaviria, M. (1974), *España a go-go: Turismo charter y neocolonialismo del espacio*, Madrid: Ediciones Turner.

Gaviria, M. (1977a), *Benidorm, ciudad nueva*, Madrid: Editora Nacional.

Gaviria, M. (1977b), *El turismo de invierno y el asentamiento de extranjeros en la Provincia de Alicante*, Alicante: Instituto de Estudios Alicantinos.

Gershuny, J.I. and Miles, I.D. (1983), *The new service economy: the transformation of employment in industrial societies*, London: Frances Pinter.

Getz, D. (1983), 'Capacity to absorb tourism: concepts and implications for strategic planning', *Annals of Tourism Research*, vol. 10, pp. 239–63.

Gilg, A.W. (1983), 'Settlement design in the Alps: the case of Leysin', *Landscape Research*, vol. 8, pp. 2–12.

Gilg, A. (1985), 'Land-use planning in Switzerland', *Town Planning Review*, vol. 56, pp. 315–38.

Gonen, A. (1981), 'Tourism and coastal settlement processes in the Mediterranean region', *Ekistics*, vol. 48, pp. 378–81.

Grafton, D. (1984), 'Small-scale growth centres in remote rural regions: the case of Alpine Switzerland', *Applied Geography*, vol. 4, pp. 29–46.

Greek Parliament (1984), *The five-year plan of socio-economic development 1983–1987*, Athens: National Publishers (in Greek).

Greenwood, D.J. (1976), 'The demise of agriculture in Fuenterrabia' in J.B. Aceves and W.A. Douglass (eds), *The changing faces of rural Spain*, New York: Schenkman.

Gunn, C.A. (1977), 'Industry pragmatism versus tourism planning', *Leisure Sciences*, vol. 1, pp. 85–94.

Gutiérrez, D. (1985), 'El club resort' in *Turismo: horizonte 1990*, Barcelona: Editur.

Hadjimichalis, C. and Vaiou, D. (1986), 'Changing patterns of uneven regional development and forms of social reproduction', unpublished paper, Athens.

Haimayer, P. (1984), 'Überlagerungen des Freizeitverkehrs in Österreich' in Österreichische Berträge zur Geographie der Ostalpen, IGU Congress, Wiener Geographische Schriften, pp. 168–76.

Ham, C. and Hill, M. (1985), *The policy process in the modern capitalist state*, Brighton: Wheatsheaf.

Hanekamp, G. (1979), 'Het wilt en bijster landt van Veluwen' in M.F. Morzer Bruijns and R.J. Benthem (eds), *Atlas van de Netherlandse Landschappen*, Utrecht: Spectrum.

de Hanni, H. (1984), 'Controlling the development of tourism: possibilities and hindrances' in E.A. Brugger *et al.* (eds), *The transformation of Swiss mountain regions*, Berne: Haupt.

Hannss, C. and Schröder, P. (1985), 'Touristische Transportlagen in den Alpen', *Dokumente und Informationen zur Schweizerischen Orts-, Regional- und Landesplanung*, April, pp. 19–25.

Hasslacher, P. (1984), 'Sanfter Tourismus-Virgental', Innsbruck: Österreichischer Alpenverein.

Heeley, J. (1981), 'Planning for tourism in Britain: An historical perspective', *Town Planning Review*, vol. 52, pp. 61–79.

Henderson, D.M. (1976), *The economic impact of tourism in Edinburgh and the Lothian region 1976*, Edinburgh: Edinburgh University, Tourism and Recreation Research Unit.

Hennessy, S., Greenwood, J., Shaw, G. and Williams, A. (1986), *The role of tourism in local economies; a pilot study of Looe, Cornwall*, Exeter, University of Exeter, Department of Geography: Tourism in Cornwall Project, Discussion Paper no. 1.

Herrera, J.L. (1984), 'Consideración turística del Camino de Santiago', *Estudios Turísticos*, vol. 84, pp. 17–31.

HMSO (1985), *Pleasure, leisure and jobs: the business of tourism*, London.

Holloway, J.C. (1983), *The business of tourism*, London: Macdonald and Evans.

INSEE (1987a), *Données sociales*, Paris.

INSEE (1987b), *Données économiques et sociales Provence-Alpes-Côte d'Azur*, Marseille.

Institut für Planungskybernitik (1989), *Norway—A study of domestic holiday demand*, Oslo: NORTRA.

Instituto Español de Turismo (1978), 'Determinación y valoración de la estructura económica del turismo español', *Estudios Turísticos*, vol. 59–60, pp. 203–25.

Instituto Nacional de Estatística (1985a), *Estatísticas do turismo 1984*, Lisbon: Instituto Nacional de Estatística.

Instituto Nacional de Estatística (1985b), *50 anos, Portugal 1935–1985*, Lisbon: Instituto Nacional de Estatística.

Janin, B. (1982), 'Circulation touristique internationale et tourisme étranger en Val d'Aoste', *Revue de Géographie Alpine*, vol. 70, pp. 415–430.

Jenkins, R. (1979), *The road to Alto*, London: Pluto Press.

Jensen, Ø. (1989), 'Overnattingsbedriftenes syn på samferdselstilbudet til og fra Nord-Norge', NF report 6/89, Nordland Research Institute.

Jurczek, P. (1986a), *Städtetourismus in Oberfranken. Stand und Entwicklungsmöglichkeiten des Fremdenverkehrs in Bamberg, Bayreuth, Coburg und Hof*, Munich: Beiträge zur Kommunalwissenschaft 21.

Jurczek, P. (1986b), 'Raumbezogene Veränderungen des Urlaubsreiseverkehrs in der Bundesrepublik Deutschland', unpublished thesis, Bayreuth.

Jurdao, F. (1979), *España en venta*, Madrid: Ediciones Ayuso.

de Kadt, E. (ed.) (1979), *Tourism: passport to development?*, Oxford: Oxford University Press.

Kahn, H. (1979), 'Leading futurologist traces next half century in travel', *Travel Trade News*, 31 January, pp. 1–8.

Kalligas, A.S., Papageorgiou, A.N., Politis, I.V., Romanos, A.G. (1972), *Myconos–Delos–Rinia: regional study of the complex of the three islands*, Athens: Ministry of State Policy, Division of Regional Planning (in Greek).

Kariel, H.G. and Kariel, P.E. (1982), 'Socio-cultural impacts of tourism: an example from the Austrian Alps', *Geografiska Annaler*, vol. 64B, pp. 1–16.

Kern, H.-P. (1986), 'Taille européenne pour Villepinte', *Le Figaro Economie*, 20 October.

Key Note Report (1986), *Tourism in the UK*, London.

King, R.L. (1981), 'Italy' in H.D. Clout (ed.), *Regional development in Western Europe*, Chichester: Wiley.

King, R. (1984), 'Population mobility: emigration, return migration and internal migration', in A. Williams (ed.), *Southern Europe transformed*, London: Harper and Row.

King, R. (ed.) (1986), *Return migration and regional economic problems*, London: Croom Helm.

King, R., Mortimer, J. and Strachan, A. (1984), 'Return migration and tertiary development: a Calabrian case study', *Anthropological Quarterly*, vol. 57, pp. 112–24.

Kitterød, R.H. (1987), 'Nordmenns ferievaner i regionalt perspektiv', *Central Bureau of Statistics of Norway*, Report 87/17.

Kitterød, R.H. (1988), 'Who spends their holiday at home' (Norwegian with English summary), *Central Bureau of Statistics of Norway*, Report 88/8.

Klöpper, R. (1973), *Die räumliche Struktur des Angebots von 'Urlaub auf dem Bauernhof—Entwicklungschancen im Rahmen des gesamten Beherbergungsangebotes in Landgemeinden*, Frankfurt: Auswetungs- und Informationsdienst, vol. 179.

Knafou, R. (1978), *Les stations intégrées de sports d'hiver des Alpes françaises*, Paris: Masson.

Knafou, R. (1985), 'L'évolution de la politique de la montagne', *L'Information Géographique*, vol. 49, pp. 53–62.

Koch, A. (1959), 'Der Urlaubsreiseverkehr. Eine Untersuchung über das Konsumverhalten der Erholungsreisenden 1958', *Jahrbuch für Fremdenverkehr*, pp. 4–70.

Koch, A. (1986), *Wirtschaftliche Bedeutung des Fremdenverkehrs in ländlichen Gebieten, Entwicklung ländlicher Räume durch den Fremdenverkehr. Forschungsberichte und Seminarergebnisse*. Bonn: Der Bundesminister für Raumordnung, Bauwesen und Städtebau, pp. 9–18.

Komilis, P. (1986), *Spatial analysis of tourism*. Athens: CPER (in Greek).

Krippendorf, J. (1984), *Die Ferienmenschen. Für ein neues Verständnis von Freizeit und Reisen*, Zurich/Schwäbisch Hall: Orell Füssli.

Krippendorf, J. (1986), 'The new tourist—turning point for leisure and travel', *Tourism Management*, vol. 7, pp. 131–5.

Krippendorf, J. (1987), *Là-haut sur la montagne . . . Pour un développement du tourisme en harmonie avec l'homme et la nature*, Berne: Kummerley and Frey.

Labasse, J. (1984), 'Les congrès, activité tertiaire de villes privilégiées, *Annales de Géographie*, vol. 93, pp. 687–703.

Lagadec, D. and Starkman, N. (1986), 'Des étoiles plein la ville', *Cahiers de l'Institut d'Aménagement et d'Urbanisme de la Région d'Ile-de-France*, no. 77, pp. 95–104.

Landini, P.G. (1973), 'Verso una conurbazione turistica negli altipiani maggiore d'Abruzzo' in *Atti della tavola rotonda sulla geografia della neve in Italia*, Rome: Società Geografica Italiana (supplement to *Bollettino della Società Geografica Italiana*, series X, no. 2).

Lanfant, M.-F. (1980), 'Introduction: tourism in the process of internationalisation', *International Social Science Journal*, vol. 23, pp. 14–43.

Langevin, Ph. (1981), *L'économie provençale*, Aix-en-Provence: Edisund, vol. 1.

Lanquar, R. *et al.* (1980), *Congrès, séminaires, voyages de stimulation*, Paris: Presses Universitaires de France.

Lanquar, R. and Raynouard, Y. (1981), *Le tourisme social*, Paris: Presses Universitaires de France, 2nd edn.

Law, C.M. (1985a), *'Urban tourism: selected British case studies'*, Manchester: University of Salford, Department of Geography, Working Paper no. 1.

Law, C.M. (1985b), *'The British conference and exhibition business'*, Manchester: University of Salford, Department of Geography, Working Paper no. 2.

Law, C.M. (1987), 'Conference and exhibition tourism', paper presented at British Regional Science Association, Stirling, September.

Lawson, F.R. (1982), 'Trends in business tourism management', *Tourism Management*, vol. 3, pp. 298–302.

Lazzeretti, L. (1986), 'Il finanziamento regionale dell'attività turistiche: primi risultati di una indagine condotta in Italia' in *Secondo rapporto sul turismo italiano*, Rome: Ministero del Turismo e dello Spettacolo.

Lecordier, P. (1979), 'Tourisme et économie régionale' in *Tourisme et développement régionale en Andalousie*, Ch. III.

Lefol, J.-F. (1987), 'Les voyages non professionnels de courte durée', *Economie et Statistique*, no. 198, pp. 37–50.

Leimgruber, W. (1985), 'Farmhouse holidays and rural development', paper given to a conference on 'The Management of Rural Resources' held at the University of Guelph, Canada, July. Available from the author at the University of Fribourg, Switzerland.

Le Monde (1986), 'Le palmarès des congrès, 8 April.

Leontidou, L. (1977), 'On urban structure and the role of planning in contemporary Greece: stereotypes vs prospects', *Architecture in Greece*, vol. 11, pp. 94–101 (in Greek).

Leontidou, L. (1981), *Employment in Greater Athens 1960–2000*, Athens: DEPOS, Public Corporation for Housing and Urban Development (in Greek).

Leontidou, L. (1990), *The Mediterranean City in transition*, Cambridge: Cambridge University Press.

Leontidou, L. (1986), 'Urbanization, migration, and the labour force in Greek cities', unpublished report for the UN, Economic Commission for Europe, Geneva.

Lewis, J.R. and Williams, A.M. (1981), 'Regional uneven development on the European periphery: the case of Portugal, 1950–78', *Tijdschrift voor Economische en Sociale Geografie*, vol. 72, pp. 81–98.

Lewis, J.R. and Williams, A.M. (1984), 'Reintegration or rejection? Portugal's retornados', *Iberian Studies*, vol. 13.

Lewis, J.R. and Williams, A.M. (1986a), 'The economic impact of return migration in Central Portugal' in King, R. (ed.), *Return migration and regional economic problems*, London: Croom Helm.

Lewis, J.R. and Williams, A.M. (1986b), 'Factories, farms and families: the impacts of industrial growth in rural central Portugal', *Sociologia Ruralis*, vol. 26, pp. 320–44.

Lewis, J.R. and Williams, A.M. (1988), 'No longer Europe's best-kept secret: the Algarve's tourist boom', *Geography* (forthcoming).

Lichtenberger, E. (1976), 'Der Massentourismus als dynamisches System: Das österreichische Beispiel' in *Tagungsberichte und wissenschaftliche Abhandlungen des 40. Deutschen Geographentages, Innsbruck 1975*, Wiesbaden: Franz Steiner, pp. 673–92.

Lichtenberger, E. (1979), 'Die Sukzession von der Agrar- zur Freizeitgesellschaft in den Hochgebirgen Europas, *Innsbrucker Geographische Studien*, vol. 5, pp. 401–36.

López Cano, D. (1984), *La inmigración en la Costa del Sol: análisis de un desarraigo*, Málaga: Diputación Provincial.

López Ontiveros, A. (1981), 'El desarrollo reciente de la caza en España in *Supervivencia de la montaña*, Madrid: Servicio de Publicaciones Agrarias.

López Palomeque, F. (1982), *La producción del espacio de ocio en Cataluña: la Vall d'Aran*, Barcelona: Universidad de Barcelona.

Loukissas, Ph.J. (1977), *The impact of tourism in regional development: a comparative analysis of the Greek islands*, Ithaca, NY, Cornell University, Graduate Field of City and Regional Planning.

Loukissas, Ph.J. (1982), 'Tourism's regional development impacts: a comparative analysis of the Greek islands', *Annals of Tourism Research*, vol. 9, pp. 523–41.

Lozato-Giotart, J.-P. (1987), *Géographie du tourisme*, Paris: Masson, 2nd edn.

Madeira: Plano à Médio Prazo, 1981–1984 (1982), Funchal: Governo Regional.

Mallon, P. (1985), 'Le tourisme rural à la croisée des chemins', *Epaces*, no. 73, pp. 4–7.

Manchester Polytechnic (n.d.), *Greater Manchester: A centre for tourism*.

Manente, M. (1986), 'Il turismo nell'economia italiana', in *Secondo rapporto sul turismo italiano*, Rome: Ministero del turismo e dello Spettacolo.

Marchena, M. (1986), 'Un análisis de los recursos turísticos andaluces', *Revista de Estudios Regionales*, vol. 6, pp. 169–95.

Marchena, M. (1987), *Territorio y Turismo en Andalucía*, Seville: Junta de Andalucía, Dirección General de Turismo.

Marinos, P. (1983), 'Small island tourism—the case of Zakynthos, Greece', *Tourism Management*, vol. 4, pp. 212–15.

Martin, E. (1986), Entwicklung der touristischen Nachfrage im ländlichen Raum, *Entwicklung ländlicher Räume durch den Fremdenverkehr. Forschungsberichte und Seminarergebnisse*. Bonn: Der Bundesminister für Raumordnung, Bauwesen und Städtebau, pp. 19–39.

Mathieson, A. and Wall, G. (1982), *Tourism: economic, physical and social impacts*, London: Longman.

Mendonsa, E.L. (1983a), 'Search for security, migration, modernisation and stratification in Nazare, Portugal', *International Migration Review*, vol. 6, pp. 635–45.

Mendonsa, E.L. (1983b), 'Tourism and income strategies in Nazare, Portugal, *Annals of Tourism Research*, vol. 10, pp. 213–38.

Mesplier, A. (1986), *Le tourisme en France*, Paris: Bréal, 2nd edn.

Michaud, J.-L. (1983), Le tourisme face à l'environnement, Paris: Presses Universitaires de France.

Middleton, V.T.C. (1977), 'Some implications of overseas tourism for regional development' in B.S. Duffield (ed.), *Tourism: a tool for regional development*, Edinburgh: Tourism and Recreation Research Unit.

Mignon, C. (1979), 'La Costa del Sol et son arrière pays', in *Tourisme et développement régional en Andalousie*. 3rd part.

Ministerie van Cultuur, Recreatie en Maatschappelijk Werk (1981a), *Structuurschema openluchtrecreatie: beleidsvoornemen*, The Hague: Stattsuitgeverij.

Ministerie van Cultuur, Recreatie en Maastschappelijk Werk (1981b), *Ruimte voor recreatie*, The Hague: Staatsuitgeverij.

Ministerie van Cultuur, Recreatie en Maatschappelijk Werk (1981c), *Nederland natuurlijk*, The Hague: Staatsuitgeverij.

Ministerie van Landbouw en Visserij (1981), *Structuurschema voor de landinrichting: beleidsvoornemen*, The Hague: Staatsuitgeverij.

Ministerie van Volkshuisvesting en Ruimtelijke Ordening (1977), *Derde nota over de ruimtelijke ordening: nota landelijke gebieden*, The Hague: Staatsuitgeverij.

Ministerie van Volkshuisvesting, Ruimtelike Ordening en Milieubeheer (1988), *On the road to 2015: a comprehensive summary of the Fourth Report on Physical Planning in the Netherlands*, The Hague, Staatsuitgeverij.

Ministry of Co-ordination (1971), *Study of employment in hotel and other tourist enterprises*, Athens (in Greek).

Mintel Publications (1985a), *Tourism special*, vol. 2, London.

Mintel Publications (1985b), *Tourism special*, vol. 3, London.

Miranda, M.T. (1985), *La segunda residencia en la provincia de Valencia*, Valencia: Universidad de Valencia.

Mirloup, J. (1984), 'Les loisirs des Français, approche géographique', *Revue de Géographie de Lyon*, vol. 59, pp. 15–28.

MNE (Ministry of National Economy, Greece) (1988), 'Five year plan for economic and social development 1988–92 (Preliminaries)', Athens: *Government Gazette*, 2 August (in Greek).

Mønnesland, J. (1989), 'Trends in regional development—main causes of unbalance during the 60s, 70;s and the 80s', in *The long-term future of regional policy—a Nordic view*, NordREFO/OECD.

Monti, S. and Vinci, S. (1984), *Mezzogiorno e sottosviluppo*, Naples: Loffredo.

Moore, K. (1976), 'Modernization in a Canary Island village' in J.B. Aceves and W.A. Douglass (eds), *The changing faces of rural Spain*, New York: Schenkman.

Morales Folguera, J.M. (1982), *La arquitectura del ocio en la Costa del Sol*, Málaga: Universidad de Málaga.

Morris, A. and Dickinson, G. (1987), 'Tourism development in Spain: growth versus conservation on the Costa Brava', *Geography*, pp. 16–26.

Morzer Bruijns, M.F. and Bentham, R.J. (eds) (1979), *Atlas van de Nederlandse landschappen*, Utrecht: Spectrum.

Moutinho, L. (1982), 'An investigation of vacation tourist behaviour in Portugal', PhD thesis, University of Sheffield.

Müller, K.H. (1985), 'Hypothese der stagnierenden Nachfrage für den Bergurlaub', *Problem Sommerfremdenverkehr in den Alpen. Referate zum 2. Hochschulkurs für Fremdenverkehr in Neustift/Brixen*, Innsbruck: Institut für Verkehr und Tourismus.

Murphy, P.E. (1982), 'Perceptions and attitudes of decision-making groups in tourism centers', *Journal of Travel Research*, vol. 21, pp. 8–12.

Murphy, P.E. (1985), *Tourism: a community approach*, New York: Methuen.

Nancy, G. (1987), 'Evaluation des exportations touristiques françaises', *Espaces*, no. 84, pp. 4–7.

Naylon, J. (1967), 'Tourism—Spain's most important industry', *Geography*, vol. 52, pp. 23–40.

Nordic Council of Ministers, *Yearbook of Nordic Statistics*.

NORTRA (1986), *Program 90—et handlingsprogram for vekst og utvikling av reiselivsnæringen*, Oslo: NORTRA.

NSSG (National Statistical Service of Greece) (1985), *Tourist statistics: Years 1982 and 1983*, Athens.

NSSG (1987), *Tourist statistics: Years 1984 and 1985*, Athens (in Greek).

OAOM & Assoc. (1976), *Chalkidiki: regional plan*, Athens: Ministry of Co-ordination (in Greek).

OECD (1974), *Government policy in the development of tourism*, Paris.

OECD (1983), *Tourism policy and international tourism in OECD member countries. Evolution of tourism in OECD member countries in 1982 and the early months 1983*, Paris.

OECD (1980–7), *Tourism policy and international tourism in OECD countries*, Paris: OECD.

OECD (1989), *National and international tourism statistics 1974–85*.

Office Fédéral de la Statistique Suisse (1986a), *Tourisme en Suisse, 1985*, Berne.

Office Fédéral de la Statistique Suisse (1986b), *Touristes suisses a l'étranger*, Berne.

Office Fédéral de la Statistique Suisse (1986c), *Moyens d'hébergement touristique en Suisse*, Berne.

Office Fédéral de la Statistique Suisse (1986d), *La balance touristique de la Suisse*, Berne.

Office Fédéral de la Statistique Suisse (1986e), *Le tourisme suisse en chiffres: édition 1986*, Berne.

Office Fédéral de la Statistique Suisse (1987), 'Le tourisme en Suisse dans le hôtels et établissements de cure en 1986', *La Vie Economique*, April, pp. 248–52.

Oglethorpe, M. (1985), 'Tourism in a small island economy: the case of Malta', *Tourism Management*, vol. 6, pp. 23–31.

O'Hagan, J. and Mooney, D. (1983), 'Input–output multipliers in a small open economy: an application to tourism', *Economic and Social Review*, vol. 14, pp. 273–80.

Opaschowski, H.W. (1982), *Freizeit-daten. Zahlen zur Freizeit-situation und -entwicklung in der Bundesrepublik Deutschland*, Hamburg and Düsseldorf: BAT Freizeit-Forschungsinstitut/Deutsche Gesellschaft für Freizeit.

Ortega Martínez, E. (1986), 'Presente y futuro del turismo de golf en España', *Estudios Turísticos*, vol. 90, pp. 23–47.

Österreichische Raumordnungskonferenz (1981), *Österreichisches Raumordnungskonzept*, Vienna.

Österreichische Raumordnungskonferenz (1985), 'Internationale und nationale Trends im Tourismus. Rahmenbedingungen für die Fremdenverkehrsentwicklung in Österreich', *Gutachten des Osterreichischen Instituts für Raumplanung*, vol. 47.

Österreichische Raumordnungskonferenz (1987a), 'Entwicklungsmöglichkeiten des Fremdenverkehrs in Problemgebieten', *Gutachten des Österreichischen Instituts für Raumplanung*, vol. 53.

Österreichische Raumordnungskonferenz (1987b), 'Zweitwohnungen in Österreich. Formen und Verbreitung, Auswirkungen, Künftige Entwicklung', *Gutachten des Instituts für Stadtforschung, Kommunalwissenschaftlichen Dokumentationszentrums, Österreichischen Instituts für Raumplanung*, vol. 54.

Österreichisches Statistisches Zentralamt (1986), 'Beherbergungs- und Gaststättenwesen 1983', *Beiträge zur Österreichischen Statistik*, no. 764.

Österreichisches Statistisches Zentralamt (1987), 'Reisegewohnheiten der Österreicher im Jahre 1984', *Beiträge zur Österreichischen Statistik*, Vienna.

Österreichisches Statistisches Zentralamt (1988), Der fremdenverkehr in Österreich im Jahre 1985, *Beiträge zur Österreichischen Statistik*, no. 808.

Pannell Kerr Forster Associates (1986), *Outlook in the hotel and tourism industries*, London.

Papachristou, G. (1987), 'In search of tourist policy', *To Vima*, 19 July, pp. 28–30 (in Greek).

Papadopoulos, S.I. (1987), 'World tourism: an economic analysis', *Revue de tourisme*, vol. 1, pp. 2–13.

Papson, S. (1979), 'Tourism, "World's biggest industry in the twenty-first century?" ', *The Futurist*, vol. 13, pp. 249–57.

Parente, A. (1980), 'L'agriturismo', in G. Corna-Pellegrini and C. Brusa (eds), *La ricerca geografica in Italia 1960–1980*, Varese: Ask.

Pasgrimaud, A. (1987), 'Le tourisme: une activité en pointe', *Ecoflash* (INSEE), no. 15.

Pearce, D.G. (1981), *Tourist development*, London: Longman.

Pearce, D.G. (1988), 'Tourism and regional development in the European Community', *Tourism Management*, vol. 9, pp. 13–22.

Pearce, D.G. and Grimmeau, J.-P. (1985), 'The spatial structure of tourist accommodation and hotel demand in Spain', *Geoforum*, vol. 16, pp. 37–50.

Pedrini, L. (1984), 'The geography of tourism and leisure in Italy', *Geojournal*, vol. 9, pp. 55–7.

Perez, M. (1986), 'L'offerta turistica' in *Secondo rapporto sul turismo italiano*, Rome: Ministero del Turismo e dello Spettacolo.

Peters, M. (1969), *International tourism: the economics and development of the international tourist trade*, London: Hutchinson.

Pinder, D.A. (1981), 'Community attitude as a limiting factor in port growth: the case of Rotterdam' in B.S. Hoyle and D.A. Pinder (eds), *Cityport industrialization and regional development*, Oxford: Pergamon Press.

Pinder, D.A. (1983), 'Planned port industrialization and the quest for upward economic transition: an examination of development strategies for the Dutch delta' in B.S. Hoyle and D. Hilling (eds), *Seaport systems and spatial change*, Chichester: Wiley.

Pinto, F.M. (1984), *O Algarve no contexto nacional: Situação regional e estrategia de actuação*, Faro: Comissão de Coordenação da Região do Algarve.

Polychroniadis, A. and Hadjimichalis, C. (1974), ' "Lyomena": a solution to the second home problem?', *Architecture in Greece*, vol. 8, pp. 54–61 (in Greek).

Pommier, Ch. (1985), 'L'impact économique de l'aménagement littoral du Languedoc-Roussillon', *Espaces*, no. 72, pp. 24–7.

Pourquery, D. (1987), 'La fin des grandes vacances', *Le Monde Affaires*, 4 July.

Préau, P. (1970), 'Principe d'analyse des sites en montagne', *Urbanisme*, vol. 116, pp. 21–5.

Préau, P. (1983), 'Le changement social dans une commune tou..stique de montagne: Saint-Bon-Tarentaise (Savoie)', *Revue de Géographie Alpine*, vol. 74, pp. 407–29, Part 1.

Préau, P. (1984), 'Le changement social dans une commune touristique de montagne: Saint-Bon-Tarentaise (Savoie)', *Revue de Géographie Alpine*, vol. 75, pp. 411–37, Part 2.

Presidencia del Gobierno (1976), *Turismo*, Madrid: Subsecretaría de Planificación.

Priebe, H. (1971), *Untersuchungen zur Regionalstruktur unterer Bayerischer Wald. Ergebnisse eines Forschungsauftages des Bundesministers für Wirtschaft und Finanzen*, Frankfurt am Main.

Prognos, A.G. (1982), *Politik, Wertewandel, Technologie. Ansatzpunkie für eine Theorie der sozialen Entwicklung'*, Düsseldorf/Vienna: Econ.

Py, P. (1986), *Le tourisme. Un phénomème économique*, Paris: La Documentation Française.

Quilici, F. (1984), 'Invito all'Italia' in *Guida Illustrata Italia*, Milan: Touring Club Italiano.

Racine, P. (1983), 'L'aménagement du littoral Languedoc-Roussillon: Bilan et perspectives', *Bulletin de la Société Langedocienne de Géographie*, vol. 106, pp. 523–31.

Ragu, D. (1985), *Le tourisme étranger en Ile-de-France*, Paris: IAURIF.

Renucci, J. (1984), 'Les résidences secondaires en France', *Revue de Géographie de Lyon*, vol. 59, pp. 29–40.

Rijksplanologische Dienst (1986), *Notite ruimtelijke perspectieven: op weg naar de 4e nota over de ruimtelijke ordening*, The Hague: Ministerie van Volkshuisvesting, Ruimtelijke Ordening en Milieubeheer.

Robert, J. (1986), 'Un contrat de pays dans la vallée d'Aulps (Haute-Savoie), *Points d'appui pour l'économie Rhône-Alpes*, no. 37, pp. 28–30.

Röck, S. (1977), 'Überlagerung von Freizeitformen. Räumliche Auswirkungen der verschiedenen Erholungsformen und ihrer Kombination (Kurz- und Langzeiter-holung)', *Raumforschung und Raumordnung*, vol. 35, pp. 224–8.

Rodríguez Marín, J.A. (1985), 'El turismo en la economía canaria: delimitación e impacto económico', in Gobierno de Canarias *et al.* (eds) *Elturismo en Canarias*, Canary Islands: Gobierno de Canarias.

Romanos, A.G. (1975), 'Mykonos: settlement protection as a motive of economic development', *Architecture in Greece*, vol. 9, pp. 197–203 (in Greek).

Roth, P. (1984), 'Der Ausländerreiseverkehr in der Bundesrepublik Deutschland. Eine Darstellung der Struktur ausländischer Gäste in der Bundesrepublik, ihre Nachfragepräferenzen, Reiseziele und Motive, Dargestellt am Beispiel ausländischer Gäste aus den USA. Grossbritannien und der Schweiz', *Zeitschrift für Wirtschafts-geographie*, vol. 3–4, pp. 157–63.

Rougier, H. (1976), 'Le tourisme hivernal dans les Alpes suisses: évolution récente et tendances nouvelles', *Information Géographique*, vol. 40, pp. 165–74.

Rovelstad, J.R. (1982), 'Tourism training strategies and programs for the 1980s',

Journal of Travel Research, vol. 21, pp. 14–18.

Rumley, P.A. (1983), 'Le tourisme Jurassien, *Geographica Helvetica*, pp. 38, pp. 73–7.

Ruppert, K. and Maier, J. (1970), 'Der Naherholungsverkehr der Münchener—ein Beitrag zur Geographie des Freizeitverhaltens', *Mitteilungen der Geographischen Gesellschaft München*, vol. 55.

Ruppert, K., Gräf, P. and Lintner, P. (1986), 'Naherholungsverhalten im Raum München. Persistenz und Wandel Freizeitorientierter Regionalstrukturen 1968/80 in *Arbeitsmaterial*, no. 116, Hannover: Akademie für Raumforschung und Landesplanung.

Salvá, P. (1984), 'Las variaciones estructurales y morfológicas en el espacio rural de la isla de Mallorca como consecuencia del impacto del turismo de massas' in *Coloquio Hispano Francés sobre Espacios Rurales*, Madrid: Servico de Publicaciones Agrarias.

Santillana, J. (1984), 'Las migraciones internas en España: necesidad de ordenación', *Información Comercial Española*, vol. 609, pp. 23–37.

Schilling, R. *et al.* (1974), 'Tourisme', *Werk*, vol. 8, pp. 908–89.

Schnell, P. (1975), 'Tourism as a means of improving the regional economic structure', in *Tourism as a factor in national and regional development*, Peterborough, Canada: Department of Geography, Trent University, Occasional Paper no. 4, pp. 72–80.

Schnell, P. (1977), 'Die Bedeutung des Fremdenverkehrs im Rahmen der Wirtschaftlichen Förderung strukturschwacher Gebiete' in *Tourism—factor for national and regional development*, Sofia, University of Sofia, Kliment Ohridski, Chair of Geography of Tourism/Union of the Scientific Workers in Bulgaria/Bulgarian Geographical Society, pp. 92–110.

Schnell, P. (1983), 'Der Fremdenverkehr in Westfalen', in P. Weber and K.-F. Schreiber (eds), *Westfalen und angrenzende Regionen, Festschrift zum 44. Deutschen Geographentag in Münster*, Teil I. Paderborn: Ferdinand Schöningh, 129–156 (Münstersche Geographische Arbeiten 15).

Schnell, P. (1986), 'Fremdenverkehr—Nachfragestruktur' in Geographische Kommission für Westfalen (ed.), *Geographisch-landeskundlicher Atlas von Westfalen*, Münster.

Scobie, W. (1989), 'Crisis talks on Adriatic slime slick', *Observer*, 20 August, p. 25.

Secchi, B. (1977), 'Central and peripheral regions in the process of economic development: the Italian case' in D.B. Massey and P.W. Batey (eds), *Alternative frameworks for analysis*, London: Pion (London Papers in Regional Science, 7).

Secretaria de Estado do turismo (1986), *Plano nacional de Turismo 1986–1989*, Lisbon: Groupo Coordenador do Plano Nacional de Turismo.

Shaw, G., Williams, A.M. and Greenwood, J. (1987), *Tourism and the economy of Cornwall*, Exeter: University of Exeter, Tourism Research Group.

Shaw, G., Williams, A.M., Greenwood, J. and Hennessy, S. (1987), *Public policy tourism in England: a review of national and local trends*, Exeter: University of Exeter, Tourism Research Group.

da Silva, J.A.M. (1986), 'Avaliação do impacto económico do turismo, em Portugal', dissertation for a Masters degree in Economics, Universidade Técnica de Lisboa, Instituto Superior de Económia.

Singh, B.P. (1984), *The impact of tourism on the balance of payments*, Athens: CPER.

Sinnhuber, K. (1978), Recreation in the mountains, *Wiener Geographische Schriften*, vol. 51–2, pp. 59–86.

Skojoldelev, E. (1984), 'Capacity utilization of Nordic tourist facilities', *Tourism Management*, vol. 5, pp. 192–206.

Skolarz, G. (1985), 'Die Reisegewohnheiten der Österreicher im Jahre 1984—Haupturlaube', *Statistische Nachrichten*, vol. 40.

Smeral, E. (1985), 'Längerfristige Entwicklung und Struktureller Wandel im internationalen und im österreichischen Tourismus' in *Österreichischer Strukturbericht 1984*, Vienna.

Smyth, R. (1986), 'Public policy for tourism in Northern Ireland', *Tourism Management*, vol. 7, pp. 120–6.

Spartidis, A. (1969), *Research on the magnitude and the characteristics of employment in tourist* enterprises, Athens: EOT (in Greek).

Stad van Amsterdam (1980), *Jaarboek*, Amsterdam: Afdeling Bestuursinformatie, Bureau van de Statistiek.

Stallinbrass, C. (1980), 'Seaside resorts and the hotel accommodation industry', *Progress in Planning*, vol. 13, pp. 103–74.

Stamm, H. (1984), *Der Urlaubstraum—ein Urlaubstrauma?* Dransfeld.

Statistics Sweden (1989), *Accommodation statistics 1988, Sweden*.

Statistisches Bundesamt (ed.) (1965), 'Urlaubs- und Erholungsreisen 1962', *Wirtschaft und Statistik*, vol. 1, pp. 38–41, Wiesbaden.

Statistisches Bundesamt (ed.) (1970), 'Ausgaben für urlaubs- und Erholungsreisen 1969, *Wirtschaft und Statistik*, vol. 8, pp. 624–626, Wiesbaden.

Statistisches Bundesamt (ed.) (1981), Urlaubs- und Erholungsreiseverkehr 1979/80. Ergebnisse des Mikrozensus 1980. *Wirtshaft und Statistik*, vol. 12, pp. 866–870, Wiesbaden.

Statistisches Bundesamt (ed.) (1986), Beherbergung im Reiseverkehr: April und Winterhalbjahr 1986—Oktober und Sommerhalbjahr 1986. Fachserie 6: *Handel, Gastgewerbe, Reiseverkehr*, Wiesbaden.

Stoelers, R. and Karssen, A. (1986), *De Vacantie atlas van Nederland*, Enschede: Intermap.

Studienkreis für Tourismus (ed.) (1986), *Urlaubsreisen 1954–1985. 30 Jahre Erfassung des touristischen Verhaltens der Deutschen durch soziologische Stichprobenerhebungen*, Starnberg.

Studienkreis für Tourismus (ed.) (1987a), *Reiseanalyse 1986. Erste Ergebnisse der Reiseanalyse des Studienkreises für Tourismus—10. März 1987*, Starnberg.

Studienkreis für Tourismus (1987b), 'Erste Ergebnisse der Reiseanalyse 1987. 17. Repräsentative Urlaubsreiseerhebung', *Animation*, vol. 8, pp. 74–9.

Sundelin, A. (1983), 'Tourism trends in Scandinavia', *Tourism Management*, vol. 4, pp. 262–8.

TCG (1981), *Tourism and regional development (Proceedings of a Meeting in the Context of the TCG Conference on Development*, Heraklion (in Greek).

Teuscher, H. (1983), 'Social tourism for all the Swiss Travel Saving Fund', *Tourism Management*, vol. 4, pp. 216–19.

Thissen, F. (1978), 'Second homes in the Netherlands', *Tijdschrift voor Economische en Sociale Geografie*, vol. 69, pp. 322–32.

Thompson, I.B. (1975), *The Lower Rhône and Marseille*, London: Oxford University Press.

Tinacci, M. (1969), 'Il litorale toscano e il litorale romagnolo: note di geografia comparata dei prezzi e delle strutture alberghiere', *Rivista Geografica Italiana*, vol. 76, pp. 353–90.

Titi, C. (1980), 'Il turismo alberghiero qualificato sulle coste liguri e venetofriuli-anogiuliane', *Rivista Geografica Italiana*, vol. 87, pp. 249–80.

Travis, A.S. (1982a), 'Leisure, recreation and tourism in Western Europe', *Tourism Management*, vol. 3, pp. 3–15.

Travis, A.S. (1982b), 'Managing the environmental and cultural impacts of tourism and leisure development', *Tourism Management*, vol. 3, pp. 256–62.

Tschurtschenthaler, P. (1985), 'Probleme des Sommerfremdenverkehrs in den Alpen' in *Problem Sommerfremdenverkehr in den Alpen. Referate zum 2. Hochschulkurs für Fremdenverkehr in Neustift/Brixen*, Innsbruck: Institut für Verkehr und Tourismus.

Tuppen, J. (1983), *The economic geography of France*, Beckenham: Croom Helm.

Tuppen, J. (1985), '*Urban tourism in France*', Manchester: University of Salford, Dept of Geography, Urban Tourism Project Working Paper no. 3.

Tuppen, J. (1987), *France under recession, 1981–6*, London: Macmillan.

Tuppen, J. (1988), 'Tourism in France: recent trends in winter sports', *Geography*, vol. 73, pp. 359–63.

UNCTC (1982), *Transnational corporations in international tourism*, New York.

Urry, J. (1987), 'Some social and spatial aspects of services', *Environment and Planning D: Society and Space*, vol. 5, pp. 5–26.

Uthoff, D. (1982), 'Die Stellung des Harzes im Rahmen der Fremdenverkehrsentwicklung in deutschen Mittelgebirgen. Eine vergleichende Analyse auf statistischer Gundlage', *Neues Archiv für Niedersachsen*, vol. 3, pp. 290–313.

Vaccaro, G. and Perez, M. (1986), 'La domanda touristica', in *Secondo rapporto sul turismo italiano*, Rome: Ministero del Turismo e dello Spettacolo.

Vaiou-Hadjimichalis, D. and Hadjimichalis, C. (1979), *Regional development and industrialization (Monopoly investment in Pylos)*, Athens: Exandas (in Greek).

Valenzuela, M. (1976), 'La residencia secundaria en la provincia de Madrid. Génesis y estructura espacial', *Ciudad y Territorio*, vol. 2–3/76, pp. 135–53.

Valenzuela, M. (1982), 'La incidencia de los grandes equipamientos recreativos en la configuración del espacio turístico litoral: la costa de la Málaga', *Coloquio Hispano-Francés sobre Espacios Litorales*, Madrid: Servicio de Publicaciones Agrarias.

Valenzuela, M. (1985), 'La consommation d'espace par le tourisme sur le littoral andalou: les centres d'interêt touristique national', *Revue Géographique del Pyrénnées et du sud-oueste*, vol. 56, pp. 289–312.

Valenzuela, M. (1986a), 'Conflicts spatiaux entre tourisme et agriculture dans les régions méditerranéennes espagnoles' in *Le tourisme contre l'agriculture*, Paris: ADEF.

Valenzuela, M. (1986b), 'La practica del esquí en la Sierra de Guadarrama (Madrid)' in *Proceedings of the VII Symposium of the IGU Commission on Environmental Problems*, Palma, Majorca.

Valenzuela, M. (1988), 'La residencia secundaria. Mito social y conflicto urbanístico en los espacios turístico-recreativos, *Urbanismo COAM*, vol. 4, pp. 71–83.

Varenne, Ch. (1986), 'Les groupements hôteliers du Massif Central', *Espaces*, no. 81, pp. 32–5.

Vera Rebollo, F. (1985), 'Las condiciones climáticas y marítimas, como factores de localización del turismo histórico y alicantino', *Investigaciones Geográficas*, vol. 3, pp. 161–78.

Vera, F. (1987), *Turismo y Urbanismo en el litoral alicantino*, Alicante.

Viken, A. (1989), *Den finske utfordring*, Alta.

Viken, A. and Sletvold, O. (1988), 'Bilturisme i Finnmark', FR report 1988:6, Finnmark Research Institute.

Vincent, J.A. (1980), 'The political economy of Alpine development: tourism or agriculture in St Maurice', *Sociologia Ruralis*, vol. 20, pp. 250–71.

Voorden, F.W. van (1981), 'The preservation of monuments and historic towns in the Netherlands', *Town Planning Review*, vol. 52, pp. 433–53.

Walsh, B. (1987), 'High heels and the new barbarians', *Times Special Report on Italy*, 17 November, p. 60.

Waters, S.R. (1967), 'Trends in international tourism', *Development Digest*, vol. 5, pp. 57–62.

Watson, A. and Watson, R.D. (1983), *Tourism, land use and rural communities in mountain areas: the Swiss approach and its relevance for Scotland*, Aberdeen: Grampian Regional Council.

Weatherley, R.D. (1982), 'Domestic tourism and second homes as motors of rural development in the Sierra Morena, Spain', *Iberian Studies*, vol. 11, pp. 40–6.

Weg, H. van de (1982), 'Revitalization of traditional resorts', *Tourism Management*, vol. 3, pp. 303–7.

Werff, P.E. van der (1980), 'Polarizing implications of the Pescaia tourist industry', *Annals of Tourism Research*, vol. 7, pp. 197–223.

West Country Tourist Board (1980), *A strategy for tourism in the West Country*, Exeter.

White, K.J. and Walker, M.B. (1982), 'Trouble in the travel account', *Annals of Tourism Research*, vol. 9, pp. 37–56.

White, P.E. (1974), *The social impact of tourism on host communities: A study of language change in Switzerland*, Oxford: School of Geography.

White, P.E. (1976), 'Tourism and economic development in the rural environment' in R. Lee and P. Ogden (eds), *Economy and society in the EEC: spatial perspectives*, Farnborough: Saxon House.

White, P.E. (1987), 'Italy: grand tour to package tour', *Geographical Magazine*, vol. 59, pp. 554–9.

White Paper (1986), 'Om reiselivet', *St. meld* 14/86, Report to the Norwegian Parliament from the Ministry of Transport.

Whysall, P.T. (1982), 'Urban conservation in the Netherlands', *Ekistics*, vol. 49, pp. 342–7.

Williams, A.M. (1981), 'Bairros clandestinos: illegal housing in Portugal', *Geografisch Tijdschrift*, vol. 15, pp. 24–34.

Williams, A.M. (1986), 'Economic landscapes of the Mediterranean', *Landscape Research*, vol. 11, pp. 8–10.

Williams, A.M. and Shaw, G. (1988), 'Tourism: candyfloss industry or job-generator', *Town Planning Review* (forthcoming).

Williams, A., Shaw, G., Greenwood, J. and Hennessy, S. (1986), *Tourism and economic development: a review of experiences in Western Europe*, Exeter: University of Exeter, Department of Geography, Cornish Tourism Project, Discussion Paper no. 2.

Winter, L. (1979), 'Quality of life in the next decade', *Vision*, July–August.

Wolf, K. and Jurczek, P. (1986), *Geographie der Freizeit und des Tourismus*, Stuttgart: Uni-Taschenbücher.

Wolfson, M. (1964), 'Government's role in tourism development', *Development Digest*, vol. 5, pp. 50–6.

Wolkowitsch, M. (1984), *Provence–Alpes–Côte d'Azur*, Paris: Presses Universitaires de France.

World Tourism Organization (1984), *Economic review of world tourism*, Madrid: World Tourism Organization.

World Tourism Organization (1986), *Economic review of world tourism*, Madrid: World Tourism Organization.

World Tourism Organization (1989), *Current Travel and Tourism Indicators*, Madrid: World Tourism Organization.

World Tourism Organization, *Yearbooks of Tourism Statistics* (various), Madrid: World Tourism Organization.

Wynn, M. (ed.) (1984), *Planning and urban growth in southern Europe*, London: Mansell.

Young, G. (1973), *Tourism: blessing or blight?*, Harmondsworth: Penguin.

Zacharatos, G.A. (1986), *Tourist consumption: the method of calculation and its use for research on the impact of tourism on the national economy*, Athens: CPER (in Greek).

Zahn, U. (1973), *Der Fremdenverkehr an der spanischen Mittelmeerküste. Eine vergleichende geographische Untersuchung.* Regensburger Geographische Schriften, 2.

Zimmermann, F. (1985a), 'Der Fremdenverkehr in Österreich — Skizze einer praxisorientierten räumlichen Fremdenverkehrsforschung aus geographischer Sicht', *Klagenfurter Geographische Schriften*, vol. 6, Klagenfurt, pp. 253–84.

Zimmermann, F. (1985b), 'Ausflugsverkehr und Kurzurlaube in Österreich unter Berücksichtigung der Überlagerung mit dem mittel- und längerfristigen Reiseverkehr', *Berichte zur Raumforschung und Raumplanung*, vol. 29, pp. 3–13.

Zimmermann, F. (1986a), 'Day trips and short-term tourism in Austria and their competition with long-term tourism', in *Big city tourism*, International Geographical Union, Commission of Tourism and Leisure, Dietrich Reimer Verlag, Berlin.

Zimmermann, F. (1986b), 'Die Bedeutung von Kultur- und Bildungsangeboten für den österreichischen Fremdenverkehr', GRAZI Karl-Franzens-Universität Institut für Geographie.

Zucker, W.H. (1986), *Urlaubsreisen 1985. Einige Ergebnisse der Reiseanalyse 1985. Kurzfassung*, Starnberg: Studienkreis für Tourismus.

Index